BLACK
BASALT

BLACK
BASALT

Wedgwood and Contemporary Manufacturers

Diana Edwards

Antique Collectors' Club

ISBN 1 85149 161 9

British Library Cataloguing-in-Publication Data
A catalogue record for this book is available from the British Library

Printed in England
by the Antique Collectors' Club Ltd., Woodbridge, Suffolk
on Consort Royal Satin paper
supplied by the Donside Paper Company, Aberdeen, Scotland

To Rodney Hampson

Other books by the same author

Tea and Sympathy: Post Revolutionary Ceramics in the Stamford Historical Society
The Castleford Pottery 1790-1821
Neale Pottery and Porcelain

*Frontispiece. Potpourri jar (minus liner) with gilded scroll band and sprigged relief Offering to Ceres bronzed and gilded. Mark: **WEDGWOOD** with No. **2/3793**, late 19th century, 7¾in. high. Royal Ontario Museum, 941.6.112.*

Contents

Colour Plate 1. First Day's Vase painted in 'encaustic' orange and iron-red dated 13 June 1769, one of six vases to be the first made at the new factory at Etruria. The reverse depicts Hippothon, Antiochus and Clymenos and is taken from Plate 129 of Hamilton's Antiquités, Etrusques, Grecques et Romaines... *of 1766. The shape is a variation of No. 40 in the Wedgwood Shape Book (with a slightly different cover) and was produced in a number of sizes from 7in. to 15¾in. Unmarked, 1769, 10in. high. By courtesy of the Trustees of the Wedgwood Museum, Barlaston, Stoke-on-Trent.*

Acknowledgements

It was Terry Lockett who propelled me into this project by suggesting me as a possible author to the publishers who were looking toward the publication of a new book on black basalt. To him and to Isabel Lockett, who have, on innumerable occasions, hosted us while on research trips to England, I owe warm thanks.

Additional thanks go to Geoffrey Godden for generously offering me his research into the *London Gazette*.

Two family members were called into service for the sake of this work. My son Mark toiled endlessly over the printing of some 500 photographs for the book, a job clearly beyond the call of filial duty. My husband, Francis Murnaghan, often worked nights and weekends to meet his obligations as a United States Federal Judge so we could make numerous research trips.

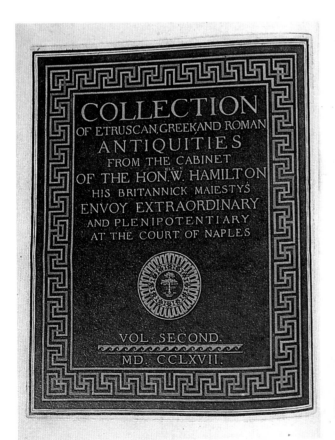
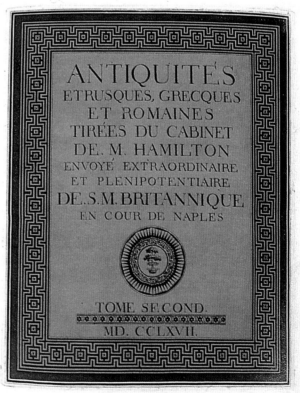

Colour Plate 2. Folio title pages from Antiquités, Etrusques, Grecques et Romaines… or, *as the English edition was translated,* Collection of Etruscan, Greek, and Roman Antiquities from the Cabinet of the Honble Wm. Hamilton. *The first volume published in Naples in 1766 did not appear in England until the spring of 1769. The catalogue, written by Pierre François Hugues, 'Baron' d'Hancarville, ran to four volumes, the last being published in 1776.*

To many others I also owe debts of gratitude: John Adeney, Antoine d'Albis, D.M. Archer, Maddy Aries, David Barker, Martin Blake, Harold Blakey, E. Myra Brown, Mary Butler Davies, Donnie Catzen, Mrs. Robert D. Chellis, Bill Coles, Robert Copeland, Oliver Fairclough, Geoffrey Fisk, Miranda Goodby, Jonathan Gray, the late Nancy and Peter Gunson, Mr. and Mrs. Jack Hacking, Pat Halfpenny, Eileen Hampson, Vivian S. Hawes, Dick Henrywood, Mr. and Mrs. Edward S. Hirschler, Mollie Hosking, Harwood A. Johnson, Dorothy Lee Jones, Peter Kaellgren, Alan Landis, Mr.and Mrs Samuel Laver, James Lomax, Volina Lyons, Pat and Philip Miller, Judith Viggers Nordin, Martin Phillips, Martha Pinello, Dr. and Mrs. Victor Polikoff, John and Jean Potter, David Pritchard, Mr. and Mrs. Martin Pulver, the late Mrs. Leonard Rakow, Kim Richardson, Louise Richardson, Gaye Blake Roberts, Laurance and Isabel Roberts, Letitia Roberts, Rachel Russell, Robert Scarlett, Arlene Palmer Schwind, Hugh Tait, and Barbara Tomlinson.

For supplying colour transparencies I particularly wish to thank Lindsay Grigsby, Bill Coles, Henry Weldon and Gaye Blake Roberts.

Special thanks go to George Miller for undertaking to provide an analysis of prices for basalt from 1795 to 1846 (Appendix I).

Above all, for research generosity *extraordinaire*, for extended hospitality, and for reading the manuscript and offering numerous constructive suggestions, and contributions of private research, I thank Rodney Hampson. It is to him I dedicate the book.

Foreword

It is now over eighty years since the publication of M.H. Grant's *The Makers of Black Basaltes* and a quarter of a century since the Holland reprint of 1967. Both the original and the reprint are now scarce items, and much new material has come to light in the intervening years. Thus a completely fresh book on the subject has been overdue for some time.

The pioneer collectors and writers on the subject whose activities are chronicled in Chapter VII devoted much of their attention to Josiah Wedgwood. This is understandable since his developments of the material, his refinements in ornament and his supreme marketing skill ensured that his factory was the market leader for most of the period when basalt was at its most fashionable. What is surprising, however, is that these early pioneers in basalt study and collection devoted as much time as they did to 'the contemporaries' and rivals of Wedgwood, and many of the manufacturers listed in Chapter IV were first brought to the attention of ceramic historians because of their basalt wares. Interest in some of the 'major — minor' potters is not a phenomenon of post-war research. As Diana Edwards indicates, the wide range of wares in the early collections disproves that contention.

Basalt is quintessentially a material for the expression of the neo-classical style. It is ill-suited to the curvilinear movement and the bold asymmetrical decoration of the Rococo and Revived Rococo styles. Thus, apart from continued production by the Wedgwood factory and a few others, the hey-day of basalt was in the period 1770-1830. Within this timespan over 170 factories are here noted as makers of the ware and the author gives us much new information on their histories and products — in all their fascinating diversity, with a wealth of illustrations hitherto unpublished.

As Diana Edwards would be the first to admit, there is still much research to be done on the subject, but the bedrock is provided here. We should all like to know why great enterprises such as Spode and Davenport appear to have marked only a small proportion of their basalt output — and the Bramelds and Minton apparently none at all. Painstaking research on individual shapes and ornamental sprigs might in future give us a few more new examples firmly attributable to individual makers. Possibly, cross-reference research with the sprig moulds used by potters making marked white feldspathic stonewares might add further to our knowledge. Though it must be acknowledged that this route is fraught with difficulties as factories traded moulds on closure, consistently bought wares from each other and freely copied the sprig designs of their competitors.

In recent years a number of important studies have appeared on individual factories — Daniel, Davenport and Dudson to name but three. These have added greatly to our knowledge of the nineteenth century enterprises. This present important book on basalt is an especially significant addition to this aspect of collecting and ceramic history. In this case the book spans the Continents, and I am now eagerly awaiting the day I find my first piece of Indian-made basalt from the Raneegungee Pottery Works!

Terence A. Lockett
November 1993

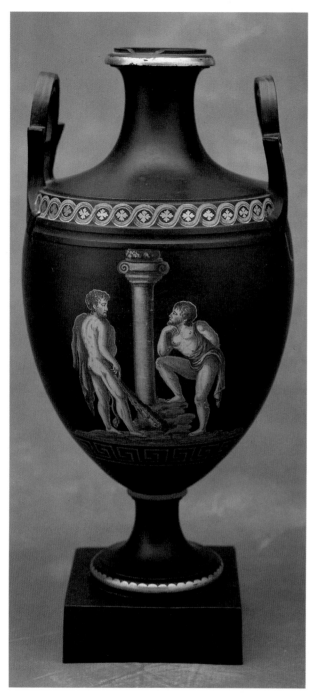

Colour Plate 3. Vase painted with 'encaustic' enamels and gilded depicting Hercules and probably his friend, Iolaus. The reverse of the vase (Colour Plate 4) has a vase draped with a floral swag resting on an elaborate scroll. This vase is a rare example of Palmer's 'encaustic-decorated' ware, and the quality attests to the threat presented by Palmer to Wedgwood & Bentley which culminated in the controversial patent dispute of 1770 (see pages 44-7). Mark: **H. PALMER HANLEY** *in wafer of base, c.1769-1770, 11in. high. Private collection.*

Colour Plate 4. Reverse of the vase in Colour Plate 3.

Colour Plate 5. Bronzed bust of Young Germanicus. The bust of Germanicus was put into production in the autumn of 1776. At the time Wedgwood wrote to Bentley: 'Germanicus' Head, the Ground will polish, but now we are begun [to] make them you cry Peccavi, & are afraid we shall make them faster than you shall be able to sell them. Away with such fears & begin to polish & sell away all before you' (E25-18717, 16 November 1776). Unmarked, 17½in. high. Grigsby collection.

Colour Plate 6. Vase and cover of ovoid shape decorated with applied relief of a putto riding a hippocampus within a husk-bordered ring above two half-figures terminating in fins, each flanking a gilded animal mask. Mark: **MADE BY H. PALMER HANLEY STAFFORDS.,** *possibly modelled by John Voyez c.1769, 17⅞in. high. City Museum and Art Gallery, Stoke-on-Trent, 170.*

Antique Collectors' Club

The Antique Collectors' Club was formed in 1966 and now has a five figure membership spread throughout the world. It publishes the only independently run monthly antiques magazine, *Antique Collecting*, which caters for those collectors who are interested in widening their knowledge of antiques, both by greater awareness of quality and by discussion of the factors which influence the price that is likely to be asked. The Antique Collectors' Club pioneered the provision of information on prices for collectors and the magazine still leads in the provision of detailed articles on a variety of subjects.

It was in response to the enormous demand for information on 'what to pay' that the price guide series was introduced in 1968 with the first edition of *The Price Guide to Antique Furniture* (completely revised 1978 and 1989), a book which broke new ground by illustrating the more common types of antique furniture, the sort that collectors could buy in shops and at auctions rather than the rare museum pieces which had previously been used (and still to a large extent are used) to make up the limited amount of illustrations in books published by commercial publishers. Many other price guides have followed, all copiously illustrated, and greatly appreciated by collectors for the valuable information they contain, quite apart from prices. The Antique Collectors' Club also publishes other books on antiques (including horology and art), garden history and architecture, and a full book list is available.

Club membership, open to all collectors, costs little. Members receive free of charge *Antique Collecting*, the Club's magazine (published ten times a year), which contains well-illustrated articles dealing with the practical aspects of collecting not normally dealt with by magazines. Prices, features of value, investment potential, fakes and forgeries are all given prominence in the magazine.

Among other facilities available to members are private buying and selling facilities, the longest list of 'For Sales' of any antiques magazine, an annual ceramics conference and the opportunity to meet other collectors at their local antique collectors' clubs. There are over eighty in Britain and more than a dozen overseas. Members may also buy the Club's publications at special pre-publication prices.

As its motto implies, the Club is an organisation designed to help collectors get the most out of their hobby: it is informal and friendly and gives enormous enjoyment to all concerned.

Introduction

Somewhat akin to James Murray, caught in a web of words while compiling the *Oxford English Dictionary*, the biographer of the black basalt industry is caught in a web of potters. The English potteries producing the ware so commonly associated exclusively with Josiah Wedgwood numbered more than one hundred and fifty and, travelling by imperceptible wires, tidings were conveyed quickly abroad where a number of Continental manufacturers flourished.

This is the second attempt to say something about the subject of basalt. The first book by Captain M.H. Grant, *The Makers of Black Basaltes*, written in 1910, still remains a classical standard reference work, and a surprisingly accurate work for its time. With tongue in cheek Grant wrote in his Preface that 'Basaltes is now so old [1910] that nothing new can be said about it'. Indeed, he proved that there was much new to be said and indeed, even with the publication of this book, there is still a great deal left for future researchers. As Nancy Gunson pointed out in her article on black basalt in the *Stonewares & Stone Chinas* exhibition catalogue (the Fourth Exhibition from the Northern Ceramic Society, held at the City Museum and Art Gallery, Stoke-on-Trent, in 1982), seventy years after Grant's book, we are not able to pinpoint the origin of the basalt body.

The contribution of Wedgwood to the history of the basalt industry has oft been acknowledged, never better than by Robin Reilly in his 1989 general opus *Wedgwood*. That Reilly and I have overlapped in some primary sources, particularly in the use of Wedgwood and Bentley MSS at Keele University is not only natural but essential in a work of this nature. Reilly's thorough use of the Wedgwood and Bentley MSS induced me, in the interest of not retreading the same territory, to rely more heavily on the Mosley (W/M) and Mayer MSS, also on deposit at Keele University Library.

That manufacturers who marked their wares have higher visibility than those who didn't is a fact which naturally skews any discussion about the subject as a whole to those who left their imprimatur on the objects. As a result, the focus of the book is directed toward marked wares in the photographs and in the text.

Though the image of black basalt has shifted through successive English, Continental and even American prisms, as researchers and writers have passed judgment on the ware, ultimately the judgment of its beauty, just as with the selection of a pearl, be it white or black, rests in the eye of the beholder.

Colour Plate 7. Vase in the shape of an amphora with ear-shaped handles encircling female masks. The vase is decorated in 'encaustic' enamels with an anthemion border at the neck and Diana and the lion. Unmarked, Wedgwood & Bentley, c.1770-5, 9¾in. high. Grigsby collection.

Colour Plate 8. Tablet of black basalt painted in 'encaustic' enamels to simulate jasper with a central oval panel painted in sepia monochrome and buff. The subject, a nymph decorating a male statue with a weary seated female surrounded by a staff and a book, has not been determined, but is taken from an engraving by Bartolozzi after a painting by Cipriani (1727-85) (Tait, 1963, 33). On 17 November 1789 Josiah Wedgwood wrote to Dr. Darwin: 'Sir W. [Hamilton] or Mr. Greville made me a present of the set of prints', referring to Bartolozzi after Cipriani (E26-19000). Unmarked, Wedgwood, c.1772-90, 14in. long. British Museum, Franks collection.

*Colour Plate 9. Oil lamp, decorated with 'Etruscan' painting. Many engravings of oil lamps by Bellori and N. Cabinet, utilized by Wedgwood as models, were to be found in Montfaucon Vol. 10. Mark: **WEDGWOOD**, c.1780-95, 5in. long. Polikoff collection.*

*Colour Plate 10. Tea cup and saucer with gilded stylized floral border. Mark: both **Wedgwood**, c.1775-80, cup: 1¾in. high, saucer: 4¾in. diameter. Mint Museum of Art, 47.1, Gutmann collection.*

*Colour Plate 11. Ecuelle, cover and stand decorated in 'Etruscan' enamels. Mark: ecuelle: **Wedgwood**, 3in. high; stand: **WEDGWOOD**, c.1775-85, 6⅜in. diameter. Mint Museum of Art, 87.23.101, Bridges collection.*

Colour Plate 12. *Cameo-medallion of Sacrifice to Aesculapius, red stoneware in basalt moulded frame with basalt sprig relief. Unmarked, Wedgwood & Bentley, c.1773-80, 2⅜in. x 2in. Grigsby collection.*

Colour Plate 13. *Garniture of three bough pots (minus cups) of basalt with 'encaustic' painted orange ground with red and white for the patera. The basalt sprig decoration is cherubs in procession with a garland of flowers. Bough pots were in production at Wedgwoods from at least 1772 (E25-18404, 13 September 1772). Mark: D-shaped pot: **Wedgwood**, 5¾in. high; flanking pot: **WEDGWOOD K**, 4¾in. high, c.1775-85. Grigsby collection.*

17

Colour Plate 14. Stirrup cups in the form of a hare and a hound. Mark: hare, **Wedgwood & Bentley** impressed behind ear, c.1775-80, 6in. high; Mark: hound: **TURNER** impressed on collar, c.1780-95, 2¾in. high. Weldon collection.

Colour Plate 15. Sleeping figure of Morpheus. Wedgwood and Bentley produced five figures (after the 'Five Boys' by Fiammingo) of Morpheus (also referred to as Somnus), the first model of which was billed by Hoskins and Oliver in 1770 (2-30950). This Morpheus rests his head on a basket of fruit. Mark: **WEDGWOOD**, c.1780-90, 5¼in. long. By courtesy of the Trustees of the Wedgwood Museum, Barlaston, Stoke-on-Trent.

Colour Plate 16. Pyrophorous vase, drum-shaped basalt with red stoneware sprig relief floral swags pendant rams' heads. Mark: **WEDGWOOD**, c.1805-10, 2¾in. high. Mint Museum of Art 87.23.96, Bridges collection.

18

*Colour Plate 17. Vase and cover, ornately gilded in the manner fashionable for a short period in the late 19th century. The swags are pendant simulated ram's head handles. Mark: **WEDGWOOD V**, late 19th century, 9½in. high. Polikoff collection.*

*Colour Plate 18. Teapot and cover, red stoneware after the Yixing with black basalt stylized floral sprigging. The finial is a basalt Fo lion of some ferocity. Mark: **SPODE** (6mm), c.1805, 5in. high. Photograph by Bill Coles.*

Colour Plate 19. Garden seat with chinoiserie figures and birds painted boldly in opaque enamels. Unmarked, Copeland & Garrett (a version of pattern 5595), c.1835-40, 18in. high. Photograph by Bill Coles.

Colour Plate 20. Potpourri jar and cover exuberantly painted in opaque enamels with Chinese flowers. Mark: **COPELAND** printed in green, pattern No. **D690** painted in red, 1858, 4½in. high. Photograph by Bill Coles.

Colour Plate 21. Potpourri jar and cover painted in opaque enamels with Chinese flowers. Mark: **WEDGWOOD**, c.1820, 9⅞in. high. Royal Ontario Museum, 970.242.52, Brown collection.

*Colour Plate 22. Vase in the form of an amphora with red stoneware sprig relief decoration of three classical figures, the central figure holding an open box (Pandora?). Mark: **TURNER**, c.1805, 10¾in. high. Grigsby collection. (Another example is in the Rakow collection.)*

Colour Plate 23. Teapot and cover of square form in the Yixing style painted in opaque enamels with swag and urn decoration. According to David Hollens, the palette and enamelling are very similar to a teapot of a different form marked Wood in the Castle Museum, Norwich. Mark: incised '17' in base, possibly Enoch Wood, c.1790, 5¼in. high. City Museum and Art Gallery, Stoke-on-Trent, 1109.

23

CHAPTER I
Black is Sterling:
Historical Antecedents of English Black Basalt

On that shore can be found round stones of many kinds of rocks, black basalt, various coloured granites, sandstones and quartz. A.S. Byatt, Possession 1990[1]

Josiah Wedgwood's encomium to basalt, 'The Black is sterling & will last for ever',[2] written to partner Thomas Bentley in 1774, was far more prescient than even he may have realized. Known as 'Egyptian black' or 'Etruscan' prior to 1773, the fabric was more specifically associated with the Wedgwood name and manufacture than with any of the other scores of manufacturers producing the wares in the eighteenth and nineteenth centuries. Llewellynn Jewitt asserted that Josiah Wedgwood first discovered the 'art of making the unglazed black porcelain' in 1766.[3] However, it was not commercially available until 30 August 1768 when Wedgwood first dispatched a 'basket containing 2 Etruscan bronze Vases'[4] for a Miss Tarleton. Since the apotheosis of the 'First Day Vases' (Colour Plate 1), which inaugurated the industrial manufacture of the 'Egyptian black' at Etruria in 1769 (black tewares, which unexpectedly served to enhance the whiteness of the hands of the pourers,[5] had been produced from 1768),[6] black basalt has enjoyed an unbroken chain of production down to the present day.

That the manufacture of black basalt is associated almost exclusively with the name of Josiah Wedgwood is both justified and inequitable: justified in the sense

Figure 1. Teapot and cover, one of the two earliest surviving examples of basalt teapots which, according to Enoch Wood, were made by John and Thomas Wedgwood before they built the Big House, Burslem. The naturalistically modelled teapot has applied sprig decoration of leaves and berries. Unmarked, c.1740-50, 3in. high. Enoch Wood collection, City Museum and Art Gallery, Stoke-on-Trent, 328.

that in modern history the Wedgwood firm is in its third century of blackware production, longer than any other manufacturer, the wares are usually acknowledged with impressed marks, and ubiquitous. The inequity emerges when one delves slightly below the surface and discovers the numerous eighteenth and nineteenth century contenders for the market Wedgwood enjoyed, the vast majority of whom did not mark their wares or pot them with a distinctiveness which would immediately identify them as to manufacturer. That the blackware industry was rife with competition amounting to some one hundred and fifty odd manufacturers heralds the success of a ware which by some accounts is a lugubrious one, and one erroneously associated with death and mourning. On the contrary, every indication points to black basalt as the rage of the 1770s, the ultimate ornamental and teaware expression of the neo-classicism which eschewed the rococo scroll for the pristine and rectilinear.

The terminology for what is almost exclusively referred to currently as black basalt went through almost as many permutations and aliases as creamware, known variously as cream-coloured and Queen's Ware. Likewise the term 'basaltes' first appeared in the Wedgwood & Bentley Ornamental Catalogue of 1773 having been referred to intermittently as 'Egyptian black' or 'Etruscan'. The sobriquet 'basaltes' or its orthographic successor 'basalt' was sporadically applied after its introduction by Wedgwood. The 1795 *Staffordshire Potteries Price Fixing Guide* lists 'Egyptian Ware' and the *Prices Current of Earthenware*, 1814 retains the original 'Egyptian Black' terminology. Early on, in August 1768, Wedgwood himself refers to his 'first fruits' as 'Etruscan bronze Vases'.[7] The use of the term 'Etruscan bronze' at that time appears to denote polished basalt vases and should not be confused with the actual bronzing of basalt vases and busts which first began in 1769, a process which does not appear to have been universally popular judging from the few surviving pieces (Colour Plate 5).

Contrary to popular opinion, Wedgwood was not the first to manufacture the black basalt body in England; eventually more than 150 potteries were in that arena. Wedgwood's visibility is stratospheric compared to that of his contemporaries owing to a remarkable correspondence with Thomas Bentley and other business alliances, a large portion of which was saved from becoming packing material for the butchers and greengrocers of Birmingham by Joseph Mayer in 1848.[8] However, research on other contemporary potters is burgeoning as primary source material is discovered in archives and personal collections, and with it a more complete picture of the potters and potteries emerges which presents Wedgwood, not necessarily as the *prima inter pares*, but places him securely in the matrix of the pottery industry. Wedgwood's audiences remain undiminished; the applause continues. However, with increased enlightenment more players are added to the stage and the perspective is magnified.

One such document, recently discovered by Pat Halfpenny, is Enoch Wood's copy of William Pitt's *A Topographical History of Staffordshire* in the City Museum and Art Gallery, Stoke-on-Trent. The book contains annotations and comments in the margins in Enoch Wood's own handwriting. Page 416 includes marginal notations divulging the manufacturer of the two early black basalt teapots from his collection (Figure 1) which have been the source of so much speculation and controversy since they were first published by Solon in 1883.[9] Given to the City Museum and Art Gallery with an attached label indicating they were made by 'Twyford', these two teapots stylistically appear to be the earliest surviving English blackwares, dating to the mid-eighteenth century, and are noted by Enoch Wood as emanating from the pottery of John and Thomas Wedgwood before they built the Big House, Burslem. In reality it seems unlikely to suppose that these are the earliest English examples of black basalt, but arguments for earlier productions of the stoneware are tenuous and speculative. Before embarking on the various hypotheses of basalt production prior to the manufacture by John and Thomas Wedgwood it would seem appropriate to discuss the properties of the basalt body and look into its historical antecedents.

The use of the word 'basalt' appears first in Pliny[10] and may be the key to the use of both the word 'basalt' and its predecessor term 'Egyptian Black': 'The Egyptians also found in Aethyopia another kind of Marble which they call Basaltes, resembling yron as well in colour as hardness'.[11] The word is originally an African word referring to an igneous rock which is dark in colour, of considerable hardness, and found in columnar formations such as the Giant's Causeway in Ireland and Fingal's Cave in the Hebrides. The ancient city of Nan Madol on the Island of Pohnpei in Micronesia is built of basalt logs quarried from nearby islands. As mentioned, the term 'basaltes' appears to have been appropriated by Josiah Wedgwood in 1773. The body utilised by the two earliest industrial manufacturers of the ware, Wedgwood and Humphrey Palmer, was composed of 20 each of Purbeck clay and of calcined iron to one of manganese.[12] It was fired in an oxidizing atmosphere at stoneware temperatures (approximately 1200 degrees centigrade). Formulas for basalt frequently made use of a colouring agent called 'carr' which is an oxide derived from iron residue in the drainage system of the mines. A Wedgwood Commonplace Book of 1789 records the Scyples [sic Cyples] Recipe for Black as composed of:

20 Blue ball clay
5 calcined carr
1 ½ calcined manganese
These to be mixed by measure in the slip[13]

Potters would have been advantageously placed in Staffordshire with the abundance of clays locally and the rich deposits of iron ore in the Apedale and Bradwell districts.[14] Carr [or car] was a principal ingredient and a valuable one. Shaw put the price at one guinea per cart load and suggested that Josiah Wedgwood 'prepared it of a superior quality in grain, and blacker in colour'.[15] The *Staffordshire Advertiser* of 26 February 1825 included an auction notice at Chesterton Manor for 'a valuable ooze of carr from coal mines and the Carr Pitts'. Manganese was available from Cornwall.

It is often claimed that one manufacturer's wares can be distinguished from another's by the texture of the basalt body. Indeed the quality of the basalt texture varies from manufacturer to manufacturer, from almost a grey, gritty texture, as the worst example, to a smooth, buttery, lustrous quality, seen, for example, on most of the wares produced by Palmer and Neale. However, the quality of the body can vary enormously within the same pot bank due to the variability in firing techniques. Frequent mention is made of formulas but very little about firing factors. Before the advent of the Dressler Oven (kiln) and sophisticated bodies to suit their purpose, the fireman's responsibility was as great as that of the thrower, turner, or decorator in

Figure 2. Jug, bucchero ware, Pre-Columbian blackware, used locally and exported to Europe. Unmarked, 6th-4th century B.C., 6½ in. high. Laver collection.

the success of the final object. Owing to the contamination factor in the iron or manganese stains associated with a refined black stoneware body, the clay would have to be prepared separately, away from the ball clays and other light bodied clays used in creamware production. The question of a separate firing remains unsolved. But chemists and technicians at the Wedgwood factory today concede that the firing process itself would not cause the iron and manganese to stain other bodies. At least in the early stages of blackware manufacture Wedgwood was firing the different bodies in the same kiln. In the same letter that Wedgwood offers his 'first fruits' to Miss Tarleton he continues:

> There are three other imperfect ones [black vases] to show you a little into *the light of our imperfections* in the manufacture of these delicate compositions…Every vase in the last kiln were spoil'd & that only by such a degree in variation in the fire as scarcely affected [*sic*] our creamcolour bisket at all.[16]

Wedgwood's Etruscan works were not ready in August of 1768, but were nearly 'ready for roofing'.[17] When completed the Black Bank consisted of over a dozen buildings.[18] However, in 1775 Wedgwood still seems to be firing several types of wares in the same kiln: 'We put a few of the Heads of fine white into every kiln we fire…'[19]

Although surviving marked examples of Spode basalt are not numerous, the factory plan also indicated a Black Bank which encompassed a square including two bottle ovens for the exclusive firing of the blackware. It is still not known whether Spode used both kilns for firing biscuit or whether one was for biscuit and the other for firing glost.[20] Swansea's pottery plan of 1802 also indicated a 'black cellar', 'black slip kiln' and a 'black shed' for firing the considerable blackware output of which, perhaps, only a couple of dozen marked items are recorded.[21]

Baitings of top quality coal placed correctly and fired to precise temperatures estimated by the use of rings (and later by the pyrometer invented by Josiah Wedgwood in 1782) could ensure a basalt yield good from the oven of 92%.[22]

These first black stonewares became commercially available in 1768; however, other potters utilized varying formulas which will be discussed individually. Prior to the eighteenth century all the prototypical blackwares, both ancient and modern, were probably fired in a reducing atmosphere at earthenware temperatures.

Basalt Antecedents

The historical antecedents of blackware production are ancient and numerous. Blackware appears to have been produced intermittently from prehistoric times down to the present. Black punctured ware, made of black clay throughout, without a slip but partly polished, has been found on several archaeological sites dating from the third century BC: in Cyprus in the early necropolis at Kalopsida as well as the late Mycenaean tombs at Enkomi, and, interestingly, also in Egypt at Khata'anah and Fayûm where the blackware was found in conjunction with scarabs and flint chips dating to the twelfth and thirteenth dynasties (2500-2000 BC).[23] The earliest examples of red and black colour on vases were in the Egyptian black and redware of the third century BC, a method introduced on the island of Cyprus.[24]

Pottery making its appearance in Cyprus during the Copper Age or pre-Mycenaean period (2500-1500 BC) was mainly indigenous, but the shapes and some of the firing techniques were derived from Egypt where the wheel was known. These Cypriot wares present very striking contrasts to the pottery of Troy of the same period.[25] The fabrics of Asia Minor represent a very primitive type of Mediterranean pottery. The original black-polished ware which developed in two separate localities, under similar conditions, evolved into the bucchero wares of Aeolis and Etruria. The earliest known Asiatic examples are from the first city of Troy (Hissarlik) in which the black colour is said to be a carbonaceous pigment in the clay. Hissarlik hand made pottery probably dates to the Middle Minoan (1900-1700 BC). A slightly later group of pots belong to a subsequent Troy population known as the Yortan civilization. Their vases were also hand made and very primitive but the black colour was produced by a chemical reduction in the iron oxide present naturally in the clay or artificially applied to the surface. In this group the most common pots were jugs copied from leather models. Pottery of the Yortan type covered the whole Bronze Age period and was introduced into regions on the other side of the Adriatic sea in at least two periods.[26]

In Italy, the blackware reached its apogee in the bucchero wares of South Etruria which were produced from the second quarter of the seventh century BC for about two centuries (Figure 2). In the archaic period bucchero pottery is a common occurrence in most Etruscan sites. Technically the bucchero wares of Central and North Etruria are inferior to those of South Etruria displaying a heavier body and less harmonious shapes. The wares of South Etruria depend on their shape alone for visual appeal. It has been suggested by many scholars that these black pottery vessels were produced as cheap imitations of far more costly bronze vessels.

The word bucchero is derived from the Spanish *bucaro* meaning 'fragrant clay'. The term was first applied to certain Pre-Columbian pottery of Central and South America made from a blackish, odorous clay. Such vases eventually found their way to Portugal and Spain[27] (and probably Italy).

All Etruscan bucchero wares were thrown on a wheel, fired in a reduction atmosphere, so that both the surface and the core are black. The deep black colour is due not only to the reduction of the iron oxides in the clay but also due to the

Figure 3. Big House, Burslem, site of John and Thomas Wedgwood's factory, built c.1750. (Photograph 1990)

combustion of carbon. It is possible that the carbon (which is organic material) was present naturally in the clay or that it might have been added artificially. The latest theory is that wood was placed in the kiln producing carbon oxides which were absorbed by the clay. The minimum kiln temperature for oxidation or reduction to have any effect on the colour of the clay is in the range of 800 degrees centigrade.[28]

The finest and earliest bucchero has a very high sheen; it is doubtful whether this was achieved by burnishing alone. It would appear that before firing the surface was coated with a thin organic wash or slip which would provide the lustrous surface approximating burnishing.[29]

Many Etruscan bucchero shapes were derived from East Greek and Corinthian prototypes. Decoration took the form of incised geometric patterns, or figures of animals such as the sphinx, griffin and centaur, or lions and panthers. Relief decoration produced in a fashion similar to sprigging on eighteenth century wares was also frequently seen on bucchero wares,[30] but human figures and mythological scenes were rarely seen.

Bucchero wares were not well represented in museum collections in England until the mid-nineteenth century, having been part of major excavations about 1817 near the present Castel Gandolfo. The British Museum specimens were given by Mr. Beldam in 1858 and Mr. Bert in 1883.[31]

Thus far the discussion has focused on wares with black bodies and black surfaces similar in aspect to black basalt. Although comparable in appearance, the Egyptian, Cypriot and South Etrurian bucchero wares probably had little or no influence on the eighteenth century blackwares produced by the earliest Staffordshire manufacturers who were far more directly influenced by the red and black figured Hellenic wares. These so-called black glazed wares were the wares published by Mountfacon, Count Caylus and Sir William Hamilton in their catalogues which were either published in English or translated into English in the 1750s and 1760s igniting the ensuing neo-classical fires. Although the discussion of these catalogues and their influence on Wedgwood follows in the next chapter, the historical affinity is one which cannot be overlooked in the present context.

In ancient times vases were made in great numbers in practically every part of Greece and more vases have survived in good condition than any other form of Greek art. Although the Greeks did not generally put treasures, such as vases, in the tombs of their dead, the Etruscans, who traded actively with Greece, often buried their dead with an array of worldly acquisitions.[32] Mid-eighteenth century excavations of Etruscan archaeological sites yielded great quantities of finely painted Greek vases of the sixth and fifth centuries BC saved for posterity by a myriad of collectors of all nationalities and conditions, who were often among the first to comment on them. Greek vase scholar Warren G. Moon likens the relationship of the emporia and Greek ceramic industry to that of the Staffordshire pottery industry in the eighteenth and nineteenth centuries with its American clientele. Americans, like the Etruscans, locally produced coarse redwares comparable to the Etruscan imitation of Greek pottery but continued to patronise the more civilized ceramic output across the sea. 'Gaudy Dutch' earthenwares were produced by the Staffordshire potters to appeal to the Pennsylvania-German Americans in the same way the Nikosthenic kyathos (one-handled cup) was made to please the Etruscan Caere.[33]

Potters, unlike collectors, are not satisfied merely with acquisitions. They need to create or imitate to gratify their patrons. The Wedgwood and Palmer imitations of Greek vases were actually closer in technique to some South Etrurian Gnathia pottery vases from Apulia than to their Greek prototypes. Instead of relying on the system reserving the figure or object in the colour of the clay by filling in the background with black glaze and then drawing in the details in reserved areas, the painters of Gnathia vases covered their surfaces with black glaze first, then painted the decoration entirely in added colours.[34] The Staffordshire potters also painted the figures on to the entirely black surface of the basalt vases in opaque enamels.

The technique for firing and decorating Greek vases was far more complicated. It is now understood, as established by Gisela M.A. Richter, that Greek vases were fired only once, but in three different phases: an oxidizing, a reducing, and a re-oxidizing phase. During the first oxidizing phase of the firing, both the vase and the glaze turned red. In the reducing phase, which would have been achieved by stifling the fire with a damp fuel, the vase and the glaze would turn black. In the final reoxidizing phase, the porous fired clay of the vase again turned red, but the glaze could not reoxidize to a red colour owing to the fact that it had sintered and sealed off its black iron oxide from contact with oxygen in the air. Therefore, the vase emerged red while the glaze remained black.[35]

Black glaze was widely utilized thoughout the Mediterranean region and the

Figure 4. Teapot and cover, light black stoneware teapot with replacement pewter spout naturalistically modelled in the Yixing manner. Long reputed to have been produced by Josiah Wedgwood at the Churchyard works, the evidence for this attribution is unsubstantiated. Unmarked, c.1750, 4in high. By courtesy of the Trustees of the Wedgwood Museum, Barlaston, Stoke-on-Trent.

technique spread across Europe to Gaul and Roman Britain. In Britain, however, the production of pottery was not an indigenous one until a temporary decline in the importation of the sophisticated Samian redwares in the first and second centuries AD. With that lacuna, and with the probable increase in the second century of orders to fill the military needs of the army on Hadrian's Wall, potters began prominently to produce two types of black burnished ware. The more primitive type, with its origins in the Iron Age people of Dorset, was black, gritty, hand made, and burnished in facets; the later ware was a greyish, finer wheel thrown ware with a more regular surface. Produced in the early second century the wares were a product of the Romanized industries of the Thames Estuary, with tributaries of pottery production located in East Yorkshire, the Doncaster region and the North Somerset marshes.[36]

During the Iron Age most pottery was fired in surface bonfires or pit clamps. This produced a reduction atmosphere which coloured the clay black throughout. Some potteries sporadically continued this practice until the sixteenth century, but after the Roman conquest most wares were fired in permanent kiln structures.[37]

The end of Roman occupation in the fourth century meant that no new coinage arrived to pay the army. Within thirty years the use of coins in general ceased, replaced by the barter system of trade. It appears that with the removal of the army, the political structure reverted into small self-governing hamlets contributing to the breakdown of trade and overall decline in the manufacture of pottery. At that time anthropologists speculate that there was a general reversion to the use of metal or wooden vessels for cooking and eating.[38]

From the fifth to the thirteenth centuries potters in Europe did not speak loudly but did not lose the language. At that time the Hispano-Moresque potters awakened an industry on the Iberian Peninsula which was to disseminate the tin glaze tradition throughout Europe and the British Isles. It is doubtful that the production of black-wares was a concomitant feature with the tin glaze industries; therefore, it seems prudent to conclude that there was a long hiatus of blackware production after the

Roman occupation of Britain until the seventeenth century when local potteries in London and the Midlands began producing black glazed jugs and drinking vessels.[39]

Speculation of a late seventeenth century blackware manufacture by the Elers Brothers at Bradwell Wood sparked by Simeon Shaw has all but been extinguished by the work of G.W. Elliott.[40] In establishing that the Elers' stonewares were slip-cast rather than thrown, as had been previously thought, Mr. Elliott exposed the improbability of a black stoneware manufacture by the brothers. The high proportion of iron and manganese oxide in the stoneware would have reduced the strength of the cast slip, as well as creating complex drying problems.[41] In direct and further refutation of Shaw, no blackware sherds have been found on the Bradwell Wood site.[42]

The Early Wares

The surviving John and Thomas Wedgwood pots manufactured before the Big House, Burslem, was built (Figure 1) are among the few early icons of the blackware industry in England. A crude portrait medallion excavated at Fenton on the Whieldon site is probably the earliest neo-classical trial piece of black basalt. Other basalt teapot fragments were also found on the Fenton Vivian site (see Figure 428). An early Yixing type naturalistic teapot in the Wedgwood Museum (Figure 4) purports to be the product of Wedgwood's Churchyard works but the foundation for this is largely speculative.

Whieldon's recipe for 'Black' survives but it appears to be an earthenware recipe, probably for black glazed Jackfield type wares:

2 pounds magnass
6 pound ocre
2 scals (iron scales)
3 Red clay
2 Tough Tom (buff-coloured local clay)
4½ white clay
½ pound flint [43]

In addition to the Cyples recipe, several other formulas survive. John Bourne of Burslem left a large legacy of pottery recipes including one for 'Egyptian Black' which carries with it a further warning:

blue clay	235
calcined ironstone	225
manganese	15
Cornish clay	15

There is no body used in the ceramic art requiring more care in examination of the water than this, principally on account of the manganese, which ought not to come in contact with lime or any calcareous earth. It requires only one fire, after which it is scoured with fine sand, and afterwards rubbed with a little oil.[44]

From about 1820 glazed blackwares became popular. A Burslem recipe of H.L. Letillier, dated May 27, 1845, entitled 'Black Shining Body' calls for:

15 Pecks	of Soft Tom slip
15 do	of red marl
2 do	of Ball Clay slip
2 do	of Iron Stone

Shining Glaze to the Above

160 pound Lead
55 pound Flint
26 pound good manganese free from iron
24 quarts Ball Clay Slip [45]

(Other recipes for 'Black' are listed in Appendix II.)

There is little evidence to indicate that the precursors of the eighteenth century black basalt production, the Italian and Cypriot bucchero wares, even the earlier Minoan and Mycenaean blackwares, inspired any of the later English industries. The two earliest industrial manufacturers of the ware, Josiah Wedgwood and Humphrey Palmer, cut a swathe through the rococo and inaugurated the neo-classical movement in the pottery industry in England with vases inspired by Hellenic examples which had been on view in the British Museum for twenty years prior to the time of their own manufactures in the late 1760s.[46] Josiah Wedgwood took credit for the invention of the body listing it among the six which he acknowledged as his own:

> *Basaltes;* a fine porcelain bisque, of nearly the same properties as the natural stone, it receives a high polish, serves as a touchstone for metals, strikes fire with steel, resists all the acids, and bears without injury, a stronger fire than the basaltes itself.[47]

Wedgwood also 'invented & brought to its present degree of Perfection that fashionable Species of Earthenware, called *The Queen's Ware...*'.[48] This startling allegation by Wedgwood's solicitors in a letter of 1771 stands in spite of the fact that other potters were making and dating creamwares as early as 1743.[49] Elliott conjectures (wrongly as we have just seen) that Wedgwood did not take credit for inventing the basalt body due both to intentional and unintentional historical use of iron oxide to colour clays. Therefore, Wedgwood felt he could not justifiably attribute any special significance to improvements to the stoneware implemented at Ivy House.[50]

The technology of the basalt fabric was in the incubus; the past, forged by a social élite anxious to protect its authority by reference to Antiquity, provided the iconography, and the rise of a prospering middle class provided the market. The prospering of all classes clamoured for urns, cassolettes and garnitures of vases for chimney-pieces.

The influence of both Count Caylus' *Compendium* and the Baron D'Hancarville's catalogue of Sir William Hamilton's collection, were tantamount to a Grand Tour or an archaeological expedition to Greece itself. It was thought until quite recently that Hamilton was one of the first to distinguish between Greek and Etruscan vases; in fact all the vases were Greek, imports into Tuscany and frequently found in Etruscan tombs. Nevertheless, Hamilton appreciated their artistic form and decoration and his influence was felt immediately in the community of potters seeking to satisfy the aristocracy, the gentry, and establish a market for the new middling classes in England's prospering economy. The first volume of his collection, *Antiquités, Etrusques, Grecques et Romaines....*was published in 1766, and advertised in London in March, 1769.

Wedgwood (and assuredly Palmer) had copies of the first volume of the catalogue early on, and Wedgwood was also familiar with the descriptions of Etruscan painting recounted by Cicero, Pliny and other ancient writers.[51] Humphrey Palmer was acquainted with Dempster's *Etruria Regalia* printed in Florence in 1724, which described the colours of the painting on Greek vases as 'Perfectly smoothe without having any glassy Appearance' (translated from the Latin).[52] That Demster was not listed in an inventory of the books in the Wedgwood and Bentley library in 1770 is a curious phenomenon, the whole subject of the classical influences and source books being touched on in the next chapter.

Thus appreciation for the sterling qualities of the black ceramic fabric, and for the potential decoration which could be applied to it, was not the province of the prophetic Josiah Wedgwood alone. Indeed, it seems to have existed from prehistoric times, not in an unbroken chain of manufacture, but rather a universal long-lived sympathy for the elegance of a body which could be burnished, painted, applied with reliefs or left unadorned with equal success.

CHAPTER II
Etruria Revived:
Early Basalt Manufacture of Wedgwood and Palmer

Poor creamcolour. They tell me I sacrifice all to Etruria *and* Vases.[1]

For all intents and purposes the manufacture of black basalt was formally inaugurated on 13 June 1769 with the opening of the Etruscan works at Wedgwood's new factory at Etruria. It was to be six months before Wedgwood delivered to Bentley the six Etruscan vases (Colour Plate 1) thrown by himself with Bentley turning the wheel. The vases, he warned, 'sho'd be finish'd as high as you please but not sold, they being *first fruits* of Etruria.'[2] 'Antique' vases (Figure 6) had been produced for a year or two prior to the opening of Etruria works but the exact date production began remains uncertain. On 23 July 1768 Wedgwood sent to Mr. Cox at the London warehouse '3 Black Marble Vases'.[3] Both variegated and marbled vases had been in production for some months having made their appearance in the late autumn of 1767.

As early as 1762, the *New York Gazette* carried an advertisement placed by Keeling and Morris for 'black Tea-pots, Milk-pots, Mugs and Bowls, and Cups and Saucers.'[4] In 1764 the firm of Bentley and Boardman in Liverpool ordered from Josiah Wedgwood '6 doz. Black Teapots 2/6 p. doz.'; 2 doz. Black Coffee Pots and 2 doz. miscellaneous Black gilt small wares.[5] Although basalt wasters and sherds exist from the Wedgwood/Whieldon partnership at Fenton Vivian and examples of some earlier basalt were produced by John and Thomas Wedgwood before they erected the Big House, Burslem (Figure 1), the blackwares offered by Keeling and Morris and ordered by Bentley and Boardman were doubtless the red-bodied, black-glazed wares generically referred to as 'Jackfield'. Wedgwood may have been experimenting with the black stoneware body as early as 1766 but there is no solid evidence of manufacture until 30 August 1768 when a 'basket containing 2 Etruscan bronze Vases' was dispatched to a Miss Tarleton.[6]

Wedgwood's interest in the 'Antique', the classical Greek and Etruscan shapes and decoration, probably antedated his manufacture of the vases by some years. The association with Dr. Erasmus Darwin in Lichfield thrust Wedgwood into

Figure 5. Vase and cover, 'Etruscan-decorated' in shades of red. The vase is copied from one in Sir William Hamilton's collection and depicts Hercules in the garden of the Hesperides. Similar to the 'First Day Vases,' shape No. 93 was offered in 6in., 8½in., 10in., 14in., 15in., 16in., and 18½in. sizes. Unmarked, Wedgwood & Bentley, c.1770-75, 13⅞in. high. Victoria and Albert Museum, C125-1956.

a circle of educated and enquiring minds providing a catalyst which ultimately fed into the experimentation and manufacture at the Ivy House and Etruria works. The inspiration and models for neo-classical objects derived from the collections depicted in books acted as sources for the Wedgwood and Bentley manufacture. By 1770, Wedgwood and Bentley had an impressive library of reference works, the inventory of which included:

L'Antiquité Expliquée par Montfaucon 15 Vols.	1722 folio	18- 0-0
Hambleton's [*sic*] *Etruscan Antiquities* 2 Vols	Do	6- 6-0
Museum Etruscum Gori 3 Vols.	Do	4- 4-0
Museum Romanem de la Chausse 2 Vols.	Do	1-16-0
Gemmae Antiquae Museum Florentinum [7] 1 Vol.	Do	3- 3-0
Turnbull's *Paintings of the Antients*	Do	2-12-1
Stosch's *Gems by Picart*		3- 3-0
Antiquities of Herculaneum 6 Vols. (Sheets)	folio	18-18-0
Recueil de Trois Cent Tetes et Sujets de Composition Graves par M. Le Comte de Caylus	4o	0-15-0
Antiquities of Venice 2 Vols.	folio	4- 4-0
Caylus' *Antiquities* 7 vols.	Do	–
Stella's *Vases of the Louvre*	folio	4- 4- 0
Plates for Ovid's *Metamorphosis*		6- 6- 0
Recueil d'antiquités Romaines	4o chiefly Vases	0- 9- 0
Verrerie par Kunckell [*sic*] et les autres	4o	1- 1- 0
Montamy	12o about	0- 3- 6
Bardon *de peinture et La Sculpture*	12o about	0- 8- 0
Dictionaire d'Antiquité	16	0- 3- 6
Lives of the Saints 10 Vols.	4o	1- 1- 0
Rossi's *Statues* at Etruria		4- 4- 0
Temple of the Muses	Do	2-10-0
Potts *Chymical Works* 4 Vols.		14-0
Hambleton's [*sic*] *Etruscan Antiquities* 1 Vol. Sr. WWW[8]		
Cherrons [*sic*] *Gems*	folio	
Stewart's [*sic*] *Athens*	Do	
Iconologie Historique par de la Fosse		
Hogarth's *Analysis*	folio	-15-0
Perriers *Statues*		
Ficoroni's *Gems*		
Middleton's *Antiquities*		
British and Irish Peerage 3 Vols.		0-12-0

Wedgwood continued to buy classical source books. In 1774 he purchased a five volume set of Grose's *Antiquities* from a Mr. Hooper for £3.15.0.[9]

Any discussion of the source books hinges on the three principal ones: the Hamilton Collection catalogue, the de Montfaucon, and the de Caylus. The subject is such a vast one that it deserves a separate volume dedicated exclusively to linking the classical relief and encaustic and Etruscan decorated wares and shapes with the individual sources.

The 1766 publication of the first volume of Sir William Hamilton's catalogue of his collection, *Antiquités Etrusques, Grecques et Romaines ...* may have inspired the rage for chimney ornaments and garnitures of vases to adorn mantelpieces, all those decorative symbols of neo-classicism. However, the movement had been afoot since the late 1730s with the excavations at Herculaneum (1738) and Pompeii (1763); Piranesi was publishing in the 1740s; Robert Adam was in Italy from 1754 to 1758 studying the art which was later to embellish the rooms at Kedleston and Osterley and other architectural monuments to his genius. In 1764, Adam's *Ruins of the Palace of Diocletian at Spalato* was published, a monumental work which further elucidated the neo-classical metier. That Josiah Wedgwood appreciated Robert Adam is evident in a letter to Thomas Bentley 7th September 1771:

> Adam is a Man of Genius & invention & an excellent Architect & Mr. Truman assured me that he knew Mr. Adam's [*sic*] kept modelers at Rome employed in copying Bas-reliefs and other things for them a conection with them would be of great use to us.[10]

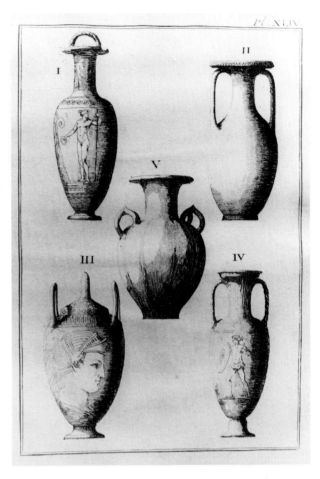

Figure 6. Plate XLIV from de Caylus' Recueil... Published in seven volumes from 1752 to 1767. By 1770 Wedgwood was in possession of all the volumes, known as The Compendium.

The earliest of these important architectural movements in England sought to perpetuate the ideas of sixteenth century Italian architect Andrea Palladio. His buildings and plans had been sought out early in the seventeenth century when English classical architect Inigo Jones (1573-1652) was travelling in Italy in the entourage of Thomas, earl of Arundel. As a late Renaissance architect Palladio published two important volumes which came out in England in 1715-16.[11] Palladio, and his Roman literary mentor, Vitruvius, became widely admired, especially in England, in the late eighteenth century. Admiring the leadership of amateur architect Lord Burlington, Palladians employed the symbols of the classical as well as the vocabulary which they felt to be consistent with the intentions of the ancients. Their aim was to be faithful to the essence and purity of Greco-Romanism, not to copy it literally. Of considerable influence was the publication of Robert Wood's *Ruins of Palmyra* and *Ruins of Baalbek* in 1753 and 1757. Wood was mentor to the Duke of Bridgewater and both Wood and Adam advised him on his purchase of antiquities. These very important works on little known classical civilizations expelled the taste for the Gothic and for the Chinese which had so dominated the rococo and baroque.[12] Piranesi's prints, in particular, offered, along with their high intrinsic value as works of art, faithfully reproduced details of ornaments which were useful to designers such as John Flaxman and Henry Webber, titans in the Wedgwood entourage. To return to Hamilton one might say that instead of inspiring the neo-classical movement, Hamilton's catalogue was the crescendo of an escalating tide of activity all organized toward addressing the excesses of the rococo with a preference for the elegant rectilinear. Wedgwood was seeking the first volume as soon as it was

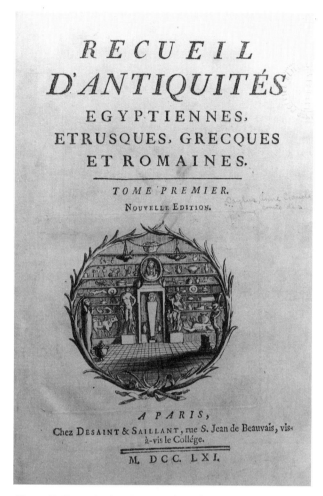

Figure 7. Count Caylus' Compendium, *first volume published in Paris in 1752.*

Figure 8. Vase, with loop handles terminating in ram's head masks. A number of choices for the pendant medallion of Apollo and Marsyas can be seen in Figure 10 illustrated in Volume I of Montfaucon. The original gem was in the Lorenzo D'Medici collection and both the Palmer and Wedgwood versions contain the 'LAVR MED' imprimatur. Mark: **H. PALMER HANLEY** *in wafer of base, c.1769-78, 9⅜ in. high. Private collection.*

available in London. In May, 1768 he wrote to William Cox: 'I pray enquire where I may get the Etruscan Antiquities when they are published, if you have not done it already.'[13] The first volume of Hamilton's catalogue was not advertised in London until March of 1769:

> IMPORTED FROM NAPLES, by T. Cadell...The first volume of the following Magnificent Work, A Collection of Etruscan, Greek and Roman Antiquities, from the cabinet of Hon. William Hamilton, His Britannic Majesty's Envoy Extraordinary at the Court of Naples. The whole will be comprised in four volumes, folio, the plates finely coloured.[14]

The terms were four guineas for the first volume on delivery, two guineas for the second volume (which appeared in 1770), and the remaining three guineas paid upon the delivery of the third and fourth volumes, which did not appear until 1776.[15]

40

Horace Walpole, author of Gothic novels and creator of Strawberry Hill in a Medieval style, was, in spite of these private other world amusements, not surprisingly among the many who purchased the volumes as soon as they appeared, Walpole purchasing the second volume on 15 May 1770.[16]

Hamilton's vases, half sold to the British Museum and the other half to Thomas Hope (resold at Christie's London in 1907), formed incomparably the finest collection of vases ever assembled by an Englishman, making his catalogue vastly influential to moulding British taste. The catalogue was an expensive production, costing Hamilton £6,000, only a little less than the price fetched by the sale of the collection to the British Museum in 1772 for £8,400. Hamilton continued to collect vases after the initial liquidation of this portion of his collection and wrote to his nephew, Charles Greville about one particular cache:

> I am sure that this mine of these vases lately discovered must fail soon, and therefore I have not let one essential vase escape Me, tho' the price be higher than it was formerly. The King of Naples has now begun to purchase them, but my harvest was luckily in first.[17]

That Wedgwood and Palmer were greatly influenced by the D'Hancarville presentation of Hamilton's collection is irrefutable. Some vases were direct copies from the catalogue such as the vase in the Victoria and Albert Museum (Figure 5; Colour Plate 1); others were adaptations which included either the shape or the decoration.

Hamilton's catalogue was clearly not the only source for the classically styled vases produced early on. Of considerable influence were the encyclopaedic tomes published in Paris by Bernard de Montfaucon in 1719.[18] The work, compiled by Benedictine monk de Montfaucon was originally published in ten folio volumes in 1719, and forms a nearly complete encyclopaedia of classical iconography and historical classical representations. Greek and Roman mythological figures as well as Egyptian are included in books whose principal sources for the deep, rich engravings include: La Chausse, Beyer, Maffei, Foucault, Gorloeus, Boissard, and N. Cabinet. Wedgwood and Bentley owned the 1722 ten volume edition (Figure 10) as well as the five supplemental volumes published in 1724 and 1757 in French and in 1725 in English. There is no way of knowing which of the French supplemental editions they owned.

Count Caylus' *Recueil d'Antiquités Egyptiennes, Etrusques, Greques et Romaines* (Figures 6 and 7) was an equally influential source, in a smaller format and, with less sophisticated engravings. Printed in seven quarto volumes in Paris, the first volume was published in 1752 and the last not until 1767. By 1770 Wedgwood was in possession of all seven volumes of Count Caylus' compendium. In a letter to Bentley in London Wedgwood wrote:

> We want an anatomical figure, w ch I sho d have bo t & think you sho d send us by the next waggon [sic] half the vols of Count Caylus & some of the other good books for Mr. Denby & us to study after.[19]

Perhaps more than any other work that of de Caylus roused Wedgwood and Bentley to copy the ancient vases. After a military career Count de Caylus studied the ancient monuments of Asia Minor, Constantinople, and Rome. On three

occasions he amassed huge collections of archaeological artefacts, each time dispersing them among royal collections. Caylus' work utilizes only his own collections, and the engravings which he personally produced from them are a unique manifestation of one man's collecting efforts. As early as 1st October 1769 in a letter to his partner Thomas Bentley, Wedgwood acknowledged the source for some vases as designs from Count Caylus.[20] Vase numbers 43-54 and number 47 were from Count Caylus, number 47 being nearly the same as one in Hamilton's *Vignets*. Vase number 33 (as well as number 21) in the shape book was also acknowledged as 'a pretty exact copy from Count Caylus'.[21]

Wedgwood and Bentley owned another of the volumes of de Caylus, *Recueil de trois cents têtes et sujets de composition Gravés par Mr. le Comte de Caylus d'après les pierres gravées antiques du Cabinet du Roi*. This work consists of about one hundred portrait busts of mythological and Roman subjects and two hundred compositions from Roman mythology. Wedgwood and Bentley seem to have used this volume to execute the following designs: Auguste et Livie (Plate 29), Tite et sa Fille Julie (Plate 34), La Vache de Myron (Plate 105), Le Taureau Dionisiaque (Plate 106), Victoire (Plate 282), Diane Chasseresse (Plate 285).[22]

Antonio Francesco Gori (1691-1757) was represented by two works in the Wedgwood and Bentley factory library, *Museum Etruscum* (1737) and *Museum Florentinum* (1731). Although they apparently only possessed one volume of the twelve volume *Museum Florentinum*, it was doubtless a source for cameos and intaglios as it contained engravings of coins and gems from private collections in Florence.

Other volumes in the factory library included *Museum Romanum* of La Chausse.

Michel Ange de La Chausse was born in Paris towards the end of the seventeenth century but lived in Rome and published many works of high quality on the antiquities of Rome, including his two volume *Museum Romanum* (1st ed. 1690; 2nd ed.1707). Originally published in one volume, the fact that the list mentions a two volume copy indicates it is the 1746 edition.

Stosch's *Gems by Picart* was the 1724 Gemmae *antiquae caelatae, sculptorum nominibus insignitae*...printed in Amsterdam by Bernard Picart.

Rossi's *Statues* refers to the *Raccolta di statue antiche e moderne data in luce...*, Rome, 1704, by Domenico de Rossi, illustrated by Paolo Alessandro Maffei.

Temple of the Muses was printed in Amsterdam in 1733 in Dutch *(De Tempel der Zang-Godinnen)* with English and French translations. The plates are engraved by Bernard Picart, who also produced the engravings for Stosch's book on gems in the Wedgwood and Bentley library.

Cherron's *Gems* is the foreshortened *Pierres antiques gravées tirées des principaux cabinets de la France* (n.d.), by Élisabeth Sophie Cheron (1648-1711). Forty-one plates are engraved by the author in this book, two of which are dated 1728.[23]

In 1762 James Stuart and Nicholas Revett published *The antiquities of Athens measured and delineated*...which was the result of their travels together to Greece. An architect, Stuart was a friend of Josiah Wedgwood which accounts for the copy in the factory library.

Nouvelle iconologie historique...of Jean-Charles Delafosse was published in Paris in 1768 and contains 168 engravings of emblems, medallions, trophies and other decorative designs.

Perrier's Statues refers to a collection of statues of Rome, *Illmo D. D. Rogerio Du Plesseis...Segmenta nobilium signorum e statuaru...* published by François Perrier (1590?-1656?) in 1638. This book contains plates of the Farnese Flora and Farnese Hercules utilized by Wedgwood.

Ficoroni's *Gems* is the *Gemmae antiquae litteratae*...published in Rome in 1757 by Francesco Ficoroni (1664-1747), a study of antique gems drawn by the author.

Middleton's *Antiquities* is the collection of the English ecclesiastical antiquarian Conyers Middleton (1683-1750), *Germana quaedam Antiquitatis eruditae monumenta...* (1745).[24]

By no means a complete discussion of the 1770 book list, the works mentioned do appear to constitute the major sources of design for early basalt shapes and decoration. However, probably some time after 1770 Wedgwood and Bentley acquired the Rev. Mr. Spence's *Polymetis or an Enquiry Concerning the Agreement Between the Works of the Romans and the Remains of the Antient Artists, Being an Attempt to Illustrate Mutually from One and Another*, London, 1747. Considered to be an ornament in every choice library, the author, Joseph Spence (1699-1768) was an intimate friend of James Thompson and a member of Pope's circle, the Dilettanti Society. Wedgwood was listed as a subscriber to the 1774 edition of the *Polymetis*

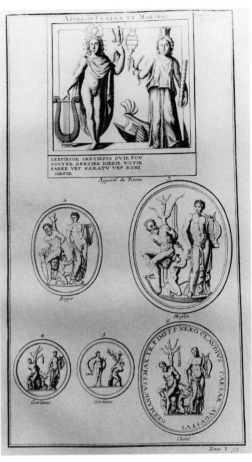

Figure 10. Plate 53, Volume I of L' Antiquité Expliquée et Representée En Figures *of Bernard de Montfaucon, 1722. The engravings by Beger, Maffei, Gorloeus, and Choul all depict the Apollo and Marsyas theme utilized by Palmer and Wedgwood and Bentley for basalt medallions on vases.*

Figure 11. Wedgwood's York Street (St. James's Square) Showrooms as illustrated in Ackermann's Plate 2, Repository of the Arts, *1809.*

whose first folio edition appeared in 1755, the third in 1774. More than thirty designs utilized by Wedgwood can be attributed to Spence's work, including 'The Judgment of Paris', 'Eros riding on a lion playing a lyre', the 'Somnus' used in zodiacial figures, the 'Three Graces' and 'Diomedes and the Palladium'.[25]

Figure 12. Vase, ovoid-shaped, engine turned with satin-stripes with a band of overlapping leaves at the shoulder, satyr's-head handles, surmounted by an acorn finial. The source for this unusual vase (which was also produced similarly by Wedgwood and Bentley) appears to be an etching signed by F. Kirschner (Frederick Kirschner, 1748-79) in the Victoria and Albert Museum (see Timothy Clifford, ECC Transactions Vol. 10, Part 3, 1978, 172). Mark: **H.PALMER HANLEY** *in wafer of base, c.1769-78, 12¾ in. high. Photograph courtesy Sotheby's New York.*

Josiah Wedgwood and rival Humphrey Palmer's red figured decoration was inspired directly by Count Caylus' *Recueil...* and by Hamilton's collection catalogues; however, the technology of the red and black figured Greek and Etruscan vases in no way approximated the process used by their English imitators. The ancient vases were decorated by painting slip on to the vases and firing in an alternate oxidation/reduction atmosphere to obtain the contrasting red or black figures. In the Wedgwood and Palmer examples a type of matt enamel was used to decorate the surface of the black basalt. Wedgwood took out a patent on this enamel process on 16 November 1769, calling it 'encaustic' painting.[26] Shortly after (or possibly before) Humphrey Palmer was also producing black basalt vases and decorating them in the 'encaustic' manner and offering them for sale in James Neale's London emporium at No. 8 St. Paul's Churchyard. In an undated draft letter

44

Figure 13. Teapot and cover. Bamboo-shaped teapots such as this one were produced popularly in the 1770s, and later. They were made by numerous potteries including Wedgwood & Bentley, Myatt, Clowes, Turner and probably Palmer. Mark: **Wedgwood**, *c.1770s, 4⅛in. high. Rakow collection.*

describing the history of the encaustic patent dispute between Wedgwood and Palmer, Wedgwood's solicitor acknowledged that the formula for this enamel was to be found in Dempster's *Etruria Regalia*.[27] Thomas Dempster's manuscript finally saw the light of day due to the efforts of Thomas Coke and Lord Leicester when it was published in Florence in 1723-4 and Palmer may have been acquainted with the work. Neale seems to have been the spokesman for Palmer, and in doing so for the first time, intimates the Palmer/Neale partnership. In a letter to Bentley on 25 October 1770, however, Wedgwood acknowledged the uncertainty of proving the fact:

> …I do not know that Palmer and Neale are partners—that matter is kept a secret, & wo'd be very difficult for us to prove, neither could we prove that Palmer has really enameled [*sic*] these things. Neale may have got them done by Giles, or some of the other enamelers [*sic*] in Town, and I think it very probable he has…[28]

Figure 14. Egg cup, finely fluted bowl with turned base. Egg cups in basalt were made at least from 1774. On 12 January 1769 Wedgwood wrote to Bentley: '[send] 6 friezed Egg cups [ceramic body unspecified] with plinth feet and nob on cover' (E96-17672). Unmarked, c.1775-1800, 2¾ high. Rakow collection.

Somewhat earlier Wedgwood was concerned with the ease by which vases could be copied. 'The Etruscan Vases are arrived— I see how the Mechanical part of the Glaze & painting is performed—all w ch may be faithfully imitated at any time.'[29]

In his own defence Neale responded that the

Figure 15. Vase and cover, scroll-handled vase with flower festoon swag and central medallions depicting the Three Graces. The source for this vase is probably an engraving of Stefano della Bella from Raccolta di Vasi diversi...(Paris, 1646).*(See Clifford,* ECC Transactions Vol. 10, Part 3, 1978, Pl. 76.) Mark: **WEDGWOOD & BENTLEY ETRURIA** *in wafer of base, c.1775, 10⅝in. high. Dwight and Lucille Beeson Wedgwood collection, Birmingham Museum of Art, Alabama.*

Figure 16. Cassolette vase and cover, starkly adorned with a simple flower festoon swag and deep vertical incisions at the shoulder. This is shape No. 151 in the Wedgwood Shape Book (with a different top, in this case one which inverts into a candlestick). It was common to couple different bases and covers according to the purchaser's requirements. Mark: **WEDGWOOD & BENTLEY ETRURIA** *in wafer of base, c.1775, 9⅜in. high. Rakow collection.*

method for producing encaustic painting was not invented by Wedgwood (and pirated by Palmer)—that Neale himself had learned the process through 'books'.[30]

On 13 October 1770 Wedgwood wrote the following to Bentley:

> I expected no less than what you have wrote [*sic*] me respecting the invasion of our Patent, and I apprehend they will persist in it to the utmost so that a tryal seems inevitable...
>
> I think we shall stand a much better chance to have it tryed in the Country,

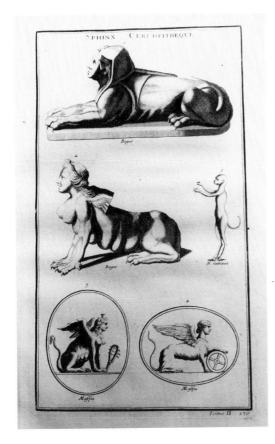

*Figure 18. Statuette modelled as an Egyptian Sphinx. In 1769 Sphinxes 6⅝in. long sold for 10/6 (17-15689). Mark: **WEDGWOOD**, c.1780-1810, 4½in. x 6⅝in., Rakow collection.*

Figure 17. Plate 130 Volume II of L'Antiquité Expliquée et Representée En Figures of Bernard de Montfaucon, 1722. Many of Wedgwood and Bentley's sphinxes and lions were based on engravings by Beger, Maffei and N. Cabinet as depicted in Montfaucon.

and shall more easily prove the invasion of the Patent against Neale than Palmer; the first thing therefore we should do in my opinion should be to purchase a Teapot from Neale, and afterwards to leave an attested copy of the Patent with him by some person who can evidence it for us. This should be done immediately as I must have the Patent sent me here that I may deliver another to Palmer.[31]

Referees were chosen to arbitrate and the resolution to the patent infringement was settled, apparently amicably, in the autumn of 1771. Very few examples of encaustic decorated wares attributable to Palmer exist (Colour Plates 3 and 4) and Wedgwood never took out any more patents.

History has dealt with the patent invasion in various and curious ways. Eliza Meteyard's unambiguous bias in Wedgwood's favour was balanced historically by Grant, who, in trying to rectify it, was probably far too partial to Palmer, the evidence for favour in that arena being insufficient to make a judgment one way or the other. However, a much earlier account was rendered by Enoch Wood in a handwritten notation in his copy of William Pitt's *A Topographical History of Staffordshire* (1817). Wood writes: 'This is the Egyptian Black clay which Wedgwood took out a patent to use Exclusively. Palmer of Hanley proved it was not *New* & voided this *Patent*'. In confusing slightly the nature of the patent, that is, not a patent for the clay itself but for the painting of the clay, Enoch Wood should not be discounted entirely. He may have been a generation away from the dispute itself, but clearly the historicity is one which fosters sympathy for Palmer. Further elucidation includes admiration for Wedgwood as Enoch Wood goes on to annotate:

Thos. & John Wedgwood who built the Big House made this Black Ware but Jos. Wedgwood made it of a Blacker Hugh & introduced it of superior

Figure 19. Statuette of a Grecian Sphinx. By 1773 at least eight models of sphinxes were listed in the first Wedgwood & Bentley Catalogue. This model must have been one of those in early production as some examples are marked Wedgwood & Bentley. Mark: **WEDGWOOD**, *c.1780-1810, 10⅝in. long, 8in. high. Grigsby collection.*

Quality in both form & Colour. I have the Original specimens (made by Thos. & John Wedgwood before the Big House in Burslem was built for them) in my museum. [Figure 1][32]

The London Showrooms

By 1766 both Wedgwood and Bentley and James Neale were operating London emporia for marketing the fashionable earthenwares and stonewares. The Wedgwood and Bentley warehouse, or showroom, at No. 5 Charles Street (now Carlos Place) was under the management of former Burslem bookseller William Cox. James Neale was trading from No. 8 St. Paul's Churchyard, the location from which he would be conducting business until his death in 1814. St Paul's Churchyard was a popular location for other Staffordshire warehousemen and served as London premises for other manufacturers of basalt later on in the century, such as Ralph Wedgwood and Samuel Hollins.[33]

Wedgwood continued to seek another venue for the London based business,[34] and by March 1768 he admonished London manager William Cox not to let the house 'top of St. Martin's Lane slip though his fingers.'[35]

The new premises were finally settled upon and in 1768 Wedgwood and Bentley acquired their first proper London showrooms in St. Martin's Lane, Charing Cross, on the north-east corner of Trafalgar Square. Later on that same year they moved their showroom portion of the business to No. 1 Great Newport Street (retaining one of the two St. Martin's Lane warehouses).[36] William Cox began as chief clerk in the London operation followed after one year by a short and unsuccessful reign with Benjamin Mather in his place. Thomas Bentley was by then overseeing the whole of the London business. The Great Newport Street showrooms served the firm until 1774 when they moved both the showrooms and the Upper Cheyne Row (Chelsea) enamelling studio to Portland House, at No. 12 Greek Street. The Great Newport Street showroom and the utensils and stock in the brick warehouse at St. Martin's

Figure 20. Pair of Triton candlesticks. On 19 November 1769 Wedgwood wrote to 'Bentley: Mr. Chambers sent me a model of the Triton candlesticks & was to have the first pair at present' (E25-18269). In 1776 tritons sold in the London showrooms for £4.4.0 the pair (W/M 1449, 19 October 1776). They proved to be a popular item and continued to be made into the 19th century. Mark: WEDGWOOD, c.1780-1800, 11½in. high. Grigsby collection.

Lane were insured for £3,000.[37] It is interesting to note that fourteen years later, in 1785, the Greek Street premises were insured for the same amount, £3,000.[38]

By 1775 the Wedgwood and Bentley inventory of all goods on hand in London was £9,568.7.4, excluding those items in the enamelling works which added another £428.19.1 to the total.[39]

The lease at Portland House expired in 1795, just months after Josiah Wedgwood's death, and new showrooms were found in St. James Square on the north side of what is joined now by Duke of York Street (formerly Duke Street). The showrooms remained at St. James until 1829 when the house was sold and not replaced by other London rooms until 1875.[40] The St. James Square showrooms were grand as depicted in Ackermann's Plate No. 2 *Repository of the Arts* published in the Strand in February 1809 (Figure 11). The plate indicates the circumference of the showroom was fitted with large glass-covered cases for ornamental wares with large round tables placed in the center of the room displaying creamware and pearlware useful wares.

Showrooms Outside London

By 1775 Wedgwood and Bentley had established showrooms or warehouses in Dublin, Bath, Liverpool and Birmingham. By January of 1773 Wedgwood was already deprecating sales in Bath and Dublin.[41] Sales in Dublin in the period from 1772 to 1775 had steadily declined from £1,225.16.10 in 1772 to £926.5.12 in 1775.[42] The Dublin inventory was the largest of all the showrooms outside London, amounting to £1,326.16.3, followed by Bath (at sightly over £800), Liverpool and

Figure 21. Large vase of Pelike shape, painted in 'Etruscan' enamel decoration. The shape (No. 110 in the Wedgwood Shape Book) was offered originally in only 11in. sizes; as this vase is 20in. high, it may be of slightly later date. The depiction, showing four women and a man in conversation with Eros flying overhead, is taken directly from Hamilton's catalogue, Volume I, Pl. 69. Nancy Ramage discovered the Flaxman drawing of the same subject in the Fitzwilliam Museum (see Ars Ceramica No.6, 1989) rendered perhaps for Wedgwood's decorators. Mark: WEDGWOOD, c.1780-1800, 20in. high. Small ewer of oenochoe form, decorated in 'Etruscan' enamels, shape No. 489. Mark: WEDGWOOD 'D', late 19th century, 8½in.high. Both Laver collection.

Figure 22. Vase of oenochoe form, painted in 'Etruscan' enamel with a figure of Vesta taken from Montfaucon Vol. I. Mark: WEDGWOOD, c. 1790, 5⅜in. high. British Museum, 1909-12-1-117, Falcke collection.

Birmingham, whose inventories consisted of much smaller stocks. Goods on hand at Etruria amounted to slightly over £3,850 in 1775.[43] In the spring of 1772, while Wedgwood was in the process of opening showrooms in Bath, he encountered Humphrey Palmer, who was apparently also considering the Spa for his own showrooms.[44] By September, 1772 Wedgwood's Bath showrooms were in full operation under his agent William Ward.[45] Nothing seems to have come of the Bath venture for Palmer.

The Blackware Trade 1769-1780

In any discussion of ceramic fabrics the wares produced by Wedgwood feature most prominently due to a preponderance of the evidence: the ware itself and the written legacy. Unquestionably Wedgwood and Bentley were principal players, and due to

Figure 23. Large vase of volute-krater shape, painted in 'encaustic' enamels of orange, red, white, cream and buff. Modelled and decorated after an Apulian vase in the Hamilton collection attributed to the Baltimore painter, the original vase was produced about 325 BC, a period which saw the final flowering of the Apulian Ornate style in vase painting. A large funerary naiskos *dominates the body of the vase; within it are a statue of a youth and his horse. On the neck there is a white female head amid an elaborate spray of meandering flowers and tendrils. The frieze at the neck, the auxiliary figures surrounding the* naiskos, *and the Greek key frieze at the base of the vase all are copied from the original, now in the British Museum (BM Cat. Vases F 284). Mark:* **WEDGWOOD Z,** *c.1790-95, 31⅜ in. high. Victoria and Albert Museum, 2419-1901, Pellatt collection. A nearly identical example is in the Zeitlin collection.*

the vast amount of original material in the archives of Keele University pertaining to the Wedgwood business, the researcher can illuminate the already impressive amount of material published on Wedgwood, particularly Meteyard and Reilly, and glean as well some information about other manufacturers operating in the Wedgwood ambit. However, the other manufacturers are shadow players, not necessarily because they were not prominent at the time, but because their business papers did not survive. As mentioned, Josiah Wedgwood was in the happy position of full recognition in his own lifetime and as a result his documents were not as readily relegated to the dustbin. His major early competitors were Humphrey Palmer and James Neale.[46] In July 1768 Wedgwood wrote to William Cox in London: 'Pray Buy a Blue neck [a Palmer vase] which you mention and send it to me'.[47] A few weeks later, as the rivals continued spying on the wares showing up in the London showrooms, the following letter was sent from Wedgwood to Cox:

> You were mentioning some time since that our blue neck'd Vases were got into the shops. I can give you the history of our pattrns [*sic*] getting there, if you can from thence tell how to remedy it, and if you cannot the Bronze Vases sent you last, will be down here in a fortnight for Copying after. The blue necks were sent here to Palmer's by Carravalla, the Person from whom I have the information was at the opening of the box, & assures me from his own knowledge that Carravalla supplies Mr. P with all my Patterns as they arrive at my rooms in London, and Fogg does the same for Bagnall & Baker and these last let any of the other potters have them, paying a share of the expence. You must try if you can recollect any particular Persons repeatedly buying a few pairs...very probably it may be some sham Gentleman or Lady equipped for the purpose with their footman or Man to carry them home to prevent discovery.[48]

Other competitors loomed on the horizon. Bagnall & Baker are mentioned above.

*Figure 24. Two vases of volute-krater shape, painted in 'encaustic' enamels. Both shape No. 128 in the Wedgwood Shape Book, the left-hand vase is a less ornately adorned version of the larger one in Figure 23.Mark: **WEDG-WOOD**, early 19th century, 13⅝in. high. The right-hand vase is decorated in opaque red and white enamels. The painting is copied from an engraving by Boitard illustrated in the Reverend Joseph Spence's Polymetis... of 1747 (see pp. 43-4). The subject is one frequently seen on relief decoration of the period depicting Venus riding on the backs of sea horses. Mark: **WEDGWOOD Z**, c.1780-95, 11½in. high. Both Laver collection.*

One early threat came in September 1769 from Boulton & Fothergill in Birmingham who promised to rival the Wedgwood and Bentley ornamental wares business. Wedgwood wrote to Bentley:

> So stand firm my friend, & let us support this threatened attack like veterans prepared for every shock... If Etruria cannot stand its ground but must give way to Soho, & fall before her, let us not sell the victorie too cheap, but maintain our ground like Men, & endeavour even in our defeat to share the Laurels with our Conquerors.[49]

Within a week Wedgwood referred to the rivals as the 'vanquished enemy', one not worth bestowing another serious thought.[50] Although Wedgwood seemed clearly concerned about Boulton impinging on his neo-classical market, the firm specialized in metal mounted natural stone vases made from marble and Derbyshire spar, not in ceramic vases.

Wedgwood continued to display that industrial uneasiness which characteristically kept him ahead in the competition:

> P—s black vases—I saw one at Mr. Bents. yesterday. The Body is very good-the shape & composition very well. The Bas reliefs are 6 of the small statues wch go round the body—Hercules, Amphale, etc....Upon the whole it

Figure 25. Large vase of volute-krater shape, undecorated. This vase, No. 128 in the Wedgwood Shape Book, was originally made in 11½in., 13¼in., 19in. and 22in. sizes. Mark: WEDGWOOD, c.1795-1820, 25in. high. Ewer, No. 60 in the Wedgwood Shape Book. This appealing form was also made by Palmer and Neale. Mark: WEDGWOOD & BENTLEY, c.1769-80, 13⅞in. high. Both Grigsby collection.

Figure 26. Vase of bell-krater shape, decorated with 'Etruscan' enamels. Vase shape 942. The top of the page in the Wedgwood Shape Book has a note, 'Drawings from Engravings by H. Moses'. Unmarked, c.1775-90, 12⅞in.high. Grigsby collection.

was better than I expected—we must proceed or they will tread upon our heels.[51]

Palmer was expanding and had let it be known within the trade that they needed a dozen 'handlers'; others such as Hollins were seeking equal numbers.[52] In another instance increased competition led to a lowering of Wedgwood's prices:

> Our painted Etruscan t pots painted as slight as possible, are ch d 12/, 10/6 & 9. Palmers I believe sell them at half the price painted with figures & borders both — Have not you lowered these t. pots?[53]

A case can be made for the infringement of Wedgwood's patent of the encaustic wares but the nervousness expressed by Wedgwood, who scrutinized Palmer's every move in the last years of the 1760s, is the first instance within the Staffordshire Potteries of the type of competition which heralded the Industrial Revolution. The wide reaching consequences of such competition were to alter dramatically the industry in technological, entrepreneurial and marketing aspects. Wedgwood and Palmer were struggling with just these problems when they began to mark their wares. Others who were less secure did not bother to acknowledge their blackwares.

Little is known of the Palmer manufacture. Documentary evidence suggests a preponderance of manufacture of ornamental wares (Figure 12). Probably the facts would bear out an equal and opposite reaction as there was a definite bread and butter trade in useful wares, albeit principally unmarked. A bamboo shaped teapot in the Miller collection in the Norwich Museum is marked with a relief 'P' on the

*Figure 27. Part tea set, painted with enamels in iron-red and white. Teapot mark: **Wedgwood**, 5in. high; saucer mark: **Wedgwood**, 5¼in. diameter; cup mark: **WEDGWOOD 2**, 2¼in. high; waste bowl, unmarked. 2½in. high; c.1775-85. Rakow collection.*

bottom (Figure 341) possibly for Palmer. Bamboo shaped teapots after Yixing models were made by a number of early basalt manufacturers including Wedgwood and Bentley (Figure 13), Myatt (Figure 310), Turner (Figure 387) and Clowes (Figure 191).

Orders to Wedgwood provide some insight into the incipient industry as a whole. A John Davenport was ordering from Wedgwoods for Lady Blount and for himself as early as July 1769.[54] By June of 1774 Davenport was providing Lady Blount with 'black egg cups' (Figure 14) and ordering for the Honorable Mr. Clifford 'two black same pans'.[55]

In an early memorandum to William Cox, Wedgwood advised his agent: 'The dark coloured Vases are the true Etruscan Vases, and are thought extreme cheap at

*Figure 28. Tray with 'Etruscan' enamel border. Mark: **Wedgwood**, c.1775, 13¾ x 10⅝in. Chellis collection.*

*Figure 29. Double-handled sugar, painted with red and white 'Etruscan' enamels. Mark: **WEDGWOOD**, c.1780-95, 3¼ in. high. Polikoff collection.*

10/6 & 9/... don't forget to call all the dark coloured Etruscan Vases'.[56]

Stock in the London warehouse in August 1769 included a variety of 'marbled' and 'blew' vases as well as a large variety of basalt ornamental wares: Etruscan candlesticks: 10 Inches at 12/-, 9 Inches @ 10/6, 10 Inches gilt @ 15/-, 9 Inches gilt @ 12/-; Etruscan Satyr's head Vases @ 10/6, and Etruscan flower festoon Vases (Figure 15) @ 18/-.[57]

The enamelling studio of David Rhodes was painting vases for Wedgwood and Bentley, presumably in encaustic and Etruscan style decoration, in September 1769. An Etruscan vase which sold undecorated for 12/- would be sold painted for 17/-. The bill from Rhodes' studio was for three months (September-November) and included some tri-colour decoration in red, white and blue.[58]

By 1769 Wedgwood and Bentley were manufacturing at least fifty different types of vases; Black vases (No. 1) 9 inches high sold for 10/6 whereas the same size 'Blue neck, white Body' vase (No. 1) without festoons sold for 8/-. Etruscan vase (No. 6) with serpent handles 6½ inches 9/-. Sphinxes 6⅜ inches long sold for 10/6 and Egyptian 'Lyons' 9 inches long were 15/-.[59] Several of Wedgwood's sphinxes and Egyptian lions followed closely engravings from Montfaucon (Figures 17, 18 and 19). Dolphin ewers were part of the London stock by the spring of 1769,[60] and late that year Mr. Chambers produced the first pair of triton candlesticks[61] (Figure 20).

The year 1769 was in no small part devoted to improving the quality and production of vases:

> You'l [sic] find some of the small Etruscan Vases not so highly polished as usual, but some good Judges here think they look the better for it, if they should want any brushing oyling [sic] please give it to them, and set them off to the best advantage, for if they are liked we can furnish you with them much better than with the more polished sort.[62]

Critical judgment from the nobility was met with respectful attention: 'Sir Watkin Wms left a note for me to wait upon him in the morning to shew me some things for the *improvement of vases* he has bro t home from his travels.[63]

Experimentation with moulds cast from marble vases was

*Figure 30. Cup, painted with 'encaustic' enamels depicting a lyre, a griffin and a triangle. Mark: **Wedgwood & Bentley**, c.1775, 2⅝in. high. Private collection, Pennsylvania.*

*Figure 31. Two sanders and covers, with bands of 'Etruscan' enamel and shell-moulded relief decoration on the covers. Mark: both **Wedgwood 2**, c.1770-80, 1½in. high and 1¾in. high. The Board of Trustees of the National Museums & Galleries on Merseyside (Liverpool Museum), 2992, 2993M, Mayer collection.*

*Figure 32. Teapot and cover, engine-turned with deeply cut vertical satin stripes and a horizontal roulette band around the middle (to disguise the seam produced by making the teapots in two parts). The teapot has a prominent, well-articulated sibyl finial which dominates the cover, becoming the focal point for the whole piece. In 1774 black teapots with 'cybils' sold for 4/6 (W/M 1449, 3 December 1774). Mark: **Wedgwood & Bentley**, c.1774-80, Gunson collection.*

*Figure 33. Teapot and cover, cylinder-shaped, satin-striped teapot with replacement pewter spout and sibyl finial. Mark: **Wedgwood**, c.1775-80, 5in. high. Polikoff collection.*

tried for a short period in 1769 but was not successful and the technique seems to have been discarded.[64]

Breakage through transportation was a chronic problem[65] but of equal concern began to be those objects which came from the kiln with some minor imperfections, too good to be abandoned but not quite perfect. In April of 1769 Wedgwood suggested pricing on quality for the first time.[66] To conceal small defects Wedgwood also bronzed imperfect blackware vases and sold them at the same price as perfect ones.[67]

In November 1769, discussing the possibility of adding figures to his stock, Wedgwood wrote:

Figure 34. Teapot and cover, moulded in the form of a cabbage leaf. Teapots in the form of cabbage leaves were produced in basalt from at least 1783. Mark: **WEDGWOOD***, c.1795, 5¾in. high. Chellis collection.*

Figure 35. Cream jug. 'Antique cream jugs' sold in 1774 for 1/6 each (W/M 1449, 19 & 26 November). Mark: **Wedgwood 5***, 4⅞in. high. Rakow collection.*

Figure 36. Teapot and cover, round bodied with parapet. Parapet teapots begin showing up on inventories sent to London in June 1775 (W/M 1449, 24 June 1775), but were probably made before that. By March 1777 Wedgwood was making some teapots without the parapet which he thought was 'in the way' (E25-18742). This teapot has a bifurcated handle at the base with applied trailing tendrils. Mark: **Wedgwood 2***, c. 1775, 4⅜in.high. Blake collection.*

Figure 36a. View of bifurcated handle in Figure 36.

I have not seen these sd black figures which have converted you to a good opinion of figure making, therefore if I shd waver a little you will not wonder...If there was any such thing as getting one sober figure maker to bring up some Boys I shod like to ingage [*sic*] in that branch. Suppose you inquire at Bow, I despair of any at Derby.[68]

By the end of 1769 Wedgwood announced that the encaustic was to be the 'principal article for the ensuing season'[69] (Figures 21-24, 26-31).

Clearly the carriage trade was smitten by the neo-classical vases, clamouring for the most recent products. In 1770 Lord Charlmont ordered a pair of Etruscan vases 20 inches high. He was careful to insist on vases made 'in imitation of Etruscan vases' He also ordered a second 'pair of any such as have been invented since'.[70]

Figure 37. Teapot and cover with parapet and sibyl finial in the popular round form which Wedgwood found easier to produce than oval teapots on 'acct of seams & other accidents' (W/M 1441, 7 September 1771). Mark: **WEDGWOOD**, c.1780-90, 3½ in. high. Virginia Museum of Fine Arts, 42.14.108.

Figure 38. Rum kettle and cover with bowed bail handle and bacchanalian boys relief decoration. Mark: **Wedgwood 5**, c.1775-80. Rakow collection.

Figure 39. Rum kettle and cover with bow bail handle and bacchanalian boys applied relief decoration. On the cover is a sibyl finial. Mark: **Wedgwood**, c.1775-80, 7in. high. Robertshaw collection.

The question arose as to which factory would supply the useful 'Etruscan' wares, the factory at Etruria, or the useful ware factory at Burslem, operated by Thomas Wedgwood under the aegis of his cousin Josiah. Bentley was particularly interested that the useful blackwares be made at Etruria where the Wedgwood and Bentley partnership would profit by them rather than give the business to the Burslem manufactory where Thomas Wedgwood received a one-eighth share of the profits.[71] In the end Bentley won, and Etruscan useful wares were manufactured at Etruria.[72]

A long and impressive advertisement in the *Gazetteer and New Daily Advertiser*, 16 January 1771, boasted of Wedgwood's international successes:

…All the crowned heads of the North of Europe have, in the course of last

*Figure 40. Rum kettle and cover with original wicker bail handle. Kettles had been made to bear wicker handles from 1773 (E25-18457). The association of rum with a bacchanal is common on Wedgwood kettles. Mark: **Wedgwood**, c.1775-80, 5¾ in. high (to top of gallery). Polikoff collection.*

year, procured themselves some of its beautiful ornamental productions, which imitate so perfectly the vases urns, ewers, lamps, tripods, etc. of Etruscan, Greek, and Roman antiquity, as well as the precious stones such as jasper, porphyry, agathe [*sic*]...; we are well informed, that there is here a foreign gentleman, who has just received orders from his Holiness, the present Pope, the Cardinal Protector of the English nation, Alexander Albani, the Grand Duke of Tuscany, and several others, for purchasing them compleat sets of these masterly performances to adorn their appartments and studios. We are further well assured, that, at this present time, Messrs. Wedgwood and Bentley are employed in making *medallions* with the effigy of the present Pope Benedick XIV, from a fine portrait in miniature which has been sent to them from Rome.[73]

This almost shameless name dropping by Wedgwood was bound to have its reaction in the form of similar flourishes by competitors:

To the Nobility, Gentry, etc.
PALMER & NEALE, Manufacturers in the Pottery, beg Leave to return

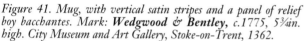

Figure 41. Mug, with vertical satin stripes and a panel of relief boy bacchantes. Mark: **Wedgwood & Bentley**, c.1775, 5¾in. high. City Museum and Art Gallery, Stoke-on-Trent, 1362.

Figure 42. Mug, ornately moulded with oak scrolls between two bands of oak leaves, the rim with an original silver mount. Mark: **Wedgwood & Bentley**, c.1775-80, 6¼in. high. Chellis collection.

their Acknowledgments to their numerous Customers; among whom are many Personages of the most distinguished Rank and Taste of this, as well as of Foreign Countries, who have honoured them with their Orders. The extraordinary Encouragement of the Public has animated their Endeavours to excel...[74]

In a letter dated 7 September 1771 Bentley urged Wedgwood to consider making oval black teapots in addition to the round ones (Figures 36 and 37) already in production. Wedgwood desisted: 'I thank you & Mr. Warwick for the drawing of the Oval T'pot, but we cannot put them in hand at present — round ones suit us much better, on acct. of seams & other accidents'[75] Their only competition remained on the Palmer and Neale front in the bread and butter useful wares trade. In a letter of 13 September 1772 Wedgwood wrote to Bentley: 'Nobody makes black T.pots but Palmers".[76] Wedgwood clearly means 'nobody else' as the firm had been producing teapots for some time. Black teapots appealed to feminine vanity by enhancing the whiteness of the pourers' hands as acknowledged by Wedgwood in a letter to partner Bentley in late 1772: 'Thank you for your discovery in favour of the black Teapots. I hope *white hands* will continue in fashion and then we may continue to make Black Teapots'.[77]

Although blackware coffee pots were in production from at least 1772, and probably had been made earlier as well,[78] it was teapots which occupied the attentions of Wedgwood among the useful wares.

All Teapots with a body of a porcelain texture & *Glazed on the inside only* will be very liable to break with hot water. ...I believe we had better not Glaze them if you can persuade the Ladies to buy them without the addition.[79]

Fluted teapots, in particular, which were made in two parts and pieced in the middle below the bands, were prone to break[80] when exposed to hot water, adding to the

*Figure 43. Inkstand, containing an inkwell and a sander. In 1776 inkstands were sold for 5/-- each (W/M 1449, 3 February 1776). Mark: **Wedgwood & Bentley**, c.1775-80, 3in. x 5⅜in. Royal Ontario Museum, 936.23.*

litany of problems faced by the manufacturer of blackware teapots.

The grapevine proved useful in prognosticating fashion trends. Although Wedgwood had been gilding his blackware pots since 1769,[81] Sir William Hamilton warned Bentley, who passed the information on to Wedgwood, that the new taste for the antique would make gilding of his pots anathema, resulting in the banishment of all gilders from the enamelling studios.[82]

Wedgwood and Bentley did not make any vases without orders for them[83] and, consequently, they had debts owing to them from an impressive list, including the Duchess of Bedford, Prince Auersberg, Lord Cathcart, Merchants Boulton and Fothergill, Lady Charlotte Dundas and Sir Lawrence Dundas, Mr. Greville, the Duke of Holstein Gluksberg, the Duke of Marlborough, and the Elector of the Palatine and the Elector of Saxony.[84]

In 1772 Wedgwood spoke of supplying Lady Wynn with a basalt tablet.[85] This must have been the tablet designed by Robert Adam for her bedroom chimneypiece at No. 20 St. James's Square. The drawings for the tablets are in the Adam collection at the Soane Museum. Originally in three panels, only the large central panel survives, the two smaller oval panels perhaps having been destroyed during the war. The remaining basalt panel is painted in natural colours with the ladies and cupids in flesh pink, the dresses in iron red, pink and blue, and the chariot in yellow, all in a matt finish, a remarkable *tour de force* for encaustic decoration.[86]

By mid-1774 Wedgwood seemed to be satisfied with the black body he was producing, acknowledging that he was still using the same proportions mixed in the first firings six years earlier. One variable seemed to be in the surface treatment of the wares, Some pieces were scoured with soap, sand and water; others left in a natural unscoured state.[87] This undoubtedly accounts for the variation in sheen seen on many Wedgwood and Bentley pieces of about the same period. In addition to the experimentation with surface treatment, Wedgwood also investigated firing the wares at a lower temperature in the biscuit oven,[88] perhaps to alleviate the fragility

*Figure 44. Butter dish, cover and stand. Mark: **Wedgwood** (on dish); **Wedgwood & Bentley** (on stand); c.1775-80, dish 3½in. high; stand 7in. diameter, Rakow collection.*

*Figure 45. Neptune and Bacchus ewers for wine and water. No. 236 in the Wedgwood Shape Book, these vases sold for 52/6 in 1776 (W/M 1449, 9 March 1776). In spite of the great cost the ewers remained popular through the 19th century and continued to be manufactured into the 20th century. Mark: **WEDGWOOD**, 19th century, 17in. high. Polikoff collection.*

*Figure 46. Vase (left), a variation of No. 81 in the Wedgwood Shape Book. This low round form with close swept handles terminating in ram's heads is attached to a shaped base. Mark: **Wedgwood & Bentley**, c.1775-80, 3¼in. high. Ewer (right). Shape No. 60 is fluted with satin stripes broken in the middle by a horizontal band of laurel leaves. The high swept handle terminates in a satyr mask and the base is moulded in a Greek key pattern. Mark: **WEDGWOOD & BENTLEY ETRURIA** in wafer of base, 13⅛in. high. Rakow collection.*

consequent to breakage in transit.

From at least 1770 the firm of plaster cast modellers, Hoskins and Oliver, were supplying Wedgwood and Bentley with plaster cast moulds taken from wax figures which in turn were modelled from drawings. Hoskins and Oliver provided both the models and the casts for many Wedgwood and Bentley ornamental wares. A bill sent to Wedgwood and Bentley covering the months May to August 1770 included several well-known examples:

Model of Morpheus	5- 0- 0
" " Cyclops	4-15-0
Finishing Infant Hercules for Modelling	
	1-11-0
Finishing Busts of Cicero and Horace	
	0-12-0

*Figure 47. Pair of vases. Shape No. 82 was intended to be made in only one size, 8¼ in. high. This low squat form is uncommon. Mark: **WEDGWOOD & BENTLEY ETRURIA** in wafer of base, 'M' on one, '7' on the other, c.1775-80, 7¾in. high. Laver collection.*

To model from the bronze of Ganymede & Bacchus	2- 2- 0
To a model of Triton from the bronze	3- 8- 0
To model the tail of the dolphin	4- 0- 0
Model back for Neptune and a mold	0-12-0
for the figure	5- 5- 0
To a model of Venus	0-12-0[89]

In January 1771 a bill was sent for:

Mold for 16 Bas reliefs	10-12- 0
Mold a tripod on six—-? of Cupid and Psyche	..1-18- 0[90]

In 1773 James Hoskins also supplied moulds of a 'likeness of Mr. Bentley, Mr. Garrick and a seal of Cicero'.[91]

By early 1773 Wedgwood was, by his own account, experimenting successfully with fine bodies for gems.[92]

Extensive inventories of basalt wares sent to London from Etruria for the years 1774 to 1776 exist in the Mosley papers of the Wedgwood archives.[93] In trying to collate the material and condense it into palatable form certain omissions are by necessity going to occur. The picture is an incomplete one at best as vases and other ornamental wares are listed in the inventories by number on a scale, which, by 1775, ranges from 1 to 511; the corresponding shapes books include drawings which survive for most of the numbered vases in the inventories sent to London.[94] By November 1774 Black vases (No. 26) 7 inches high were selling for 12/-, 8½ inches 18/- and 10 inches 21/-. In teawares, slop bowles 2/-, plain sugars 2/-, and antique cream jugs 1/6 (Figure 35).[95] Black upright Teapots sold for 4/-, with 'cybils' [finials] 4/6 (Figure 33).[96]

Busts of Zingara (Figure 52), Vestal, Homer (Figure 53), Aristotle, Plato and Shakespeare were in production and selling for 18/- each. One of Cleopatra (no size indicated) was 10/6, while a black bust of Voltaire (no size; see Figure 54) was 15/-. Various black lamps were being sold for 5/- and 7/6 ;a 'Toylet candlestick' or chamberstick, was 3/6.[97]In December 1774 busts of Rousseau appear on the inventory at 10/6 as well as black figures of Apollo and Mercury at 21/-.[98]

Figure 48. Vase, based on an original by sculptor Edme Bouchardon (1698-1762) published in Gabriel Huquier's Second Livres de Vases Inventes par Edme Bouchardon. This vase, No. 11 in the Wedgwood Shape Book, substituted the mermaid handles for mermen handles (see Timothy Clifford, ECC Transactions Vol. 10 Part 3, 1978, Pl. 78 a,b). In both versions the figures rest on a giant oyster shell. The vase is unmarked because it would have been marked in the plinth which it lacks. Other versions are marked Wedgwood & Bentley, c.1775-80, 9½in. high. By courtesy of the Trustees of the Wedgwood Museum, Barlaston, Stoke-on-Trent.

Figure 49. Vase with high swept handles terminating in female masks (as in Apulian krater vases of the third century BC), and embellished with a moulded relief procession of cupids carrying a garland of laurel and berries. This was shape 1263 in the Wedgwood Shape Book. Drawings of vases such as this one (6in. high) appear in inventories sent from Etruria to London in 1776 priced at 6/- each (W/M 1449, 4 May 1776). Mark: **Wedgwood**, c.1776-80, 8in. high Grigsby collection.

Wedgwood and Bentley subcontracted George Palethorpe to rivet holes, fire and grind plinths for vases, and join various black basalt objects by riveting wings on sphinxes, and extensive work relating to ornamental wares. Palethorpe also pierced holes in teapots and gilded dolphin vases.[99]

Nathan and Pollard were among a number of firms utilized by Wedgwood and Bentley to polish and mount seals and make settings for jewellery. Pollard sent several bills extending from 1774 to 1787.[100] Between 1776 and 1790 Bentley and White in Birmingham also provided mounts for seals and cameos.[101] Other Birmingham firms mounted seals, cameos and buttons. William Smith, who worked for Wedgwood between 1774-90,[102] seems to have had a number of partners. In addition to those bills under his own name, others exist for: Smith & Bodern 1774-5,[103] John Smith 1775-6[104] and W & R. Smith 1788-90.[105]

By March of 1775 figures of Ganymede and the Eagle (£1.1.0), heads of the King of Poland (2/-), Dr. Franklin and Newton (2/6 each) and Hanibal [sic] (Figure 58)

(1/6) are being sent to the London showrooms.[106] The Prince of Anhalt Dessau ordered the figure of Ganymede and the Eagle in March of 1775.[107] At this same time black fluted teapots, made at least since 1772, appear on the inventories at 4/-. Cameos and intaglios both individually and for bracelets and other jewellery generally sold for about 1/- a piece.[108] In June of 1775 Parapet teapots enter the inventories at 4/6 (Figures 36 and 37), with 'figures' (sprig relief figures) at 5/-. A 'Black Watch Case', 11 inches high went for 27/-. Black double lamps were also sold for 27/-.[109] In early 1776 a bust of Hypocrates [*sic*] was listed at £1.11.6.[110] By January 1776 large amounts of jasper are being sent to London with fewer basalt vases. Garden pots of all varieties (Figure 51; Colour Plate 13), popular throughout, continue to be seen prominently on nearly all inventory lists. The price on black parapet teapots, 4/6, and with figures, 5/-, remained the same as the year before with plain black teapots sold at 4/-, with figures 4/6. 8 Inch busts (Socrates, Aristotle) were 18/-; 7 inch (Newton, Locke, Prior (Figure 55), Congreve) 15/-. Black inkstands 5/- (Figure 43) inkpots 2/-.[111] Black coffee pots were offered at 7/6 each. Busts of Montaigne and Rousseau appear in these papers at this time.[112] By February 1776 parapet teapots had increased in price to 5/6 with fluted and plain upright remaining the same at 4/-. Replacement covers

Figure 50. Vase and cover, a variation of shape No. 98 which, unlike the drawing in the Wedgwood Shape Book, includes a medallion of Hercules and the Nemean lion. The vase has Egyptian-head handles and a sibyl on the cover. Mark: WEDG-WOOD & BENTLEY ETRURIA in wafer of base, c.1775-80, 15in. high. Polikoff collection.

Figure 51. Pair of bulb pots, Wedgwood shape No. 1322 decorated with the popular flower pot motif: cupids in a procession with garlands. Mark: Wedgwood on both, with painted No. 55 and 55-2, c.1774-80, 4¼in. high. Rakow collection.

*Figure 52. Bust of Zingara. Appearing on the 1774 inventory of busts sent to London (W/M 1449, 26 November), Zingara was modelled by Richard Parker. The large figure sold for 18/-. Although Zingara may have been a popular figure of a Marylebone Gardens burletta produced in 1773 as suggested by Meteyard (Choice Examples of Wedgwood Art, 1879), Alison Kelly points out that this figure was of classical origin and Canova also made copies of the classical bust (Kelly, Decorative Wedgwood, 33) illustrated in Maffei's Raccolta di statue antiche... (1704) which constituted part of the Wedgwood and Bentley library in 1770. Mark: **Wedgwood & Bentley**, c.1774-1800, 15½in. high. Laver collection.*

*Figure 53. Bust of Homer. John Cheere supplied the model for a bust of Homer in February 1774 (Kelly, Decorative Wedgwood, 48). By 26 November 1774 busts of both Zingara and Homer appear on the inventories being sold for 18/- each (W/M 1449). Mark: **WEDGWOOD & BENTLEY** in base, bust also impressed **HOMER**, c.1774-80, 14½in. high. Chellis collection.*

for both teapots and for vases were special order items with a vase cover costing as much as 10/6. Sphinx candlesticks (Figure 104) appear at £1.11.6 and hares' heads (stirrup cups) at 2/6[113](Colour Plate 14). A pair of griffin candlesticks was 5/5. Bas-reliefs of Antony and Cleopatra 15/- and 'toylet' candlesticks remained the same price as 1774 at 3/6.[114]

Jasper continued numerically to outstrip basalt in inventory sent from Etruria to London, but basalt objects remained strongly prominent, although fewer variegated vases were to be seen by 1776. In March 1776 there is an entry for: 24 English Poets in black @ 1/- (each); and 23 ditto with frames 1/6. These would, of course be the self-framed medallions and cameos such as those seen in Figures 66-68; 70; 72, 73. Entries for Cupid and Psyche in black at 5/- and Medusa in black at 1/6 appear

*Figure 54. Miniature bust of Voltaire. Full-size busts of Voltaire were being sold for 15/- in late 1774 (W/M 1449. 26 November 1774). Caster (left), sander for inkwell (right). Square inkpots and sanders sold for 2/- each in 1775 (W/M 1449, 24 June 1775). Mark: bust, **Wedgwood & Bentley** on truncation, c.1778-80, 4¼in. high; caster, **WEDGWOOD**, c.1780-1800, 3½in. high; sander, **Wedgwood & Bentley**, c.1775-80, 1¾in. high. All Chellis collection.*

along with 'Black Vases No. 236 Neptune & Bacchus 52/6' (Figure 45) and 'Black Lamps with 2 handles' at 10/6 and antique ewers at 1/6 each (Figure 46 right).[115] The following week 110 Greek heads (cameos) appear on the inventory at 1/- each.[116] A new listing described as 'fluted sugar dishes' sold for 3/- along with vases and some teapots at previous prices.[117]

By 1776 extensive entries for 'heads", both Roman Emperors and Empresses, the Caesars, (Figures 66 and 67) etc. appear on Wedgwood and Bentley inventories. For the most part they continued to be sold at the same price as other cameos, that is at one shilling each, but some, probably larger, were going for 1/6. The lists do not distinguish between cameos and intaglios. Black tablets, of undisclosed subject matter (13 inches), were offered at the same time for £1.7.0. the pair. This inventory also included 'Black Vase Candl No. 125' (cassolettes presumably) for 15/- each and Sphinx candlesticks for 15/-.[118]

In May 1776, 7 inch black vases (not numbered but with small drawings beside the entry) with high swept handles, narrow necks and flaring lips sold at 7/6 with similar 6 inch examples selling at 6/- each. A new item lists 'Fluted Buckets & Ladles' for 2/6 each with plain ones going for 2/-. Low fluted ewers were 1/6 with plain ones at 1/3; parapet teapots remain at 4/6 with smaller ones (or possibly seconds) at 3/6, with figures on those at 4/-.[119]

Weekly deliveries arrived in London from Etruria and by May of 1776 the inventories began indicating some 'imperfect' examples at lower prices, although the

*Figure 55. Bust of Prior. By 3 February 1775 busts of Matthew Prior were being offered for sale in London for 15/- (W/M 1449). Mark: **Wedgwood & Bentley**, c.1775-80, 15¼in. high. British Museum, I 716.*

*Figure 56. Bust of Mercury. In May and June 1779 Hoskins and Grant provided Wedgwood with moulds for several busts including one of Mercury (Meteyard, 1879). However, since no bust of Mercury appears in any Wedgwood catalogues of the 18th century, it may date to after 1788. Mark: **Wedgwood**, c.1782-90, 20⅜in. high. British Museum, 1909-12-1-103, Falcke collection.*

*Figure 57. Bust of Minerva. Busts of Minerva (about 22in.) were listed in the 1779 Wedgwood and Bentley catalogue. Mark: **WEDGWOOD** impressed in base, **MINERVA** on back, c.1780-95, 19½in. high. Grigsby collection.*

idea of pricing on the basis of quality had been discussed between the partners since 1769.[120] For example a perfect tablet of the Feast of the Gods (Figure 77) would sell for £1.1.0, imperfect for 10/6. An imperfect Silenus tablet was included in the same inventory for 12/-, but there was no perfect one to compare it with. The same list included '1 Black Figure Morpheus' at £5.5.0 (Colour Plate 15).[121]

The second listing in these papers for black coffee pots occurred in May 1776. They were selling for 5/- each. In a previous listing earlier in the year black coffee pots were selling for 7/6, but neither are described so comparisons are not possible. The same inventory included an entry for 'wafer boxes' (for ecclesiastical use) at 1/6 each; pateros [sic] (pateras are goblets made for the Spanish market) 3/-.[122] Black candlestick vases in styles fluctuating from Nos 3-131 ranged in price from 7/6 for No. 3 to 15/- for No. 125. Black Etruscan vases 7 inches high sold for 7/6; 6 inch went for 6/-.[123] In June 1776 two large (20 inch) 'figures of Neptune & Tryton' were sent to London priced at £15.15.0. At the same time 'Black heads' (medallions) of Satyr and Indian Bacchus were 2/6 each while Marcus Aurelius and Antonius were 1/6 and framed examples of Erasmus, Pompey and Prince Eugenie were 2/6. The variations in pricing continue with Cicero, Middleton and Socrates going for 2/-. Presumably the popularity of the subject did not reflect itself in the pricing.

Teawares sent down to Greek Street were priced as follows: sugar dishes 2/6,

*Figure 58. Medals of Hannibal and Coriolanus, referred to as 'heads', were sold in 1775 for 1/6 each (W/M 1449, 15 March 1775). Mark: Hannibal, **Wedgwood & Bentley**, c.1775-80; Coriolanus, unmarked, c.1775-80, 1½in. diameter. Both Polikoff collection.*

*Figure 59. Portrait medallion of Josiah Wedgwood (1730-95) in silver gilt frame modelled by William Hackwood (oven book 13, 20 April 1782; Reilly and Savage, 1973, 333). Unmarked, **'WH'** on truncation, c.1782, 5in. high. British Museum, I-91.*

*Figure 60. Portrait medallion of Dr. Erasmus Darwin (1731-1802) in integral moulded frame. The medallion is modelled after a portrait in oil painted by Joseph Wright of Derby in 1770. Not in the 1779 catalogue, it was produced shortly thereafter and is attributed to William Hackwood (Reilly and Savage, 118). Mark: **WEDGWOOD**, c.1780-95, 6in. high. British Museum, 1909-12-1-128. Falcke collection.*

plains basons [*sic*] 2/-, fluted basons [*sic*] 2/6, antique cream jugs 1/6. Other ornamental wares included black and white bough pots (jasper) 2/- and black vase with drapery No. 40 31/6, black vase with festoon No. 1 £1.7.0.[124]

Square ink pots sold for 2/-,[125] and dolphin tripod (vases) went for 27/- each.[126] On 27 June 1776 a long, more detailed description of vases and prices was sent down with the London shipment and included some Etruscan decorated wares (Figures 5, 21-24, 26-31; Colour Plate 1). It is worth while to repeat that as early as September 1769 David Rhodes' enamelling studio was decorating wares for Wedgwood and Bentley in red, white and blue,[127] but listings of wares sent from the factory to London in 1774-1776 do not indicate Etruscan wares until 27 June 1776. Among

*Figure 61. Portrait medallion of Sir William Hamilton (1730-1803) in integral gilded frame. An especially popular figure for Wedgwood, Hamilton's portrait was kept in production from the first ornamental catalogue of 1773 to the last in 1787. It was modelled by Joaquim Smith in 1772, possibly to honour the accession of the first part of Hamilton's collection to the British Museum. Mark: **Wedgwood** (blurred impression), c.1773-80, 6⅛in. high. British Museum, 1909-12-1-127, Falcke collection.*

*Figure 62. Cameo-medallion of Hugo Grotius (1583-1645) with moulded and gilded integral frame. Dutch theologian and jurist, the cameo medallion was listed in the oven book for 12 September 1779 (Reilly and Savage, 1973, 179). Mark: **Wedgwood**, c.1779-80, 3⅞in. high. British Museum, 1901-12-1-126. Falcke collection (ex-Carruthers collection).*

Figure 63. Portrait medallion of Charles Emmanuel II (1634-75), Duke of Savoy, in integral frame. The medallion was listed in the 1773 ornamental catalogue. (A paper label on the back indicates that the medallion was the property of Mr. Joseph Mayer, potter [son of Elijah Mayer] and that it was a gift to Mayer from the Wedgwood family.) Coincidentally, another example was given to the British Museum by Mr. Joseph Mayer of Liverpool in 1853. Unmarked, c.1770-80, 8in. high. Laver collection.

other ornamental wares ('Black vase No. 1 — Lion' £2.12.6; Black & red Toilet Candlestick 2/6; Black Tablet 4 x 3 inches 2/-) were '2 Etruscan vases No. 108 12 inches 12/- each'. Once again imperfect items, labelled 'not fine', were sent to London at reduced prices.[128]

A large lot of Etruscan vases came down to London in July 1776 and included vases numbered 43, 93, 121, 183 in varying sizes. Comparative pricing on Etruscan vase No. 93 (Figure 5) would be as follows: 10 inch 15/-, 8 inch 9/-, 5 inch 5/-. On No. 183 a 9 inch vase would be 10/6, 7 inch 7/6 and 6 inch 6/-.[129]

At one point Wedgwood lamented: 'We have no Greek painted Vases left, if we had a set or two, *not too high priced*, we sho'd probably sell them. However, it is necessary to keep up a show when the good people come to see us'.[130]

Teapots were also numbered according to shape. A large (9 inch) teapot, No. 80 with medallions was 13/-; No. 12 (7 inch) teapot with 'Boys' 9/-, the same No. 12

Figure 64. Tablet of Bacchus and panther with integral moulded and gilded frame. The subject is taken from a frieze of the monument of Lysicrates at Athens. The first medallion seems to have been made in November 1772 for Sir Watkin Williams Wynn (Meteyard, Memorials of Wedgwood, 1874). Unmarked, Wedgwood & Bentley, c.1772-80, 11½in. x 14½in. Victoria and Albert Museum, 4-1884.

Figure 65. Bas-relief of Cassandra grasping the Palladium in integral moulded frame. Modelled by John Bacon, the medallion is labelled as 'Cassandra, a fine figure in high relief, from a gem in the King of France's cabinet' in the 1779 Wedgwood & Bentley Catalogue, but the medallion was in existence by 1773. Unmarked, c.1773-90, 11in. high. Grigsby collection.

teapot fluted 11 inches high was 10/-, and the same style plain 9 inches high was 10/6.[131]

By 1776 black 'medals' of King George III and Queen Charlotte sold for 1/- (Figure 70). Personal coats of arms could also be commissioned at more than three times the amount. For example, three 'medals' bearing the arms of the Murray family were sold to one Col. Murray for 10/6.[132] Seals were made to order for the Pugh, Watts, Park, Ordd, O'Gorrman, and Pearson families and delivered to London in the autumn of 1776.[133]

By mid-1776 variegated vases were still being sent to London for sale but not in great quantity. Black vases continued in prominence. In Etruscan wares one begins to see forms other than vases decorated in the Etruscan manner appearing on the inventories. For example, Etruscan ewers (numbering 43, 93, 142, 153, 162, 165, 183); a 10 inch ewer sold for 12/-. Inventories begin to show the red and black wares with which Wedgwood is so often associated, although other manufacturers such as Spode, and Turner, were also making these wares (Figure 406; Colour Plates 18, 22). For example red and black candlesticks (no size) were listed for 2/6 (a pair?),[134] and red and black fluted teapots sold for 1/6 each.[135]

Figure 66. Cameos of Six Emperors of Rome appeared frequently in inventories of wares going down from Etruria to London from 1776 (W/M 1449, 27 April 1776) selling for 1/- each. Marks: all **Wedgwood**, c.1775-80, all 2in. x 1¾in. Rakow collection.

*Figure 67. Cameos of the twelve Empresses of Rome. Marks: all **WEDGWOOD**, c.1780-95, all 2in. x 1¾in. Rakow collection.*

Figure 68. Cameo-medallion of Domitilla, wife of Vespasian, 10th Roman Emperor, in integral moulded and gilded frame. Mark: Wedgwood & Bentley, c.1775-80, 3⅜in. x 2⅝in. Chellis collection.

Figure 69. Medal of Gregorius V Pont. Max. Sold for 6d. each or 3d each if one took the whole set. The heads of the popes were struck as medals. Unmarked, c.1775-80, 1¾in. diameter. Polikoff collection.

Eye-bath cups were made in basalt and sold at 1/- the dozen.[136]

One black tablet depicting the death of Cato's son sold at the magnificent sum of £5.5.0,[137] and another of a Roman procession brought the same amount later on that year.[138] Producing tablets was a challenge. As late as 1773 Wedgwood wrote to Bentley: 'I will make you gems & Seals Enough, but the black Tablets we cannot manage cleverly'.[139] Nevertheless, Wedgwood admitted that tablet making was the nicest branch of their business but that it required a longer series of his attention and efforts than he could possibly give.[140] A glimpse into the labour involved emerged in a letter from Wedgwood to Bentley:

> The tablets for Miss Milnes are come out of the oven today, & are pretty good. They have been 5 or 6 weeks in drying & burning—cost some Guineas modeling & moulding & are very bad things to make.[141]

Dolphin tail ewers had been made since 1769, but in these inventories dolphin tail vases make their appearance in the wares sent to Greek Street to be sold in October

Figure 70. Pair of cameo-medallions of George III and Queen Charlotte in integral moulded and gilded frames, modelled by William Hackwood. Marks: both **Wedgwood**, Geo.III marked '**WH**' (William Hackwood) in relief on the front, c.1775-80, 4⅛in. x 3¼in. Grigsby collection.

Figure 71. Intaglio seal of Theseus raising a stone. Mark: **Wedgwood & Bentley**, c.1775-80, 1in. x ¾in. Royal Ontario Museum, 975.192.6. Brown collection.

Figure 72. Cameo-medallion of Joseph of Austria mounted as a pendant. The 1779 catalogue does not list Joseph of Austria, but it is listed in 1787. The mark of Wedgwood & Bentley would seem to indicate a manufacture before Bentley's death on 25 November 1780. Mark: **Wedgwood & Bentley**, c.1779-80, 2⅜in. high. Chellis collection.

Figure 73. Cameo-medallion of 'Montagne' modelled by Pesez. Wedgwood wrote to Bentley:'I observe Pesez, the artist, to whom we owe most of these Heads, is a very strong mannerist, & has given a Family likeness to them all in the thickness of their Lips & peculiar bold opening of the Nostril...I sorted out his Heads, as the production of the same Artist, before I saw he had put his name on them' (E25-18688, 7 September 1776). Mark: **Wedgwood**, 'PESEZ' in truncation, c.1776, 3⅜in. x 2¼in. Chellis collection.

1776, appended to the entry is a price of 31/6.[142] About the same time there are entries for 'winged Sphinx candlesticks' (Figure 104) at 31/6 each or £3.3.0 the pair. Tritons (Figure 20) were 42/-, £4.4.0 a pair and black coffee pots had diminished in price to 4/6.[143]

By the autumn of 1776 there was also an apparent decline in the popularity of black teapots, but in a letter to Bentley Wedgwood admitted he could not let the market go:

> MAKE NO MORE BLACK TEAPOTS!... Our Black Teapots sell very well at Dublin & Bath & a few at Liverpool & will always be the most saleable part of our stock—20 or 3 times 20 crates of Black Teapots, such as ours, will not frighten me & we cannot leave off & begin such staple articles *abruptly*

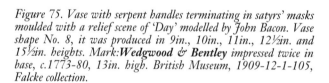

Figure 74. Bas-relief of 'Day' in integral moulded and gilded frame, modelled by John Bacon and listed in 1773 ornamental catalogue. Unmarked, c.1773-80, 8⅛in. high. Grigsby collection.

*Figure 75. Vase with serpent handles terminating in satyrs' masks moulded with a relief scene of 'Day' modelled by John Bacon. Vase shape No. 8, it was produced in 9in., 10in., 11in., 12½in. and 15½in. heights. Mark:**Wedgwood & Bentley** impressed twice in base, c.1773-80, 13in. high. British Museum, 1909-12-1-105, Falcke collection.*

without quite deranging us. So we shall make as few as we can, but not leave them quite off.[144]

An invoice for purchases made by Sir Nigel Gresley, Bart. on 14 October 1776 included several basalt items of both ornamental and useful wares: 3 black vases ornamented with medallions and drapery festoons £4.14.6 (3 metal branches were included in this order of vases); 1 black fluted sugar dish 3/-, 1 black parapet teapot 5/-; 1 ditto less sibyl top 4/6; 1 black fluted low shape ditto 4/-; 1 ditto larger 4/6. Wedgwood charged 2/6 for the box and the order was sent totalling £5.18.0. For reasons which are not specified the three black vases were returned along with the branches and credited back to the Gresley account on 11 November.[145]

By the autumn of 1776 wares were sent down to London with the famous 'Dancing Hours' relief decoration[146] (Figure 82). Several other well-known relief themes were included in the list: 'Boys & goat', 'Cupid & Marriage' and the 'Triumph of Bacchus' (Figure 84).[147] The Dancing Hours depicted the classical Horae, personification of the hours of the day and was one of Wedgwood's most popular relief decorations.[148] The design has traditionally been attributed to Flaxman as it was intended, in some instances, to be executed in tablet form, and to act as a frieze to the Marriage of Cupid and Psyche. A letter from Wedgwood to Bentley[149] suggests how Wedgwood placed his chimney ornaments. In this case the Marriage

Figure 76. Slave medallion in white jasper and black jasper relief, integral moulded basalt frame. An abolitionist, Josiah Wedgwood produced this small medallion in 1787 for free distribution to those in support of the cause. The model, produced by William Hackwood, was based on a design by Henry Webber. Unmarked, c.1787, 3¾in. high. British Museum, 1909-12-1-260, Falcke collection.

Figure 77. Tablet of Feast of the Gods, gilded and with integral moulded frame. Based on a Renaissance bronze by Guglielmo della Porta, the Feast of the Gods was being produced at least by 1773. The unevenness of the tablet indicates the firing problems about which Wedgwood was complaining (E25-18433, 2 January 1773). A perfect plaque of Feast of the Gods sold for £1.1.0, imperfect for 10/6 (W/M 1449, 11 May 1776). Unmarked, c.1773-80, 8¼in. x 11⅜in. British Museum.

of Cupid and Psyche formed the central panel flanked on either side by two panels of the 'Dancing Hours' while two oval medallions were inset into the columns of the surround. The Dancing Hours appears to be the earliest surviving work by Flaxman in which classical figures appear. The source is Bartoli's 1693 prints which were reproduced in Montfaucon.[150] Scholars admit that Flaxman's design exhibits a fluidity and freedom which is uniquely his own[151] and ultimately derives from his particular genius. The 'Dancing Hours' theme was employed by several other Staffordshire potters, including Neale and Turner.

'Boys & Goat' is another Flaxman design which emerges in this same group sent down to Greek Street for sale in late 1776. Caylus may have provided the source for the procession with the goat (Vol. III, Pl.LVI). Nevertheless, just as with the 'Dancing Hours', the figures are appealingly and charmingly Flaxman.

The 'Triumph of Bacchus' (Figure 84) is the fourth design included in the list. Several engravings of the 'Triumph' are depicted in Montfaucon, Vol.II, and may have served as sources for the designer, who is believed to have been Hackwood. Further discussion about the modellers and designers employed by Wedgwood and Bentley will follow in this section.

In November 1776 Wedgwood was sending a Bust of the Madonna to London and charging 31/6. At the same time he was also offering 'fluted pillar candlesticks', presumably modelled as Corinthian columns.[152] Late 1776 inventories show a considerable number of items, presumably utilizing cameos and intaglios, were mounted as jewellery in gold, some with pearls, and sent to Greek Street. A gold bracelet with pearls, not further described, sold for £3.3.0.[153]

Caneware, as the buff bodied stoneware was called, was in production from late November 1776, having been in experimental stages as early as July 1771.[154] The first caneware teapots were sold at nearly half the price of black basalt ones, some for even less than that. They were priced at 2/6, 2/-, and 1/6, but descriptions are sadly lacking. The same shipment included 'Greek paintings of Diana, Adonis, etc' for

Figure 78. Tablet of a Bacchanalian Sacrifice, bronzed. Bronzed basalt was made from 1769 but there are few surviving pieces. In Wedgwood Memorials *(Pl. XXI) Meteyard illustrated another one of these tablets, based on a Clodion bas-relief, marked Wedgwood & Bentley. Mark:* **WEDGWOOD**, *c.1780-95, 19⅜in. long. British Museum, 1911-10-17-1, bequest of F. E. Hallett, Esq.*

42/- each and '2 Black Judgements of Paris' at 5/- each.[155]

'1 Gilt Vase Pot Pounce (1st mint)' at 42/- was sent down on 30 November 1776 and the next month statues of Apollo, Venus, Bacchus and Mercury (Figure 56) at 21/- each were also in the London inventory.[156] Black statues of these four had been in production at the same price since at least December 1774.[157] 10 black 'Fox Heads' stirrup cups (Figure 87) were sent along with the statues to London to be sold for 2/6 each.[158]

Busts of George II went for 21/- whereas a bust of Venus brought £2.2.0.[159] These are the last inventories for the year 1776 which provide a fairly comprehensive idea of what was available in the London showroom along with comparative prices. The last inventory in this lot is dated 11 September 1779. The first item is an imperfect Figure of Ceres for £3.3.0. followed by busts of Garrick, Shakespeare, Bacon, and Horace also at £3.3.0.

By March 1777 Wedgwood was making some teapots without the parapet, which he thought was 'in the way'.[160] He began making what he described as 'Bow handled Bassrelief Lip Spouted Teapots', and writing to Bentley about them he said: 'Few Ladies dare venture at anything out of the common stile 'till authorised to do so by their betters. I hope some of these will seize upon our…teapots."[161] Tritons with branches were offered in the same letter at two guineas for the figures alone, the branches being additional. By 1777 tripods were also in the Wedgwood and Bentley inventory,[162] though the mould for a Cupid and Psyche tripod had been made by Hoskins and Oliver as early as 1771.[163]

In 1778 Mary Whitbread of Bedwell Park made a gift of a large black basalt, neoclassical baptismal font to St. Mary's Church, Essenden. An identical font is at Cardington in Bedfordshire and another font, previously in use from 1783 to 1865 in the church of St. Margaret at Moreton Sea, Shropshire, is now in the Lady Lever Art Gallery, Port Sunlight.[164] While perhaps not the very largest pieces of black basalt produced, these fonts compete for the title.

Concerned about aiming his wares in the direction of wealthier clients, Wedgwood discussed the possibility of a less expensive line for country shops in a letter to Bentley: 'I will endeavour to make some cheap black & cane teapots; indeed, I have done so, but when they are finished they seem too good for the purpose'.[165]

In May and June of 1779 Hoskins and Grant (Oliver had died and James Hoskins

Figure 79. Oval tablet of the Judgment of Hercules, modeller unknown, but early versions are listed in the 1773 catalogue. Mark: WEDGWOOD J, c.1780-95, 9in. x 12in. Chellis collection.

had taken a new partner) provided Wedgwood with moulds for library busts of Bacchus, Ariadne, Mercury (Figure 56), Alexander, Shakespeare, Garrick, Julius Caesar, Zingara (Figure 52) and Chrispagnia.[166] Casts of Cupid and Psyche and Aurora as well as a sitting figure of Venus, a mould of Sterne, and a sitting figure of Mercury were also supplied at that time.[167]

By 1779, of course, printed lists of the ornamental wares produced by Wedgwood and Bentley were available, the documentation from 1779 being updated with catalogues of wares every few years.

Proportionately little is known about the other manufacturers operating in the ambit, or in the wake as the case may be, of Wedgwood and Bentley. Occasionally

Figure 80. Oval tablet of a Frightened Horse modelled by George Stubbs. Wedgwood wrote to Bentley on 21 August 1780 that 'Mr. Stubs [sic]...nearly finished his tablet' (Wedgwood MS LHP). Mark: WEDGWOOD (modern copy), 8¾in. x 14¼in. By courtesy of the Trustees of the Wedgwood Museum, Barlaston, Stoke-on-Trent.

Figure 81. Tablet of Venus at Vulcan's Forge, observing while he forges the armour of Achilles. The tablet is not listed in any of the 18th century catalogues. Mark: **WEDGWOOD**, *c.1790 to early 19th century, 6¾in. x 10¼in. Chellis collection.*

Wedgwood discussed his competitors in letters to Bentley, for instance in February 1778 he wrote: 'Mr. Palmer sells his 3 sizes of black flat fluted Teapots with Sybil [*sic*] tops at 18/--the long dozns, that is @ 9d., 12d., & 18d. Per pot which we sell at 50 or 60/--!'[168] His competitors undercut Wedgwood's prices but not necessarily the quality of the product. Certainly, Palmer was a major competitor until 1778 when bankruptcy forced him out of the business. Thereafter, Neale wares, of uniformly high quality, continued to carry away some of the business which would have otherwise gone to Wedgwood. It seems likely that by the mid-1770s Spode must have been manufacturing black stoneware. Recalling that Wedgwood had written in 1772 that 'Nobody makes black T.pots but Palmers'[169] suggests that other manufacturers must have gone into production some time later. It would stand to reason that most potteries of any consequence would not wait long to cash in on a market of burgeoning popular interest.

One hitherto unrecognized manufacturer, Thomas Barker, was operating the Foley pottery at Fenton in the 1760s and 1770s. A number of redware teapots with pseudo-Chinese seal marks were excavated by S.J. Greaves and her crew in 1973-4.[170] The site appeared to have a *terminus post quem* of 1775. Since the excavations, however, the City Museum, Stoke-on-Trent has acquired a basalt teapot (Figure 212) marked with same pseudo-Chinese seals seen on the redware pots excavated at the Foley site. It appears that Thomas Barker was also dabbling in the manufacture of blackwares, which were extremely finely grained and potted. A date of 1770 has been assigned by archaeologists for the manufacture of most of the stonewares with seal marks, and, in spite of Wedgwood's remark in September 1772 that 'Nobody makes black T.pots but Palmers',[171] a range from 1770 to a little later seems to be a prudent date for the Foley teapot.

Figure 82. Milk jug with cover with moulded relief decoration of the 'Dancing Hours' modelled by Flaxman, satin-striped cover with sibyl finial. Mark: **Wedgwood**, *c.1776-80, 5½in. high. Rakow collection.*

Figure 83. Chocolate pot and cover, of upright drum-shape with satin-striped base with relief decoration of Lady Templetown figures. The dome cover is topped by a sibyl finial. Mark: **WEDGWOOD**, *c.1785-95, 6¾in. high. Johns Hopkins University, Homewood House Museum.*

Judging from the shapes of John Turner's early pieces he was manufacturing black-wares in the 1770s (Figure 387). Turner competed in both the useful wares market and in ornamental wares (Figure 386) as well, producing basalt of beautiful quality.

William Greatbatch was also producing blackwares (Figure 222) competitively throughout the 1770s and until 1782 when the factory closed. The Greatbatch site has been thoroughly discussed in David Barker's monograph on the subject.[172] William Clowes was also making blackwares in the 1770s (Figure 191).

However, for the most part, the largest number of competitors for the Wedgwood market in black basalt were manufacturing in the 1780s and 1790s and on through the first quarter of the nineteenth century. The discussion, factory by factory, of these fellow manufacturers occurs in Chapter IV.

Wedgwood Designers and Modellers

The list of Wedgwood designers and modellers who worked in basalt is one which, just as a discussion of encaustic sources of design, is so vast as to require a separate volume. The intention at this point is briefly to list major modellers, some of whom, such as Flaxman, Hackwood, Stubbs, and Webber are well known. There are many others about which little or nothing is known.

Among those is Daniel Greatbatch who was a master potter in charge of vase modelling in 1769.[173] By and large Greatbatch remains an unknown. Meteyard does not mention him and Reilly only alludes to him as the 'principal vase modeller".[174]

William Wood was a modeller for Wedgwood from the late 1760s. He was the brother of Enoch Wood and worked with Charles Denby in modelling medallions and bas-reliefs taken from gems and plasters.[175] Denby also executed drawings from

Figure 84. Vase depicting the Triumph of Bacchus modelled by William Hackwood. Several engravings of the Triumph of Bacchus are included in Montfaucon Vol. II and moulds for the relief were executed in 1769. A variation of Wedgwood shape No. 239, it was listed in the 1773 catalogue and is mentioned in inventories of wares going from Etruria to London from 1776-78. This particular vase was advertised by Gered's London in the Antique Dealer's Fair 1955 as having formerly been in the Grant collection. Mark: **WEDG-WOOD & BENTLEY ETRURIA** in wafer of base, c.1770-80, 12in. high. Copy photograph from file in Victoria and Albert Museum.

Hamilton's catalogue. Vase shape No. 48 was described by Wedgwood as a 'unique, taken from a drawing of Mr. Denby's'.[176] William Wood was part of the group which included William Hackwood and Henry Webber, along with Wedgwood, who formed the team of modellers of the Portland Vase, so he undoubtedly executed other important pieces which have not been attributed to him. Denby appears to have been multi-talented for during the time he was senior modeller at Etruria he was also temporarily employed as a painter in the Rhodes decorating studio in London helping to complete the Husk service for Catherine the Great.[177] A sacrifice medallion was modelled by Denby for Wedgwood and Bentley.[178]

Jean Voyez has been mentioned as a modeller of promise who did not work out for Wedgwood's purposes in 1768-9; however, there remain five examples of his enormous gifts as a modeller while he was employed by Palmer (see Palmer, Chapter IV; Figures 336-338).

John Flaxman, jun., began working for Wedgwood and Bentley in 1775 when he was twenty years old. Constable speculates that he may have been encouraged to unite art with industry as a result of not winning the gold medal of the Royal Academy.[179] However, his father had worked intermittently as a modeller for Wedgwood and Bentley and probably in the first years of his employment many of the designs attributed to him were indeed those of his father. The first surviving bill, for March and April 1775, is receipted by John Flaxman, jun. with a note appended 'for my father'.[180] Several works executed during that time have been attributed to Flaxman, sen., on the basis of that bill, including the famous wine and water ewers (Figure 45). However, Flaxman's casts for the Neptune and Bacchus ewers were based on models by Clodion and probably not the models for the ensuing pair which suggest an earlier source, possibly Renaissance bronzes.[181] Although the younger Flaxman is primarily acknowledged for his drawings from classical sources for jasperware, probably one of his first works was of the Dancing Hours which was executed in basalt and appeared in the London showrooms in 1776.[182] As heretofore mentioned, previous research has dated the relief modelling of the Dancing Hours to 1778 (Figure 82) in accordance with a letter published in Farrar.[183] The original letter in the Wedgwood archives is undated and was probably placed in the Farrar letters contextually, not sequentially. The same inventory in which the Dancing Hours was listed included (2 November 1776) 'Boys & Goat' and 'Cupid & Marriage' (The Marriage of Cupid and Psyche), both probably also Flaxman designs. Because Flaxman was an artist he was not an inexpensive ornament in the Wedgwood entourage. In 1777 Wedgwood wrote to Bentley:

— Having laid all our bassrelief [sic] Goddesses & ladies upon their backs on a Board before me in order to contemplate their Beauties, & to increase their number, I instantly perceiv'd that the six Muses we want might be produc'd from this lovely group at half the trouble & expence they will be procur'd from Flaxman, & much better Figures.[184]

Bentley had placed the order before receiving the letter from Wedgwood to countermand the execution of the Muses. As a result a tablet with the six Muses was rendered by Flaxman in 1777.

The Apotheosis of Homer, more famous in jasper but also produced in basalt (Figure 85), was perhaps Flaxman's most famous design for Wedgwood. The source for the design is a scene from a krater vase in the Hamilton collection, Vol. III, page 31. The subject appears in the Wedgwood and Bentley catalogue of 1779 and the jasper example and blackware examples probably date to the previous year, to 1778.

Traditionally attributed to Flaxman on stylistic grounds, Flaxman exhibited a bust of Mercury at the Royal Academy in 1781 and offered a cast to Wedgwood in 1782.[185] Black figures of Mercury had been in production at the Wedgwood factory since at least 1774,[186] but the first mould for a bust of Mercury seems to have been supplied by Hoskins and Grant in the spring of 1779, described as a 'large Antique Bust of Mercury'.[187]

Unless one can firmly identify that the drawings for the Hoskins and Grant mould emanated from Flaxman, which seems unlikely considering he offered the cast three years later, it is necessary to disabuse ourselves of the notion that the first Mercury bust was a Flaxman origination. Is this figure the Hoskins and Grant bust (Figure 56) or one cast from the Flaxman offering? The bust does not appear in any of the eighteenth century Wedgwood catalogues which appears to make most examples very late in that century or products of the nineteenth century.

Mrs. Mary Landré was providing casts for Wedgwood and Bentley at least by 1769 and probably a year earlier.[188] Considerable speculation exists about which casts came from her studio. The Sleeping Boys modelled after Duquesnoy originals and the Death of A Roman Warrior have been commonly attributed to her workshop without positive proof. Her invoice listings are imprecise, for example '4 Groops of Boys' or '6 Passions or Vices' or 'a Battle piece' leave much to the imagination. However, 'The Drunken Silenus', 'Apolow and Dafne' [sic], and 'Antique heads of the 12 Cesers [sic] and Empresses' (Figures 66 and 67) are all familiar subjects.[189] The Drunken Silenus was adapted by numerous other potters, including Adams, Benjamin Adams, and Castleford.

John Coward was another of Wedgwood's modellers in the early years of Etruria. Coward was sending drawings to Wedgwood for his inspection; one of which was chosen was for a cast of an 'Antique Boat',[190] possibly an inkwell similar to the one in Figure 105 or 106.

At the same time John Bacon the elder, a more prominent modeller, was providing

Figure 85. Vase depicting the Apotheosis of Homer. More famous in jasper, the vase, modelled by John Flaxman around 1779, was also produced in basalt. Mark: WEDGWOOD 'V', late 18th - early 19th century, 17in. high. Victoria and Albert Museum, 2402-1901.

models for Wedgwood and Bentley. Bacon, who initially worked at the Coade Artificial Stone Manufactory in Lambeth, received the first gold medal ever given for sculpture at the Royal Academy in 1769 for his bas-relief of Aeneas bearing Anchises from the burning of Troy.[191] Contemporaneously John Flaxman was studying at the Royal Academy Schools while James Tassie, another Royal Academician, commenced work for Wedgwood producing numerous impressions in 'Sulfer' [sic] and enamel.[192] Portrait medallions of George III and Queen Charlotte are generally acknowledged to be the work of John Bacon.[193] Bacon reputedly modelled the 'Night' and 'Day' (Figures 74 and 75) relief scenes listed in 1773 catalogue.

James Tassie was a formidable Wedgwood rival for the seals trade. Wedgwood confided to Bentley in 1776:

Mr. Tassie & Voyez, between them, have made terrible depredations upon our Seal trade. [Figure 412] The former by making them more beautiful, & the latter by selling them cheaper & carrying them to market himself. It will be a credit to emulate the one & the other we may fight in our own way, as far as we think prudent, & as may *benefit our Dignity*.[194]

Other potters, such as Turner, were capitalizing on the Wedgwood reputation for fine seals, cameos and intaglios. One unknown manufacturer, in particular, was producing intaglios impressed with the name WADGWOJD (Figure 466), the similarity in names being clearly not coincidental. Another unidentified potter who marked his intaglios 'W. DICKSON' (Figure 206) seems to have been operating contemporaneously as well.

In 1769 Mr. P. Theodore Parker sent a bill for modelling statues of Flora, Spencer, Seres [sic] Hercules, Juno, Prudence, Milton, Shakespeare and 3 'Doggs'.[195] That same year Thomas Pingo also provided moulds for Wedgwoods.[196]

Henry Webber has been called 'an unjustly neglected eighteenth century sculptor'.[197] In 1776 he won the Royal Academy Gold Medal for sculpture for 'The Judgment of Midas'. Webber was the last of the generation of sculptors who, while working in the neo-classical metier, incorporated an appreciation for the Baroque, and he was the first artist to take up full-time employment in the ceramic industry, beginning work for Josiah Wedgwood in 1782. Webber's connection with Wedgwood may have been initiated by John Bacon, whose studio he joined after leaving school. Webber's designs for Wedgwood were numerous and include: Triumph of Mars, A Boy Leaning on his Quiver with Doves, Cupid Sharpening his Arrows, Hebe, and Sacrifice to Hymen and Sacrifice to Concordia, the latter being listed as a pair (No. 259) in the 1787 catalogue.[198] The Commercial Treaty between France and England (1786)[199] afforded the opportunity of new design to Wedgwood who wrote at that time to Flaxman:

Figure 87. Stirrup cup in the form of a fox head. In 1776 fox heads stirrup cups were sold by Wedgwood & Bentley for 2/6 (Wedgwood MS W/M 1449, 14 December). Mark: **WEDGWOOD**, *c.1780-95, 5½in. high. Collection of the Newark Museum, New Jersey E49.306, gift of John B. Morris, 1949.*

Montfaucon in his *Antiquities* Vol. 1, Part 2, p. 349 speaking in the manner in which Virtue is represented says, *In Gordiano pio Virtus augusti exprimitur per Herculam exuiras leones gestantem & clave innixum.* I have got Mr. Webber to sketch me this Hercules to represent Virtue & the implem'ts of war sacrificing upon an altar sacred to Commerce, but this is not meant by any means to preclude any alteration or better mode of expressing the same thing, which will probably occur to you...[200]

In the 1787 catalogue the Commercial Treaty with France is number 256 under Bas-Reliefs, Medallions and Tablets.

Webber spent from July 1787 to the end of 1788 in Europe. In 1788 Webber was in Rome where he spent some time overseeing the work of several Italian artists commissioned to make models for Wedgwood reproduction. Accounts exist from April 1788 to September 1790 for charges made by such artists as Angelo Dalmazzoni, Angelino Fratoddi, Angelini, Camillo Pacetti, Manzolini, Mangiarotti and Cades for models in wax made from the Capitoline Museum.[201] By the end of 1788 Webber was back in Etruria and he continued to work for Wedgwood until 1795. After Webber left Rome an English resident named Jenkins handled Wedgwood's affairs with the Roman artists.[202]

The explanation of the bas-reliefs from Webber's third expedition was sent to Wedgwood on 12 December 1789. Designs executed by Pacetti included: Priam kneeling before Achilles begging the body of his son Hector, The Fable of Prometheus, Luna, Diana & Diana Lucina, Esculapius and Hygeia, The Simulacrum of Hygeia, A Faun with three Spartan bacchantes, Endymion sleeping on the rock with Latonius visited by Diana, M. Aurelius making his son Commodus Cesar [sic], Apotheosis of Faustina, and The Life of Achilles.

Angelini designs included: The nine Muses, Apollo with the muse Erato, Pluto carrying off Proserpine, The whole fable of Meleager, Two Fauns, two bacchantes and a Silenus, The top of the urn of the Muses, Three Nymphs and three Silenuses, Several geniuses representing the pleasures of the Elysian fields in games, dancing and banqueting.[203]

Angelino Fratoddi was responsible for designs of the shell cameos including: A Woman making an oblation to Hygeia; Livia making an oblation to Mars; Tellotes at the golden altar; Infant Jupiter nursed by Rhea (from a Greek bas-relief in the palace Giustiniani); Juno; Iris and the Bona Dea; Mercury; Apollo; Diana and Lucifera; Antiope exciting her sons Zerus and Amphion to avenge her banishment by tying Dirces to the horns of a wild bull; Paris taking an arrow from Cupid and desiring Cupid to strike Helen; Paris and Helen; Andromache weeping over the ashes of Hector; A child whose destiny is being considered in the presence of his mother; A writer of comedy and tragedy and an allegorical figure of poetry; An offering to the goddess of Health; Sitting figure of Venus with Cupid and two Nymphs decking her; Nemides, goddess of Earth, and the tripod of Delphos.[204]

William Hackwood was hired in 1769 by Josiah Wedgwood. Although originally hired for a period of five years, Hackwood actually remained with the firm until 1832.[205] Perhaps the most prolific of the modellers employed by Wedgwood, Hackwood was responsible for most of the heads of the Illustrious Moderns.[206] According to Wedgwood Mr. Tebo was 'busting' them out for Hackwood to finish.[207]

The association between Josiah Wedgwood and George Stubbs was fostered by Thomas Bentley, but shortly after Stubbs began work for Wedgwood on the Frightened Horse plaque in 1780, Bentley died. The first Frightened Horse plaque was probably executed in blue and white jasper and produced before Bentley's death in November because it is marked WEDGWOOD & BENTLEY. Another was subsequently produced in basalt (Figure 80).[208] Stubbs continued to work in various mediums for Wedgwood and in 1785 completed another basalt plaque of The Fall of Phaeton, a design which he had been working on since 1780.[209]

John Charles Lochée and Joachim Smith and others such as Pesez (Figure 73) worked as plaster cast modellers for Wedgwood in the mid-1770s making portrait heads of figures of the day. By the mid-1780s other artists joined Flaxman, Webber and Hackwood in the Wedgwood entourage, particularly Lady Templetown and Lady Diana Beauclerk.

Lady Templetown provided models of a serene and contemplative nature such as her well-known Domestic Employment (Figures 145, 267, 287-289, 292, 295, 327, 391), and Friendship consoling Affliction. Lady Diana was renowned for her child bacchanals which featured plump babies cavorting mischievously. Lady Diana's babies were frolicking and bumptious while Lady Templetown's figures were tranquil, but both infected the designs emanating from the other Staffordshire potters. Many of their designs appear in the 1787 Wedgwood catalogue.

Esteem for the name Wedgwood was such that the firm was being approached by independent modellers with drawings and proposals for models. In 1790, on Wedgwood's advice, cameo maker, R. Burley of Birmingham, sent a drawing of a vase along with an offer to make cameos.[210]

The London plaster shops or mould makers were a common link with all the Staffordshire potters. Establishments such as those run by John Cheere, John Flaxman, Charles Harris, Mrs. Landre, Hoskins and Oliver and subsequent partners, Peter Vanina[211] and others, in which sculpture and similar ornaments were available in whole or in part, were essential to the survival of a pottery industry not simply interested in providing functional vessels, but ones which would incorporate the art of the past with current popular themes.

Wedgwood's Foreign Markets

The earliest surviving record by Bentley and Boardman for an American trade was an order for Boston in 1764 for cauliflower, pineapple wares, cream coloured earthenware and blackware.[212] By 1768 Wedgwood seemed to be considering certain trading possibilities in Philadelphia with William Logan, Esq.[213] Certainly by 1769 Wedgwood began heavily exporting to America and by 1771 the firm was exporting great quantities.[214]

Many Continental markets were established by 1769: such was the firm's early success abroad that Wedgwood and Bentley's Amsterdam agent, John Du Burk, ransacked the London showroom in April 1769, taking with him fifty vases, and leaving none for local patrons.[215] Du Burk continued as agent in Amsterdam until 1777 but it was not an altogether happy arrangement for Wedgwood. By 1776 Wedgwood was complaining to Bentley that Du Burk had turned out to be a 'Bad Man as well as a fool...'[216] In 1773 Joseph Cooper had joined Du Burk, thus ensuring some English oversight in the troubled Amsterdam business.[217] Cooper was the London printer of both the 1773 and 1774 catalogues as well as the catalogue of the Frog Service for Catherine the Great. Through Du Burk and Cooper, Wedgwood and Bentley marketed a great deal of ornamental basalt as well as useful teaware, although breakage in transit continued to plague the transactions.[218]

Frankfurt dealer Baumgartner began ordering from the firm in late 1769.[219] Meteyard says that Baumgartner was also responsible for introducing the Etruscan painted vases of the factory into Italy.[220] By early 1770 Thomas Bentley was in communication with St. Petersburg through the English envoy to the Russian court, Lord Cathcart. Particularly anxious to secure the patronage of the Russian élite, Bentley had sent Lord Cathcart two sets of the latest vases by way of introduction to the firm's merchandise. He even went as far as marking the prices on the vases themselves.[221] The wares were immediately successful. Lady Cathcart wrote to Josiah Wedgwood:

St. Petersburg 7 October 1770

Sir,

I give you the trouble of this letter by post, without waiting for other opportunities, because I can give you the pleasure of knowing that your commissions of this year have been extremely successful... Mr. Welden tells me her Imperial Majesty is vastly pleased with what was executed by her Command...Mr. Welden will also tell you that Her Majesty has kept all the Vases & Dejeunié [sic] you sent to me as Samples, and that they were much liked.

Yours most Humb'l Ser'v,

S. Cathcart[222]

To avoid offence, Wedgwood kept the merchants informed about his personal communications with Lady Cathcart. In a letter to Messrs. James Jackson in St. Petersburg he informed them of the nature of the articles sent to Lady Cathcart to be presented to Her Imperial Majesty: vases, urns, and bas-reliefs after Etruscan, Greek and Roman models. He suggested that since the articles were highly priced they would be worth the attention of the merchants.[223] Survival of documentation of basalt orders going to Russia after the early 1770s is scant, but demand for neoclassical ornamental wares appears to have continued. In 1786, there was a large commission placed through Messrs. Cooper, Palmer & Perkins, St. Petersburg, for bas-reliefs of: Triumph of Ariadne and Bacchus, Offering to Aurora, Cupid and Psyche and four bas-reliefs made from Cipriani's design engraved by Bartolozzi representing Minerva visiting the muses and Vulcan visiting the muses.[224] These appear to have been intended to be made of jasper but the order also contained some medallions and some small vases of unspecified composition.[225] In 1798 a large order was placed by dealer H.S. Wagnon in St. Petersburg for 100 black teapots in various shapes and sizes.[226] Wagnon continued ordering from Wedgwood and Byerley through at least 1804.

*Figure 88. Salt in the form of a dolphin. Mark: **WEDGWOOD**, c.1790-1810, 4¾in. high. Grigsby collection.*

Basalt was being exported to France at least as early as 1774 and probably much earlier.[227] The third edition of the catalogue in French (1774) included a lengthy, graphic description of a Wedgwood and Bentley inkwell (Figure 89).[228] After the Treaty of Commerce between England and France in 1786 Wedgwood established two depots for marketing wares, one at Rue St. Honoré, with M. Daguerre attending, and the other at the House of Sykes and Compagnie, Place Palais Royal.[229] Dominique Daguerre was actually a Paris furniture dealer who included large quantities of Wedgwood in his stock. Daguerre's business crashed at the time of the French Revolution and he escaped to England for a short while before returning to Paris in 1791 to continue the Wedgwood trade.[230] Prior to the revolution several other French merchants were actively selling Wedgwood blackwares, including Messrs. Bruneau Maubran & Co., Paris, who were ordering seals, intaglios, medallions and plaques.[231] M. J. Boulanger, Paris, complained in a letter to Wedgwood in 1789 that cameos did not sell.[232] Another dealer, John Savaers, argued that, though recognising the price for Wedgwood wares was higher than those of other manufacturers, the price was truly out of proportion.[233] Savaers complained that Wedgwood's black ware assortment was too small and that each teapot should have a figure on the cover, not just the 'Buttons', and that the teapots and milkpots were in general 'too little'.[234] In the early nineteenth century M. Jean Bourdon, Paris, was ordering '100 Theyeres noires form grande nouvelles, 30 [Theyeres] moyenne, 10 ditto petites.'[235] Too extensive to quote here, but among the Wedgwood manuscripts at Keele University, is a list of the French accounts from the 'green book' of export sales for 1790.[236]

In addition to the Staffordshire Price Fixing Agreements (*see* Appendix I), Wedgwood produced several extensive lists of factory prices including basalt and other dry bodies, one around 1806 or later (the handwritten manuscript is undated). The 1817 and 1836 printed English price lists include Egyptian Black, Cane and Red-bodied wares but by 1845 no black or other dry bodies are listed in the English price list. The 1845 French price list included *Basalte* among the other earthenwares when the English edition did not. By 1845 the factory had reduced the offering of teaware to two shapes, Nos. 43 and 146, but were offering a variety of other wares, including Barberini and other vases.[237]

In Dresden, Henrietta Ch. Conradi was acting as a Wedgwood agent for many friends, and in 1777 planned to open a warehouse in Bohemia.[238] In 1790 she was continuing her basalt orders which included black fluted teapots, coffee pots, cream jugs and sugars.[239] Just as the English, Germans were also interested in black tea services of 'the newest fashion'.[240] Hamburg merchants Phillip & Otto von Oxen placed an order in 1790 for 'large, choicest vases for Chimneypieces for a German Prince'.[241]

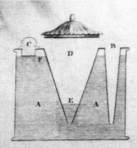

Des ECRITOIRES en Porcelaine Noire, fabriqués par les Sieurs WEDGWOOD et BENTLEY.

DE parmi tout le grand Nombre des Ecritoires et d'Encriers qu'on a inventé jusqu'ici, celle, qui est representée dans la Figure ci-dessus, est la meilleure et la plus commode : et comme elle est d'une Invention tout neuve, il en faut une Description.

EXPLICATION DE LA FIGURE.

A A. La Citerne, remplie d'Encre jusqu'à F.

B. Des Tuyaux pour les Plumes, qui sont formées en bas, ce qui empêche qu'il n'y entre point d'Air.

C. Une petite Ouverture, qui va à la Citerne, avec un Bouchon très serré.

D. Un Cone, par où l'on remplit la Citerne, en tirant premierement le Bouchon à C.

On verse l'Encre dans le Cone, jusqu'à ce qu'il soit plein, après quoi on remet le Bouchon dans sa Place ; puis on vuide l'Encre hors du Cone, soit en versant, ou par une Eponge, aussi bas que E, alors l'Encre restera dans la Citerne, à la Hauteur de F, et agira en Fontaine ; la Plume puisant l'Encre par le Cone D, au Point E.

Les Avantages et Propriétés de ces Ecritoires.

L'Ouverture graduelle du Cone fait, qu'on n'est pas sujét de se salir les Doigts, ou la Plume, comme on fait avec les autres très communes.

Le Bout du Cone etant etroit, previent que la Plume ne grâte contre le Fond.

La Surface de l'Encre n'est pas exposée à l'Air, autrement qu'au petit Point E, ce qui en previent l'Evaporation ; et l'empêche de se gâter en s'epaississant comme il arrive dans tous les Encriers communs, où il y a une grande Surface necessairement exposé à l'Air.

Ce qui recommande ces Encriers encore davantage, est, qu'ils sont composés d'un Jaspe ou Porcelaine noire, très fine et bien lié, qui n'est jamais corrodé par l'Encre, et ne l'absorbe point : aussi ils se laissent finir et achever avec la derniere Delicatesse ; comme on en finit constamment un grand Nombre, qui meritent bien d'être placés parmi les plus beaux Productions de l'Art.

Ces Encriers se vendent separament, comm n representés dans l'Estampe ci-dessus ; ou bien avec des Sabliers, Oubliers, &c. forment plusieurs Especes des Ecritoires, tant utiles qu'embellies des Ornemens : les Prix sont de Six Sols, et montant graduellement selon la Beauté de l'Ouvrage, leur Grandeur, et les Formes, jusqu'à environ Huit Chelins la Piece.

Messrs. WEDGWOOD et BENTLEY, prennent la Liberté de recommander à Messieurs les Marchands étrangers, qui voudroient bien acheter de leurs Oeuvrages, d'addresses les Ordres à leurs Correspondens ordinaires en Angleterre ; car la grande Attention que leur Manufacture demande constamment, et leur Situation, rendent les Soins des Commissions, et d'une Correspondence étranger et extensive, extremement difficile.

The largest Frankfurt dealers of Wedgwood blackware were Behagel and Son. They were actively ordering from Wedgwood and Byerley between 1797 and 1806. Black basalt 'oval boat Escritoires' (Figures 105 and 106), tea and coffee wares, and bas-reliefs requesting 'boys' and 'Dancing figures' were part of orders placed in 1798 and 1800.[242]

In Warsaw, Munkenbeck & Co. were ordering black beehive teapots as well as other black basalt tewares in 1802.[243] Wedgwood sent black tewares to St Helens[244] and to Neufchatel;[245] to Antwerp he sent tewares as well as basalt chambersticks and double salts.[246]

In Leghorn (Livorno) Giuseppe Fantechi was a principal merchandiser of Wedgwood wares with orders extending from 1783 to 1802. His market was apparently a sophisticated one, as orders exist for black vases, escritoires, inkpots, bas-reliefs and tablets, statues and tripods.[247]

Documentation for Wedgwood exports to America is scant, but documentation for the other manufacturers also producing basalt is nearly non-existent. Complicating the obvious obscurity of data on export and use in America is the almost complete lack of archaeological evidence. A few sherds exist from excavations undertaken systematically in Williamsburg from the 1930s on, but with one exception, a Neale basalt teabowl fragment (Figure 334), there are no excavated examples attributable to a specific manufacturer. Another major colonial and federal period town which has enjoyed numerous archaeological testings is Portsmouth, New Hampshire. A basalt fragment of a teapot base marked with the letters KER appears to be from a teapot of BARKER manufacture (Figure 149). Other areas in

Figure 89. Des Ecritoires en Porcelain Noire. *The document which discusses the function of basalt inkwells is from the third edition of the Wedgwood and Bentley catalogue in French, 1774. Wedgwood MS W/M 1851.*

Figure 90. Partially reconstructed teapot from H.M.S. DeBraak, *a British warship sunk at the mouth of the Delaware River (USA) in 1798. Unmarked, c.1790-5.*

colonial American archaeological sites have also yielded very little blackware.

Just how much basalt was being used in American households and what economic factors prevailed to make the purchase of basalt possible is a study which has not been made. That the blackware existed in some households is shown in inventories and through newspaper advertisements. For example, the 1780 Baltimore County inventory for Thomas Lloyd listed '1 black stone coffee pot'.[248]

In 1795, Philadelphia stationer and bookseller, William Young, advertised 'a variety of Wedgwood inkstands' for sale in his shop.[249] In 1796, New York china merchant Ebenezer Young, was offering 'Tea Pots Egyptian Black 3s'. [250] In an inventory of Mount Vernon taken in 1799/1800, listed in the contents of George Washington's home was '1 Egyptian China' [Teapot] in the Closet under Frank's [the butler] Direction. It was valued at fifty cents.[251] A basalt coffee pot at Mount Vernon may have been acquired by the Washingtons in Philadelphia with the teapot.[252] A letter to Thomas Jefferson from his daughter, Martha Randolph, written on 11 July 1805 asked for some additions to the tea equipage at Monticello: 'The tea pots are too small consequently a large black one with two cream pots to match would add to both the comfort and appearance of the board, the plated ones being so much worn as to shew the copper.[253] A family inventory after Jefferson's death recorded '1 wedgewood teapot' and '1 wedgewood sugar dish' which may have been basalt but were more likely to have been jasper.[254]

Montreal merchant, Elias Smith, complained in his letterbook entry for 10 October 1799 of the loss, due to breakage in transit, of an entire crate of Egyptian black valued at five guineas.[255] Stock in the probated inventory of Portsmouth, New Hampshire china and textile dealer, Abraham Isaac, in 1803 included twenty Egyptian black teapots valued at one shilling each and seven glazed black teapots at nine pence each.[256] Abraham Isaac may have been the merchant who supplied William Neil of Portsmouth with the 'three black teapots' listed in the probated inventory of his estate in 1826.[257]

Among the contents of the H.M.S. *DeBraak*, a British warship that sank at the mouth of the Delaware river in May 1798, was a basalt teapot with a widow finial (Figure 90) and a cream jug.[258]

In Cornwall Philip Moore, probably a merchant, was ordering 'Round black teapots' directly from Wedgwood and Byerley in 1813 along with other popular wares. His letter came with the admonition to send the goods via Liverpool as they were cheaper and faster than wares sent via Bristol.[259] One wonders if American merchants also found the Liverpool route more expeditious. At any rate great quantities of basalt do not appear to have adorned American homes. For instance, the Governor of Maryland, Charles Ridgely, boasted one sole 'Black Teapot' in the inventory of his estate taken after his death in 1829.[260]

Business papers exist in the Baker Library, Harvard University, for Boston china dealer Horace Collamore extending from 1807 to 1853. In Collamore's price list for Staffordshire pottery of 1814, Egyptian black oval teapots were 12/- and 18/- each, oval coffee pots 21/-, round 'thread', fluted [tea]pots 12/-, round satin striped [tea]pots 14/-, bowls thread, fluted 15/-, bowls figures 15/-, round milk jugs and creams, not fluted 15/-, ditto figures 18/-, oval milk jugs and covers 26/-, round image or figure teapots 16/-.[261] It is interesting to compare these prices with those of the Wedgwood 1815 price list[262] which sold flat fluted teapots for 36/- per dozen. Collamore was selling what would be a 3 shilling teapot in England for 12 shillings in America.

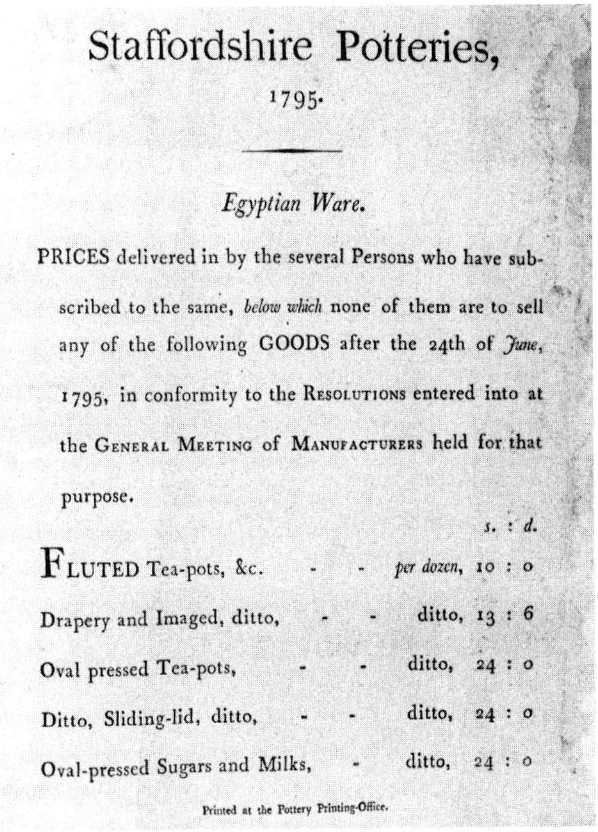

Marketing at Home 1786-1800

London is larger and more lovely than ever. The increasing population, riches, splendour are scarcely credible. Its superiority to all other capital cities is very striking.

Mrs. Thrale, March 1787

After Boulton and Watt's steam engine was incorporated into the works at Etruria (probably later than the 1782 date often suggested),[263] the Wedgwood production doubtless increased, along with the general efficiency of the factory. Merchandising was encouraging, in the sense that markets existed for wares produced domestically; however, competition from foreign merchandise loomed as an omnipresent threat. One Manchester dealer, John Bury, acknowledged that the business was brisk in foreign china and glass but not in Staffordshire ware which was sold too low for the ladies of Manchester to be interested.[264]

Basalt, jasper and caneware continued in popular demand both in useful and ornamental wares as well as for jewellery, buttons, and cane handles. Wedgwood continued to subcontract individuals and companies to mount such oddments. In 1786 a Wolverhampton steel manufacturer, Mr. Haselwood, was placing cameos and intaglios into metal mounts for buttons and cane handles.[265]

Basalt enjoyed great popularity between 1785 and 1795. Basalt teawares were being ordered from Wedgwood by Birmingham merchant, Joseph Barnet in 1787[266] and 'Egyptian Black with broad flutes' by St Catherine's London dealers, Hardress, Mantz and Co.[267] Edinburgh merchants George and John Taylor were placing frequent orders to Wedgwood for Egyptian black teawares from 1788 to 1793, ordering 'fluted Black Teapots, Teapot stands, Sugar basins, etc.'[268]

Individual customers were still being treated with the inimitable Wedgwood courtesy. When Lady Banks or Thomas Webb of Sterling Park placed a small order for basalt and creamware they often received a reply personally from Josiah

Staffordshire Potteries,
1795.

Egyptian Ware.

PRICES delivered in by the several Persons who have subscribed to the same, *below which* none of them are to sell any of the following GOODS after the 24th of *June*, 1795, in conformity to the RESOLUTIONS entered into at the GENERAL MEETING of MANUFACTURERS held for that purpose.

		s. : d.
FLUTED Tea-pots, &c.	per dozen,	10 : 0
Drapery and Imaged, ditto,	ditto,	13 : 6
Oval pressed Tea-pots,	ditto,	24 : 0
Ditto, Sliding-lid, ditto,	ditto,	24 : 0
Oval-pressed Sugars and Milks,	ditto,	24 : 0

Printed at the Pottery Printing-Office.

Figure 91. Egyptian Ware prices from the Staffordshire Price Fixing Agreements entered into by the Committee of Manufactures of 1795, the first existing document fixing prices for basalt (see Appendix I). Photograph courtesy City Museum and Art Gallery, Stoke-on-Trent.

Wedgwood.[269] The hand of the potter may have been less in evidence by 1790, but the hand of the businessman was not, and the potter walked frequently in tandem with that of the businessman:

> Josiah Wedgwood to Thomas Byerley   December 22, 1790
> I beg my comp't to Mr. Hope and wish to acquaint him that his Etruscan Table service is in great forwardness & will be ready very soon. What has occasioned it to be so long in hand is the difficulty in making the red upon the black instead of the black upon the red as we used to do.[270]

A Committee of Manufacturers had been organized to fix prices and to oversee problems within the pottery industry as a whole. By 1790 those manufacturers who regularly attended meetings of the committee consisted of Josiah Wedgwood (in the chair), Jacob Warburton, Richard Mare, Ralph Wedgwood, George Taylor, John Glass, and Benjamin Godwin.[271] Subscribers to the committee were far more numerous and in 1795 prices were fixed on 'Egyptian Ware' (Figure 91).

Another copartnership was established among the potters on 25 May 1797 to purchase clay co-operatively and directly from the manufacturer, without the intervention of third parties. The agreement was for twenty years and each party contributed £20 toward the establishment of the concern. The Potters Clay Company, as it was called, included Josiah Wedgwood II and Thomas Byerley, John Rogers, George Rogers, Anthony and Enoch Keeling, John Mare, John Blackwell, William Adams, Ralph Baddeley, John Yates and William Yates, Samuel Hollins, Edward Keeling, Elijah Mayer, James Whitehead and Charles Whitehead, Edmund John Birch, John Breeze, Ephraim Booth, Hugh Booth and Joseph Booth, James Bulkely and William Bent, and John Davenport.[272]

The sudden death of Josiah Wedgwood in 1795, after only a short illness, closed the door on an unexcelled era of prosperity and technological innovation in the English pottery industry. A notice appeared in *The Times* on Saturday 10 January 1795 and simply said: 'Died, on Saturday, the 3d inst., Josiah Wedgwood, F.R.S. of Etruria, in the county of Stafford.'

Other manufacturers and retailers were selling the blackwares but documentation on these warehousemen is extremely patchy. Neale and Bailey of St. Paul's Churchyard were selling basalt, along with other ceramics and glass, to Messrs Bird, Savage and Bird, London: Black oval teapots 2/- and 2/6 each, sugar basins 1/9, milk pots 1/-, double black ink 3/-, single ditto 9d.[273] In 1798 and 1800 merchant William Wills of Exeter placed orders for basalt through Wedgwood and Byerley, in some instances specifying wares produced by other factories, namely Wilson and Turner.[274] Further discussion about these and other manufacturers occurs in Chapter IV.

CHAPTER III
Wedgwood in the Nineteenth Century

Society, an ample allowance of society, this is the first requisite which a mother should seek in sending her son to live alone in London; bars, routs, picnics, parties; women, pretty, well-dressed, witty, easy-mannered; good pictures, elegant drawing-rooms, well got-up books, Majolica and Dresden china — These are the truest guards to protect a youth from dissipation and immorality.
A. Trollope, *The Three Clerks* 1857

Majolica and Dresden china represented the society of which Trollope was writing. Black basalt was indeed by 1857 out of fashion. Not so, however, during the first quarter of the nineteenth century which continued to sustain this curious and enduring stoneware.

After Wedgwood's death, the firm, composed of Josiah Wedgwood II and Thomas Byerley, continued in the tradition of serving individuals by acknowledging orders for specific requests. In 1800, Mr. Blane ordered two tritons for a single light

Figure 92. Drawing Book for Black Ware 1800 (Hartley, Greens & Co., Leeds Pottery). No. 26, a beehive teapot, the beehive shape being the rage at home and abroad during the early years of the 19th century. The unpublished Drawing Book is on deposit at the Leeds City Art Gallery Library.

Figure 93. Ewer or rhyton in the form of a female head, traces of bronzing. No. 196 in Wedgwood's Shape Book, the ewer may be taken from a 4th century BC bronze, probably Etruscan, now in the Louvre (Tait, 1963, 36). Aileen Dawson (1984, 43) suggests another source, a drawing in the Royal Library Windsor commissioned by the 17th century antiquarian Cassiano dal Pozzo. Mark: **WEDG-WOOD K**, probably late 18th century. 10in. high. British Museum, 1909-12-1-106, Falcke collection.

for his home at 25 Portman Square and was charged 36/-.[1]

Suppliers of raw materials or blackwares were an integral part of the manufacturing process. Cornish manganese for colouring the stoneware body black was supplied by Hall, Harding Co. of Newcastle to Wedgwood and Byerley in the early years of the nineteenth century.[2]

At the same time the rage both at home and abroad was for the fashionable beehive teapots. As early as 1791 merchants were clamouring for the beehive teapots. By 1802 merchants abroad were requesting the shape specifically.[3] At home beehive teapots sold for 12/-, 18/- and 24/- per dozen.[4] In the early years of the nineteenth century the Leeds Pottery were also producing their version of the beehive tewares (Figure 92) along with Spode,[5] the Don Pottery, Keeling, Toft & Co. (Figure 268), and others. By 1811 Wedgwood made beehive teapots in two versions, either plain or fluted.[6] It was the only teapot shape specified time and again from 1791, and seemed to be especially popular with foreign markets.

By 1808 the new low oval shape as well as red and black Egyptian teawares were also highly desirable.[7] The new low oval teawares, following silver and porcelain fashion, were not popular in all areas of the country. In Durham, merchant Elizabeth Haswell reproached Wedgwood by saying: '…the black Tea Potts & Milk Pots of the low Pattern they are an article that may stand 20 years before I can sell one…'[8] Other dealers were unable to sell 'Bronze Ware'[9] (Figures 93 and 113; Colour Plate 5).

Figure 94. Tablet of Venus in her car drawn by swans with attendant cupids, modelled in 1778 (Meteyard, Memorials, 1874). This is No. 245 in Class II of the 1787 catalogue. Mark: **WEDGWOOD O**, late 18th-early 19th century, 6½in. x 8½in. Rakow collection.

*Figure 95. Déjeuner tray, with silver inlay. Referred to as 'Silver Etruscan' by Wedgwoods, a 'déjeuner for one with bowl' sold for £1.17.6 in 1795 (17-15861, 24 January 1795). Mark: **WEDGWOOD**, c.1791-1814, 12⅜in. long. British Museum, 1909-12-1-123, Falcke collection.*

*Figure 96. Teapot and cover with silver Etruscan decoration. The round parapet teapot has a band of wheat sheaf silver Etruscan decoration and a spaniel finial. Mark: **WEDGWOOD**, c.1800, 5½in. high. Royal Ontario Museum, 970.242.104, Brown collection.*

Major nineteenth century ceramic trends extended to the basalt produced by Wedgwood and by many other manufacturers of blackware: wares made in the Egyptian style, wares decorated with 'Black Chinese Flowers', and blackware decorated with silver inlay. The early nineteenth century saw a rekindled interest in wares painted in the Etruscan style as well.

Black Egyptian wares and red and black Egyptian wares (Figures 102 and 103) had been made since the 1770s when the influence of Montfaucon[10] and Caylus[11] was an

*Figure 97. Group of 'Etruscan' decorated wares of the 18th and 19th century. The fashion for 'Etruscan' decoration on basalt extended into the 19th century and the more restrained the decoration, the more difficult it is to distinguish from the earlier wares. Mark: oil lamp, **WEDGWOOD**, c.1780-95, 5½in. long; inkwell, '**Wedgwood 3 No. 18**', c.1770-80; cup and saucer, **WEDGWOOD 2**, c.1795-1810. Chellis collection.*

*Figure 98. Calyx-krater vase with 'Etruscan' decoration. Mark: **WEDGWOOD A**, '43' painted in red; c.1795-1810, 7⅞in. high. Rakow collection.*

extension of the Grand Tour, tantamount to bringing the classical wonders of Greece and Rome into one's home with Greek style vases on the chimney-piece, cameos of the Heads of the Roman Empresses and Caesars in the curio cabinet, and a pastille burner in the shape of a pyramid (Figure 380) or a sphinx couchant (Figures 18 and 19) on the sideboard. One of the most popular forms from the first period Egyptian production was the canopic vase (Figure 108), taken directly from volume four of Montfaucon. By early 1771 nozzles were being added to canopic vases to convert them into candlesticks.[12] But all of these forms were revived, and often embellished, in the early nineteenth century stimulated by interest in Napoleon's Egyptian campaign of 1798.

As mentioned, black relief decoration on red stoneware had also been made since the 1770s but enjoyed renewed interest in the first decade of the nineteenth century. That Wedgwood had been experimenting with red decoration on the black body since late 1790 (and finding difficulty in achieving satisfactory results in finishing the Etruscan table service in this combination for Mr. Hope) we do know.[13] However, the red on black and the black on red, or *rosso antico*, was a happy and popular alliance also produced by a number of other potters outside the Wedgwood sphere, Turner (Colour Plate 22), Spode (Colour Plate 18), and Baddeley at Eastwood

*Figure 99. Kantharos-shaped pastille-burner, with liner and insert, painted with 'Etruscan' enamels. Mark: **WEDGWOOD**, c.1805-20, 8⁹⁄₁₆in. wide. British Museum, 1909-12-1-119, Falcke collection.*

*Figure 100. Jug with 'Etruscan' decoration. Mark: **WEDG-WOOD OHN/Y 112**, probably November 1860 (but the date letters could be November 1886), 5in. high. Rakow collection.*

(Figures 136 and 137) to name but a few.

The Wedgwood factory offered the same vases in several bodies (Figure 109): Incense Vase No. 658 was available in 'Plain black, Cane Gadrooned or Red and black'. The red and black combination was more expensive. Incense vase No. 657 (4½in. high) in plain black was 2/9, in red and black 4/- and in black flat fluted 3/3. The red body with black relief decoration was the more successful of the two combinations, and the *rosso antico* was favoured within the country. Oxford dealer, Mrs. Lydia Butler, was placing orders for Egyptian lamps, red and black[14], for red and black Egyptian teapots[15], and for red Egyptian [low parapet teapots] with black ornaments in 1813.[16] She was ordering relatively little plain black teaware.[17]

Exuberant enamelling with opaque colours in the *famille rose* and *famille verte* palette was particularly effective decoration on the black basalt body and was popularly produced in the 1820s and 1830s (Figure 101; Colour Plate 21). Copeland and Garrett (and later Copeland) also produced similarly decorated basalt (Colour Plates 19 and 20), and the Lowesby factory in Leicestershire produced remarkably fine blackwares decorated in the same fashion (Figure 276).

Applied decoration in silver, called 'Silver Etruscan,'[18] and silver inlay, began to be seen on wares produced by Wedgwood in 1791[19] (Figures 95 and 96) and was manufactured thereafter by numerous other potters, who, by and large, did not mark their wares. It was an effective, pleasant decoration but could not stand up to the test of time as it tended to tarnish and disappear into the black body.

The Egyptian revival resuscitated interest in the Etruscan painted wares, but by the early nineteenth century most of the important painters were gone. Aaron Steele seems to have been the only major painter remaining active and thus became a valuable asset to the Wedgwood firm,[20] which had begun production of large painted

*Figure 101. Vase decorated with 'Chinese flowers' in opaque enamels. Mark: **WEDGWOOD**, c.1820, 8⅞in. high. Polikoff collection.*

*Figure 102. Oil lamp, rosso antico, with sun face and other embellishment in redware on a basalt body. Mark: **WEDGWOOD**, c.1805-15, 5½in. long. Polikoff collection.*

*Figure 103. Candlestick of sphinx pilasters on shaped base, rosso antico, Mark: **WEDGWOOD W**, c.1805-10, 7½in. high. Chellis collection.*

*Figure 104. Sphinx candelabrum, modelled in one piece of unpolished basalt. Sphinx candlesticks were being made at least by early 1776 and cost £1.11.6 the pair (W/M 1449, 14 February 1776). The early 19th century interest in Egyptian motifs caused a second wave of wares, such as this one, to be produced. Mark: **WEDGWOOD S**, c.1805-20, 14¼in. high. The Board of Trustees of the National Museums & Galleries on Merseyside (Liverpool Museum), 3028M, Mayer collection.*

96

*Figure 105. Inkstand in the form of a boat (minus liners and covers) with ram's-head handles and three cups with bacchanalian boys in relief. Inkstands in boat form had been made since 1769 when Wedgwood wrote to Bentley, 'I forgot to pay the Modeller for a cast of an Antique Boat...' (96-17673, 20 March 1769). However, the rage for classical and Egyptian inkwells followed the Napoleonic Egyptian campaign of 1798. Mark: **WEDGWOOD**, c.1805-10, 4½in. high. Grigsby collection.*

*Figure 106. Inkstand in the form of an Egyptian boat. Mark: **WEDGWOOD**, c.1805-10, 5⅛in. x 12in. Chellis collection.*

*Figure 107. Pair of dolphin candlesticks and an Egyptian sphinx couchant. Dolphin candlesticks were popularly produced from 1800 and the sphinx couchant was first produced in 1769. By 1773 there were eight models listed in the ornamental ware catalogue. The sphinx and other exotic Egyptian ornaments enjoyed a revival after 1798. Marks: all **WEDGWOOD**; candlesticks c.1800-20, 8⅝in. high; sphinx c.1798-1810, 5⅞in. long. Photograph courtesy Sotheby's New York.*

Figure 108. Canopic vase decorated with moulded relief signs of the zodiac. Mark: **WEDGWOOD**, c.1800-15, 9⅜in. high. Grigsby collection.

Figure 109. Drawings of incense vases and descriptions of the bodies in which they were manufactured by the Wedgwood factory. No date, c. 1800-10 (Wedgwood MS 54-30033).

vases. One patron for such vases was the Marquis of Lansdowne who sought 'Etruscan Vases' for his library in 1813.[21] Wedgwood was still making vases thirty-four inches high and larger in 1829.[22]

About the same time a variety of pastille burners entered the factory repertoire (Figures 110, 112 and 113). Popular in the last decade of the eighteenth century and through the first quarter of the nineteenth century, the pastille burner was essentially a device for burning incense, the incense in this case being cones of charcoal dipped in fragrant oils or extracts, which masked unpleasant odours in rooms without proper ventilation or septic systems. As late as 1836 Lady Granville, the wife of the British Ambassador to France, received a gift of 'gilt and brown pastilles' from the Turkish Ambassador.[23] Pastille burners in the black basalt body were decorated in current fashion, bronzed (Figure 113), painted in encaustic and Etruscan colours, produced in red and black stoneware, and many modelled in an Egyptian motif (Figure 112 and 113). One pastille burner (as well as other wares), boldly painted in red block letters on the base, has a curious date which has baffled scholars: 2 February 1805 (Figure 112a).[24]

Figure 110. Incense vase and cover for burning pastilles. The relief decoration of garlands of flowers pendant to female masks and a rosette fretted band at the shoulder of the vase add neo-classical touches. Mark: **WEDGWOOD**, c.1800-20, 7½in. high. Rakow collection.

Figure 111. Pair of oil lamps. Oil lamps used in the 18th century were frequently converted into pastille-burners for incense in the late 18th century or early in the 19th century. Mark: **WEDGWOOD**, c.1790-1810, 8⅛in. high. Grigsby collection.

Figure 112a. Mark on base of pastille-burner in Figure 112.

Figure 112. Pastille-burner (minus cover) situated on a disc base with a tripod of Egyptian motif. The base (Figure 112a) bears the full name Josiah Wedgwood and a curious date, 2 February 1805. Gaye Blake Roberts has suggested (see fn.24 Chapter III) that the date may have been an important one for trials for firing of wares of various bodies. Mark: **WEDGWOOD** impressed plus the red printed mark in Figure 112a, 1805, 7in. high. Chellis collection.

Figure 113 Pastille-burner and cover, bronzed. Very similar in form to Figure 112 but bearing the cover which was missing on the previous piece. The perforations on the cover would allow the perfume of the pastilles to escape. Mark: WEDGWOOD 2, c.1805-10, 7¾in. high. Chellis collection

Figure 114. Nelson's Column with attendant lions probably made by the Wedgwood factory shortly after the erection of the monument in Trafalgar Square in 1842. Mark: WEDGWOOD C * on column; lions, all WEDGWOOD, c.1842, 21¾in. high. National Maritime Museum, Sutcliffe Smith collection.

The original tripods, introduced in the 1770s, were oil lamps and were refitted to accommodate pastilles in the early part of the nineteenth century. Production of pastille burners in basalt was not the exclusive territory of the Wedgwood factory, although other factories, such as the Cambrian Pottery, Swansea (Figure 177), and Turner (Figure 386), which were also making their own versions, are not numerous.

Another vase, a more modern tinderbox and precursor to the match, was the pyrophorus vase of which there were a number of styles made during the second and third decades of the century (Colour Plate 16). They were clever devices and Wedgwood is given credit for first introducing the idea into a decorative ceramic vessel. The pyrophorus vase contained slivers of wood tipped with sulphur coated with a paste of potash, and sugar which could be ignited when brought in contact with a concentrate of sulphuric acid. The sulphuric acid had to be kept in a glass container and the matches in a wooden box. When the sliver of wood or match was

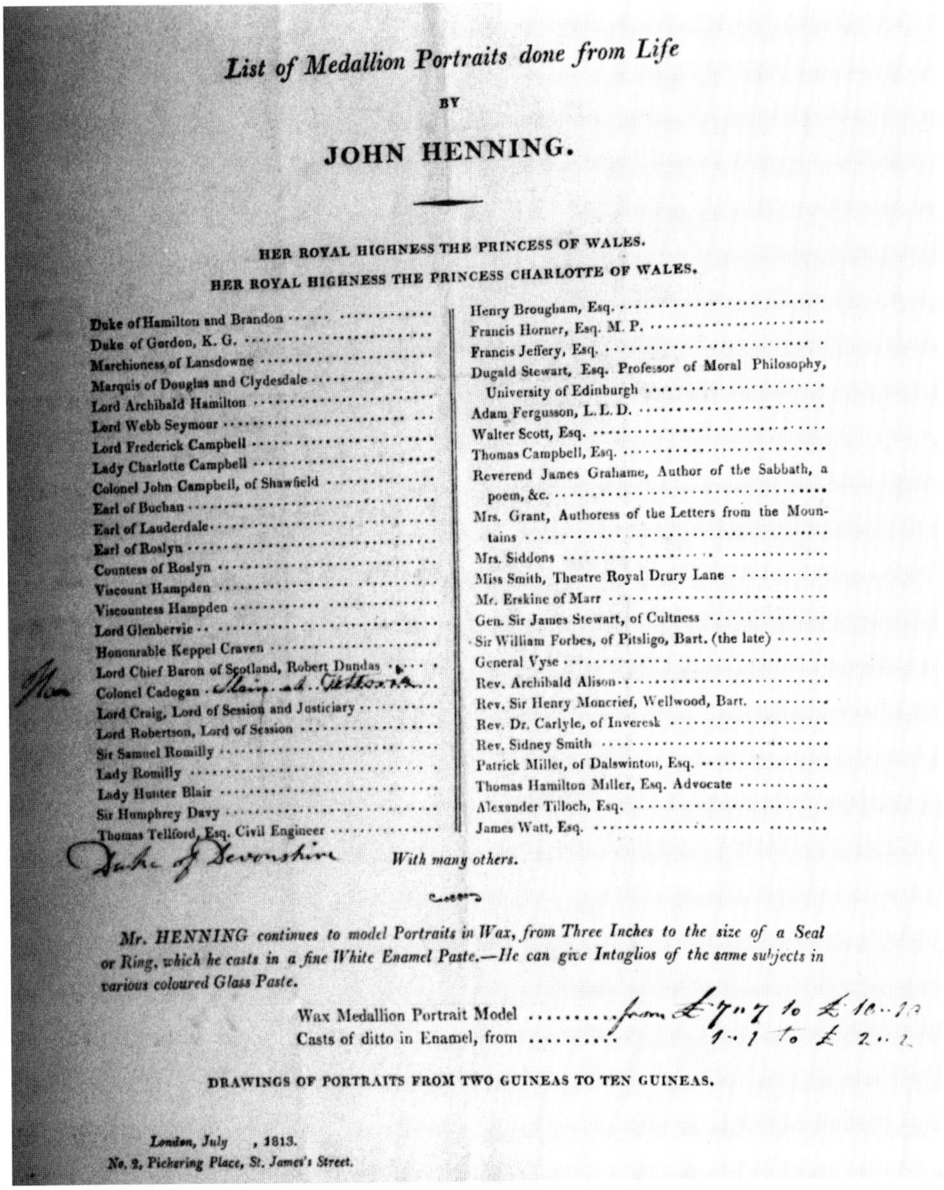

List of Medallion Portraits done from Life

BY

JOHN HENNING.

HER ROYAL HIGHNESS THE PRINCESS OF WALES.
HER ROYAL HIGHNESS THE PRINCESS CHARLOTTE OF WALES.

Duke of Hamilton and Brandon
Duke of Gordon, K. G.
Marchioness of Lansdowne
Marquis of Douglas and Clydesdale
Lord Archibald Hamilton
Lord Webb Seymour
Lord Frederick Campbell
Lady Charlotte Campbell
Colonel John Campbell, of Shawfield
Earl of Buchan
Earl of Lauderdale
Earl of Roslyn
Countess of Roslyn
Viscount Hampden
Viscountess Hampden
Lord Glenbervie
Honourable Keppel Craven
Lord Chief Baron of Scotland, Robert Dundas
Colonel Cadogan
Lord Craig, Lord of Session and Justiciary
Lord Robertson, Lord of Session
Sir Samuel Romilly
Lady Romilly
Lady Hunter Blair
Sir Humphrey Davy
Thomas Tellford, Esq. Civil Engineer
Duke of Devonshire

Henry Brougham, Esq.
Francis Horner, Esq. M. P.
Francis Jeffery, Esq.
Dugald Stewart, Esq. Professor of Moral Philosophy, University of Edinburgh
Adam Fergusson, L. L. D.
Walter Scott, Esq.
Thomas Campbell, Esq.
Reverend James Grahame, Author of the Sabbath, a poem, &c.
Mrs. Grant, Authoress of the Letters from the Mountains
Mrs. Siddons
Miss Smith, Theatre Royal Drury Lane
Mr. Erskine of Marr
Gen. Sir James Stewart, of Cultness
Sir William Forbes, of Pitsligo, Bart. (the late)
General Vyse
Rev. Archibald Alison
Rev. Sir Henry Moncrief, Wellwood, Bart.
Rev. Dr. Carlyle, of Inveresk
Rev. Sidney Smith
Patrick Miller, of Dalswinton, Esq.
Thomas Hamilton Miller, Esq. Advocate
Alexander Tilloch, Esq.
James Watt, Esq.

With many others.

Mr. HENNING continues to model Portraits in Wax, from Three Inches to the size of a Seal or Ring, which he casts in a fine White Enamel Paste.—He can give Intaglios of the same subjects in various coloured Glass Paste.

Wax Medallion Portrait Model .... from £7..7 to £10..10
Casts of ditto in Enamel, from .... 1..1 to £2..2

DRAWINGS OF PORTRAITS FROM TWO GUINEAS TO TEN GUINEAS.

London, July , 1813.
No. 2, Pickering Place, St. James's Street.

Figure 115. List of portrait medallions modelled by John Henning, July, 1813 (3-2617).

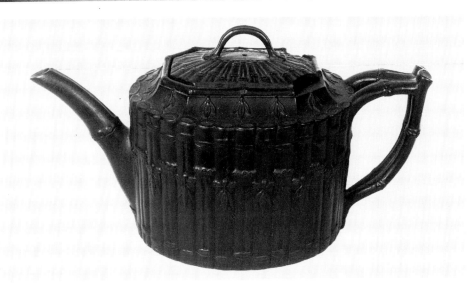

Figure 116. Teapot with sliding cover, moulded in an oval with columns of bamboo forming the body and a bifurcated bamboo handle. Mark: ***WEDGWOOD****, c.1810, 5⅛in. high. Rakow collection.*

*Figure 117. Two cups and saucers, the one on the left unpolished with engine-turned satin stripes, the one on the right polished basalt with husk border and swag relief decoration. Marks: both **WEDGWOOD**, c.1800-10, cups 2¼in. high; saucers, 5¼in. diameter. Rakow collection.*

*Figure 118. Large bowl, moulded with leaves and bell flowers. Mark: **WEDGWOOD**, c.1820-40, 5⅛in.high x 12in. diameter. Collection of the Newark Museum, New Jersey, E55.59, gift of John B. Morris, 1955.*

Figure 119. Spittoon, polished basalt with satin-striped body and horizontal chequered mid-riff band, glazed interior. Mark: WEDGWOOD, c.1795-1820, 3¾in. high. Grigsby collection.

Figure 120 Hedgehog crocus pot and tray. A form which had been made from at least 1783, the hedgehog crocus pot was particularly popular in the second decade of the 19th century with Wedgwood the major, perhaps only, manufacturer. Mark: WEDGWOOD on tray, c.1810-20, 5½in. high x 10¼in. diameter. Chellis collection.

dipped into the acid a chemical reaction took place which ignited it so a candle or fire could be lit. Pyrophorus vases, easily confused with inkwells, are distinguished by holes of different sizes in the top.[25] Some are combinations of both. Competitors began to cash in on the lucrative market and by 1813 Spode was also making pyrophorus vases.[26]

Historical events frequently provided Wedgwood and other manufacturers with the opportunity to produce commemoratives. Nelson's victories were immortalized on teawares, particularly by Elijah Mayer and Moseley but by others as well (Figures 296, 297 and 306), as were Wellington's (Figures 451 and 452). In the collection of commemorative basalt in the National Maritime Museum is a replica of Nelson's Column at Trafalgar Square (Figure 114), probably made by the Wedgwood factory shortly after the monument was erected in 1842.

Portrait medallions of national heroes and men of the day continued to be produced but with less response from the buying public. One modeller, John Henning, who applied for a position at the company in 1813, boasted a long list of portrait medallions produced from life models (Figure 115).[27]

Figure 121. Crocus pot and tray in the form of a jar. Mark: WEDGWOOD, c.1810-20, 4½in. high. Polikoff collection.

Some dealers continued to stock the plain low oval teapots, coffee pots and low oval parapet teapots, but the market for these unembellished blackwares was not spirited.[28]

A list of black basalt sold by London china dealers Thomas Goode from March 1828 through December 1830[29] contains names of those who bought from them, and prices, but does not specify the manufacturer of the blackwares. By 1828 black basalt had plummeted in price, a teapot going as low as 1/- on the retail market. Black basalt continued to be sought after by the carriage trade, although perhaps less assiduously than fifty years earlier. The Hon. William Ponsonby, Viscount Clifden, Lord Braybrooke, Earl Gower, R. Adam Dundas, Esq., and His Serene Highness the

Figure 123. Pot-pourri jar (minus cover) with a sprig relief of Offering to Ceres bronzed and gilded. Mark: **WEDGWOOD, 2/3793**, late 19th century, 7¾in. high. Royal Ontario Museum, 941.6.112.

Figure 122. Barberini vase in polished basalt. The basalt version of the Portland vase was produced by Wedgwood in 1845 and sold for 4/6. Mark: **WEDGWOOD**, c. 1845-50, 6¼in. high. Polikoff collection.

Figure 125. Small tablet, possibly taken from a south German or Netherlandish 17th century original, perhaps a carved boxwood. Mark: **WEDGWOOD** in an arc, probably 19th century, possibly not English (see Chapter VI, Bodenbach and Vranov nad Dyji, Moravia, manufacturers who used the Wedgwood mark spuriously), 3⅛in. x 4¾in. Victoria & Albert Museum, c. 101-1926.

Figure 124. Venus Victrix. Mark: **WEDGWOOD**, c.1850-60, 20in. high. Polikoff collection.

Figure 126 Small tablet. Like Figure 125, this one also presents difficulties in attribution as well as dating. The tablet depicts a lady and a birdseller. Mark: **WEDGWOOD**, *19th century, possibly European (see remarks Figure 125), 2⅛in. x 3in. Grigsby collection.*

Figure 127. Figure of a fallow deer by John Rattenbury Skeaping A.R.A. (1901-1980). Mark: **WEDGWOOD**, **'J. Skeaping'** *inscribed, c.1927, 6½in. high. Polikoff collection.*

Prince Esterhazy were among those who purchased basalt teawares and inkstands from Goodes in the last two years of the 1820s.

After 1810 few new shapes, apart from commemorative wares, appear to have been added to the Wedgwood repertory, and from 1830 little or no Etruscan decorated wares seem to have been produced. After 1846 no Egyptian black wares appeared on the price lists (see Appendix I). One popular form which had been made on and off since before 1783 was the hedgehog crocus pot (described variously as 'Porkiopins' or 'for snodrops pots')[30] (Figure 120). The pot is filled with moss and planted with crocuses which then grew through the holes in its back. Crocus pots were popular in a variety of shapes (Figure 121) but are often confused with pot-pourri vases and

Figure 128. Three animal figures by Ernest William Light. The animals were originally issued in 1913 with glass eyes; at least one more set with moulded eyes was reissued in 1935. Marks: all **WEDGWOOD**, *c.1913; alighting bird 6½ in. high, poodle 3in. high, cat 4⅛in. high. Polikoff collection.*

pastille burners. A letter from Hackwood, Dimmock and Company to Josiah Wedgwood, Esq. in 1813 requested '6 blk Hedge hog crocus pots' and confirms that at that time Wedgwood was the only manufacturer of these hedgehog pots. [31]

Although 1846 was the last edition of the printed price list of the Staffordshire potters for Egyptian Black useful wares, some grand ornamental wares continued to be produced on through the century. A basalt version of the Barberini Vase was produced by the Wedgwood factory in 1845 and sold for 4/6 (Figure 122).[32] Other dramatic ornamental wares were revived for the 1862 Exhibition, including the popular wine and water ewers (Figure 45), which had always been most effective in the black body. Large basalt vases in the classical Greek style and in Renaissance revival styles were modelled by Hugues Prôtat for both the Paris Exposition Universelle of 1867 and the London Exhibition of 1871.[33] By mid-century basalt busts and large figures for libraries and entry halls were being manufactured to a scale befitting the Victorian household (Figure 124). Reilly illustrates a large variety of Victorian library busts and figures in *Wedgwood Vol. II* (pp. 460-472).

During the late nineteenth and early twentieth centuries animal figures were popularly produced in basalt. Wedgwood employed modellers to design specifically for that market including John Skeaping A.R.A. (1901-80) (Figure 127) and Ernest William Light (Figure 128).

A black basalt catalogue was issued in 1914 by Wedgwood which included composite shapes from nearly all the salient periods of basalt production including the round parapet of the 1770s, the silver shapes of the 1790s, and the low oval fluted, low round and Arabesque shapes of the early nineteenth century, some of which remain in factory production today.

CHAPTER IV
The Competitors

Abbott and Mist, 82 Fleet Street, London 1802-09
James Mist, 82 Fleet Street, London 1809-18?

Andrew Abbott and James Underhill Mist were London retailers and decorators from August 1802 until 1809. Abbott (1743-1819) had begun as a gilder of black ware, then became a clerk for London warehouseman, William Bacchus, whose shop was on Thames Street.[1] In 1780 Abbott was admitted to the freedom of the City of London by redemption and referred to as 'chinaman and Potter'.[2] By 1781 Abbott was in partnership with John Turner as *Bailey's Northern Directory* lists Turner & Abbott as 'Staffordshire-potters china and glass men, 9 Old Fish Street' (London). By 1782 Turner and Abbott had moved their shop to 81 Fleet Street, and by 1784 it was next door at 82 Fleet Street. In January 1785, *The Morning Herald and Daily Advertiser* placed a long advertisement for Turner and Abbott describing the manufacture of 'Egyptian Black...some elegantly mounted with silver spouts and chains...'[3] Tunnicliff's directory of 1787[4] of the principal merchants of Staffordshire included Turner and Abbott and appended to their names, 'Potters to the Prince of Wales'.

There are marked examples of Turner intaglios of Hippocampi[5] which may have been ordered by Wedgwood, but Wedgwood produced quantities of his own marked intaglios and cameos which would discount any theory of immoderate sub-

*Figure 129. Sander with two bands of undulating roulette decoration. Mark: **MIST 4**, (James Mist was a London retailer, not a manufacturer), c.1810-18, 2⅛in. high. Royal Ontario Museum, 970.242. 100, Brown collection.*

*Figure 130. Flower pot and stand, not basalt but white stoneware with relief decoration on a dark brown ground: Jupiter and the eagle, Sportive Love, Britannia and Fame with a tablet inscribed 'Howe and Nelson'. Mark: **MIST LONDON**, c.1810-18, pot: 3¼in. high; stand: 4in. diameter. Victoria & Albert Museum, Schreiber collection, 564.*

contracting of crests, seals and the like.

After John Turner's death in 1787 William and John Turner, jun. maintained the partnership with Abbott. The business prospered in the years just prior to the outbreak of war with France, that is from 1788 to 1792, dropping somewhat in 1793, but regaining in 1794. The Turner brothers were withdrawing heavily from the profits of the business while the other partners, Abbott and Newbury (Abbott had acquired a business partner, Benjamin Newbury), were ploughing their profits back into the business. By the time the Turners and Abbott and Newbury dissolved their partnership, 1 August 1792,[6] the portion of the business owned by the Turner brothers had dropped to less than one third. The Turners continued to supply Abbott and Newbury who continued to operate out of Fleet Street until Newbury left the partnership in 1802 to be replaced by James Underhill Mist. Account books indicate that Abbott and Mist sold wares of other manufacturers of black basalt, including: R. Baddeley, J. & E. Baddeley, Chetham & Woolley, Chetham & Co., Davenport, Forrester & Mayer, John Heath, Keeling, Toft & Co., John Mare, Elijah Mayer, William and John Turner, Wood & Co., Wood & Caldwell and Robert and David Wilson.[7] The partnership between Mist and Abbott was dissolved on 25 March 1809[8] and Mist continued running the business alone from the Fleet Street emporium which he had presumably leased from Abbott in 1809 following the dissolution of the partnership. The final settlement between Mist and Abbott was protracted until 1814 when Mist was overcome by debts and 'dishonesty'.[9] However, it is possible that Mist did not vacate the premises at No. 82 Fleet Street until 1818 when it was then leased to J. & J. Davenport.[10]

Black basalt exists with the impressed mark '**MIST**'. Surviving examples consist mainly of inkwells, etc. (Figure 129); however, there is a cache-pot in the City Museum, Stoke-on-Trent and a '**J. MIST**' flower pot and stand in the Victoria and Albert Museum (Figure 130). Turner may have been supplying the Mist marked

*Figure 131. Vase and cover, polished basalt with moulded relief decoration consisting of centurions on horseback, and simulated handles of female masks. The shoulder and base are decorated with foliage. Mark: **ADAMS**, c.1790, 10½in. high. Rakow collection.*

wares or, in Hillier's opinion, seconded by Tony Thomas, some lesser potters may have been supplying the wares marked with the Mist name, as the quality is variable.[11] It would seem that the marked Mist wares might date from 1809 to possibly as late as 1818, during the period when Mist was operating the business alone and not in a partnership.

Marks: MIST, MIST LONDON, J. MIST, J. MIST 82 FLEET STREET LONDON

William Adams (and Sons), Greengates Works, Tunstall, Staffordshire c. 1787-1805; **Benjamin Adams** 1805-20

There were four William Adams operating potteries in the Stoke-on-Trent area in the eighteenth and early nineteenth centuries, three cousins and a son of one of the cousins.[12] The William Adams who made basalt operated the Greengates Works, Tunstall. Others may also have produced blackware. Confusion reigns when trying to sort out the two William Adams listed in the Burslem Land Tax records during the eighteenth century. A William Adams is listed in the Land Tax records for Burslem in 1781 as paying taxes on three properties. By 1784 William Adams owned four properties in Burslem, only one of which he was occupying himself, the other three being let to John Bourne, Mr. Heath, and John Graham, jun. This appears to be the William Adams of the Brick House, Burslem and Cobridge, noted for creamware and pearlware, but probably not as a manufacturer of stonewares. From 1784 to 1788 William Adams and Company were occupying two premises owned by Thomas Wedgwood of Etruria. This must have been the Brick House Works originally owned by William Adams (I), then occupied by Josiah Wedgwood before the move to Etruria, and after the move to Etruria operated by his cousin Thomas as the useful wares works for the Wedgwood factory. William Adams was in a partnership for a short period in the mid-1780s with John Hales[13] and from 1786 to 1792

*Figure 131a. Mug, with glazed interior, exterior boldly embellished with neo-classical figures. Mark: **ADAMS**, c.1800. Gunson collection.*

109

with a Mr. Heath,[14] probably Thomas Heath of the Hadderidge, Burslem. Both *Bailey's Northern Directory* (1784) and Tunnicliff (1787) listed only one William Adams and Company as 'Manufacturers of cream-coloured Ware, China glazed Ware painted'. This was the same Cobridge manufactory which ceased production in 1831, and as mentioned, probably did not make basalt wares but certainly could have.[15]

The Greengates factory in Tunstall operated as William Adams & Sons from 1745 to 1805,[16] from 1784[17] under William Adams II and from 1805-20 under his son Benjamin Adams, who was apprenticed under Josiah Wedgwood at the Brick House and probably went with Wedgwood to Etruria.[18] The beautiful stoneware produced by Adams attests to the high degree of attention paid during his Wedgwood apprenticeship. One of the William Adams was a participant in the Potters Clay Company co-partnership of 1797 which had formed the co-operative to purchase clay directly from the manufacturers without the intervention of third parties.[19]

The rare basalts marked by Adams (Figures 131 and 131a) compete successfully with the beautiful jasper wares more commonly associated with the factory. The one piece of basalt, in the Rakow collection, is of the highest quality, fine grained, satin smooth, expertly modelled, equal to anything produced by Wedgwood, Palmer or Neale. Sir Isaac Falcke, the British Museum's great ceramic benefactor, noted that he had an Adams marked intaglio of very fine quality, 'equal to Wedgwood's best period'.[20]

There is a group of basalt wares marked with an impressed 'A' (Figures 442-444) which may be the products of one of the Adams factories; however, the paucity of basalt wares attributable to the factories makes comparisons futile, so only an extremely tentative 'possible Adams' attribution is credible. (*See* Cambrian Pottery, Swansea for further conjecture on the 'A' marked wares.)

Mark: ADAMS (Other marks, less common, have been noted on jasper: **ADAMS & CO, W. ADAMS**)

Samuel Alcock & Co., Cobridge, Staffordshire, c.1826-53
Samuel Alcock, better known as a manufacturer of porcelain and earthenwares, had a small output in basalt. The published material on Alcock, has, in the main, concentrated on his porcelain production.[21] As a major mid-nineteenth century manufacturer, Alcock operated twenty ovens in 1836.[22] As with the porcelains the rare Alcock basalt is distinguished by the numbers in the base. One teapot form peculiar to Alcock, and looking earlier than it is, has a round body with characteristic sprig decoration in white (Figure 132).
Mark: four numerals incised in base; letters and numerals impressed

Richard Meir Astbury, Foley Pottery, Fenton, Staffordshire, late 18th-early 19th century; 151 Drury Lane, London c.1790
Richard Meir Astbury (1765-1834), Valentine Close and Robert Barber Wolf were Staffordshire warehousemen trading from 151 Drury Lane, London, in 1790.[23] Any pottery attributed to the Fenton manufactory is only speculative. One teapot in the Norwich Museum (Figure 133) marked **ASTBURY** can be dated by shape to the period Richard Meir Astbury was potting at Fenton, but no basalts have been identified from his pottery so the attribution is tentative.
Marks: ASTBURY (?), R.M.A. (recorded on other wares)

Figure 132. Teapot and cover, round body with white sprig relief decoration and a sibyl finial. Mark: '1592' incised in base; impressed in base 'S 78 9', Samuel Alcock, Cobridge, c.1840, 5½in. high. Royal Ontario Museum, 970.242.77, Brown collection.

*Figure 133. Teapot and cover, cylinder-shaped with vertical fluting and horizonal bands of Greek key moulding at the shoulder and base. The finial (minus head) is a seated female holding a spray of flowers in her right hand. Mark: **ASTBURY** (possibly Richard Meir Astbury, Foley Pottery, Lane End), c.1790, 5⅞in. high. Castle Museum, Norwich, Miller collection.*

Figure 134. Teapot and cover, naturalistically moulded in the form of a tree trunk. The finial, a figure of Britannia, is crudely modelled with a cat-like visage. Hobson, Catalogue of English Pottery in the British Museum, *feels the piece is probably the work of Thomas Astbury (1725-88). Mark:* ASTBURY, *c.1770-75, 4⅝in. high. British Museum, G40, Franks collection.*

Thomas? Astbury, Lane Delph, Staffordshire working period c.1725-72? (d.1788)
The Astbury family of potters have their names entwined with those of the Elers[24] and frequently intermarried with the Twyford family, another one of the ascendant pottery families. Joshua Astbury, the potter patriarch of the family, died in 1721. His will[25] was still being disputed by his son Joshua (1715-1744) in 1733. The elder Astbury, in addition to his son by the same name, had two daughters, Anne Astbury (b.1717), who married John Twyford, and Mary Astbury, who married potter John Mare; by 1758 Anne Astbury Twyford was a widow.[26]

Another branch of the family yielded John Astbury (d.1744), father of Thomas, both potters of Lane Delph in Fenton. Thomas Astbury was perhaps the man who produced the well-potted black basalt teapot in the British Museum (Figure 134). John Astbury was involved in the complicated will of his forebear Joshua Astbury (d.1721). The pottery which he left to his son, also Thomas, seems to have been passed to the Baddeleys by 1772.[27] Thomas Astbury died in debt and his estate was divided among his creditors on 7 November 1788.[28] The process of deduction leaves the historian with Thomas Astbury as a possible potter of the black basalt tewares which stylistically date from the 1770s; however, there were other Astburys operating pot banks which could have made these fine blackwares (*see* **Richard Meir Astbury**).
Mark: ASTBURY

H. Aynsley & Co., Commerce Street, Longton, Staffordshire 1873-present
Aynsleys occupied the works originally carried on by Chetham and Woolley (1796-1807), followed by various members of the Chetham family and successive partners until some time after 1865.[29] In 1873 the works passed into the hands of H. Aynsley and Company who, according to Jewitt, manufactured the usual array of earthenwares, including Egyptian black.[30] No examples of their blackware production have been identified.

William Baddeley, Eastwood, Hanley, Staffordshire 1802-22
The Baddeley family were among the numerous Staffordshire pottery families who were operating more than one pottery successively, or occasionally, as in this particular family, successively and simultaneously.

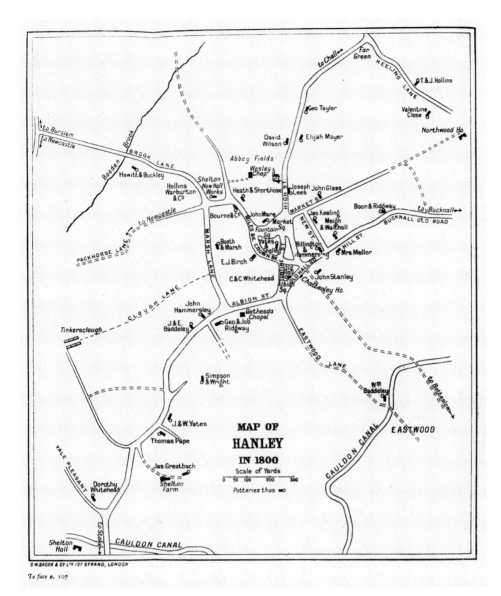

Figure 135. Map of Hanley in 1800 published by G.W. Bacon & Co., 127 Strand, London. J.C Wedgwood had this map redrawn by Bacons for publication in his book, Staffordshire Pottery and its History *(London 1912). The map indicates the locations of all the potteries in Hanley in 1800/02.*

John Mallet has thoroughly documented a pottery forebear, John Baddeley, in his E.C.C. paper 'John Baddeley of Shelton'.[31] From 1759-61 John Baddeley was making 'red' and 'black' wares in Shelton as well as 'China'.[32] Another branch of the family, William Baddeley, was the potter who produced earthenware and basalt in Eastwood, Hanley, in the first two decades of the nineteenth century. William Baddeley's factory was located on Eastwood Lane on the north side of the Cauldon canal. Another pottery was being operated by sons of John Baddeley, John and Edward Baddeley,[33] on Albion Street, Shelton from at least 1784 until the partnership dissolved in 1811.[34]

William Baddeley I was paying taxes in Burslem in 1781 and then disappeared off the record. (To add confusion a Baddeley & Co. reappeared on the Burslem tax records in 1812 paying taxes on one property owned by themselves and occupying another property owned by Earl Parker.) In September 1789 the *London Gazette*[35] published a dissolution of partnership notice between:

*Figure 136. Small vase, red-ware with basalt relief decoration of a cherub on one side and Venus and Cupid on the reverse, basalt scroll handles. Mark: **EASTWOOD**, William Baddeley, c.1805-10, 3⅞in. high. British Museum, 1909-12-1-114, Falcke collection.*

*Figure 137. Small urn (minus cover), redware of low round form with basalt floral decoration and prominent basalt scroll handles. Mark: **EASTWOOD** (impressed on side of foot), William Baddeley, c.1805-10, 4in. high. Royal Ontario Museum, 984.18.31, Brown collection.*

Figure 138. Coffee pot and cover of hexagonal vertical shape laid out in panels separated by columns, sprig relief of a nymph dancing with cymbals, swan finial. Mark: EASTWOOD (impressed on outside footrim below spout), William Baddeley, c.1815-20, 9¾in. high. City Museum and Art Gallery, Stoke-on-Trent 650.P.37.

Figure 139. Cream jug, glazed and moulded with the Duke of Wellington charging on Copenhagen at the Battle of Waterloo. Mark: EASTWOOD (impressed in footrim under spout), William Baddeley, c.1815-20, 3¾in. high. Rakow collection.

William Baddeley of Fenton Low and John Pope in the city of Dublin, Pot seller, in the business of manufacturers and vendors of earthenwares carried on by us at Fenton Low…

24th Day of September 1789
William Baddeley
John Pope
Charles Harrison

A number of bills of receipt exist between William Baddeley and Josiah Wedgwood II for services rendered by Wedgwood and Byerley for the period 1799 to 1801. It appears that Wedgwood was providing workmen to assist Baddeley as the bills are for wages paid and wages due including interest.[36]

William Baddeley II was listed in 1807 in the rate records as occupying a property owned by Josiah Wedgwood in Shelton, which must have been his residence. Another entry for 1807-8 exists for the pot works located in Hanley. Holden's triennial *Directory* of 1805 lists William Baddeley as 'Egyptian black manufacturers, Shelton' and the same directory for 1809-11 lists him as 'Egyptian-black-manufacturer, Hanley'. The 1818 and 1822 Staffordshire directories describe William Baddeley as a 'fancy and ornamental earthenware Manufacturer' in Eastwood. The business was put up for sale by auction in 1822 as the *Staffordshire Advertiser* for 22 June printed the following notice:

Auction Hanley 2 July 1822 small potworks and house in Eastwood, land connecting to canal used as wharf, now occupied by William Baddeley and used by him for some years as a Black and Caul [probably a misprint for Cane] manufactory, apply William Baddeley, or Ward, solicitor, Newcastle.

Baddeley basalt (Figures 136-147) is usually[37] stamped with the mark **EASTWOOD** on the front edge of the footrim (Figure 142a). Grant suggested that

*Figure 140. Cream jug with floral scroll relief moulding. Mark: **EASTWOOD**, William Baddeley, c.1810, 3⅛in. high. Robertshaw collection.*

*Figure 141. Cream jug with basketweave moulding and central reserve panels depicting Poseidon on a dolphin. Mark: **EASTWOOD** (impressed on footrim below spout), William Baddeley, c.1810, 3⅜in. high. Hacking collection.*

since William Baddeley's father [grandfather], John Baddeley, 'stole' the process for cutting with the lathe, Baddeley impressed the factory name on the outside of the footrim, under the spout of teapots, to avoid obliteration by the lathe.[38] Basalt manufactured at Eastwood is of generally high quality, perhaps tending to density and a slightly granular surface similar to graphite, but with pleasant proportions. The forms, often divided into columns, frequently have parapet collars and lids with the characteristic finials with the reverse swan neck (the Leeds Pottery also featured reverse swan neck finials on teapots, shapes Nos. 28 and 30 in the *Drawing Book*). However, many have conventional swan finials facing forward. Shapes in general can be confused with many produced by the Leeds Pottery.

Following early nineteenth century fashion Baddeley produced red stonewares with black sprig relief decoration (Figures 136 and 137), as well as gilded basalt (Figure 146). Commemorative wares depicting Wellington's victory and other

Figure 142a Impressed mark of sugar box and cover in Figure 142.

*Figure 142. Sugar box and cover with naturalistic relief decoration and a central figure of Zephyr, reverse neck swan finial. Mark: **EASTWOOD** (Figure 142a), William Baddeley, c.1810, 5⅛in. high. Gunson collection.*

Figure 143 Teapot and cover, oval parapet teapot with lower body moulded in diamond quilted pattern, the upper two-thirds in floral and geometric and floral relief decoration. Mark: *EASTWOOD* (below spout), William Baddeley, c.1810, 7½in. high. Gunson collection.

Figure 144. Two cream jugs, the one on the left to accompany the teapot in Figure 143, the one on the right to accompany the sugar box in Figure 142. Marks: both *EASTWOOD* (on footrim below spout), William Baddeley, c.1810, 3½in. high (left), 4⅜in. high (right). Rakow collection.

Figure 145. Cream jug, oval shape laid out in shepherd's crook columns with a central relief from the Domestic Employment series designed by Lady Templetown for Wedgwood and copied by many other potters. Mark: *EASTWOOD* (on footrim below spout), William Baddeley, c.1810. Blake collection.

Figure 146. Cream jug of oval shape, gilded, with a figure from Domestic Employment. Mark: *EASTWOOD* (on outside base below handle), William Baddeley, c.1810, 4in. high. Blake collection.

117

events of national historical significance were also produced at Eastwood (Figure 139).

Jewitt suggested, with questionable authority, that William Baddeley used the impressed EASTWOOD to confuse the unwary and possibly pass off his wares as Wedgwood by intentionally impressing the prefix EAST lightly and leaving the clearly impressed suffix WOOD.[39] In fact, the impressed **EASTWOOD** is usually clearly visible, often on an outside footrim beneath a spout or handle.

Mark: EASTWOOD

Bagnall & Baker, Shelton, Staffordshire c. 1768
Josiah Wedgwood wrote at least one letter concerning the little known firm of Bagnall and Baker. Written on 31 August 1768 to William Cox Wedgwood stated that 'Carravalla supplies Mr. P. [Palmer] with all my Patterns as they arrive at my rooms in London, and Fogg does the same for Bagnall & Baker...'[40] Charles Bagnall of Shelton had previously been a partner with Joshua Heath[41] and was a potter of considerable experience about which little is known. No basalt is attributable to the firm.

W. Bailey & Company, Lane End, Longton, Staffordshire, working period 1805-17
Pottery retailers and decorators,[42] William Bailey and Company were selling stoneware teapots, described in their inventories as 'eagles, octagon',[43] which could either have been feldspathic stoneware or basalt.

Ball & Company, High Street, Longton, Staffordshire, 1802
Mather & Ball, High Street, Longton, 1805-20
Mather & Ball occupied works owned by T. Alcock between 1807 and 1820. They produced black glazed ware, stoneware and lustre. No marked pieces are known.[44]

Banks & Thorley, New Street, Hanley 1875-79; Boston Works, High Street, Hanley 1879-87; **Banks & Co** 1887-8; **Edward Banks** 1888-89
Jewitt said that among the many Victorian earthenwares produced by Banks and Thorley was 'jet' and stoneware.[45] The term 'jet' became current Victorian lexicon for describing the black stonewares referred to previously as 'shining black' and popularized by Riley and Cyples earlier on in the century. No marked 'jet' wares have been recorded for this factory.

Barker
There were several Barkers in Staffordshire in the pottery industry as well as Barkers in Yorkshire in Mexborough, at the Don Pottery and at Swinton. The marked Barker basalt (Figures 148-153) is often difficult to attribute with certainty to Staffordshire or to Yorkshire. Thomas Barker, the probable potter involved with the Foley Pottery, Fenton, Staffordshire, will be discussed under **Foley Pottery**.

John Barker, Lane End, Longton, Staffordshire, c.1784-1802
Richard Barker, Flint Street, potter 1784-1810, manufacturer c.1820-35
Bailey's Directory of 1784 and the 1787 Tunnicliff directory listed John Barker as a

manufacturer of 'Cream coloured, China glaze and Blue wares' with no mention of Egyptian black. William Barker was listed simply as a 'potter' in the two directories and as a 'dish maker' in the 1820, 1822/3 directories. His address was given as Commercial Street. Richard Barker was a 'potter' at No. 126 works on the east side of Flint Street from 1784 until 1810. From 1820 to 1835 Richard Barker is listed in the directories as an 'earthenware manufacturer' at the same location. No mention of Egyptian black is made in any of the directory listings. Wedgwood and Byerley supplied John Barker with fire bricks in 1793[46] and in 1800 they were either firing bricks for Barker or possibly firing kiln loads of pottery for him.[47]

Barkers & Myatt, Fenton?, Staffordshire, c.1821
A partnership was dissolved between James Barker, John Barker, Joseph Barker and John Myatt on 25 March 1821 with John and Joseph Barker to continue the business.[48] Both Barker and Myatt marked basalt exists (*see* **Myatt** Figures 310 and 311) so it is likely that this manufactory produced basalt, but designating any particular example to the factory is impossible.

John and Joseph Barker, High Street, Lane End, Longton, Staffordshire, c.1818-31[49]
The 1822-3 directory listed J & J Barker as manufacturers of earthenware, 'shining black' and as lusterers and enamellers. As with other Barkers mentioned one cannot make the specific attributions of basalt to this factory either.

Barker & Company, Low Pottery, Rawmarsh, Yorkshire, 1790s-1812;
Jesse Barker 1809 and **Peter Barker** 1811, Mexborough Pottery, Mexborough, Yorkshire, 1809-late 1820s; **Samuel Barker**, Mexborough Pottery late 1820s-1848; Don Pottery late 1830s-1848 or later[50]
Peter Barker and John Wainwright were partners in the Low Pottery, an early eighteenth century pottery in Rawmarsh, from the 1790s until 1812 when Peter Barker left to join his brother permanently in the Mexborough enterprise. John Wainwright continued the Rawmarsh operation until his death c.1830.

Mexborough had been established in 1800 by Robert Sowter and his partner

Figure 147. Three milk jugs typical of William Baddeley's factory. Marks: all EASTWOOD (on footrim under spout), 5⅜in. high (left), 6¼in. high centre and right), c.1815-20. Rakow collection.

119

*Figure 148. Teapot and cover, with fine fluted lower body and cover, recumbent lion finial. Mark: **BARKER**, probably Staffordshire, c.1790. 3¾in. high. Rakow collection.*

*Figure 149. Partially reconstructed teapot with cylindrical fluted body and Greek key band at shoulder and base. Excavated from a house site on Deer Street, Portsmouth, New Hampshire, which was standing in 1783. According to archaeologist, Aileen Agnew, who excavated the site and wrote the report, the fill appeared to be around 1785. However the date on the teapot would be somewhat later, 1790-1800. Mark: **KER** (presumably BARKER), probably Staffordshire, c.1790-1800. Strawbery Banke Museum, Inc.*

William Bromley. Apparently the owners were adventurers in the pottery business[51] and the workmen were those who had been formerly at Swinton. The pottery was let to Jesse Barker in 1809 after having been sold piecemeal in thirds to speculators, most of whom were corn factors. Jesse Barker and Peter Barker purchased the pottery in 1811 and the following year Peter divested himself of the Rawmarsh interest and moved to Mexborough operating the pottery until Jesse's son Samuel took over the business in the late 1820s. By 1838 Samuel had inherited his father's interest and purchased his uncle Peter's share. By the late 1830s Samuel Barker was operating the Don Pottery as well as the Mexborough Pottery, both of which were active under Samuel Barker until at least 1848.[52]

It is not possible to attribute with any assurance the **Barker** marked basalt (Figures 148, 150-153), nor to conscionably assign a Staffordshire or Yorkshire attribution.

Figure 150. Cream jug moulded in panels with sprig relief decoration. Mark: **BARKER**, probably Yorkshire, c.1810-15, 4⅛in. high. Victoria & Albert Museum, 3661-1901.

Figure 151. Teapot and cover of polished basalt. Characteristic of many Yorkshire stonewares, the teapot is divided into panels and has a gallery into which the cover is set. The central relief is a mourning figure. Mark: **BARKER**, probably Yorkshire, Jesse and Peter Barker, c.1810-15, 5¾in. high. Rakow collection.

This uncertainty unfortunately extends to the sherds excavated in North America (Figure 149). Obviously a North American trade existed for at least one of the manufacturers and the pottery was sufficiently established to warrant impressing a factory name which would be recognised. It is likely that more than one of the Barker factories impressed the name.

Thomas Barker, *see* **The Foley Pottery, Fenton**

Thomas Barlow, Market Street, Longton, Staffordshire, 1849-65 or later
Thomas Barlow occupied the old Cyples pottery and manufactured black and lustred wares but no marked pieces are known.[53]

George Barnes, High Street, Lane End, Longton, Staffordshire, c.1795
Barnes & Buxton, High Street, Lane End, 1799-1802

Figure 152. Teapot and hinged cover, glazed basalt of oval shape with central relief of a mourning figure and an obelisk. Mark: **BARKER** (each letter is impressed separately), c.1810-15, 6¾in. high. Castle Museum, Norwich, Miller collection.

Figure 153. Teapot and cover press-moulded with plain pillars flanking central panels sprigged with Venus disarming Cupid and Cupid Asleep. Mark: **BARKER**, probably Yorkshire, Jesse and Peter Barker, c.1810-15, 6½in. high. Gunson collection.

*Figure 154. Punch pot with bail handle terminating in satyr's head masks. Deeply cut satin stripes top and bottom are interspersed with a band of sprig relief children dancing with musical instruments. The cover has a widow finial. Mark: **B&W 10** (in rectangular die on base), **IG** at base of handle, probably Birch and Whitehead, c.1797-98, 9⅞in. high. Rakow collection.*

G. & W. Barnes, High Street, Lane End, 1804
G. Barnes, Hog's Lane, 1817-25[54]
According to the 1822-3 directory George Barnes was a manufacturer of Egyptian black as well as an earthenware dealer. Hampson points out that there are also some twenty-five sprig moulds in the Spode works marked BARNES which could have been used by the firm for making sprigs for black basalt and other stonewares.[55] Little more of consequence is known about the firm. For a short period George Barnes was in partnership with William Barnes in the Lane End manufactory, but the liaison dissolved in 1804, the business then being carried on exclusively by George Barnes[56] until 1825. Frustratingly, and in spite of the marked sprig moulds, no specimens have been identified which are marked or attributable to the firm.

Bates and Bennett, Lincoln Pottery, Sneyd Green, Cobridge, Staffordshire, 1868-c.1895
Bates and Bennett occupied the pottery formerly owned by John and Robert Godwin and manufactured Egyptian black along with other popular Victorian earthenwares.[57] No known examples of their blackwares have been identified.

Birch & Whitehead, c.1797-98
Edmund John Birch, Crown Bank, Shelton, Staffordshire, 1797-1814
Edmund John Birch and Christopher Charles Whitehead formed a partnership for wares which seems to have included fine black basalts (Figures 154 and 155). The 1800 map of Hanley (Figure 135) shows the location of the two potteries as adjacent to each other on the west side of Tontine Street and Crown Bank, just north of Albion Street. Although the attribution of wares impressed '**B & W**' could have been given to other partnerships (Godden suggests the possibility of Breeze and

Figure 155. Sugar box and cover of rare octagonal form divided by fluted columns with four of the eight panels depicting dancing musical children. Mark: **B&W** (in rectangular die in base), c.1797-98, 6½in. high. Gunson collection.

Figure 156. Jug with lower half fluted and upper portions sprig decorated with Amalgamation of Peace destroying implements of War, and a French Revolutionary Figure. A nearly identical jug illustrated in Stoneware & Stone Chinas, pl.111,124, is marked Keeling, Toft & Co. Mark: **Birch/IG** at base of handle, c.1805-10, 3¾in. high. Photograph courtesy Geoffrey Godden.

Figure 157. Jug similar to Figure 156 in shape and with similar sprig relief subjects but with a different modeller's initials. Mark: **Birch/ ES** at base of handle, c.1805-10, 4⅛in. high. Gunson collection.

Figure 158. Sugar box and cover with base fluted half way up and fluted cover, widow finial. Sprigged relief subjects on upper half of body include Amalgamation of Peace destroying implements of War. Mark: **Birch/'PM'**, c.1805-10. Royal Ontario Museum, 970.242.57, Brown collection.

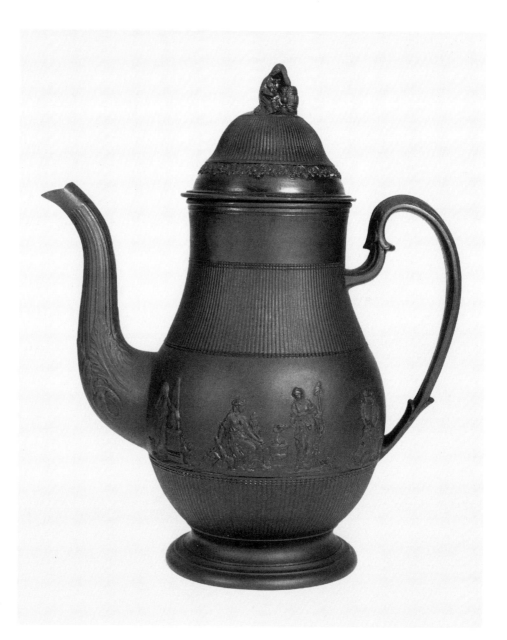

*Figure 159. Large coffee pot and cover of baluster shape with characteristic fluting and sprig relief associated with the previous Birch basalt pieces. In addition to Amalgamation of Peace destroying the implements of War, there is Poor Maria, and Venus on her shell sprig relief decoration. Mark: **Birch**, c.1805-10, 12in. high. Collection of the Newark Museum, New Jersey E24.17.71, gift of Mrs. Samuel Clark, 1924.*

Wilson), the similar quality of the body and modelling of marked **B&W** wares to those marked **Birch** is too striking to overlook. The use of exact sprig relief decoration is never a fully conclusive reason for attributing a piece to a factory, but can weigh the scale when considered in conjunction with other characteristics. In this case both **B&W** and **Birch** wares utilized similar sprig relief decoration, such as the woman with flowing robes with a rod in her right hand, an uncommon sprig which is seen also on **W(***)** basalt. They also both used the widow finial with frequency, as did many other potters.

Both Dr. and Mrs. Leonard Rakow and Nancy Gunson have published articles about the rare **B&W** marked pieces in their collections.[58] The Rakows point out the unusual sprig decoration of children dancing around playing various musical instruments which is seen only on **B&W** marked wares and some Neale marked stonewares. The widow finial is also the one used by Neale.[59] The wary will point out that all this leads to an attribution more closely affiliated with the Breeze and Wilson (Robert Wilson being the potter for both Neale and early Wilson wares) than the Birch hypothesis. However, the wares look too early to be from the short-

Figure 160. *Teapot and cover of round parapet shape with urn and swag relief decoration and a widow finial. Mark:* **Birch**, *c.1800, 5¼in. high. Castle Museum, Norwich, Miller collection.*

Figure 161. *Teapot and cover globular fluted teapot with parapet, widow finial. Mark:* **Birch**, *c.1800, 4¾in. high. City Museum and Art Gallery, Stoke-on-Trent.*

Figure 162. *Teapot and cover, round body with bamboo-reeded, engine-turned decoration and a parapet neck, widow finial. The handle, spout, widow finial and general shape correspond to marked Birch wares. This teapot has only the modeller's initials. Mark: 'JB', possibly Birch, c.1800-05, 6in. high. Royal Ontario Museum, 970.242.72, Brown collection.*

lived Breeze/Wilson partnership dissolved in 1811. Future research will undoubtedly reveal more specific information about the manufacturer.

The few documented wares are impressed with a rectangular die with **B&W**, sometimes a numeral and frequently a potter's mark **IG** or **JG** at the base of the handle. The Rakows have documented three pieces so marked, one in Grant, another in the Birmingham Museum and the third, a punch pot in their own collection (Figure 154). Lending credence to the Birch connection, Geoffrey Godden reported a fourth marked with the **IG** potter's initials, on a **Birch** marked piece (Figure 156).[60]

Edmund John Birch was another member of the Potters Clay Copartnership of 1797 as were James and Charles Whitehead, the sons of Christopher Charles Whitehead. The latter was listed as a potter in Shelton in the 1784 and 1787 directories and in various other directories until 1815. He died in 1818.[61] Neither the sons nor Birch were listed in the 1784 and 1787 directories. Some other correspondence exists to indicate that there were two elder brothers(?) — Christopher and Charles Whitehead who were producing red stoneware and selling it to Josiah and Thomas Wedgwood in 1777.[62] The map of 1800 (Figure 135) also corroborates with the listing of the pottery as 'C & C Whitehead', but many other documents simply list the one name, Christopher Charles Whitehead. Prior to 1793[63] James Whitehead, John Whitehead and Charles Whitehead were in a pottery partnership

*Figure 163. Partial teaset with round cylinder-shaped teapot, the various sprig decorations common to Birch wares seen as well as some Aesop fable relief scenes. Mark: all **Birch**, c.1800-05, teapot 5⅝in. high, sugar 5in. high, cream jug 4in. high. Grigsby collection.*

with Ephraim Chatterley in Hanley which was dissolved on 6 November 1793.[64] The business was carried on by the three Whiteheads without Chatterley.

Just one pottery to the north was the former pottery operated by Heath and Bagnall of Shelton, transferred to Edmund J. Birch on 15 March 1797 and insured by the Salop Fire Insurance Company:

> Sett of pottworks in one connected building in Shelton £500. Utensils £150. Stock of earthenware £250; sliphouse situated on the banks of the navigation [canal]; two houses near £40.[65]

By the end of 1798 Birch and Whitehead had dissolved their short partnership[66] and the Birch business was carried on under the name of E.J. Birch & Co. The White-heads continued on separately in their own business to be followed by the sons.

Some interesting correspondence exists in the Wedgwood archives between Birch and Josiah Wedgwood II over the lease of a 'Hall' from Wedgwood to Birch in 1810 for a period of twelve years.[67] Further insight into Birch's prosperity is elucidated by correspondence between Wedgwood and Birch at the time Wedgwood was in Paris (early March to 17 May 1810) seeking his aid in getting Birch's son into 'any Respectable School near Paris…where he can speak nothing but French, and devote his leisure hours to writing and accounts, which probably may hereafter be useful to him.'[68]

Birch was one of the most prolific and accomplished manufacturers of basalt (Figures 156-167, 169 and 170). The body, of intense blackness, was extremely compactly potted, fine and dense. The Victoria & Albert Museum has a teapot with silver decoration but silver was not a common addition to the basalt palette. Mentioned earlier, the widow finial was used on wares manufactured by the Birch

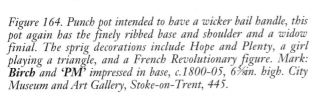

Figure 164. Punch pot intended to have a wicker bail handle, this pot again has the finely ribbed base and shoulder and a widow finial. The sprig decorations include Hope and Plenty, a girl playing a triangle, and a French Revolutionary figure. Mark: **Birch** *and* '**PM**' *impressed in base, c.1800-05, 6⅜in. high. City Museum and Art Gallery, Stoke-on-Trent, 445.*

Figure 165. Group of teawares and covers all characteristic of Birch basalt. Marks: all **Birch**, *sugar box right* **Birch** '**CC**', *c.1805-10, sugar boxes 5½in. high, jug 6⅜in. high. Rakow collection.*

and Whitehead partnership and by those marked by Birch alone. The Birch wares seem to be fairly consistently marked by the manufacturer with, from time to time, the addition of initials by other individuals, presumably the modeller. '**PM**', '**IG**', '**ES**' and '**CC**' are some of the extraneous modellers' initials recorded on Birch wares and can be seen in conjunction with the Birch mark or occasionally by themselves. Grant suggests that '**RD**' may be another one of Birch's modellers[69] but the example illustrated in Figure 441 is not sufficiently like any other marked Birch wares to warrant its being illustrated with the other Birch pieces (*see* **Yates** for comments on this piece). The teapot marked '**JB**' (Figure 162) has enough Birch attributes to be included among the others as a possible Birch piece. David Gaimster (*Northern Ceramic Society Newsletter* No.67) notes the excavation of a Birch teapot in Duisburg, Germany, which suggests that Birch engaged in a European trade. The output appears to be limited almost exclusively to useful wares; however, one curious medallion with Pan piping to a dancing bacchanalian baby exists impressed **Birch** (Figure 170). The medallion is inscribed 'CHEIRON 1782' in relief on the front.
Marks: B & W; Birch; in addition some modellers' initials are also seen: **PM, IG, ES, CC, JB** (?)

*Figure 166. Bowl with sprig depictions of Hope and Plenty, and boy with a hoop. Mark: **Birch**, c.1805-10, 4¼in. x 7⅞in. Rakow collection.*

*Figure 167. Jug with satin stripes and ear-shaped handle. Mark: **Birch**, c.1800-10, 3⅛in. high Royal Ontario Museum, 970.242.38, Brown collection.*

John and William Birks, Market Street and High Street, Longton, Staffordshire, 1796-1806

Hampson indicates that the Birks were producing Egyptian black and that although no marked pieces are known, black stoneware sherds have been excavated at the Gladstone Pottery from the period the Birks were working and may have been manufactured by them.[70]

John Bourne, Burslem, Staffordshire, c.1787

Tunnicliff's directory of 1787 lists John Bourne as a manufacturer of 'China glaze, blue painted, enamelled, and cream-coloured Earthenware'. However, a receipt for Egyptian Black is number 56 in the *Ceramic receipts for many years used by the late John*

Figure 168. Cream jug of oval shape laid out in panels with swag and floral relief. The handle is ear-shaped as in Figure 167. Unmarked: possibly Birch, c.1800, 3¾in. high. Robertshaw collection.

*Figure 169. Jug with spreading foot and vertical satin-stripes. Mark: **Birch**, c.1800-10, 4½in. high. City Museum and Art Gallery, Stoke-on-Trent, 2654.*

Figure 170. Rare medallion of Pan piping to a dancing bacchanalian baby with relief inscription on lower front 'CHEIRON 1782.' Mark: Birch, 11½in. x 9in. Grigsby collection.

Figure 171. Teapot and cover, oval form in convex panels with simple relief fence and foliage pattern around base, recumbent lion finial. Mark: BRADLEY & CO., c.1796-1800, 4¼in. high. Victoria & Albert Museum 3392-1901.

Bourne of Burslem.[71] The receipt reads:

blue clay	235
calcined ironstone	225
manganese	45
Cornish clay	15

No specimens have been attributed to this Bourne factory.

Bradley & Company, Coalport Pottery, Shropshire, 1796-1800
Interest in Bradley and Company was sparked by Roger Edmundson's comprehensive history of the pottery and its wares published in the *Northern Ceramic Society Journal* 4 (1980-81). Bradley and Company were the only earthenware producers at Coalport, and not connected with the porcelain producing factories in Coalport. Although they were in business for only four years there are enough marked wares in existence to attest to a variety of earthenware production including black basalt.

At this point only three basalt pieces have been found with the **BRADLEY & CO COALPORT** mark, all silver shaped teapots, two of which are illustrated in Figures 171-172. The third is illustrated in Roger Edmundson's article. All have straight spouts, conventional handles with leaf moulding at the top and lion finials. The shapes are characteristic of the late eighteenth century following closely popular silver forms. The body itself is often, but not always, rough, and grey in colour, as if by overfiring.
Mark: BRADLEY & CO COALPORT

Brameld & Co. *see* **Swinton**

John Breeze, Greenfield Works, Tunstall, 1801(?)-12; **Jesse Breeze**, Greenfield Works, c.1810-22
John Breeze and his son Jesse were probably significant manufacturers of basalt wares[72] although none is specifically identified with their pottery. Although the *Victoria History of the County of Stafford* gives the date of 1801 as the purchase of the Smithfield estate where John Breeze established the Greenfield Works, he was clearly operating some sort of pottery prior to that as he was in the Potters Clay Company Copartnership in 1797.[73]

*Figure 172. Teapot and cover moulded in oval form in vertical convex panels with leaf foliage. A central panel has an elliptical reserve with a sprig relief of Apollo, recumbent lion finial. Mark: **BRADLEY & CO.**, c.1796-1800, 4¼in. high. Victoria & Albert Museum, C204-1901.*

Brown & Cartlidge, Burslem, c.1810.

Mintons were being supplied with large quantities of Egyptian black teapots and other blackwares during the year 1810 by Brown & Cartlidge, Burslem.[74] Perhaps this was a partnership involving James Cartlidge who was producing blackwares in Burlsem at the time, or this may have been the retail arm of the same business.

Brown & Malkin, c.1787.

Probably retailers, the sole documentary evidence for their existence is a receipt from Messrs Wedgwood who 'bought of Brown & Malkin 2 jugs Black 6/- @ 0.2.0'.[75] Malkin, of course was an old pottery manufacturing name, but the Brown/Malkin partnership is not documented. Sarah Brown was the predecessor at Samuel Mayer's pottery in Hanley according to Jewitt[76] but the eighteenth century Malkins appear to have been concentrated in Burslem, not Hanley.

William Bullock, Liverpool, Merseyside, c.1800-40(?)

Grant illustrated a marked **(W. BULLOCK)** and dated (July 1st 1805) tripod cantharis[77] of excellent quality and unusual modelling with howling grotesques (Figure 173). The manufacturer was the brother of celebrated Regency cabinet maker George Bullock. The date on the vase refers to the so-called Garrard's Act of 1798 'for encouraging the art of making new models and costs of busts, and offer other things therein mentioned.'[78]

William Bullock founded a museum in Liverpool around 1800 and opened up the museum in London in 1812 in the Egyptian Hall, Piccadilly. The museum contained ornithological and conchological specimens as well as bronzes and apparently basalts. An advertisement appeared in *Gore's General Advertiser* for 6 June 1805 beneath an engraving of pyramids: 'W. BULLOCK, JEWELLER, SILVERSMITH, AND CHINA MAN at the Museum and Bronze Figure Manufactory, CHURCH STREET, LIVERPOOL.' He boasted a 'complete assortment of every article in the Bronze Figure and Ornamental Business.'[79] Probably William Bullock or his father was the modeller named W. Bullock to whom John Baddeley of Shelton paid £21.19.6 for providing models to Reid and Co. in 1761.[80] It would appear that the basalt bearing Bullock's name was modelled by William Bullock but

Figure 173. Cassolette vase of Regency style in basalt (left) bearing the impressed mark on the front edges of the three small tablets above the feet: **W. BULLOCK. PUB. JULY 1 1805,** *8¾in. high. Ex-Grant collection. A bronze and giltmetal cassolette oil lamp of Regency style (right), also by sculptor William Bullock of Liverpool, c.1805, 11in. high. Photograph courtesy Christie's London.*

produced by some other manufacturer, probably the Herculaneum Pottery, Liverpool, and sold and marketed by Bullock from his museum in Liverpool. Bullock apparently died in obscurity some time after 1840.[81]
Mark: W. BULLOCK

Harrison & Burn, Barbican, London, c.1801
Burn & Co, Raneegungee, India, first quarter of the 19th century
John Harrison and Thomas Burn were Staffordshire warehousemen in the City of London whose partnership was dissolved on 6 October 1801.[82] The company business remained in the name of Thomas Burn who apparently moved the business out to India, operating under Burn & Co. Grant illustrated a vase of black basalt marked **BURN & CO** in the centre of a belt on which was written **RANEEGUNGEE POTTERY WORKS**. Grant described the piece as made of native clays and of a quality to correspond to wares made by Shorthose & Heath or Hartley & Greens.[83] No other wares with the Burn mark are recorded.

Cambrian Pottery, Swansea, 1764-1870
    Coles Family 1764-86
    Coles & Haynes 1786-1802
    Haynes & L.W. Dillwyn 1802-10
    Dillwyn & Co. 1810-17
    T. & J. Bevington 1817-24
    L.W. Dillwyn 1824-31

*Figure 174. Engraving of the
Cambrian Pottery, Swansea
unsigned, published by Coles
& Haynes, 1791.*

L.L. Dillwyn (son) 1831-50

Evans and Glasson; D.J. Evans 1850-7

Invoices in the Royal Institution of South Wales indicate that black basalt was being
made at least as early as 1790 at the Cambrian Pottery.[84] Included are a sugar box
and a cream jug priced at one shilling three pence each and a teapot 'with lock cover'
for one shilling four pence.[85] Swansea was probably exporting to North America by
1792 as indicated in an advertisement in *Dunlap's Daily American Advertiser*
(Philadelphia) for 23 June 1792 which offered 'from Swansea Assorted earthenware
in crates.'

The pottery (Figure 174), located on the river Tawe, was one mile up the river
from the pier head, which extended 800 feet into the bay. Sea vessels loaded and
discharged their cargoes in the Tawe about two miles from the pottery, providing a
convenient natural access for transport. The 1802 plan of the pottery included a
black cellar, black shed and a black slip kiln.[86] In spite of the obvious relevance of the
'black bank' very few marked examples of Swansea basalt have been discovered.
Those that have exhibit a broad range of shapes, including some dramatic ornamental wares like the reclining Anthony and Cleopatra (Figures 175 and 176), some
examples of which are signed by the modeller 'G. Bentley 22 May 1791', as well as
impressed **SWANSEA**, the mark commonly associated with the pottery. A pastille
burner in the shape of a vase is in the National Museum of Wales collection (Figure
177). The sprig relief decoration appears to commemorate the death of Nelson and
was probably made shortly after 1805, at the height of fashion for both pastille
burners and Nelson commemoratives. In the Meagher bequest to the Glynn Vivian
Art Gallery, Swansea, are three more Swansea examples of basalt, a coffee pot and
two inkwells. It is interesting to note that in addition to the impressed **SWANSEA**
factory mark are letters '**A**' on the handle base of the coffee pot, '**B**' on one inkwell,
'**D**' on another. The series of '**A**' marked wares (Figures 442-444) mentioned as
conceivably denoting one of the Adams factories now extend in possible attribution

Figure 175. Figure of Mark Anthony reclining. Mark: **G BENTLEY, SWANSEA** *May 22, 1791, 11in. long. Victoria & Albert Museum, 3501-1901.*

Figure 176. Figure of Cleopatra reclining. Mark: **SWANSEA**, *c.1791, 12in. long. The National Museum of Wales, Cardiff, 3092.*

*Figure 177. Pastille burner (left) in the form of a vase with sprig relief decoration commemorating the death of Nelson. Mark: **SWANSEA**, c.1805-10, 13¼in. high. Jug, with fluted body. Mark: **SWANSEA**, c.1805-10, 4¾in. high. The National Museum of Wales, Cardiff, 2522, 2523.*

to Swansea manufacture, particularly the coffee pot (Figure 442) with the **'A'** impressed at the base of the handle. True black in colour and fine grained, Swansea basalt is smooth to the touch approaching almost technical perfection. Grant conceded that Swansea basalt was equal to anything produced by Enoch Wood or Neale in both conception and execution and was only surpassed occasionally by Wedgwood or Turner.[87]

During the second Dillwyn occupation of the Cambrian Pottery (1824-50) Dillwyn succeeded in producing some excellent quality Etruscan vases; however, they were low fired, red bodied earthenware vases painted with a black slip, rendering in effect a black body only superficially. These vases, therefore, not being stoneware of the Egyptian black variety, fall out of the scope of this book.

In addition to works already cited the most important general work on the subject is E. Morton Nance's *The Pottery & Porcelain of Swansea & Nantgarw* (London: B.T. Batsford Ltd., 1942).

Marks: SWANSEA (plus letters **'A'**, **'B'** and **'D'** have been found; also modellers' names are found on basalt, such as **'G. Bentley'** accompanied by a date).

Carlisle Works *see* **Cyples & Ball**

James Cartlidge, Knowl Street, Burslem, Staffordshire, c.1787-1820; **Cartlidge and Beech**, Moorland Road, Burslem, 1822-26
S. and J. Cartlidge were listed as potters in Burslem in the 1787 directory. Both James Cartlidge and the partnership with Beech advertised the production of Egyptian black in the directories from 1818 to 1823. The partnership terminated with the death of James Cartlidge on 28 July 1826. The sale of the pottery was advertised in *The Staffordshire Advertiser* for 25 November 1826:

> Auction Burslem utensils &c of Cartledge [*sic*] and Beech, declining business, including Egyptian Black, [printing] presses, manufactory also to be let, vacant.

There is some question about whether the business actually continued until 1828 as other advertisements appeared offering the remainder of the utensils.[88] By October 1828 the pottery was definitely no longer in operation and was described as 'potworks *late* occupied by Cartlidge and Beech'.[89]
No wares produced by this manufactory have been identified.

Richard Cartledge, Golden Hill, Tunstall, Staffordshire, c.1818-20
The Commercial Directory 1818-1820 lists Richard Cartledge as producing 'black ware'. Nothing else is known of the manufactory.

Thomas Cartlidge, Burslem, Staffordshire, c.1823-24
The *London Gazette* carried a dissolution of partnership notice (27 March 1823) between Thomas Cartlidge and Benjamin Cork on 1 April 1823.[90] Eighteen months later a second partnership between Thomas Cartlidge and John Walton noted as 'manufacturers of earthenware, Burslem' dissolved.[91] It is not known if black basalt was part of their output, but it seems likely since John Walton was also listed in the 1822 directory as a 'Black and Figure Manufacturer' and potters with the surname Cork manufactured blackwares in Burslem (*see* **Cork and Condliffe**).

Castleford Pottery *see* **David Dunderdale & Co.**

John Catherall, nr. Buckley, Flintshire (brickworks); Chester, Cheshire (pottery shop), c.1815
A few business papers and price lists exist in a group of papers known as the Catherall Papers in the Clwyd Record Office (North Wales) which indicate that John Catherall was attempting to start an earthenware manufactory near his brickworks near Buckley, probably at Buckley Mountain. John Daniel was seeking employment with Catherall and wrote: 'I have receipts for all under glaze colours, and Enamel colours, and could gild any shining black you should make or if preferable silver it.'[92] A Mr. T. Simpson of Hanley replied to various queries raised by Catherall with the following: 'The Egyptian Black Teapots, you must have Fired too hard, or too quick; I conceive it is the latter, by having some of them good- the price you can get for shining black, would be good in the Potteries, if you can get

*Figure 179. Teapot and cover, polished basalt of oval shape with vertical engine-turned satin stripes, widow finial and original silver tip to spout. Mark: **SALOPIAN**, c.1790-95, 5¾in. high. Thomas collection.*

*Figure 178. Cream jug, oval with bamboo-moulded base and sprig decoration of Hope and Plenty and Sacrifice to Minerva. Mark: **SALOPIAN** (probably the retail trade mark of Thomas Turner, London. The pieces bearing the **SALOPIAN** mark were not manufactured at the Caughley factory), c.1790, 6in. high. Gunson collection*

them up as cheap.'[93] Nothing else about this attempt at blackware manufacture in Flintshire is known.

Caughley Works (Thomas Turner), Nr. Broseley, Shropshire, 1775-99
There is no definitive proof that Caughley ever produced basalt, but due to the association of the few marked **SALOPIAN** basalt teawares with the Caughley factory it is necessary to address the problem here. In fact all the evidence works against such a notion. The quality of the Salopian basalt is dark and lustrous, often with a high sheen and fine engine turning. Grant speculates that due to the unusual nature of basalt production at what has been assumed to be an exclusive porcelain manufactory, the wares may have been made at Coalport by Bradley and Company, hypothesizing that neighbour Thomas Turner may have been involved in the Coalport enterprise.[94] However, the marked Bradley & Co. wares bear no resemblance to the Salopian basalt either in texture or form. In discussing excavations at Caughley on three tips of kiln rubbish undertaken by Dr. A.J.W. Houghton, Grant-Davidson reported on the basalt recovered. He noted that 'basaltes of good quality, thinly potted, and some with moulded floral reliefs was found in small quantity'.[95] In the opinion of Roger Edmundson these sherds could have been broken whole pieces discarded on the site and unless they are actually factory wasters should be regarded as probably not of Caughley manufacture.[96] Who then manufactured the **SALOPIAN** (Figures 178 and 179) marked wares?

Thomas Turner was also a retailer with a London warehouse and showroom. It is the opinion of Mr. Edmundson that Turner commissioned the basalts from other potteries, thus forging the alliance with his own porcelain manufactory by marking them **SALOPIAN**.
Mark: SALOPIAN

Charles Chatterley (Charles & Ephraim Chatterley), Hanley, late 18th century
Shaw included Charles Chatterley along with Humphrey Palmer among 'the chief manufacturers of the improved kinds of Pottery in Hanley'. He added that Chatterley (and Palmer) also made the 'dry bodied pottery, then acquiring celebrity'.[97] This probably included basalt, although no wares are attributed to the pottery.

Charles and Ephraim Chatterley had a large European trade jointly operated with John and William Yates out of No. 31 St. Paul's Churchyard in the early 1790s, probably marketing wares of many manufacturers including those produced by James and Charles Whitehead, nephews of the Chatterleys.

Samuel Chatterley, Hanley, Staffordshire, c.late 18th-early 19th century
Samuel Chatterley is described by John Ward, *The Borough of Stoke-Upon-Trent...*, as a noted maker of Egyptian black. Grant allowed that Chatterley made 'excellent Black Egyptian for tea and coffee sets' from the middle of the end of the eighteenth century,[98] but his name has systematically eluded the records, including the directories. Charles and Ephraim Chatterley are recorded in the eighteenth century directories as potters in Hanley. The few references to Samuel Chatterley which have been uncovered are random and do not relate to a black basalt production. In 1760 a Samuel Chatterley was buying porcelain from Reid & Co.[99] In 1807/8 an S. Chatterley owned the property occupied by Keeling, Toft & Co. and paid taxes of £1.9.2.
The wares reputed to have been made by this firm have not been identified.

*Figure 180. Teapot and cover, oval polished basalt with unusual engine-turned lower third comprised of vertical undulating lines. The sprig decorations include Hope and Plenty, the Amalgamation of Peace destroying the implements of War. The finial, missing its head, is the Mother and Child associated with the factory. Mark: **Chetham & Woolley, Lane End—R.W.** incised in cursive in base, c.1790s, 8in. high. City Museum and Art Gallery, Stoke-on-Trent.*

Chetham & Woolley, Commerce Street, Lane End, Longton, Staffordshire, c.1794-1809
(Mrs. Ann) Chetham & Woolley, 1807-09
Mrs. Ann Chetham, 1809-11
Chetham & Son, 1814-21
Chetham & Robinson, 1822-24
James Chetham and Richard Woolley were in partnership from at least 1794 to 1807 until the death of Chetham. His widow succeeded him and continued in business with Woolley until his departure in 1809. By 1814 Mrs. Chetham had taken her son, Jonathan Lowe Chetham into partnership until her own death in 1821. Jonathan Chetham was joined by John Robinson in 1822 and Robinson's son Samuel joined them in 1834. John Robinson died in 1840 and Samuel seems to have left them also as J. L. Chetham is sole proprietor until his own death in 1861.[100]
Chetham and Woolley were sending their wares to London Staffordshire warehouseman Thomas Wyllie from 1794 to 1799[101] and supplied Mintons with twelve dozen black inkstands in 1808 charging them £3.8.0.[102] Hillier states that London dealers Abbott & Newbury, and later Abbott & Mist bought ware from Chetham & Woolley for decoration and resale between 1801 and 1808,[103] as did the Herculaneum Pottery warehouse in Liverpool during the 1807/08 period.[104]
Identification of the wares is open to some conjecture. It has long been assumed that the Venus and Cupid finial was exclusive to the Chetham and Woolley manufactory because of one signed teapot with the Venus and Cupid finial (head missing) in the City Museum and Art Gallery, Stoke-on-Trent (Figure 180). In excavations, however, around the general area of the firm's works in Chancery Lane (Stoke-on Trent), several fragments have been found of black basalt as well as white stoneware and pearlware, but no Venus and Cupid finials (Figure 181). Owing to the fact these were from disturbed levels it is impossible to date them to one of the

a.

b.

c.

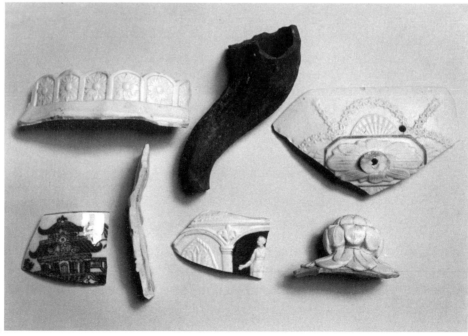

d.

Figure 181. a. Group of three fragments of covers from the Chetham site 1800-20; b. Group of two gallery pieces and one base fragment from the Chetham site 1800-20; c. Two spouts from the Chetham site 1800-20; d. A group of white stonewares and a basalt and a pearlware fragment from the Chetham site c.1800-20. City Museum and Art Gallery, Stoke-on-Trent.

Figure 182. Teapot and cover, round form with fine bamboo-moulded lower half of body and beading at shoulder. The undulating gallery, Mother and Child finial, spout, and finely reeded cover have all been associated with marked examples of Chetham and Woolley or fragments excavated from the factory site. Unmarked, attributed to Chetham & Woolley, c.1805-10, 4¾in. high. Private collection.

Figure 183. Teapot and cover, polished basalt with lower portion engine-turned with diagonal bars, shoulder with a bust scroll and leaf motif, and Mother and Child finial. The central portion is decorated in sprig reliefs which include Charlotte at the Tomb of Werther and Sportive Love. Unmarked, attributed to Chetham & Woolley from gallery, cover, finial and spout, c.1805-10, 6¼in. high. City Museum and Art Gallery, Stoke-on-Trent, 2709.

several partnerships. David Hollens' article in the *ECC Transactions* Vol. 11, Part 3 entitled 'Some Researches into the Makers of Dry Bodies' links a group of stonewares bound by the Venus and Cupid finial accompanied by a band of oak leaves on the top of the cover. Several of these examples are ones he illustrates in the article and others bound similarly are illustrated here in Figures 180 and 182-4. The link for all these wares is the teapot in the City Museum with the incised factory signature (Figure 180). However, at least one other manufacturer, Samuel Hollins, utilized the Venus and Cupid finial making any attribution by finial alone uncertain.

Figure 184. Teapot and cover, round-bodied with fine bamboo-engine-turned base and shoulder interspersed by swag sprig relief decoration. The gallery, spout, cover and finial have all been associated with Chetham and Woolley. Mark: *JW* impressed on underside of cover, possibly Chetham & Woolley, c.1800, 6⅝in. high. Royal Ontario Museum, 970.242.75, Brown collection.

There are a few pieces stamped with a **CHETHAM & WOOLLEY** mark in white stoneware; one in the Weldon collection in New York is a large traditional hunt jug with the brown enamel neck which is impressed with the name at the base of the handle. Unfortunately no basalt wares have been discovered similarly impressed. It appears that the manufacture of basalt was continued into the Chetham and Robinson partnership as the 1822 directory lists 'Egyptian black' among the other wares produced by the factory. In addition to the Hollens article further information on the Chetham family is available in the *Northern Ceramic Society Newsletter* No. 19 or in the reprint of the article in *Echoes and Reflections*, 1990.

Marks: Chetham & Woolley Lane End RW (incised in cursive); **CHETHAM & WOOLLEY**. Initials are recorded in other bodies: **C & R, C.R.S., J.L.C., J.R. & F.C.**

Richard Woolley *see* **Woolley**

Church Gresley Pottery, Church Gresley, Derbyshire, 1790-late 19th century
Jewitt indicated that after the Church Gresley Pottery was taken over by Mr. T. Green in 1871 their production included, in addition to cane coloured, Ironstone, Rockingham mottled, and buff, black lustre ware.[105] No examples are attributable to this manufactory.

Ralph and James Clews, Cobridge Works, Cobridge, Staffordshire, 1813-34
Ralph Clews (b.1788) and James Clews (b.1790) went into business for themselves late in 1813. A letter to Josiah Wedgwood II dated 7 September 1813 signed by James Clews discusses the brothers' intent to begin an earthenware manufacture and inquires about the prices of plaster and raw materials.[106] George Miller and Nancy Dickinson have provided much of our current knowledge about the Clews brothers and particularly their trade with America.[107]

James Clews began work for Andrew Stevenson in 1811 or before. In 1813 the Clews took over the Bleak Hill Works formerly occupied by Peter Warburton, which continued to be owned by Mary Warburton and let to the Clews.[108] 1817 was the first listing for the Clews in the land tax records. They were established in property formerly occupied by Warburton but owned by William Adams of Cobridge.[109] By 1816 they were engaged in an American trade exporting large amounts of blue printed earthenware through Bolton and Ogden in Liverpool, to Ogden and Day in New York.[110] Although the Clews produced high quality black basalt (Figures 186-190) no listings for the blackware occur in the invoices sent to America.[111] Bankruptcy forced the brothers out of business in 1834.

The basalt manufactured by the Clews is sometimes glazed, almost approaching the 'jet' wares of the later part of the century. But in many instances the wares are unglazed. Decoration tended toward engine-turned geometrical designs and floral sprig decoration. But sherds excavated on the site, which could date from the Warburton or Clews manufactory (Figures 185), indicate that some classical revival swag relief was produced as well.

MARK: CLEWS

Figure 185. Fragments of teawares from the Warburton/Clews factory site in Cobridge, c.1795-1834.
City Museum and Art Gallery, Stoke-on-Trent.

Figure 186. Small teapot and cover; sugar box and cover, engine-turned diagonal striped decoration. Marks: both CLEWS, c.1815-20, teapot 4½in. high, sugar box 4¼in. high. Rakow collection.

Figure 187. Tea cup, engine-turned chevron decoration. Mark: CLEWS, c.1815, 2¾in. high. Robertshaw collection.

Figure 188. Small jug with horizontal and vertical engine-turned decoration. Mark: CLEWS, c.1820, 5in. high. Gunson collection.

William Clowes, Longport, Burslem, Staffordshire, c.1778-1800
By 1778 and probably before that date William Clowes (1745-1822) was operating a manufactory in Longport as well as a London wholesale pottery business. *The London General Evening Post* ran an advertisement on six days in May 1778 which read:

STAFFORDSHIRE WARE, sold by WILLIAM CLOWES at [*sic*] Co. at 112, in the Minories, where Merchants and Dealers may be supplied with any Quantity on the shortest Notice, and on the most reasonable Terms, or at their Manufactory, at Longport, near Burslem, Staffordshire.[112]

Figure 189. Sugar box and cover, exuberantly moulded with flowers. This form was also made in earthenware with an orange/brown glaze highlighted with copper lustre and blue (see Miller, An Anthology of British Teapots, Pl. 1418). Mark: **CLEWS**, c.1825, 5¾in. high. Gunson collection.

Figure 190. Sugar box (minus cover), moulded with leaves and flowers, basketweave lower third. Mark: **CLEWS**, c.1825. City Museum and Art Gallery, Stoke-on-Trent.

In 1787 Clowes and Williamson were mistakenly listed as potters in Fenton in the directory. Clowes apparently resided in Burslem as he took out an insurance policy in 1781 for household goods and wearing apparel totalling £400.[113] He was listed as paying taxes on property in Burslem from 1786 through 1806.[114] Land Tax records are very general resources owing to the fact that they give only three pieces of information: owner's name, occupier's name and tax assessment. Therefore, it is impossible to tell from land tax records if, by 1787, Clowes was simply residing in Burslem or operating a pottery in Burslem, or both. At some point his uncle, Hugh Henshall,[115] entered into the business as the dissolution of partnership notice appeared in the *London Gazette* on 18 November 1800:[116]

Figure 191. Teapot (minus cover) of fine quality. The bamboo-shaped body was a popular early form following Yixing red stoneware prototypes of the 17th and 18th century. Mark: **W. CLOWES**, William Clowes, Burslem, c.1770s, 4¼in. high. Mint Museum of Art, Delhom collection.

Figure 192. Teapot and cover with globular fluted body, sibyl finial to cover. Mark: **W. CLOWES**, William Clowes, Burslem, c.1775-80, 4in. high. Essex Institute, Salem, Massachusetts, 170.

William Clowes
H. Henshall   Longport
A. Williamson

Partnership dissolved 11 November 1800 to be carried on by Henshall and Williamson.

William Clowes was also one of the ten original partners in the New Hall Porcelain Works begun in 1781 but was reputed to be only a 'sleeping partner';[117] he was one of the four remaining in 1810 when the copyhold was bought.[118] A William Clowes, probably his son who was also William, was a workman in the Davenport factory.[119]

A number of blackwares are attributable to the factory, boldly impressed **W. CLOWES**. The earliest is a teapot in the bamboo shape (Figure 191) similar to ones produced by Wedgwood and Bentley, Turner, and Myatt. Another globular shaped teapot with a reeded body (Figure 192), perhaps nearly contemporary with the bamboo shaped one, is in the Essex Institute, Salem, Massachusetts. Clowes was among the few potters to engage in an ornamental ware production and the candlestick in the British Museum (Figure 194) attests to the success of the venture. The few existing pieces impressed with the manufacturer's name indicate a wide range of shapes and forms may have been produced by the factory but not yet identified.

Mark: W. CLOWES

Clulow and Company, Lower Lane, Fenton, Staffordshire, c.1802

Only speculatively a black basalt manufacturer, the single known example emanating from this pottery is a white feldspathic stoneware teapot in the Newark Museum.[120] It seems likely basalt was also produced. The partnership was one which included, in addition to Robert Clulow, Joseph Rogers, John Hampson and Daniel Morris and was located at Lower Lane. On 5th February 1802 this partnership was dissolved to be carried on under the name of Robert Clulow & Co.[121]

Caleb Cole, Newfield, Newcastle-under-Lyme, Staffordshire, c.1792 to early 19th century

Little is known about this manufacturer but on 10 October 1792 Cole insured the buildings of his pottery for £350, stock and utensils for £100.[122]

One document pertaining to this possible blackware manufacturer is an advertisement in the *Staffordshire Advertiser* for 30 October 1802:

Auction Caleb Cole's earthenware utensils and farm stock at Newfield, common and engine lathes, stove pots and pipes, copper plates, presses, black clay, made up clay &c.

No other information about the pottery has come to light.

James Collinson, Golden Hill, Tunstall, Staffordshire, c.1818-20

The *Commercial Directory* for 1818/19 and 1820 listed a James Collinson as producing blackware in Golden Hill. No wares have been identified.

*Figure 193. Coffee pot and cover, with fluted mid-riff, ear-shaped handle and widow finial. Mark: **W. CLOWES** (impressed on handle), William Clowes, Burslem, c.1790, 10in. high. The National Museum of Wales, Cardiff, 500.*

*Figure 194. Candlestick in the form of a woman carrying an urn on her head. Mark: **W. CLOWES**, William Clowes, Burslem, c.1780-1800, 9in. high. British Museum, 158-511, Sheldon collection.*

John Cooper, Hill Top Works, Church Gresley, Derbyshire, 1810-late 19th century.

Started in 1810 by John Cooper, The Hill Top Works carried on as Cooper & Massey and Cooper & Banks, produced among other popular nineteenth century wares, 'black lustre'.[123] No blackwares have been identified.

W.T. Copeland (and Sons), Spode Works, Stoke-on-Trent, Staffordshire, 1847-present.

William Taylor Copeland had been a partner with Thomas Garrett in the Copeland

*Figure 195. Partial teaset painted with flowers in opaque enamels. Marks: all **COPELAND & GARRETT**; painted in enamels **5595/1**, additional marks impressed: cream jug '**36**', 2½in. high, sugar box '**21**', 3¾in. high, teapot '**18**', 4½in. high, c.1835-40. Rakow collection.*

145

and Garrett firm which succeeded the Spode enterprise in 1833. In 1847 Garrett retired, leaving Copeland to sole ownership of the firm. Copeland was highly successful, employing over eight hundred workers[124] and producing a large variety of ceramics, both utilitarian and ornamental. Basalt did not, by this time, comprise a large portion of the stock of any of the mid-century factories but the lovely covered jar (Colour Plate 20) attests to the superb quality available in wares beautifully painted with opaque Chinese style flowers.

For reference works on the Copeland and Copeland and Garrett factories *see* next entry, Copeland and Garrett.

Marks: COPELAND; COPELAND LATE SPODE (impressed or painted).

Copeland and Garrett, Stoke-on-Trent, Staffordshire, 1833-47
The large firm of Copeland and Garrett produced some beautifully painted basalt wares (Colour Plate 19; Figure 195) in the the manner of Wedgwood Etruscan wares and with Capri style enamel flowers. The opaque enamels produced dramatically effective decoration on the austere body. An Etruscan painted vase was exhibited by the firm in the 1851 Exhibition.[125] The wares were often impressed with the shape number and painted with a painter's number. In 1836/7 Copeland and Garrett were the second largest firm in the Potteries after Davenport, paying taxes on twenty-five ovens.[126]

A monograph by Alan Townsend dedicated to the Copeland partnerships is in preparation. Meanwhile, other books include sections dedicated to the Copeland and Garrett/Copeland periods (but none treat basalt production): Godden, *Victorian Porcelain* (Herbert Jenkins, London, 1961) and *Staffordshire Porcelain* (Granada, London, 1983), A. Hayden, *Spode and His Successors* (Cassell, London, 1924) and William Burton, *A History and Description of English Porcelain* (Cassell, London, 1802). Other catalogues include material from the Copeland periods: *Spode Copeland 1765-1965* (catalogue written by Robert Copeland and published by Spode in English and Norwegian, 1966), and *Spode.Copeland 1733-1983* (Pat Halfpenny ed., City Museum and Art Gallery, Stoke-on-Trent, 1983).

Mark: COPELAND & GARRETT; the mark **C & G** has been noted on porcelains.

Cork and Condliffe, Queen Street, Burslem, Staffordshire, c. 1834-43 or later
Pigot's 1834 directory lists this firm as producing 'Egyptian black'. In 1836/7 Cork and Condliffe were paying rates to the Potteries Chamber of Commerce on two [bottle] ovens.[127] Cork and Condliffe were still in operation in 1843.[128] Nothing else is known about the pottery which became Cork & Edge in 1846, and Cork, Edge and Malkin in 1860. No blackware examples are known.

Cyples, Longton, Staffordshire
   Joseph Cyples II, Lane End, 1784-89
   Mary Cyples, works No. 132, 1791-1802
   Lydia Cyples, Market Street, 1811-32
   William and Richard Cyples, Market Street, 1832-40
   Cyples, Barlow and Cyples, Market Street, 1841-44
   Cyples & Robey, Market Street, 1845-46
   Cyples & Barker, Market Street, 1846-47

Cyples & Hughes, High Street (Carlisle Works), 1845-46
Cyples & Ball, High Street (Carlisle Works), 1847-48

All of the Cyples factories from 1784 until 1848 were listed in the various directories as having produced 'Egyptian black'.[129]

A Wedgwood Commonplace Book of 1789 records a receipt for Black annotating 'Scylpes' [*sic*] as the originator:

> 20 Blue Ball Clay
> 5 calcined carr
> 1½ calcined manganese
> These to be mixed by measure in the Slip.[130]

Between 1824 and 1828 Lydia Cyples sold ware amounting to £253 to the Herculaneum Pottery warehouse in Liverpool[131] probably for export.

On 11 December 1847 the *Staffordshire Advertiser* printed this notice:

> Auction 4 January 1848 earthenware and china manufactory 1605 super yards Market Street, Longton, 'long celebrated for manufacture of Egyptian Black', several years ago worked by late Mrs. Lydia Cyples, since by Cyples, Barlow & Cyples, Cyples & Robey, recently Cyples and Barker...apply William Cyples.

Because of the preponderance of Egyptian black which must have been produced by the several Cyples partnerships in the two factories, it is difficult to assign any piece to one particular partnership. However, the shapes would seem to indicate that many were made during the tenure of Lydia Cyples at Market Street (Figure 196). The key to manufacturer and dating rests uncertainly on style. The pots in general are glazed basalt, often with engine-turned embellishment. The wares are bold in design and sturdy in appearance, the high sheen imparting strength to the aggregate. Marked wares by Cyples are by no means common, but large numbers of unmarked

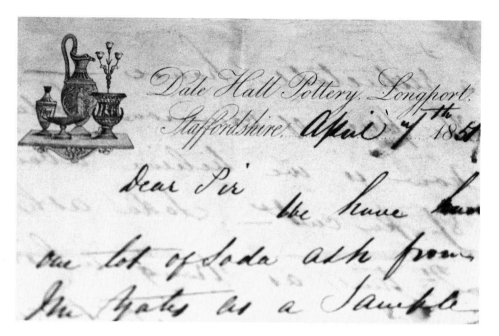

Figure 197. Letterhead from the Dale Hall Pottery, Longport, April 7, 1851 (Wedgwood MS 36-27842).

Figure 198. Teapot and cover, engine-turned chevron pattern to lower third with sibyl finial on cover. The sprigged decoration includes Poor Maria, Sportive Love, Hope attended by Peace, Art and Labour, and the Bourbonnais Shepherd. Mark: DAVENPORT over an anchor, c.1810, 4½in. high. Lockett collection.

glazed basalt wares exist, many probably produced at the other Cyples factories.
Mark: CYPLES (occasionally **I CYPLES**).

Dale Hall Pottery, Longport, Staffordshire, c.1790-late 19th century
Commencing in 1836, during the occupation of the pottery by Thomas, John and Joshua Mayer, the Dale Hall Pottery probably made black basalt wares. They produced a large variety of Victorian stonewares, jaspers and elaborately decorated ornamental wares which were shown in the 1851 Exhibition as well as the 1876 Exhibition in Philadelphia. A printed letterhead from 1851 illustrates the type of wares produced by the pottery (Figure 197). Jewitt also illustrates drawings of a number of pieces.[132] No basalt wares have been attributed to this factory, although

Figure 199. Sugar box and cover similarly decorated to teapot in Figure 198 but with a raised crimped gallery and fine diamond rouletting at shoulder. Mark: DAVENPORT over an anchor, c.1810, 5½in. high. Gunson collection.

Fig, 200. Sugar box and cover with engine-turned chevron body and fine diamond rouletting at shoulder, raised, crimped gallery and sibyl finial. Unmarked, Davenport, c.1810, 4½in. high. Cleaver collection.

some marked basalt plaques with upper case **MAYER** (Figures 304 and 305) could conceivably be the products of this pottery.
Marks: T.J. & J. MAYER; MAYER; MAYER BROS.

Davenport, Longport, Staffordshire, c 1794-1887
The large firm of Davenport has been recently expertly documented by Terence Lockett and Geoffrey Godden in their book entitled *Davenport China, Earthenware & Glass 1794-1887*.[133] Therefore, as with other major potteries whose histories have already been explored, it is not necessary to dwell on a pottery history which is available in another volume.

It appears that John Davenport may have been in some kind of business, probably as a dealer in earthenware and glass, in Burslem as early as 1783 as a John Davenport was paying taxes on one property owned by himself and occupying another property owned initially by Anthony Keeling, then by a Mr. Swinnerton. By 1791 he owned both properties and continued to occupy the two through the end of the eighteenth century. The above is conjecture or preamble, because we cannot be certain that this is our John Davenport (b.1765). However, it may very well be as John Davenport was listed as a 'Manufacturer of Earthenware' in 1791 in a Sun Fire Insurance policy issued on his small Burslem potworks.[134] We do know that prior to going into business for himself in Longport in 1794 he was a partner with Thomas Wolfe, probably acting a Wolfe's manager in the Liverpool warehouse. He participated in the Potters Clay Copartnership of 1797 along with many other prominent late eighteenth century manufacturers who benefited by buying clay co-operatively.[135]

The Davenport pottery paid rates on the largest number of ovens in 1836/7 in all of the Potteries, thirty in all.[136] In addition to making the standard earthenwares, Davenport manufactured a variety of stonewares, particularly caneware, and porcelain. Judging from its relative rarity basalt was not a key player in the output of

Figure 201. Teapot and cover with engine-turned body and rouletting at shoulder and gallery. Mark: **DAVEN-PORT** over an anchor, c.1820, 4in. high. Royal Ontario Museum, 970,242, 103, Brown collection.

the factory. Lockett suggests that stylistically basalt seems to have been made by the firm from about 1805 until around 1830.[137]

Wedgwood & Byerley were 'buying in' wares from Davenport as well as from other manufacturers to complete orders. Middle men, such as Thomas Hawkins, filled the orders, for a commission of five per cent on the total bill, often combining the wares of a number of manufacturers in doing so.[138] In addition to Wedgwood and Byerley, other retailers, such as Abbott & Mist, London, were selling Davenport wares in the early part of the nineteenth century.[139]

Davenport had a large export trade to the Continent and to North America. A number of basalt pieces are found in North American private and museum collections,

Figure 202. Cream jug to accompany teapot in Figure 201. Mark: **DAVENPORT** over an anchor, c.1820, 3⅝in. high. Royal Ontario Museum, 970.242.96, Brown collection.

Figure 203. Teapot and cover of unusual form for Davenport basalt. The body is decorated prominently with grape and vine leaves, and the central panel of Pan and Mercury is framed by rose sprig relief. Unmarked, Davenport, c.1825-30, 7in. high. Hacking collection.

Figure 204. Milk jug or hot water jug and cover to teapot in Figure 203 sprig decorated with a relief of Vulcan. Mark: DAVENPORT over an anchor, c.1825-30, 5⅞in. high. Hacking collection.

Figure 205. Sugar box and cover to accompany milk jug and teapot in Figures 203 and 204. The sugar box has simulated ring handles. The central sprig relief has a cupid figure which according to T.A. Lockett has 'a curious bowler hat...on the back of his head'. Unmarked, Davenport, c.1825-30, 5¾in. high. Hacking collection.

although that, even combined with a large trade in other wares, does not constitute grounds for a large overseas trade in blackwares. Too few Davenport marked pieces exist to justify such an assertion, although many unmarked basalt wares may have been produced by the pottery. Most of the known shapes are illustrated in Figures 198-202. One set of three teawares (Figures 203-205), discovered in Portugal, is of an unusual form for Davenport basalt and of considerably later date, probably the end of the

Figure 206. Two intaglio seals of monograms. Mark: W. DICKSON on both. Maker unknown, probably 18th century. Rakow collection.

second decade of the nineteenth century or into the third decade. The earlier wares frequently have engine-turned decoration and rouletting. Some combine engine-turned portions of the body with rouletting and sprig decoration.

Marks: DAVENPORT, Davenport, both above an impressed anchor; **Davenport** (less frequently).

W. Dickson

Two black basalt intaglio seals (Figure 206) in the Rakow collection are impressed **W. DICKSON** on the reverse. Nothing is known about the manufacturer and these appear to be the only recorded blackwares with this mark.

Dillwyn of Swansea, *see* Cambrian Pottery

Don Pottery, Swinton, South Yorkshire, 1801-35
Greens, Clark & Co., 1801-10
John and William Green, 1810-23
Green & Co., 1823-35

The Don Pottery was built in 1801 on the bank of the canal in the Parish of Swinton, near Mexborough. The pottery was founded by John Green a former partner in the Hartley and Green's Leeds Pottery venture and in the Swinton Potteries until he became bankrupt in 1800. The original venture consisted of three other partners: Richard Clark, a ropemaker in Leeds, and John and William Brameld of the Swinton Pottery. Several other partners joined in 1803. John Green died in 1805 and his younger son William became a partner. By 1823 the firm was solely owned by the Green family and remained so until bankruptcy of the Green brothers forced the sale of the Don Pottery in 1835.[140]

The pattern book (actually a shapes book) for 'Queen's or Cream-Coloured Earthenware' was issued in 1807[141] and a factory bill head for 1808 included all the popular bodies and decoration as well as 'Egyptian Black' among the factory's output.[142]

Egyptian black produced by the Don Pottery is fugitive. Grant admits to not having seen any marked examples;[143] indeed, there may be none. However, some shapes are easily confused with those produced by Hartley, Greens and Company at the Leeds Pottery. A comparison of Figure 235, probably manufactured at Leeds with a white stoneware teapot incised 'Made by Enoch Barker at the Don Pottery'

Figure 207. Teapot and cover, the most popular form associated with Castleford stonewares, and only one of two teaware shapes apparently produced in basalt. Mark: **D.D. & Co., CASTLE-FORD POTTERY,** *David Dunderdale & Co., Castleford, c.1800-05, 7in. high. Castleford Museum, Wakefield Metropolitan District Council.*

Figure 208. Sugar box and cover (not mate) en suite with teapot in Figure 207 and hot milk jug in Figure 209. The central relief is of Zephyr. Mark: Figure 208a, c.1800-05, 4¾in. high. Rakow collection.

Figure 208a. Mark on sugar box in Figure 208.

(Pl. 1375, Miller, *An Anthology of British Teapots*) serves to illustrate the posible confusion which could arise in identifying pieces from these two factories.

In addition to the works cited, there is an article by T.G. Mandby, 'Neglected Don Pottery', *Antique Collector*, September, 1986.

Marks (on earthenware): **DON.POTTERY; DON; GREEN**.

James Donovan, Dublin (Ireland), c.1770s-1829

In the same category as James Mist and Neale & Bailey, Donovan was a retailer and probably never a manufacturer. Large firms like Mintons were supplying Donovan with a variety of pottery and porcelain for his Irish clients.[144] However, just as with Mist there are numerous earthenwares marked with Donovan's several imprimateurs. Grant even describes a [basalt] tea service decorated with Aesop's fables in the style and quality of Shorthose and Heath and their school stamped DONOVAN.[145]

153

David Dunderdale and Company, Castleford Pottery, Castleford, West Yorkshire, 1790-1821

The Dunderdale saga is one which also has been explored in a single monograph.[146] Its history is not unlike that of many other smaller potteries outside Staffordshire. The pottery was initiated by David Dunderdale II and John Plowes in 1790. Relative to other Yorkshire potteries of the period the Castleford Pottery was a fairly large concern being insured for a total of £3,700 in 1790.[147] By the end of the decade the elder Dunderdale was dead and his son by the same name succeeded him in the business. The Dunderdales were not a pottery family, but woolstaplers from Leeds. However, David Dunderdale became a leader among the county potters, assuming the Chair on 21 March 1796 of the first organization of Yorkshire potters, modelled on the Staffordshire Committee of Manufacturers.[148] John Plowes also appears not to have been associated with the manufacture of pottery before the Castleford venture, but he did go on to Ferrybridge after leaving Castleford in 1803 and stayed there until his death in 1812. The pottery suffered the financial misadventures of the period: an economy battered by intermittent wars and economic blockades, as well as a glut of consumer goods. It finally succumbed in 1821.

An earthenware shapes book was issued in 1796,[149] but as with other books of this nature, it has little relevance for the stoneware shapes produced by the pottery.

The name Castleford was a sobriquet, even in the nineteenth century. Lady Charlotte Schreiber remarked in her *Journals* about finding in 1871 'a little piece of Castleford Pottery...at Jesusa's [Madrid]'.[150]

The Castleford Pottery produced the earthenwares and stonewares popular at the time with an emphasis on the feldspathic stonewares associated with the pottery. Porcelain[151] may have been manufactured as well. A small and specific group of black basalt was produced (Figures 207-210), all taken from the same moulds as the tewares seen in the white feldspathic stonewares. In fact, it appears that the basalt was restricted to just two of the styles seen in the feldspathic stonewares.

Marks: D.D. & Co., CASTLEFORD POTTERY; D.D.& Co., CASTLEFORD; D.D. & Co.

Eastwood Pottery *see* **William Baddeley**

Gordon Elliott, North Staffordshire, working period 1978-present

Gordon Elliott worked at the City Museum and Art Gallery, Stoke-on-Trent, from 1953 to 1978. He was Keeper of Ceramics when he left and went to the North Staffordshire Polytechnic as a lecturer in ceramic history in the Art History Department. Specifically interested in the technology of the pottery industry, he studied pottery making and decided to reproduce a piece from every significant period to learn how it was done. He began with Roman pottery and by the time he reached the eighteenth century he was exceptionally competent. Some pieces which he gave as presents received such an enthusiastic response that he was encouraged to produce wares on a commercial basis.

Among the wares produced was fine quality basalt. The basalt was confined to hand pressed plaques, cameos and medallions, of subjects such as Josiah Wedgwood and Thomas Bentley. Elliott produced a series of commemorative portrait plaques modelled by John Bromley which included Sir Winston Churchill, Sir Christopher

Figure 209. Hot milk jug and cover, en suite with teapot (Figure 207) and sugar box (Figure 208). Mark: **D.D. & Co.** *CASTLEFORD POTTERY, c.1800-05, 6⅜in. high. Yorkshire Museum, Hurst collection.*

Figure 210. Jug, hexagonal shape, slightly different from the basalt commonly associated with the Castleford pottery. However, the relief decoration and handle are common to Dunderdale stone-wares. Mark: **D.D. & Co. CASTLEFORD POTTERY**, *c.1800-05. Castleford Museum, Wakefield Metropolitan District Council, CAS 1544.*

Figure 211. Two cameos depicting Sacrifice to Hymen and The Marriage of Cupid and Psyche. Mark: **Elliott**, *Gordon Elliott, Staffordshire, c.1985, both 2½in. x 3in. Private collection.*

Wren, Hugh Bourne, John Wesley and Joseph Smith. A special pair of plaques with portraits of Queen Elizabeth and Prince Philip made for their jubilee was commissioned from Bromley and Elliott by Thomas Goode of London. Other plaques included subjects such as the Marriage of Cupid and Psyche and Sacrifice to Hymen (Figure 211).[152]

Mark: Elliott

Ferrybridge Pottery *see* **Knottingley Pottery** and **Ralph Wedgwood & Co**.

Foley Pottery, Fenton, Staffordshire, c.1765-75

In 1973-4 an excavation of a waste tip of early pottery was undertaken by the Archaeological Society of the City Museum, Stoke-on-Trent. Through research undertaken by David Barker,[153] it now seems probable to conclude that the occupying potter of the Foley during the period in which these sherds were produced was Thomas Barker. Although the recovered sherds included a large number of red stonewares, white salt-glazed stonewares and other early creamwares (and no black basalt), the seal marked group of red stonewares identified by Robin Price as Group III[154] type with pseudo-Chinese seal marks have been identified by David Barker as coming from the Foley site. One whole teapot, in a basalt body, with the same seal mark has been a recent acquisition of the City Museum and Art Gallery, Stoke-on-Trent (Figure 212). It is beautifully potted and Yixing inspired, as were many of the red stoneware sherds recovered. With David Barker's research it seems admissible to suggest that this teapot was also from the Foley Pottery, probably produced by Thomas Barker between late 1772[155] and 1775. No other blackwares have been identified.

Ford, Lewis & Co., Shelton (Hanley), Staffordshire, c.1822

The 1822 directory listed the firm of Ford, Lewis and Company as 'earthenware and shining black manufacturers'. The partnership between the two owners, Lewis Ford and Thomas Ford was dissolved on 23 November 1822 and the firm was to continue in operation as L. Ford and Company.[156] No blackwares have been attributed to this manufactory.

J. Ford and J. Gibson, Tunstall, Staffordshire, c.1840

The pottery was located on the East side of the turnpike going from Brownhills to Tunstall.[157] *The Staffordshire Advertiser* published the following notice on 12 December 1840:

> Partnership dissolved, J. Ford and J. Gibson, Tunstall, Egyptian ware manufacturers.

John Gibson apparently continued manufacturing blackware until 1844 when Gibson's landlord, experiencing financial trouble, was forced to auction off the property to his creditors.[158] No wares have been attributed to this manufactory.

Forrester and Meredith, Lane End, Longton, Staffordshire, c.1784-87

These partners are not identified but they are listed in both *Bailey's Directory* (1784) and Tunnicliff (1787) as 'Manufacturers of Queen's Ware, Egyptian Black, Red China and various other ware'.

John Forrester and Charles Harvey of Lane End were in a partnership which was dissolved in 1798. Both individuals carried on business separately.[159] Charles Harvey and John Harvey then erected the Stafford Street Works, Longton.[160] John Forrester was again dissolving a partnership in 1802 with one Thomas Mayer.[161] In 1802 John Forrester continued to carry on business alone. Nothing else is known about the businesses or their products.

Garrett & Fletcher, 'Castleford Pottery', Castleford, West Yorkshire, c.1822-44

The pottery was built by Joseph Garrett early in the nineteenth century east of the Ferrybridge Road in Castleford. Garrett had been associated with the Hunslet Pottery, Leeds and he also worked at the Swillington Bridge Pottery before building the pottery in Castleford.[162] By 1822 the pottery appears to have been exclusively in the hands of Isaac Fletcher who was listed as a pot-maker and manufacturer of

Figure 212. Teapot and cover, Yixing inspired with cylindrical undecorated body and finial in the form of a dog with a ball in its mouth. Mark: **Pseudo Chinese seal**, attributed to Thomas Barker, Foley Pottery, Fenton, c.1770-75. City Museum and Art Gallery, Stoke-on-Trent.

Figure 213. Teapot and cover, of globular shape with engine-turned vertical and horizontal decoration. Mark: **J. GLASS HANLEY** (in rectangular die on base), c.1795-1800, 4⅜in. high. Castle Museum, Norwich, Miller collection.

'Black' in the 1822 Directory of the County of York. When the pottery was advertised to let in 1844 the plan included 'two large kilns for making Black and Stone Wares...[163] Nothing is known of the wares produced, nor are there any known marks.

Gibson and Sons, Albany Pottery, Burslem, Staffordshire, c.1885-
The Pottery Gazette Diary of 1888 illustrates a group of fashionable Victorian teapots including the 'jet' bodies manufactured by Gibson and Sons.[164] Gibson and Sons was previously Samuel Gibson and Robert Sudlow whose partnership was dissolved in 1884.[165] Both firms were manufacturing large quantities of teapots as well as jet. Nothing else is known of the blackware production.

John Gilbert and Co., Burslem, Staffordshire, c.1794-1803
John Gilbert and Co. of Burslem were operating a pottery described as an earthenware manufactory, for which an insurance policy was taken out in 1797 totalling £1,000.[166] Gilbert was in operation prior to 1797 as he was supplying Staffordshire warehouseman Thomas Wyllie with pottery to sell in London from 1794-6.[167] In 1803 he took out another policy on the works for nearly the same value. At that time the policy described Gilbert as 'John Gilbert of Clough Hall...Gent'.[168] One piece of basalt marked **GILBERT** has recently been discovered, a cream jug in a private collection. Although one cannot ascertain with complete certainty that this is the Gilbert, it seem likely that the manufacturer may have been John Gilbert.
Mark: GILBERT

John Glass, Market Street, Hanley, Staffordshire, c.1784-1838
Surprisingly Grant does not mention John Glass but Glass was a major producer of black basalt in the salient period of its manufacture. John Glass is a good example of how misleading the directories can be for in none is he mentioned as a manufacturer of Egyptian black.
    The pottery was located on the north side of Upper Market Street (now Huntbach Street), Hanley, just up from Market Square. Glass was a subscriber to the Committee of Manufacturers in 1790.[169] In 1792 the Salop Fire office insured:

> John Glass of Hanley, Potter. His house and another adjoining £100. Household goods £150. Sett of Pottworks connected £250. Stock of earthenware £400. Blocks and Molds £100; Total £100[170]

*Figure 214. Teapot and cover, melon-shaped with ribbed fluting interspersed with vines and berries. The rare finial depicts a merman blowing from a conch shell. This shape is known to have been produced by Samuel Hollins in a drab-green stoneware with blue enamel stripes. The finial on the Hollins example is a Mother and child. Mark: **J. GLASS HANLEY** (in rectangular die on base), c.1790-1800, 5in. high. Rakow collection.*

There was an addendum added to the policy on 12 September 1794.

> The stock of earthenware and the blocks and molds being removed to Mr. Richard Mare's sett of Potworks in Hanley, continue to be insured there.

Richard Mare, also a potter with John Mare in a neighbouring pottery on the north side of Market Square, was occupying the house 'adjoining' the Glass potworks. Glass must have been experiencing success since by 1794 the pottery buildings could not contain all his wares. By 1795 the business had expanded to include two works, the one 'Pottworks insured for £400…and a Second sett of Pottworks connected for £250. Total £1400.'[171] By 1797 Glass was occupying his own dwelling house, formerly occupied by Richard Mare, and a note appended to the insurance policy added that the excess stock continued to be housed at the works of Richard Mare.[172]

At some point John Glass contracted a partnership with John Taylor and from 1798 to 1800 Glass and Taylor were selling their wares through Staffordshire ware-

*Figure 215. Teapot and cover of oval form with sprig relief of Hope and Plenty and Britannia (on reverse). Mark: **J. GLASS HANLEY** (in rectangular die on base), c.1810, 6¾in. high. Rakow collection.*

*Figure 216. Teapot with hinged cover, the same form as the one in Figure 215 except with hinged cover. Mark: **J.GLASS HANLEY** (in rectangular die on base), c.1810, 5¾in. high. Rakow collection.*

Figure 217. Coffee pot and cover with engine-turned chequered decoration. Mark: ℐ.GLASS HANLEY (in rectangular die on base), c.1790-1800, 8¼in. high. Rakow collection

Figure 218. Hot milk jug (minus cover) with finely ribbed vertical base and reeded strap handle with acanthus leaf terminal. Mark: ℐ.GLASS HANLEY (in rectangular die on base), c.1790-1800, 5⅜in. high. Hirschler collection.

houseman Thomas Wyllie in London,[173] but by 4 January 1801 the partnership was dissolved.[174] In 1800 Glass and Taylor supplied Thomas Wyllie with '46 Doz Round Black Teapots', overcharging for them.[175] Tax records indicate that in 1807/8 John Glass rented out a pot works to Breeze and Leigh and by 1818 the directories were listing the manufacturers as John Glass and Sons. The dissolution of the partnership between the elder Glass, John Glass the Younger, and Richard Dean Glass occurred on 9 January 1821.[176]

The blackwares produced by the John Glass and subsequent partnerships displayed a wide range of shapes and decoration as well as technical prowess. One particular teapot (Figure 213) is somewhat roughly potted with a granular surface. Most other examples from the pottery demonstrate the high degree of technical achievement of which the pottery was capable, pleasing forms and interesting decoration (Figures 214-221). However, they are easily mistaken for almost identical ones produced both by William Baddeley at Eastwood and by the Leeds Pottery. Like Eastwood, Leeds, and others, teapots produced by Glass can be found with hinged covers (Figures 219 and 220). One teapot in the Merseyside Museum, Liverpool, with a curious embossed mark on the base (Figure 239) corresponds almost completely to a marked J. GLASS HANLEY example in the Gunson collection (Figure 219), the only differences being the shape of the handle and spout. To add to the confusion the shape of the body and spout are nearly identical to number 29 (Figure 240) in the Leeds *Drawing Book*, the distinction there being the finial, and the hinged lid. (However, #29 Drawing Book shape carries with it an appendage 'and with Hinges'). The mark (Figure 239a) a cursive double L (or H) raised figure is no help in identifying the pottery. Is it Glass, Eastwood, Leeds or a fourth manufacturer not yet identified?

Mark: J. GLASS, HANLEY

*Figure 219. Teapot with hinged cover, identical in body to Black-ware Drawing Book shape No. 29 of the Leeds Pottery but with different handle and spout. **J. GLASS HANLEY** teapots are frequently mistaken for wares produced by both the Leeds Pottery and by William Baddeley at Eastwood as John Glass pieces are often moulded and sprigged almost identically. Mark: **J. GLASS HANLEY**, c.1800-20, 7¾in. high. Gunson collection.*

Figure 220. Teapot with hinged cover, easily confused with both Eastwood marked pieces and Leeds pottery examples having the same body shape and moulding as #29 in the Drawing Book of 1800, but with identical spout, handle and finial as the one in Figure 219, marked by J. Glass. Unmarked, John Glass, Hanley, c.1800-20, 6⅛in. high. Temple Newsam House, Leeds, 4.74.46.

Thomas and Benjamin Godwin, New Basin, Navigation Road, Burslem, Staffordshire, c. 1783-1834; **Thomas Godwin**, 1834-54

A receipted invoice from Thomas and Benjamin Godwin indicates they were in an earthenware manufacturing business in Cobridge at least as early as 20th May 1783: 'Mr. Wedgwood & Co.bought of Thomas & Benjamin Godwin 3 Doz. Chamberpots and 3 Doz Bowls'.[177] The Godwins were listed as earthenware manu-facturers in various locations in Burslem and Cobridge in the local directories from 1784 to 1834. Benjamin Godwin was a subscriber to the Committee of Manufacturers in 1790.[178] At least by 1806 Benjamin Godwin occupied property in Burslem formerly owned by Isaac Warburton (the executor was William Adams). The Sun Fire Insurance Company insured the property on a set of pot works for

*Figure 221. Sugar box and cover, London-shaped with vertical indented moulded base and strawberry moulded band around the upper body. Mark: **J.GLASS HANLEY** (in rectangular die on base), c.1820, 4⅝in. high. Rakow collection.*

*Figure 222. Group of teaware sherds from the William Greatbatch site, Fenton, dating from c.1770-82. The teapot base (3½in. diameter) has a **pseudo Chinese seal mark**. City Museum and Art Gallery, Stoke-on-Trent.*

£300, the house for £100.[179] An 1807 rate indicates that Godwin was in another partnership operating as Godwin & Co. and occupying a second property owned by Joseph Boon.[180] This was apparently the partnership with Ralph Stevenson which was carried on in Cobridge as Stevenson and Godwin. Their dissolution of partnership occurred on 10 November 1810 and indicated they were indeed 'Earthenware Manufacturers'.[181] The 'Upper Manufactory' was to be carried on by Benjamin Godwin & Sons (Benjamin Endor Godwin and Stephen Godwin) and the 'Lower' one by Ralph Stevenson.[182] By 1813 the property was owned by Jacob Warburton, with Godwin continuing as occupier. The property continued to be listed variously in both Thomas and Benjamin Godwin's names through 1820 in the tax records and in the directories. By 1822 some directories are listing the pottery as Benjamin Godwin and Sons, a partnership which had been in existence since 1810.

In 1815 Thomas and Benjamin Godwin received of Josiah Wedgwood, Esq. 'one pound nine shillings & nine pence being the return of 4 1/2 on the £ from the Dividend made upon [the] Kingswell Estate'.[183]

Some information about the blackwares sold by the Godwins has been discovered by Ann Eatwell and Alex Werner. In 1821 Benjamin Godwin was selling '14 doz. oval black Teapots 21/-', in 1823 '2 doz black teapots 2 patterns 17/-', and in the same year '2 doz oval Black teapots 17/-'.[184]

The partnership was dissolved due to the death of Benjamin Godwin in 1834, the official dissolution being on 15 January.[185] Thomas Godwin paid rates on three ovens in 1836-7[186] and appears to have continued in business until 1854.[187] No blackwares have been identified from any of the Godwin manufactories.

William Greatbatch, Lower Lane, Fenton, Staffordshire, c.1762-82
The small basalt production of William Greatbatch was identified during the excavation of the Greatbatch waste tip in Fenton in 1979. In a recent book on the potter entitled *William Greatbatch, A Staffordshire Potter*,[188] David Barker states: 'The basalt sherds from the Greatbatch site suggest that this was never an important line for him and that he steered clear of vases and other ornamental wares'.[189] Greatbatch wares appear to have been largely unadorned tea and coffee wares (Figure 222). Of the five black basalt sherds recovered from the site the only embellishment is one piece with an undulating reeded pattern and one finial with a partial widow knop. Barker dates all these wares from 1770 to 1782. The recognizable forms are either cylindrical or round bodied and the only markings are impressions of an initialled seal mark in the base of one of the teapot sherds (Figure 222). No extant pieces have yet been associated with the pottery.

Greens, Bingley & Co. *see* **Swinton Pottery**

S. Greenwood, Fenton, Staffordshire, c.1770-80
Nothing is known of this manufacturer. Jewitt indicates that a potter named Greenwood was operating in Fenton from about 1770 to 1780 but gives no other information. Were it not for the existence of a black basalt vase in the British Museum (Figure 223), the Greenwood name would be relegated to oblivion. The very handsome vase is not unlike those produced by Wedgwood and Bentley and Palmer and Neale, if a bit heavier and slightly more awkward in execution. Grant

feels the one distinguishing, perhaps unique, feature in the Greenwood vase is the band of oak leaves at the shoulder.[190]
Mark: S. GREENWOOD

Hackwood, Dimmock & Company, Hanley, Staffordshire, c.1802-27; **William Hackwood** 1827-43
William Hackwood, Thomas Dimmock and James Keeling were in a partnership producing earthenwares and china in the first quarter of the nineteenth century. Black basalt was among various wares produced by the pottery although not stated in any directory descriptions of the firm's output. Although the dissolution of partnership for the three did not occur until 1827,[191] the 1818 directory lists 'Hackwood, Dimmock & Co. earthenware Manufacturing' and James Keeling as 'earthenware manufactrs. Hanley'. According to the *Parson's & Bradshaw Directory* (1818), James Keeling was involved in another manufacturing business of his own in New Street, Hanley. After the dissolution of the partnership William Hackwood, jun. was responsible for the debts incurred by the firm[192] and apparently continued in the business until 1843.[193] William Hackwood is listed in 1836-7 as paying rates on four ovens and Hackwood and Keeling on five ovens in Hanley,[194] but little else is known of the businesses after that.

Another Dimmock, Timothy Dimmock, was involved with the firm. A letter to Josiah Wedgwood, Esq. from Hackwood, Dimmock and Co. in 1813 and signed by Timothy Dimmock requested from Wedgwoods '6 blk Hedge hog crocus pots...knowing no other in the trade that manufactures them...'[195]

Although Grant was not very complimentary about the quality of Hackwood basalt calling it 'gritty, grey, refusing polish',[196] the examples which are illustrated (Figures 224-227) here do not adhere to that deprecation. The wares were competently potted and utilized most of the decorative techniques available at the time, from engine turning and rouletting to sprig-moulded relief. Far from being gritty, the surfaces of most Hackwood basalt are smooth and pleasant to the eye as well as the touch. The mark includes the impressed **HACKWOOD** or **HACKWOOD & CO.** often plus a number. One milk jug in the Temple Newsam House collection is impressed **HACKWOOD 80**.[197]
Marks: HACKWOOD; HACKWOOD & CO. (often including a number, '**24**', '**30**', '**36**', etc.)

John and Ralph Hall, Sytch Pottery, Burslem, Staffordshire, 1802-22; Swan Bank Works, Tunstall, Staffordshire, c.1811-22; **Ralph Hall**, Swan Bank Works 1822-49
Although no black basalt has been identified as having been manufactured by any of the Hall potteries, an invoice in the Horace Collamore papers at the Baker Library Harvard University from John and Ralph Hall 26 December 1815 lists among the many earthenware items '1 doz. Blk Glazed Teapots' and '2/3 doz. Black Teapots'.[198]

Hall is listed in the Burslem tax records as owning and occupying property from 1812. On 1 January 1822 John Hall of Burslem and Ralph Hall of Tunstall dissolved their partnership.[199] Ralph Hall continued to operate the Swan Bank Works, Tunstall and reputedly produced excellent quality blackwares as well as other earthenwares.[200]

Figure 224 Sugar box and cover (not mate), round-bodied with engine-turned basketweave decoration, raised crimped neck, sibyl finial. Mark: **HACKWOOD 36**, *Hackwood, Dimmock & Co., Hanley, c.1810, 4⅝in. high. Royal Ontario Museum, 970.242.55, Brown collection.*

Figure 223. Vase (minus cover) with classical swags pendant rams head simulated handles and draped over a central rosette medallion. The shoulder has a band of oak leaves and the base has vertical sprigged leaf embellishment. Mark: **S.GREENWOOD**, *c.1775-85, 9⅜in. high. British Museum, K30, Franks collection.*

Ralph Hammersley, High Street Works, Tunstall, Staffordshire, c.1860-88
According to Jewitt, Hammersley produced 'common jet' wares but none of these has been identified.[201]

Ralph Harding, Shelton, Staffordshire, c.1822
Judging from the shapes of the few pieces of black basalt impressed **HARDING** it seems likely they were produced in the 1820s. Ralph Harding was listed in the 1822 directory in Shelton and Godden suggests him as a possible potter to have produced the covered sugar (Figure 228).[202] There is another teapot impressed **HARDING** in the Victoria and Albert Museum. Nothing else is known to help define this pottery.
Mark: HARDING

W. & J. Harding, New Hall Works, Hanley, Staffordshire, 1862-72
The only indication that this pottery made blackware comes from a notice in the *Staffordshire Advertiser* on 26 September 1863: 'Wanted, 2 turners to turn boxes, jars, etc., another to work at engine lathe to turn black &c. Apply W.&J.Harding, New Hall Pottery, Hanley'. Nothing else is known about the pottery or its blackwares.

Figure 225. Sugar box and cover, round with diagonal striped pattern and floral band at top and around cover, button knop, c.1810-20, 4in. high. Milk jug with sprig relief of Amalgamation of Peace burning the implements of War, c.1810, 5⅛in. high. Marks: both HACKWOOD. Blake collection.

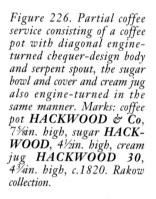

Figure 226. Partial coffee service consisting of a coffee pot with diagonal engine-turned chequer-design body and serpent spout, the sugar bowl and cover and cream jug also engine-turned in the same manner. Marks: coffee pot HACKWOOD & Co, 7⅝in. high, sugar HACKWOOD, 4½in. high, cream jug HACKWOOD 30, 4¾in. high, c.1820. Rakow collection.

Figure 227. Two cream jugs. Left, glazed and moulded with stylized and realistic flowers. Mark: HACKWOOD & Co., c.1815, 3¾in. high. Right, engine-turned with chequered diagonal stripes and sprig-decorated with a floral band. Mark: HACKWOOD 24, c.1820, 4⅝in. high. Rakow collection.

*Figure 228. Sugar bowl and cover elegantly turned and undecorated. Mark: **HARDING**, probably Ralph Harding, Shelton, c.1825, 4in. high. Photograph courtesy Geoffrey Godden.*

John Harrison, Tunstall, Staffordshire, c.1838-41

In his 1843 book *The Borough of Stoke-on-Trent* John Ward named John Harrison as a manufacturer of China toys and black Egyptian. Nothing else is known of this pottery or its wares.

Hartley, Greens & Co., Leeds Pottery, West Yorkshire, c.1781-1830

The pottery, built in 1770, originally operated as Humble, Greens and Company. By 1776 William Hartley was a partner in the firm of Humble, Hartley, Greens and Co. Richard Humble retired in 1781 and the firm traded as Hartley, Greens and Company. From 1785 to 1806 the Leeds partners and Swinton partners agreed to amalgamate the two potteries and John Green seems to have been in charge of both until 1800 when he left the firm. By 1806 the two potteries had separated.[203] Hartley died in 1808[204] and his son William Hartley, jun. took over his father's portion of the partnership until he moved to London in 1820,[205] just after the partners of Hartley, Greens and Co. sold out to merchants and creditors. The pottery continued under new management until it was sold again at auction in 1850.[206] A detailed description of the pottery history can be found in Donald Towner's *The Leeds Pottery* (London: Cory, Adams & Mackay, Ltd., 1963) and *Creamware* (London: Faber & Faber, 1978) and Heather Lawrence's *Yorkshire Pots and Potteries* (Newton Abbot: David & Charles, 1974).

Black basalt was a relatively late introduction into the beautiful creamware repertoire of the Leeds Pottery. *A Drawing Book for Black Ware* was issued in 1800 which included ninety shapes, some identified as Staffordshire in origin, others such as Nos. 4 to 17 correspond to Swinton drawing book shapes and are so identified.

The shapes from Swinton often have animal finials, lions and spaniels, or widow or button finials, whereas the Leeds shapes in the drawing book have either widow

Figure 229. Teapot and cover, the oval shape, No. 30 in the Drawing Book for Black Ware of 1800, *is divided into panels by shepherd's crook columns. The central sprig relief is Hope and Plenty and the cover has a reverse-neck swan finial. Mark:* **LEEDS * POTTERY** *(in footrim), c.1800-20, 6⅞in. high. Gunson collection.*

Figure 230. Shape No. 30 in the Drawing Book for Black Ware of 1800 *of Hartley, Greens & Co. The manuscript* Drawing Book *is in the Leeds City Art Gallery Library.*

Figure 231. Teapot (minus cover), shape No. 41 in the Drawing Book *(note that applied portions, such as handles, spouts and finials do not always correspond to the drawings in the original). The oval body is finely fluted with horizontal and vertical engine-turned decoration. A band of leaves is at the shoulder and the teapot would have had a cover with a widow finial (see Figure 232). Mark:* **LEEDS * POTTERY** *impressed twice. c.1800-20, 4¾in. high. Temple Newsam House 16.290/47.*

Figure 232. Shape No. 41 in the Drawing Book for Black Ware of 1800, *Hartley, Greens & Co., Leeds.*

finials, swan or floral knops. The reverse neck swan finial found on some Eastwood basalt is also seen on some Leeds blackware (Figure 229). No other animal finials or sibyl finials seem to have come from the Leeds repertory itself.

Teawares often follow exactly drawing book prototypes, but handles, spouts and finials, all easily interchanged, can vary. The teapot in the Norwich Museum (Figure 235) is identical to No. 86 in the *Drawing Book* except for the finial which is found commonly on Leeds blackwares and can be seen on numerous teapots in the *Drawing Book* as well as on No. 81 (Figure 233).

In an effort to make their wares competitive, the Leeds Pottery was in communication with Wedgwood as early as 1789 consulting their price list and offering Wedgwood a copy of the Leeds prices. Regarding the Leeds price list Josiah Wedgwood responded to Mr. Fesquit with the following remark: 'You will have observed…that my prices are somewhat higher….My manufactures are of a superior

Figure 233. Teapot and cover, a London-shaped teapot which one would have been tempted to date later if it were not in the Drawing Book for Black Ware of 1800 (shape No. 81). Mark: **LEEDS POTTERY**, *c.1800-20, 6⅛in. high. Castle Museum, Norwich, Miller collection.*

Figure 234. Shape No. 81 in the Drawing Book for Black Ware of 1800, *Hartley, Greens & Co., Leeds.*

Figure 235. Teapot and cover, shape No. 86 in the Drawing Book. *This is very similar to earthenwares produced by the Don Pottery. However, if a careful comparison is made with the earthenware examples (illustrated No. 1375, Miller, An Anthology of British Teapots), the evidence is weighted in favour of a Leeds attribution which corresponds exactly (except for the finial) with the Drawing Book (see Figure 236). Unmarked (incised '26'), Hartley, Greens & Co, Leeds, c.1800-20, 7¼in. high. Castle Museum, Norwich, Miller collection.*

Figure 236. Shape No. 86 in the Drawing Book for Black Ware of 1800, *Hartley, Greens & Co., Leeds.*

kind'.[207] Apparently, the Leeds Pottery continued in communication with Wedgwoods and attempted to some extent to observe the Prices Current maintained by the Staffordshire pottery industry. In 1817 Hartley, Greens & Co. wrote to Wedgwood thanking them for the latest copy of the Prices Current and apologized for not having one of their own to pass on in return: 'We have hitherto managed to make the Prices agreed upon by you in 1814 go down, except in a few instances we have allowed an extra amount of a few pence'.[208]

Stylistically Hartley and Greens' basalt seems to be rather restricted in dates from about 1800 to around 1820, or a little later. Since Hartley left the business in 1820, it would stand to reason that nothing with the impressed mark **HARTLEY, GREENS & CO.** *could* be later than 1820. However, many blackwares simply bear the impressed mark **LEEDS POTTERY**. These may have been produced after 1820, after Hartley's departure, but it is not a reliable dating tool as some pieces of the same form, for example teapots of shape No. 87 in the *Drawing Book* (Figure 237), can be found bearing either signature. It appears that the Leeds Pottery utilized the same designs issued in the *Drawing Book* for a considerable period, from

Figure 237. Milk jug and teapot and cover, shape No. 87 in the Drawing Book. This is a famous Leeds Pottery mould seen in many other bodies, including those decorated with lustre. The London shape has prominent strawberry moulded decoration. There are nine plaster blocks for the strawberry moulding from the pottery at Temple Newsam House. The teapots are found with both the Hartley Greens imprimateur or the simple Leeds Pottery impressed mark. Mark: both **HARTLEY GREENS & Co. LEEDS POTTERY**, c.1800-20, teapot 5⅛in. high, milk jug 4in. high. Temple Newsam House, Leeds, 1905.1, 4.107/46, teapot Hollings collection.

Figure 238. Shape No. 87 in the Drawing Book for Black Ware of 1800, Hartley, Greens & Co., Leeds.

Figure 239. Teapot with hinged cover, nearly identical in form to No. 29 (Figure 240) in the Blackware Drawing Book of Hartley, Greens and Co. This teapot is distinguished only by its finial, a stylized floral knop instead of a swan. A curious mark in relief (Figure 239a) is previously unrecorded leaving this piece open to speculation, possibly Hartley, Greens & Co., c.1800-10, 7in. high. The Board of Trustees of the National Museums & Galleries on Merseyside (Liverpool Museum), 1313M, Mayer collection.

Figure 239a. Mark for teapot in Figure 239.

168

Figure 240. Shape No. 29 in the Drawing Book for Black Ware of 1800, *Hartley, Greens & Co., Leeds.*

Figure 241. Cream jug. This relates to shape No. 29 in the Drawing Book. *The central relief is the Bourbonnais Shepherd. Mark:* **LEEDS * POTTERY**, *c.1800-20, 4½in. high. Temple Newsam House, 11.102/69.*

Figure 242. Three sugar boxes. Left relates to Drawing Book No. 29. Unmarked, Hartley, Greens & Co., 5in. high. Centre relates to shape No. 38 in the Drawing Book. Mark: **LEEDS * POTTERY**, 4⅞in. high. Right is a variation of shape No. 35. Mark: **LEEDS . POTTERY**, 4⅜in. high. All c.1800-20. Temple Newsam House, Leeds, 4.101/46; 4.96/46; 4.62/46, Hollings collection.

Figure 243. Teapot, cover and stand, No. 79 in the Drawing Book, the central panel depicts the Amalgamation of Peace burning the implements of War. Mark: on both teapot and stand **LEEDS * POTTERY**, c.1800-20, 6½in. high. Rakow collection.

Figure 244. Cream jug, of oval shape, a variation of teapot shape No. 79. Mark: **HARTLEY GREENS & Co. LEEDS POTTERY**, c.1800-20, 4⅞in. high. Rakow collection.

Figure 245. Teapot and cover, shape No. 35 in the Drawing Book. The oval teapot has the central depiction of the Amalgamation of Peace burning the implements of War. Mark: **LEEDS . POTTERY** plus an incised 'X', c.1800-20, 6⅛in. high. Temple Newsam House, 4.91/46, Hollings collection.

Figure 246. Cream jug, oval shape relates to No. 47 in the Drawing Book. Mark: **LEEDS * POTTERY**, *c.1800-20, 4in. high. Blake collection.*

Figure 247. Waste bowl, with basketweave lower third, wide fluted mid band and upper band of applied leaves. Mark: **LEEDS.POTTERY** *on inside foot, c.1790-1820, 3in. x 5⅞in. Temple Newsam House, 4.108/46, Hollings collection.*

Figure 248. Tea cup and saucer of the same pattern as the bowl in Figure 247. Mark: saucer: **HARTLEY GREENS & Co.**, *c.1790-1820, saucer 5⅞in. diameter, cup 2¾in. high. Rakow collection.*

Figure 249. Tea cup and saucer, with fine ribbed body. Mark: **HARTLEY GREENS & Co. LEEDS POTTERY**, *c.1790-20, saucer 6in. diameter, cup 2½in. high. Rakow collection.*

Figure 250. Teapot and cover (not mate) corresponding to shape No. 22 in the Drawing Book. Mark: **LEEDS.POTTERY**, c.1800-20, 4¾in. high. Temple Newsam House, 4.102/46, Hollings collection.

Figure 251. Tea canister of round form with engine-turned chequered decoration. Mark: **LEEDS. POTTERY**, c.1800-20, 4in. high. Mint Museum of Art, Delhom collection.

Figure 252. Two mugs (probably for chocolate), both of which are thrown in a cylindrical form. The mug on the left has an engine-turned chequer-pattern similar to several teapots in the Drawing Book for Black Ware, particularly Nos. 56, 68, and 70. The right-hand mug has applied relief decoration which relates to teapot shape No. 86 (see Figure 236). Marks: Left, unmarked, Hartley, Greens & Co., Leeds; right, **HARTLEY GREENS & Co, LEEDS POTTERY**, both c.1800-20, both 2½in. high. Temple Newsam House, 4.69/46; 4.70/46, Hollings collection.

Figure 253. Hot milk jug and cover (left) with fine basket-weave engine-turning to base and sprigged leaf border near the neck. The cover has a widow finial. Mark: **LEEDS * POTTERY**, c.1800-20, 5⅛in. high. Jug (centre) with engine-turned diagonal chequered pattern to lower half. Mark: **LEEDS * POTTERY**, c.1800-20, 4¼in. high. Jug (right) with fluted body. Mark: **TURNER**, c.1790, 4½in. high. Gunson collection.

172

Figure 254. Three milk jugs of baluster shape. Marks: all **LEEDS . POTTERY**, *c.1790-1820, left and centre 5¼in. high, right 4⅞in. high. Temple Newsam House, 4.105/46; 4.93/46; 11.103/ 69. Hollings collection.*

Figure 255a. Mark on coffee pot in Figure 255.

Figure 255. Coffee pot (minus cover), press-moulded, similar in form and decoration to those produced at Eastwood by William Baddeley. This coffee pot is marked: **HARTLEY GREENS & Co. LEEDS * POTTERY** *on the outside footrim (see Figure 255a), c.1810-20, 9½in. high. Robertshaw collection.*

1800 to 1820 or later. From time to time the wares resemble some made by other Staffordshire potteries, particularly Eastwood and J. Glass, Hanley. One teapot in the Merseyside Museum, Liverpool, has a curious raised cursive double L, or H (Figures 239 and 239a) mark on the base. It is almost identical in shape and decoration to *Drawing Book* shape No. 29, save for the finial which is a knop, not a swan. Similarly shaped teapots (Figure 219) exist marked **J.GLASS HANLEY**, the difference being in the handle and spout. The body is identical in both cases to that of *Drawing Book* shape No. 29. The case is only slightly weighted in favour of Leeds being the manufacturer over Glass, or perhaps there was yet another firm adding to the confusion?

A small group of blackwares (Figures 351-356) have tentatively been identified as the products of the Leeds revival firm of James Wraith Senior and John Morton. For further discussion of these *see* **Senior & Morton**.
Marks: HARTLEY, GREENS & CO., LEEDS * POTTERY;
LEEDS.POTTERY

Figure 256. Coffee pot (minus cover), press-moulded, similar to the one in Figure 255, but with slight variations in applied relief on the body and handle. The central panel depicts Hope and Plenty. Mark: **LEEDS.POTTERY**, c.1800-20, 8¼in. high. Temple Newsam House, 4.81/46, Hollings collection.

Figure 257. Coffee pot and cover, thrown in a pear-shaped form with basketweave engine-turning to base and scroll and urn applied relief decoration. There is a raised, crimped gallery and a domed basketweave cover with a widow finial. The scroll and urn relief decoration are seen on three teapots (Nos. 17, 31, 83) in the Drawing Book. Unmarked, Hartley, Greens & Co, Leeds Pottery, c.1790-1820, 10⅝in. high. Temple Newsam House, 4.79/46, Hollings collection.

Figure 258. Coffee pot and cover, thrown, pear-shaped with engine-turned chevron decoration to body, acanthus leaf-moulding to spout and domed ribbed cover with widow finial. Mark: **LEEDS . POTTERY**, c.1790-1820, 9⅛in. high. Temple Newsam House, 4.97/46, Hollings collection.

Figure 259. Coffee pot and cover, thrown pear-shaped coffee pot with applied acanthus leaves at base and sprig decoration of Hope and Plenty. The domed cover has a band of leaves and a matt ground. Mark: **LEEDS. POTTERY**, c.1790-1820, 9⅛in. high. Temple Newsam House, 4.80/46, Hollings collection.

*Figure 260. Pair vases, polished basalt with satyr head handles, laurel swag, and bacchanalian boys relief decoration. The prototype for these vases may have been the one produced by Turner (Figure 261) in white stoneware. Mark: **HERCULANEUM '2'** impressed inside upper lip of both and also in the white stoneware bases (not shown), c.1800-10, 12¼in. high. Rakow collection.*

Herculaneum Pottery, Liverpool, Merseyside, 1796-1840

The Herculaneum Pottery was started in the last days of 1796 by Samuel Worthington and immediately boasted sixty employees, forty of whom had transplanted themselves from Staffordshire to accept the job.[209] By 14 January 1797 Worthington had taken out an insurance policy on the pottery, located at Harrington[210] (Toxteth) totalling £2700.[211] The manufacture never featured basalt as a strong suit for earthenware destined for the American market was the principal objective. The Herculaneum warehouse became a major depot for Staffordshire potteries sending wares to America. Potteries such as William Adams of Cobridge, J. & E. Baddeley, John Barker, Hackwood, Dimmock & Co, Hicks & Meigh, Thomas Holland, James Keeling, Lockett & Co., Minton, Shorthose & Heath, Spode, Wood & Caldwell and Yates were but some of the basalt-producing manufacturers who were using the factory for shipping to North America. In spite of the concentration on earthenwares, during the 1800 to 1810 period a number of fine quality stonewares, including some Egyptian black, were manufactured. The formula was a fairly standard one: 100 blue clay, 60 ochre, 40 magnas [manganese], 20 iron scales.[212] Although very little Herculaneum basalt survives, the quality of the body and the execution of the modelling can be almost startlingly sophisticated. The vases in the Rakow collection (Figure 260) are examples of such subtle execution as to rank them high on the scale of basalt vases in general. However, the prototype may have been ones produced by Turner (Figure 261) which in all likelihood antedate the Herculaneum examples. In any case the Turner caneware vase is of a finer breed yet and although it is impossible to tell the date it seems reasonable to assume that Turner being the older, bigger brother, and a major stoneware manufacturer, may have spawned the modeller who translated his work to Liverpool. Other Herculaneum vases exist (Figure 262) which do not demonstrate the skill manifest in the Rakow pair but which are classically pleasing and tolerably well executed. The body manufactured by the pottery is

Figure 261. Vase in caneware with octagonal polished basalt plinth. The relief decoration is identical to the vases in Figure 260. Mark: TURNER, c.1790-1810, 13¼in. high. Rakow collection.

Figure 262. Vase with scroll handles and band of Greek key relief at shoulder. The central relief is Boys and Goat. The texture is dull, with a graphite appearance. Mark: HERCULANEUM, c.1790-1810, 14½in. high. City Museum and Art Gallery, Stoke-on-Trent, 2645.

variable, often tending to a harsh aspect and gritty texture, but the forms inevitably please. Nevertheless, the output of basalt was either minuscule, the survival low, or most unmarked, because the few known examples can be counted in single digits (Figures 260 and 262-5). The Herculaneum pottery may have made portrait busts. Smith illustrates a bust of Nelson[213] which may have been produced at Toxteth.
Mark: HERCULANEUM

Hicks & Meigh, Hill Street, Shelton, Staffordshire, 1803-22; **Hicks, Meigh & Co**. (or **Hicks, Meigh & Johnson**) 1822-35

The partnership of Richard Hicks and Job Meigh, which after 1822 included a third partner named Johnson, was not one commonly associated with the production of black basalt. The firm's products included a range of earthenware, ironstone, and china popularly associated with the early years of the nineteenth century. However, an invoice discovered by Ann Eatwell and Alex Werner indicated that the firm was producing 'black china' in the period from 1811 to 1813.[214] One can only surmise that blackware was manufactured before and after those dates as well. Although the firm was a large one, employing some 600 hands in the 1830s,[215] no black basalt has been identified with the pottery.

Figure 263. Sugar box and cover, oval with basketweave moulded body and a central reserve oval panel depicting Venus on her shell being transported by dolphins. Mark: **HERCULANEUM**, *c.1805-10, 5½ in high. City Museum and Art Gallery, Stoke-on-Trent.*

Figure 264. Cream jug of oval form, the cartouche flanked by a spray of foliage tied at the base by a bow. The central panel has a relief of the Dipping of Achilles while the reverse depicts the Sacrifice to Hygeia. Mark: **HERCULANEUM**, *c.1800-10, 4½in. high. Rakow collection.*

Fig, 265. Oval medallion of Mary Queen of Scots in a basalt oval frame. The medallion is creamware with a polychrome transfer print of Mary Queen of Scots. Both frame and medallion are impressed **HERCULANEUM**, *c.1805, 6⅛in. high. Mint Museum of Art, Delhom collection.*

Thomas Holland, Burslem, Staffordshire, c.1774-1815; **Ann Holland & Co**. c.1815-1840s or later

Holland was a manufacturer of black basalt wares over a considerable period of time, but, once again no blackwares are attributable to his pottery. In fact, no wares of any kind have surfaced with the Holland imprimatur.

The earliest documentation of the existence of this pottery is an invoice dated August 1774 indicating Thomas Holland sold wares to Mr. Joseph and Thomas Wedgwood.[216] Both the 1784 *Bailey's Directory* and the 1787 Tunnicliff Directory listed Holland as a 'Manufacturer of black and red-China Ware and Gilder'. Holland made his appearance late in the Burslem tax records, not until 1805 when he is listed until 1815 as renting property from a Mr. Thacker. Holland must have died around 1815 because in 1816 the same property was occupied by John Davenport for one year before being put back in the name of the Holland family. Mrs. Holland is listed as occupying the property in 1817, and 1819.

Meanwhile, in 1809, before his death, Holland was selling to 'Messrs Wedgwood: 20 10 Groce Trials — 0.10.0.'[217]

By 1822 the directories listed the factory as Ann Holland & Co. and either 'shining black Manufacturers' or ' black earthenware Manufacturers'. A recipe for Thomas Holland's shining black glaze was passed on to Mr. T. Simpson of Hanley through Henry Steel in 1815. It is the following:

60 lbs Litharge
18 lbs Flint
11 lbs Manganese
18 quarts White Slip, not too thin[218]

Evidently, some time after the death of Thomas Holland, Ann Holland took John Pearson of Burslem into partnership and the firm traded as Holland & Pearson until the dissolution of their partnership on 25 March 1831. The business, carried on by Ann Holland,[219] was still operating in 1843.[220]

Samuel Hollins, Vale Pleasant, Shelton, Staffordshire, c.1769 to early 19th century

Samuel Hollins was a major figure in the potteries in the late eighteenth century about whom only fragments are known. His pottery, located on the Cauldon Canal in Vale Pleasant, was a large and apparently prosperous one and Hollins was an esteemed member of the Potteries community. He was a member, rising to Mayor in 1796,[221] of the Mock Corporation of Hanley formed by the élite citizens of the district.[222] Certainly the name of Samuel Hollins is principally associated with his partnership in the New Hall Porcelain Works, also located in Shelton. However, judging from the few surviving examples attributable to Hollins, he was an importantly competent potter in his own right.

All the directories refer to Samuel Hollins simply as a 'potter' in Shelton. It is not known when the pottery began but one Hollins pottery was calling for nearly a dozen handlers in 1769.[223] Invoices in the Wedgwood archives indicate that by 1777 Wedgwood was 'buying in' from Samuel Hollins in such quantities that the listings for the wares, which were all 'octagon-shaped', filled several pages of paper.[224]

In 1797 he was one of the active partners in the Potters Clay Company Co-

Figure 266. Coffee pot and cover, pear-shaped with fine basket-weave base and domed cover with Mother and child finial. The sprigged central relief depicts the Death of General Wolfe and Mercury. The late owner of the piece attributed it to Samuel Hollins on the basis of the finial and the depiction of the Death of Wolfe. Unmarked, c.1790-1800, about 11½in. high. Robertshaw collection.

partnership formed co-operatively to buy clay directly from the manufacturers without third party intervention.[225]

Wedgwood and Hollins were producing in tandem, an arrangement not unusual in the potteries where one needed to call on a competitor to fill out an order to a customer or dealer. In 1798, dealer James Collison from Leicester, inquired of the Wedgwood Company about manufacturing replacement pieces for a service purchased from Samuel Hollins[226] and in 1801 Messrs Wedgwood and Co. bought 'red China Teapots, Bowles, Sugar Boxes and Cream Ewers' from Samuel Hollins.[227] In 1805 and 1806 Samuel Hollins was supplying wares to London Staffordshire warehouseman Thomas Wyllie.[228]

One can get an idea of the extent of Samuel Hollins' holdings in Shelton through a description of his insurance policy held by the Salop Fire Insurance Office:

> Samuel Hollins of Shelton, Potter. House £50. House and stables in the tenure of (?) Goodwin £100; Snape's house and bakehouse £35; seven dwellings £105; Brewhouse £10. Large quadrangle range of workshops and warehouses £500; Second range of workshops and hovels £200; third range of clay and crate warehouses £100; Stock in quadranglar range £800; Stock in second range £50; Utensils and working tools in all buildings £200. Fixtures therein £100; Mr. Hollins' household goods £260; His wearing apparel £40; Total £3000, 13 December 1790.[229]

By 1808, when another policy was taken out, Samuel Hollins had insured the quadrangle workshops and warehouses 'in occupation of Messrs. T. Hollins Junior and Co.'[230] One assumes that by that time Samuel Hollins was retired from the active business of potting. He died in 1820.[231]

Hollins also operated a London emporium in partnership with William Sutton in St. Paul's Churchyard where they were described as 'dealers in earthenware'.[232] The partnership dissolved in 1793 and nothing more is known of the business.[233]

Hollins is principally associated with the superb refined dark red stoneware impressed with his name. However, he also produced excellent stoneware in other unusual colours, such as teal. One teapot produced by J. Glass, Hanley (Figure 214), has a nearly identical twin marked Hollins in drabware with blue enamel decoration. Both are in the Rakow collection and in writing about them the Rakows suggest that Samuel Hollins might be the originator of the Venus and Cupid finial, the one feature which distinguishes the Hollins teapot from the one produced by Glass.[234]

On the strength of the Rakow paper several collectors attribute black basalt pieces in their collections to Samuel Hollins, one such example being the very fine coffee

pot in Figure 266. However, a caution is required. There are no known marked Samuel Hollins black basalt wares; nevertheless, it seems extremely likely he was a manufacturer as he was making and marking other coloured stonewares.
Mark: S.HOLLINS; HOLLINS

T.& J. Hollins, Keeling Lane, Far Green, Shelton, Staffordshire, c.1792-1820; **T.J.& R. Hollins** c.1818-22
The 1800 Map of Hanley (Figure 135) shows the pottery of Thomas and John Hollins as located on the north side of Keeling Lane in the Far Green area of Hanley. There is some uncertainty about when Thomas Hollins the Younger took over Samuel Hollins' pottery but it must have been in the last years of the 1790s. The family were apparently operating another pottery in Hanley in 1792 as an insurance policy was taken out by: 'Messrs. Hollins and Sons of Hanley, Potters. Sett of Pottworks in one connected range...' (£1350 total).[235] Two policies were taken out on 15 July 1808 on the pottery in Shelton, formerly occupied by Samuel Hollins. The descriptions differ substantially enough from the 1792 policy to confirm that the two 1808 policies are describing another potbank entirely. It is worth reproducing them:

> Samuel Hollins of Shelton, Esq. His dwelling house in his own occupation £500. His household goods and other insurable property therein £300. His dwellings house and two stables adjoining in the occupation of Goodwin £100. His dwelling house and bakehouse adjoining in the occupation of — Snape £35. His quadrangular range of workshops and warehouses in the occupation of Messrs. Thomas Hollins Junior and Company £500. His second range of workshops and Hovels in the occupation of said Messrs. T. Hollins Junior and Co. His third range of clay and crate warehouses (also in their occupation) £100. His seven dwelling houses adjoining (under one roof) £105. Total £1840.[236]

> Messrs. Thos. Hollins the Younger and Co. of Shelton, Potters. Their stock in trade in their quadrangular range of workshops and warehouses £1500; their stock in trade in their second range of workshops and Hovels £150; their utensils, working tools and fixtures in the two ranges and in a third range of clay and crates warehouses thereto £350. Total £2000.[237]

Both were taken out on the same day, 15 July 1808. Samuel Hollins was insuring the buildings on his property while his nephew Thomas Hollins, jun., as occupier, was insuring the stock and utensils. If these two insurance policies are compared with the one Samuel Hollins took out in 1790 (*see* entry for Samuel Hollins), it is evident that Thomas Hollins, jun. was occupying the former pottery of his uncle. Thomas and John were also operating the smaller pottery, probably owned by their father, on the Keeling Road in Far Green.
Certainly Thomas Hollins, jun. was manufacturing black basalt. Invoices exist in 1810 to 1812 which confirm that Hollins was selling 'black Dutch teapots, handld teas black' (could be black printed).[238] Unfortunately, this is another case where there are no identifiable blackwares from the manufactory.

By 1818 the directories began listing the pottery as 'Hollins, Thomas, John and Richard, earthenware Manufacturers, Upper Hanley'. What happened to the Vale Pleasant pottery is unknown, as the 'Upper Hanley' designation clearly means the Far Green pottery. Perhaps there were two independent operations for a time, one operated by Thomas Hollins, jun. alone, the other by Thomas and John and eventually Richard.

In 1814 T.J. & R. Hollins hired a Mr. James Potts away from Wedgwood.[239]

By 1819 Richard Hollins appeared to be in financial difficulty and notes of debt began to appear.[240] By 1822 Hollins furthered his indebtedness to Josiah Wedgwood II[241] and after several unsuccessful attempts to collect, Wedgwood finally settled in 1826 by taking his pews in the church in lieu of the debt.[242] Meanwhile, the pottery had succumbed. The dissolution of partnership occurred on 3 June 1822.[243]

Mark: T. & J. HOLLINS

George Hood, Highgate Pottery, Brownhills, Burslem, Staffordshire, c.1831-46
The pottery was established by George Hood in 1831 who purchased the land in 1831 from Mr. Randle-Wilkinson and built the manufactory. It was evidently a fairly large manufactory as George Hood paid rates on seven ovens operating at his pottery in 1836-7.[244] The works changed hands in 1846 when they were bought by William Emberton and thence carried on by his sons after his death in 1867.[245] The only indication that the earlier owner, George Hood, manufactured basalt wares was a listing in Pigot's directory for the firm which indicated they manufactured 'Egyptian black'. No known wares have been identified.

Hyslop-Hall, Cut Bank Pottery, Ouseburn, Newcastle upon Tyne, Northumberland, c.1857
The *Staffordshire Advertiser* 4 April 1857 advertised a small pottery to be let making black and Rockingham teapots, yellow bakers &c. Apply Charles Hyslop, Quayside, or present tenant Mrs. E. Hall, Cut Bank Pottery, Ouse Burn, Newcastle-on-Tyne. Nothing else is known of the pottery or its products.

Jarvis, Wilkinson and Fieldhouse, Longton, Staffordshire, c.1851
The *Staffordshire Advertiser* of 18 October 1851 disclosed the partnership dissolution on 16 October of William Jarvis, Thomas Wilkinson and James Fieldhouse, debts going to James Fieldhouse who was to continue the business with Thomas Minshull (a minor). According to the newspaper the trio were 'manufacturers of Black and Rockingham wares'. The succeeding partnership between Fieldhouse and Minshall lasted only two months before it too was dissolved (*Staffordshire Advertiser*, 3 January 1852 reported the partnership ended 16 December 1851). William Jarvis had been a manufacturer of Egyptian black earlier (*see* William Jarvis). Nothing else is known about this partnership or their products.

William Jarvis, Great Charles Street, Longton, Staffordshire, 1818-32
Pigot's 1822 directory listed William Jarvis as a manufacturer of Egyptian Black. He was subsequently in a partnership manufacturing Black and Rockingham wares with Thomas Wilkinson and James Fieldhouse (*see* above entry). No marked pieces are known.

John Johnson, Tunstall, Staffordshire, c.1834

Pigot's directory of 1834 listed John Johnson of Tunstall as a manufacturer of Egyptian black. John Johnson had been in a previous partnership in the manufacture of earthenware in Burslem with William Godwin and Thomas Rowley operating as Godwin, Rowley and Johnson. That liaison was dissolved in 1832.[246] No known basalt wares from these two potteries have been discovered.

Anthony Keeling, Shelton and Tunstall, Staffordshire, c.1759?-1810; **Anthony and Enoch Keeling**, Tunstall, c.1795-1814

Anthony Keeling was one of the most important potters in Staffordshire in the incipient years of industrialization. He is also one of the most enigmatic in terms of his own wares. Known primarily as one of the original partners in the New Hall Porcelain Works, Keeling was an important potter in his own right, undoubtedly producing porcelain,[247] and acknowledged by the directories as producing 'Egyptian Black'.[248] Frustratingly, no basalt pieces are attributable to this important potter.

Keeling (b.1738) married Enoch Booth's daughter, Ann, in 1760.[249] He was probably involved in some sort of business with Enoch Booth prior to the marriage but by August 1764 he was producing 'fine Blue Teapots' and selling them to Josiah Wedgwood.[250] This must be the so-called Littler's blue salt-glazed teapots and if so, Keeling was prominently producing and selling them to Wedgwood in the following years as well. Geoffrey Godden discovered another invoice in March 1765 which included 6½ dozen 'Mazarine Blue' teapots as well as accompanying other tea-wares.[251] In 1766 Wedgwood continued buying from Keeling.[252] Keeling was operating two potteries, one in Shelton where in *Bailey's Directory* of 1784 he was simply listed as 'potter', and one in Tunstall, where the same directory listed him as a 'Manufacturer of Queen's Ware in general, blue painted and enamelled, Egyptian Black...'

The 'Egyptian Black' and other earthenwares were produced at Tunstall. Burslem Land Tax (which included Tunstall) began being assessed and collected in 1781. Keeling first appears on those records in 1783, but as an owner of property being occupied by a John Davenport. By 1786 Keeling was occupying two properties himself, the one owned by him and previously occupied by John Davenport and another property owned by the Rev'd W. Wright. By 1791 Keeling had sold the property he owned but remained the occupier of the property owned by Wright. The last year Keeling appeared on the Burslem tax list was 1814. Some years the firm was listed as A. & E. Keeling, other years as simply Anthony Keeling. In 1797 Anthony and Enoch Keeling were participating in the Potters Clay Copartnership.[253] Another Keeling, Edward Keeling, who was a partner in one of the china manufacturing businesses with Anthony Keeling, was also on the list. In 1798 Anthony and Enoch Keeling were ordering 'Cornwall clay' from Wedgwood & Byerley, probably for their china manufacturing business in Shelton.[254] A letter in the Wedgwood archives from Anthony Keeling to Thomas Byerley, Esq. dated 9 February 1804 indicated that Keeling was in debt to Wedgwoods and offered Byerley his own share in the Hendra Clay and Stone concern for which he advanced £635 against a portion of the unpaid debt to Wedgwoods. Byerley declined by return post 11 February 1804.[255] Apparently Anthony and Enoch Keeling took a partner into the Tunstall business, a David Ogilvy, jun. The partnership, probably undertaken for financial reasons, was dissolved on 9 September 1809.

> Partnership dissolved between Anthony Keeling, Enoch Keeling and David
> Ogilvy, jun. Potters and China Manufacturers at Tunstall. All persons to pay
> said debts to Anthony Keeling or Enoch Keeling.[256]

It seems prudent to conclude that the Keelings were in business in Tunstall until
1809, or possibly receiving debts until 1810, yet they remain on the tax records
through 1814. It appears that Anthony Keeling gave up potting as his business was
leased to Robert Winter until 1812, when Keeling advertised the works and his
house to be let.[257] By March 1814 Keeling's house and effects were advertised to be
auctioned on account of 'changing his residence'.[258] This was occasioned by his move
to Liverpool where he died 14 January 1815, aged seventy-six.[259]

Up to this point the history has concerned the activities in Tunstall which mainly
constituted the earthenware portions of the business, but possibly some china
production as well. (The dissolution of partnership in 1809 described the partners as
'Potters and China Manufacturers'.) However, Geoffrey Godden has discovered
another dissolution of partnership notice in the *London Gazette* which was formed
between Anthony Keeling, Samuel Perry, Edward Keeling, John Shorthose, Thomas
Heath and Thomas Shelley in Hanley for the production of china. This firm dissolved on 11 November 1792.[260]

Although this partnership does not actually concern a study of the basalt
producing potters, it is useful in shedding light on the extent of the activities of
Anthony Keeling. Edward Keeling, one of the partners, who potted at Hanley from
at least 1781, sold his pottery in 1804. James Keeling of Keeling, Toft & Co.
succeeded Edward Keeling (*see* next entry). Anthony Keeling died in Liverpool in
1815.

As mentioned, no known basalt wares have been identified from the Anthony
Keeling or A. & E. Keeling manufactory.

Edward and Joseph Keeling, Keeling Lane, Hanley, Staffordshire, c.1787-1804
The 1787 directory listed Edward Keeling of Hanley as a potter. He was apparently
in another partnership with Joseph Keeling but little is known of their manufactory
or their wares. A notice in the *Staffordshire Advertiser* of 8 December 1804
constitutes nearly the total knowledge available about the pottery:

> To be let or sold, potworks in holding of Joseph Keeling, Keelings's Lane,
> declining on account of ill health-earthenware mfy., 'particularly in the
> Egyptian Black line' and a house in the possession of Edward Keeling
> adjoining-apply him or Tomlinson [solicitor].

Staffordshire Advertiser of 31 August 1805:

> Auction 30 tons black clay, flint &c., property of Joseph Keeling, at his mfy.,
> Keeling's Lane, Hanley.

Little is known about their wares although there is one bowl (Figure 267) in the

Figure 267. Waste bowl with applied relief of Domestic Employment, Sportive Love. Mark: *JOSEPH KEELING O*, c.1790-1800, 3¼in. high. Victoria & Albert Museum, 2638-1901.

Figure 268. Teapot and cover, in the popular beehive shape with engine-turned diagonal stripes and sibyl finial to cover. Mark: *KEELING TOFT & CO.*, c.1800-15, 5⅝in. high. Royal Ontario Museum, 970.242.67, Brown collection.

Figure 269. Sugar bowl (minus cover), pear-shaped with a spreading foot and lion mask simulated handles; the sugar is engine-turned with a diagonal striped pattern. Mark: *KEELING TOFT & Co.*, c.1800-15, 3⅜in. high. Royal Ontario Museum, 970.242.5, Brown collection.

Victoria and Albert Museum which Grant described as of 'dull, poor workmanship' and design, marked **JOSEPH KEELING O**, which stands as the sole identifying product of their manufactory.[261]

Keeling, Toft & Co., Hanley, Staffordshire, late 18th century to 1824-27?

Keeling, Toft & Company was a large and complicated manufactory which, by the early years of the nineteenth century, was probably operating from four sites in Hanley. One site was the former Mellor works on the south side of Old Hall Road as it becomes Hill Street. The 1800 Map of Hanley (Figure 135) shows this property as being occupied by Mrs. Mellor. By 1802 an insurance policy indicated that Keeling, Toft and Company were occupying the Mellor pottery.[262] If the pottery was listed in Mrs. Mellor's name in 1800 William Mellor was probably deceased by that time, and William Mellor was one of the original partners in Keeling, Toft and Company. The partnership, therefore, probably predates 1800. The other original partners were: James Keeling, Thomas Toft, Philip Keeling, John Howe, Samuel Hatton and Thomas Dimmock. John Howe retired in 1801 and Samuel Wright and James Graves were added to the firm. All this information is detailed in the dissolution of partnership notice in the *London Gazette* published on 16 September 1806.[263] The firm was listed as being 'manufacturers of Porcelain and Earthenware'.

James Keeling was operating another pottery nearby on the east side of New

Figure 270. Teapot and cover, round-bodied with parapet, the whole being decorated with wide satin-stripes. The cover has a sibyl finial of the Wedgwood type. Mark: **KEELING TOFT & Co.**, *c.1800, 5⅜in. high. Gunson collection.*

Figure 271. Milk jug en suite with teapot in Figure 270. Mark: **KEELING TOFT & Co.**, *c.1800, 5¼in. high. Gunson collection.*

Figure 272. Two teapots and covers with cylindrical bodies engine-turned at the base decorated with the Amalgamation of Peace burning the implements of War. The left-hand teapot has a widow finial, the right-hand one a sibyl. Mark: both **KEELING TOFT & Co.**, *c.1800, 5¼in. high and 6½in. high. Rakow collection.*

Street from some time before 1800. In 1801 he insured his potworks, listed as 'an earthenware manufactory' for £600.[264] By 1807-8 Keeling, Toft & Co. were also tenants of James Greaves Potworks, the New Pot works on the same property, and another property owned by Samuel Chatterley. An 1802 insurance policy with the Sun Fire Company listed 'Messrs. Keeling, Toft, and Co. of Hanley…earthenware Manufacturers on their stock and utensils in a set of Potworks all communicating…£800'. The 'all communicating' probably referred to the James Greaves and New Potworks on the same property. The Chatterley property was also nearby on the south side of Old Hall Road. The 1818 *Commercial Directory* listed Keeling, Toft & Co. as operating from Charles Street Hanley and James Keeling as continuing to operate the New Street site. To add to the confusion, there were two James Keelings, one of Hanley, the other from Shelton. As can be seen in the dissolution of partnership notice of 1813, both James Keelings were involved in a partnership which, for a time, traded as Keeling, Mayer & Co.[265]

Some time before 1813 Elijah Mayer the Younger had joined the group which by that time consisted of: James Keeling of Shelton, James Keeling, Thomas Toft,

Sampson Wright and Philip Keeling, all of Hanley, Thomas Dimmock of Shelton under Harley, William Hill and John Aston (Executors named in last will of Samuel Hatton ...), Dealers in black glazed earthenware under the firm of Keeling, Mayer & Company, dissolved on 3 November 1813. This appears to be the retail end of the business.

The dissolution of partnership notice appeared in the *London Gazette* on 4 July 1828:

> Notice is hereby given that the Partnership heretofore existing and carried on between James Keeling, Thomas Toft, Thomas Dimmock, Sampson Wright, John Hatton and Philip Keeling, as manufacturers of Earthenware at Hanley...in the firm of Keeling, Toft, and Company was dissolved by mutual consent on the 11th day of November 1824 [*sic*]. All just debts due or owing from the said concern will be received and paid by the said Thomas Toft.
>
> _____30th June 1828...[266]

In 1808 and 1809 James Keeling was sending wares down to London Staffordshire warehouseman Thomas Wyllie to be sold under his own name. In 1812 and 1813 Keeling, Toft & Co. were sending their wares to Thomas Wyllie as well.[267] All along (and as late as 1824) James Keeling was taking out insurance policies on his own pottery on New Street and appearing in separate listings as a potter in the directories. That he was one of the two James Keelings involved in the retail business of Keeling, Mayer & Co. is assured, but it is not certain that he was the one also operating as a principal partner in Keeling, Toft & Co. At any rate James Keeling in and of himself is not known for the manufacture of black basalt, whereas Keeling, Toft & Co. most assuredly are. James Keeling was manufacturing stoneware 'octagon eagle Shaped' in 1809-10.[268] These could very well be basalt but could also be feldspathic stoneware.

The tradition of making black basalt was in place at the William Mellor's pottery in Hanley before Keeling, Toft and Company were manufacturing there. Jewitt suggests that both Mellor and Keeling, Toft & Co. manufactured Egyptian black for the Dutch market.[269] Elijah Mayer may have provided the Dutch connection.

The blackware manufactured by the firm incorporated common forms, including the beehive form (Figure 268) which was particularly popular abroad. Beehive teawares were far and away the most frequently sought after single shape in the correspondence to the Wedgwood Company from European merchants from 1791 into the second decade of the nineteenth century. Other more conventional shaped satin striped globular teawares were produced (Figure 270) as well as cylindrical teapots with fluted bases. Widow and sibyl finials continued clearly in demand into the nineteenth century (Figures 270 and 272). The quality was consistent, the body being dense, compact and generally well potted.
Mark: KEELING, TOFT & CO.

Kilnhurst Bridge Pottery, Kilnhurst, South Yorkshire, 1784-1863 or later
Heather Lawrence gives a history of the Kilnhurst Bridge Pottery and mentions that at the sale of the pottery in 1854, transferring the ownership from Charles Robinson to Richard Bedford, the property comprised, among its other buildings, a 'black

kiln'.[270] No known wares of any description have been identified with the Kilnhurst Bridge Pottery but it is likely they were producing black basalt.

Kingfield Pottery, Glasgow, Scotland, late 18th century to early 19th century
Jewitt says that one John Anderson worked this pottery producing eighty dozen black earthenware teapots per week. The ware was unmarked and may not have been Egyptian black stoneware.[271]

Knottingley Pottery, Ferrybridge, West Yorkshire, 1793-present; *see also* **Ralph Wedgwood & Co.**
The Knottingley Pottery, or Ferrybridge Pottery as it is often called, has a long and complicated history. For a complete pottery history the best reference is Heather Lawrence's *Yorkshire Pots and Potteries*. Some few basalt teawares marked **FERRY-BRIDGE** are located in various Yorkshire museums (Figures 426 and 427) and appear from the shape and decoration to be of late eighteenth century or early nineteenth century manufacture, that is, either during, just before, or just after Ralph Wedgwood's tenure in the pottery.

Other well-known potters were also involved in the Ferrybridge works, including John Plowes of the Castleford Pottery. The pottery was large. An insurance policy taken out in its early years indicated that by 1795 they were operating four ovens, four slip or clay houses, and three warehouses and packing chambers.[272]

Further policies taken out in 1801, 1806 and 1813 expanded the coverage on the original premises.

The basalt produced by the Knottingley Pottery at Ferrybridge is a little heavy in its execution and decorated with engine-turned patterns popularly used in both Staffordshire and Yorkshire.
Mark: FERRYBRIDGE

Lakin & Poole, The Hadderidge, Burslem, Staffordshire, 1792-96; **Lakin & Co.**, Bourne's Bank, Burslem, Staffordshire, 1797-99; **Thomas Lakin (& Co.)** Stoke-on-Trent, Staffordshire, c.1810-17
Thomas Lakin produced fine black basalt when in partnership with John Ellison Poole and Thomas Shrigley. An insurance policy on their pottery business in Burslem was taken out on 1 December 1792 totalling £1000.[273] Lakin left the partnership on 31 December 1795 and Poole and Shrigley continued carrying on business[274] in Burslem. Poole paid taxes on two properties in Burslem through 1798; however, no black basalt wares have been specifically associated with the Poole and Shrigley business after Lakin left, although it seems likely they continued to manufacture blackwares at The Hadderidge.

By 1797 Lakin was in business for himself in a smaller manufactory in Burslem at Bourne's Bank insured for £400.[275] This was short lived and by November 1799 the pottery at Bourne's Bank was being advertised for sale.[276] Soon after Lakin was taken into the Davenport business and remained there until the early years of 1810, after which he removed to Stoke and continued potting until about 1818. Lakin spent the last years of his life at the Leeds Pottery and died in 1821.[277] The latter part of the history is attenuated owing to the fact that it probably does not relate to the documented blackware production which seems to have been relegated to the Poole,

Figure 273. Teapot with hinged cover. Quintessentially Lakin and Poole in shape and decoration this is only one of three recorded pieces marked as such. Mark: **POOLE LAKIN & CO**. *impressed in footrim. This narrow oval form was also produced in caneware, and seems to have been employed by Thomas Lakin only when he was in partnership with John Ellison Poole from 1792-95, 5⅝in.high. Blakey collection.*

Figure 274. Teapot and cover, polished basalt boat-shaped body with indistinct animal finial. The shape and general embellishment would lend itself to a Lakin attribution. Mark: large **L** *in relief on base, attributed to Thomas Lakin, c.1795-1800, 6in. high. Castle Museum, Norwich, Miller collection.*

Shrigley partnership with Lakin which marked their wares **POOLE, LAKIN & CO**.

Very few black basalt pieces have survived from this pottery. Both marked and unmarked wares of identical form exist. One teapot (Figure 273) in the Blakey collection marked **POOLE, LAKIN & Co**. has a twin unmarked example in the Gunson collection. Another similarly shaped teapot in the Miller collection in the Castle Museum, Norwich (Figure 274) which resembles all the Lakin and Poole teapot shapes is marked with a large 'L' on the base. It is possible that this teapot is a product of the Bourne Bank period when Lakin was on his own. The shape is appropriate for the 1790s, not a shape from the second period in the nineteenth century when Lakin was also in business for himself. A fine quality vase from the Poole, Lakin and Co. period is in the City Museum and Art Gallery, Stoke-on-Trent (Figure 275). Both the vase and the teapots are an excellent tribute to the talents of a man who seems to have produced an astounding variety of wares in a very few years of manufacture.

Marks: POOLE, LAKIN & Co., 'L'(?), LAKIN (although no blackware has been found with the mark, wares in other bodies are marked simply **LAKIN**).

Jonathan and George Leak, Commercial Street, Burslem, c.1810-14

Jonathan and George Leak were 'Egyptian Black' manufacturers who began advertising the sale of their pottery on Commercial Street in the *Staffordshire Advertiser* by 6 October 1810. The pottery apparently did not sell for it was advertised again on 25 April 1812 to be sold at auction. By 1813 Jonathan and George Leak had formally dissolved their partnership.[278] Once again in 1814 the pottery, described as adjoining the railroad from Sneyd colliery to Burslem Branch canal, was to be auctioned.[279] Jonathan Leak apparently continued in the manufacture of pottery as he is listed in the *Commercial Directory* of 1818, 1819 and 1820 as producing 'Egyptian' in Burslem. Jewitt described Jonathan Leak as 'a clever potter, who after some strange vicissitudes, went to Sydney, where after a time, discovering a valuable bed of clay, he established the first pottery in Australia'.[280] Nothing else is known of the pottery or its products.

Timothy and John Lockett, Burslem, c.1784-1801

There were Lockett pottery enterprises in Longton and in Burslem, the one in

Figure 275a. Coffee pot of ovoid shape with finely reeded lower third of body and domed lid with reverse neck swan finial. Mark: **LOCKETTS & CO.**, *probably George Lockett & Co., c.1805-16, 8in. high. Rakow collection.*

Figure 275b. Mark on coffee pot in Figure 275a.

Figure 275. Vase of ovoid form with engine-turned lower body and interlaced rings at neck. The sprigged relief is Hope and Plenty. This is one of two known vases so marked, the other being in the National Museum of Wales, Cardiff. Mark: **POOLE LAKIN & Co.**, *c.1792-96, 7¾in. high. City Museum and Art Gallery, Stoke-on-Trent.*

Burslem operated by Timothy and John Lockett predating the Longton factories. Timothy and John Lockett were billed as 'White Stone Potters' in *Bailey's* 1784 directory. This is, of course, far from conclusive evidence that they produced black basalt. However, the fact that they were firing at stoneware temperatures combined with marked Lockett examples of black basalt issues an imperative to look into their manufacture. However, there is little evidence to elucidate the argument one way or the other. Indeed, nothing conclusive.

Timothy Lockett was a tax collector in Burslem for the first year the taxes were collected and recorded in 1781.[281] He is listed from 1781 to 1786 as occupying property in Burslem owned by John Richards, which may be a personal residence for Lockett. By 1790, however, Timothy Lockett was occupying two other properties, one owned by himself and another property let by the executors of 'Church Wedgwood', the old, or part of the old, Thomas and Josiah Wedgwood pottery. The confusion lies in the fact that the two properties were both taxed at the same rate — £0.5.6.[282] In 1795 Lockett was listed for the first time as owning the 'Church Wedgwood' property in addition to the other property. Lockett continued to pay land taxes on the two properties through at least 1801. By 1805 Timothy Lockett was no longer personally occupying either site, both of which were let to others. Timothy and John Lockett formally dissolved their business partnership on 7 November 1800[283] which roughly corroborates the land tax research data. John Lockett remains on the Burslem tax records through 1819 paying a very modest rate of £0-1-0.

No basalt has been associated specifically with this pottery. Although there are known examples of basalt wares impressed **LOCKETTS & CO.**, these are probably the products of the Longton Locketts (*see* next entry) who were operating from three sites over a long period.

Lockett & Shaw 1796-1804, King Street, Longton, Staffordshire; **George Lockett & Co.**, King Street, Longton 1805-16; **Lockett, Robinson & Hulme**, King Street, Longton 1816-18; **Lockett & Hulme**, King Street, Longton 1819-26; **John Lockett & Son**, King Street, Longton, 1827-35; **John and Thomas Lockett**, King Street, Longton, 1836-40, King Street and Market Street, 1841-55; **John Lockett**, King Street and Market Street, 1855-post 1865[284]

Besides the King Street and Market Street works, the Locketts potted from Chancery Lane from 1822 to 1858. The King Street works was no. 133 on Allbut's Map of 1802. At the death of John Lockett II (1733-1835) a valuation was made of his property at the King Street works. It included a 'Black Slip House, with slip kiln, ocre ark and tubs, Manganese', etc. This portion of the pottery was known as the 'Top Bank'. The 'Lower Bank' was the Chancery Lane works and was at least in part a repository for stock.[285] John Lockett II was listed in the 1822 directory as 'China, etc. Manufacturer'. Clearly from the description of the pottery site in 1835 the etcetera included the manufacture of 'Egyptian black'. Lockett and Shaw were black manufacturers[286] and Lockett and Hulme were listed as manufacturers of 'Egyptian Black' as well as 'china and earthenware' in the same directory. There are other indications that Lockett and Hulme were manufacturing blackware. Mintons bought black basalt teapots from Locketts between 1803 and 1809.[287] In 1819 they sent to Staffordshire warehouseman Thomas Wyllie in London '3 doz.(24) oblong teapots black basket' and '3 doz. oval black teapots (24) flower basket'.[288] This seems to be a single sale but the descriptions are more complete than many general listings. At the 1862 Exhibition the Locketts showed: '…black Egyptian wares…Egyptian black and black lustre ware-teapots, sugars and creams, in oval and round shapes, of a variety of patterns'.[289] Two marks have been noted and both are very rare: a basalt teapot in the British Museum with white stoneware reliefs is marked **J. LOCKETT**, probably the product of the John Lockett & Son partnership from 1827-35. A basalt teapot (minus cover, Figure 275a) from the Gunson Collection impressed **LOCKETTS & CO.** is a difficult mark to pinpoint. We may never know which of the partnerships so marked their wares, possibly George Lockett & Co..
Marks: LOCKETTS & CO.; J. LOCKETT

Lowesby Pottery, Leicestershire, c.1835-45
According to Jewitt the Pottery at Lowesby was launched by Sir Frederick G. Fowke, Bt. in 1835 and produced vases of distinction. The idea for the pottery was generated from home experimentation by Fowke with the local clay. Determining

*Figure 276. Pair of bottles, gourd-shaped red earthenware with black dip decorated with exuberant flowers in enamels. Mark: **LOWESBY '4'** and a **fleur de lys** impressed (Leicestershire), c.1835-45, 9⅛in. high. Victoria & Albert Museum, 44-1899, Rathbone collection.*

that they were successful as garden pots, he set out to make the business commercially viable.[290] The vases and other ornamental wares were not usually black bodied ware, and thus the inclusion of this pottery in this book is questionable, but they were redwares with black dip decorated with exuberant floral painting (Figure 276) and sometimes gilded. Apparently some useful domestic wares were also produced. Unlike most other blackwares, the unusual Lowesby wares drew upon no earlier English blackware traditions, appearing to call upon the forceful character of the Turkish Isnik wares, apparent precursors to, in some instances, William Morris and William De Morgan's inspired creations.

The wares seem to have been moderately successful as a London studio for decoration and retail sales was opened in King William Street under the management of a Mr. Purden. However, the enterprise was shortlived. A notice in *The Sheffield and Rotherham Independent* of 10 June 1848 announced the sale at auction of the remaining stock of the Lowesby Pottery, 'of ornamental, terra-cotta vases and flower pots...none having been made for some time'.[291] The arms of Sir Frederick G. Fowke, the founder of the works are a fleur-de-lis, argent. The imprimatur of the pottery represents the armorial bearing of the family and the name of the estate,

Lowesby Hall. An upper case **LOWESBY** sometimes without the fleur-de-lis underneath, is impressed on the base of the wares.
Mark: **LOWESBY** (with or without an impressed fleur-de-lis)

John and Richard Mare, Market Square, Shelton, Hanley, Staffordshire, c.1770-85; **Richard Mare**, Hanley, 1785-94 or later; **John Mare**, Market Square, Shelton, Hanley, 1785-1808; **John and Matthew Mare**, Market Square, Shelton, c.1808-14; **Matthew Mare and Co.**, Shelton, c.1814; **John Mare**, John Street, Shelton, 1814-26

The Mare family are a challenge when one is presented with the various threads of the family which are interwoven in complicated ways, with several partnerships within the family operating from more than one site simultaneously. Just how much black basalt was made by the family is a conundrum. At least one family member, John Mare, was manufacturing and marking some blackwares **I. MARE** and John and Matthew Mare were also producing basalt. Therefore, it seems likely that other family members were participating in the manufacture of the popular stoneware.

The Mare family had resided in Hanley at least since the early years of the eighteenth century.[292] John and Richard Mare were among the potters who signed the 1770 Staffordshire Price Fixing Agreement.[293] They were listed simply as 'potters' in Hanley in *Bailey's* 1784 directory but their partnership was dissolved on 11 November 1785 and both potters continued operating out of their own works.[294]

In February 1786, Richard Mare took out a small insurance policy on his Hanley pottery totalling £400.[295] Mare was among the subscribers to the Committee of Manufacturers in 1790.[296] By 1792 he had greatly increased the amount of the insurance on his expanded pottery for a total valuation of £1,500.[297] In 1794 an insurance policy taken out by John Glass indicated that Richard Mare's pottery was housing stock as well as blocks and moulds from the John Glass works.[298] The *Staffordshire Advertiser* of 17 June 1797 published a notice that the 'creditors of Richard Mare, Hanley, potter deceased send account to John Mare, Junior, Hanley'. Unfortunately, little else is known about Richard Mare or his products.

There is a little more information about John Mare. In 1791 his pottery on the north side of Market Square was insured for a total of £1,000.[299] John Mare was exporting to America by 1795[300] and in that year one letter to an American client, William C. Lake, laments his inability to process the order for shipment due to 'the negligence and drunkenness of my workmen [as] we have had a Wakes here wch has caused from a week to ten days play...the workmen have done little business in hopes of having their wages advanced...'[301] John Mare was recorded in Enoch Wood's list of prominent potters of 1794 and 1797 as well as a list of leading manufacturers in 1802.[302] He was a participant in the Potters Clay Copartnership of 1797[303] and Wedgwood and Byerley were buying in some wares from John Mare in 1799 and 1801.[304] Between 1798 and 1802 receipts exist that indicate that Wedgwoods and Mare were borrowing, lending, buying and selling raw materials from each other.[305] This practice continued in the years 1808 to 1810 when the firm was the partnership of John and Matthew Mare.[306] Wedgwoods continued buying in ceramics as well from J. & M. Mare.[307] The partnership of Abbott and Mist in London decorated and sold wares of John Mare in the years between 1801 and 1808,[308] and some blackwares described as 'oval Teapots black' were sent down to

Figure 277. Teapot and cover (not mate). Oval bombé-shaped teapot with bamboo-reeded base and swag sprig relief decoration. Mark: **I. MARE**, c.1790-1800, 4⅞in. high. Castle Museum, Norwich, Miller collection.

Figure 278. Bowl, with spreading foot, fluted base and swag-decorated sprig relief. Mark: **I. MARE**, c.1790-1800, 3in. high. Gunson collection.

·London to be sold by Thomas Wyllie in 1810.[309]

The partnership with Matthew Mare, contracted some time between 1808 and 1810, was dissolved in 1814. Initially one partner, Thomas Hollins of Manchester, who probably maintained only a financial interest in the pottery, was listed in a dissolution of partnership notice which appeared in April in the *London Gazette*.[310] Some days later the partnership between the principals, John and Matthew Mare, was also formally dissolved.[311]

In that year John Mare took over a pottery adjoining the King's Head Inn on John Street in Shelton which was worked until 1826 when John Mare, the younger, became bankrupt.[312] The bankruptcy notice in the *Pottery Mercury* appeared on 1 March 1826.[313] His factory was offered for sale at auction in 1827,[314] and he died in 1832.[315]

Documented black basalt produced by John Mare is rare, so rare that Grant does not mention it. Two known pieces (Figures 277 and 278) are attractively potted in a neo-classical style with relief swags and a finial with a mother suckling her infant. The bombé oval shape may be the one described as being sold to Wyllie in London, but the description ('oval teapots black') is characteristically vague.
Mark: I. MARE

Marsh and Willett, Kiln Croft Works, Silvester Square, Burslem, Staffordshire, c.1829-34
This was the works formerly operated by James and William Handley until their bankruptcy in 1828,[316] when it was taken over by Marsh and Willett (c.1829). The firm was listed in Pigot's 1834 directory as producing 'Egyptian black'. Samuel Marsh was formerly in a partnership with William Goodwin which was dissolved in 1829.[317] The notice of the dissolution of partnership between Marsh and Willett, which appears to have been more of a reorganization than a dissolution, was published in the *Staffordshire Advertiser* on 3 October 1829 and indicated that the partnership with Willett would continue. Subsequently, however, Marsh's name is not often linked with Willett and by 1836 Samuel Marsh is listed as paying taxes on three ovens in Burslem, but there is no mention of Willett.[318] There are no identified examples from the Marsh and Willett pottery.

Nehemiah Massey, Bourne's Bank, Burslem, Staffordshire, c.1834-43 or later
Pigot's 1834 directory listed Nehemiah Massey as operating from Newcastle Street and producing 'Egyptian black and lustre'. The *Staffordshire Advertiser* printed a notice for the sale of the pottery on 9 May 1840:

Figure 279. Sugar bowl and cover. An elegant, boat-shaped sugar bowl dramatically free of decoration, c.1790-1800. Mark: **E. Mayer '12'**, *5¼in.high. Gunson collection.*

Figure 280. Two mugs, the left one with a fluted base and relief sprigging of a sheep, ram, goat and a dog; the right undecorated. Marks: both **E. Mayer**, *c.1790-1800, 3⅛in. high and 2½in. high. City Museum and Art Gallery, Stoke-on-Trent.*

Figure 281. Teapot and sliding cover, hexagonal and nearly free of embellishment except for a restrained daisy chain at the shoulder and a modest gadrooned gallery, c.1800-10, 6⅝in. high. Inkwell, polished basalt with vertical satin stripes, c.1790-1830, 2⅝in. high. Marks: both **E. Mayer**. *Rakow collection.*

194

Figure 282. Sugar box and cover and cream jug en suite (except different finial) with teapot in Figure 281. Mark: sugar box **E. Mayer**, cream jug unmarked, c.1800-10, 6¼in. high and 5⅛in. high. City Museum and Art Gallery, Stoke-on-Trent.

Figure 283. Coffee pot and cover, elegantly unadorned except for a moulded spout and an ear-shaped handle. A widow finial sits atop a domed cover. Mark: **E. Mayer**, c.1790-1810, 12¼in. high. City Museum and Art Gallery, Stoke-on-Trent.

Figure 284. Hot milk jug, teapot and coffee pot and covers, all polished basalt with satin striped engine-turned bodies and covers, all with widow finials. Marks: all **E. Mayer** in footrim, c.1800, left 6⅜in. high, centre 5⅛in. high, right 7½in. high. Rakow collection.

Auction at potworks of Nehemiah Massey, Bourne's Bank, Burslem. Stock in trade includes engravings, blue printed, painted, edged, dipt, and C.C. ware, Egyptian Black and Rockingham.

According to Ward, Massey was still in the pottery manufacturing business in Burslem in 1843.[397] No specimens from this factory are known.

Elijah Mayer, High Street, Hanley, Staffordshire, c.1787-1834
By the time Elijah Mayer came on the scene in 1787, it might have been assumed that the principal outposts of basalt manufacture had been stormed. Most of the major players had been on the scene manufacturing basalt for over a decade, some for nearly two decades. But of those potters who marked their wares, leaving aside

Figure 285. Open salt with fine ribbed bulbous body. Mark: **E. Mayer**, c.1800-30, 1½in. high. The Board of Trustees of the National Museums on Merseyside (Liverpool Museum), 918.

Figure 286. Two cream jugs of upright form, glazed inside, with fine fluted base (left) and satin stripes with a band of platinum lustre leaves and grapes (right). Marks: both **E. Mayer**, c.1800-10, 4⅞in. high and 5½in. high. Rakow collection.

Figure 287. Teapot and cover, glazed basalt, the lower third and shoulder with rouletted decoration. The sprig reliefs include the Domestic Employment motifs generated by Lady Templetown. Mark: **E. Mayer**, c.1790-1800, 6⅛in. high. City Musem and Art Gallery, Stoke on Trent.

Figure 288. Teapot and cover in glazed basalt with lower third in diagonal chequered engine-turned design. The sprigged decoration includes Power of Love, Cupids procession, Cupids with torches, Domestic Employment, widow finial. Mark: **E. Mayer**, c.1790-1800, 4½in. high. Gunson collection.

Wedgwood, Elijah Mayer was probably the most prolific of the manufacturers of black basalt. According to Shaw, Elijah Mayer was an agent for Mr. Charles Chatterley in Holland.[320] By 1783 he was an enameller of earthenware in Hanley operating from the High Street. In that year 'Elijah Mayer of Hanley, Enameller...' took out an insurance policy on his house, and warehouse ('no kiln therein'), business and personal goods as well as stock in trade.[321] By 9 August 1787 Mayer made it clear in an emendation to the same insurance policy that he was now in the earthenware manufacturing business having altered his buildings to include a quadrangle with a 'Pottwork and wareroom'.[322]

In 1790 a letter from Amsterdam dealers S. Chuman & Co. to Wedgwood and Byerley indicated that they were dealing with Mayer & Co.[323]

Elijah Mayer was a participant in the Potters Clay Copartnership of 1797.[324] The Wedgwood papers have invoices for the years 1788 to 1806 indicating that Mayer was both buying in and selling to Wedgwoods as well as being supplied with raw

Figure 289. Waste bowl en suite with the teapot in Figure 288. Mark: **E. Mayer**, c.1790-1800, 3⅛in. high. Rakow collection.

Figure 290. Teapot and cover, cylindrical-shaped with fluted base and cover with widow finial. The relief sprigging includes the cupid and lion and cupid pulling a faun, two popular reliefs found on E. Mayer wares. Unmarked, Elijah Mayer, c.1790-1810, 5⅛in. high. Private collection.

Figure 291. Sugar box and cover en suite with the teapot in Figure 290. Mark: **E. Mayer**, c.1790-1810. Private collection.

Figure 292. Kettle intended to have a wicker bail handle. The beading to the modest gallery adds a distinct touch not seen frequently on Mayer teawares. The sprig relief includes the Dipping of Achilles and Domestic Employment. Mark: **E. Mayer**, c.1790-1810, 6½in. high. City Museum and Art Gallery, Stoke-on-Trent.

materials.[325]

Elijah Mayer was among the earliest of the manufacturers to recognize the health hazards presented by lead glazes. 'In the manufacture of china it is most important…[to] do away entirely with the use of White lead…' Mayer wrote.[326] He estimated that the 'number of persons in the district whose labour exposes them to the noxious exhalations of White Lead' at three hundred fifty.[327]

Mayer was also concerned that his wares be competitive with the French in foreign markets, a concern doubtless shared by the community of potters selling to the Continent.[328]

In 1805 Elijah Mayer took his son of the same name into the business, trading as Elijah Mayer and Son. Like his father, who seemed to be carrying on two businesses, one manufacturing pottery in Hanley, the other marketing abroad as Mayer & Co., Elijah Mayer the Younger was, in addition to being a partner in the manufacturing

Figure 293. *Chocolate pot and cover, of cylindrical form with applied sprigs of Cupid and lion and Cupid and the faun. The widow, so frequently seen on Mayer basalt, sits prominently atop the cover. Mark:* **E. Mayer,** *c.1790-1800, 6in. high. Gunson collection.*

Figure 294. *Sugar box and cover of faceted oval form with ring simulated handles and a crimped gallery with sibyl finial. The interlaced rings at the shoulder are often among the restrained embellishment seen on Mayer stonewares. Mark:* **E. Mayer,** *c.1790-1800, 3¾in. high. Chellis collection.*

Figure 295. *Coffee pot and cover with high domed cover and widow finial. The relief decoration is that seen commonly on Mayer basalt: Cupid and faun and scenes from Domestic Employment. Mark:* **E. Mayer,** *c.1790-1800, 10⅜in. high. Photograph courtesy Sotheby's, New York.*

business, a partner in a firm trading as Keeling, Mayer & Co., 'Dealers in Black Glazed earthenware'. The dissolution of this partnership occurred in 1813.[329]

Wedgwood and Byerley continued to buy in from Elijah Mayer in 1807 using Thomas Hawkins as the agent.[330] The works were carried on by Elijah the Younger (who died in 1813), and grandson Joseph Mayer (*see* next entry). The 1818 and 1822 directories list the works as Elijah Mayer and Son, earthenware manufacturers, High Street and Parson and Bradshaw (1818) also listed Elijah Mayer as 'earthenware commission dealer'.

Geoffrey Godden notes a possible link between marked E. Mayer stonewares such as the one illustrated in Miller and Berthoud, *Anthology of British Teapots*, Plate 1122 in the Victoria and Albert Museum and a Billingsley marked teapot in the same institution.[331]

Mayer blackwares are of the highest quality, consistently finely potted, turned and embellished. Stylistically, they seem to span the range of the pottery's existence from the last two decades of the eighteenth century at least on through the second decade of the nineteenth century. Mayer basalt has a slightly bluish cast to the body. The widow finial, which is often used, is somewhat different from Wedgwood's widow. On Mayer pieces the legs face straight ahead whereas the legs of the Wedgwood widow veer to the left. Finials primarily consist of the widow, stylized floral knops, and ring loop and Greek key geometric designs. Mayer effectively, almost

Figure 296. Two teapots and covers. Moseley and Mayer teapots commemorating the Victory at Trafalgar are almost identical: the major difference is the Greek key band at the shoulder heads to the left on Mayer basalt and to the right on Moseley. The Mayer teapots also have a band of leaf foliage around the base of the spout (Figure 296a) which the Moseley ones do not. Mark: left **MOSELEY**, right **E. Mayer**, c.1806-10, 5¾in. high. City Museum and Art Gallery, Stoke-on-Trent.

Figure 296a. Detail of distinguishing leaf relief band at base of spout on E. Mayer Trafalgar commemorative teapots.

Figure 297. Sugar bowl and cover, part of a teaset to commemorate Lord Nelson's triumph at Trafalgar. The wares are press-moulded with a vermiculated ground inset by a cartouche depicting the symbols of victory. Mark: **E. Mayer**, c.1806-10, 5¼in. high. Rakow collection.

Figure 297a. Reverse detail of Trafalgar commemorative sugar box in Figure 297. The cartouche occasionally has the minute incised signature 'W. Hackwood' on the lower right front.

dramatically, utilized the undecorated or sparsely decorated body (Figures 279, 281-283). In effect it is a bold move as the piece must be satin to perfection to remain undecorated. Mayer produced several Egyptian campaign and Trafalgar commemorative teawares. The Trafalgar teawares are almost identical to those produced by Moseley (Figures 296 and 297), except for two distinguishing features. The band

Figure 298. Sugar box and cover, teapot and cover of oval form with wide ribbed base and ring simulated handles (on sugar box) and ring finial on both. The sprigs are Domestic Employment, Power of Love and Cupid's procession. Marks: **E. Mayer**, c.1800, 5⅛in. high and 5¾in. high. Robertshaw collection.

Figure 299. Sugar box and cover and cream jug in low oval form with ribbed base and a band of stylized flowers and scrolls at the neck. Marks: **E. Mayer**, c.1800-10. 4⅝in. high and 3⅜ in. high. Rakow collection.

Figure 300. Part teaset moulded overall in scrolls and flowers with a stipple ground. Marks: cream jug and sugar **E. Mayer**, teapot: an incised **5** in base, c.1810, 4½in. high and 5⅜in. high. Rakow collection.

Figure 301. Teapot and cover of oval form, the body moulded of simulated bamboo. This imaginative treatment provided an attractive shape which, in spite of its unusual form, adhered to contemporary styles. Mark: **E. Mayer** in footrim, c.1810, 6½in. high. Rakow collection.

Figures 302 and 303. Pair of tablets. The subjects, popular on stoneware by many manufacturers, are Bacchanalian Boys and Boys and Goat. Marks: **E. MAYER** (it appears that all of Mayer's tablets and medallions are marked in upper case; whereas the hollow wares were in upper and lower case), c.1790-1830, 10½in. x 15½in. Rakow collection.

201

of Greek key decoration at the neck goes to the left on the Mayer examples and to the right on the Moseley ones. The leaf style relief around the base of the spout on Mayer pieces as illustrated in Figure 296a also sets them apart from Moseley wares. The cartouche which has 'Pro Patria' on one side and the Trafalgar commemorative symbols on the other is very occasionally signed in minute print 'W. Hackwood' on the lower right face.

Some ornamental wares were manufactured, particularly tablets and medallions, all marked in upper case (whereas the teawares are impressed uniformly in upper and lower case), some of which may have been manufactured in the Joseph Mayer works. However, at least one pair of tablets (Figures 302 and 303) has the upper case mark **E. MAYER** definitely placing it among those wares produced by Elijah Mayer. The two other medallions marked simply **MAYER** (Figures 304 and 305) have a distinctive look, less refined than the other **E. Mayer** marked wares, opening up the possibility for speculation by another manufacturer, possibly the later Joseph Mayer works. A few basalt wares are decorated with platinum lustre (Figure 286) and pieces were occasionally glazed on the outside (Figures 287 and 288). The marks were usually simply **E. Mayer** but Jewitt said that some wares are marked **E. Mayer & Son**.

Marks: E. Mayer; E. Mayer & Son, MAYER

Joseph Mayer & Co., High Street, Hanley, Staffordshire, c.1814-28; Church Works, High Street, Hanley, c.1828-31

According to the Victoria County History Joseph Mayer worked from at least two potteries in the High Street, Hanley,[332] including in the last years the site of the former Palmer/Neale/Wilson pottery, the Church Works. The records are all vague. The 1818-19-20 *Commercial Directory* listed Joseph Mayer and Son as earthenware manufacturers without specifying what line they worked in, so it is possible they did not manufacture black stoneware at all. No known blackwares are specifically associated with the Joseph Mayer manufacture. Although it is tempting to speculate that the few pieces simply marked with upper case **MAYER** may be the products of this works (Figures 304 and 305), there is nothing to substantiate this. It seems that Joseph Mayer left the Church Works in 1831, letting it to his cousin, William Ridgway, while Mayer retained some warehouses for storage of some of his father's wares.[333]

A few letters were exchanged between Joseph Mayer and the Wedgwood factory in 1814 and 1815 but they are not very illuminating. In 1814 Mayer requested a price list from Wedgwoods,[334] and Mayer was buying clay from the Wedgwood factory in 1815.[335] There is still another letter which indicates that Abraham Wedgwood made a gift of a cameo of Josiah Wedgwood to Joseph Mayer on 15 February 1832.[336] Since the letterhead on that and the other correspondence between Joseph Mayer and Abraham Wedgwood is Hanley, it seems likely it is the Hanley Joseph Mayer, and not the Liverpool man of the same name, who received the gift of the cameo.

Joseph Mayer died on 28 June 1860 and an auction of the 'extensive stocks of superior antique black drab lustre enamelled and other wares...black and brown teapots, jugs &c' began being advertised in the *Staffordshire Advertiser* on 15 September 1860. The first auction was held on 22 October. A second sale was

*Figure 304. Cameo-medallion of Shakespeare in profile in a rectangular panel with a vermiculated ground. Mark: **MAYER**, c.1800-30, 2½in. x 3½in. Rakow collection.*

*Figure 305. Round tablet depicting the Birth of Venus. Mark: **MAYER**, c.1800-30, 5⅞in. diameter. Rakow collection.*

advertised for 17 December including 'twenty large lots of the beautiful antique cane, brown, black, enamelled and lustre ware and China…also a large stock of black Egyptian ware, of various patterns and excellent quality. This fills a large warehouse, but will be divided into lots to suit purchasers'.[337] The remaining stock, including moulds and biscuit ware, as well as Mayer's paintings by Van Dyke and Lucas Van Leyden, as well as a large quantity of antique pottery ware were sold at a third auction on 16 February 1861.[338] Joseph Mayer left a personal estate of about £200,000 in 1860 followed by trails of litigation from distant family members.[339]

Figure 305a. Trade card Mayer & Newbold Pottery, Longton (1817-32). Courtesy, The Winterthur Library, Joseph Downs Collection of Manuscripts and Printed Ephemera, 62x2.

Figure 306. *Cream jug with vermiculated ground and Greek key border. The central cartouche depicts the victory at Trafalgar in 1805. Almost identical commemorative teawares were made by Elijah Mayer and by Moseley, the distinguishing feature being the Greek key border which runs right in the Moseley wares (see Figures 296 and 297). Mark:* **MOSELEY** *impressed in the broad footrim, c.1806-10, 4⅜in. high. Gunson collection.*

Figure 307. *Sugar box (minus cover), oval with scroll moulded relief at base and applied shell central cartouche with cupids in a car pulled by lions. Mark:* **MOSELEY** *(in a curve), c.1801-22, 2⅞in. high. British Museum, R 11.*

Jewitt confirms that all the pottery sold at auction in 1860 was indeed the very same that had been stored in the warehouses at the Church Works in 1832, all wares from Elijah Mayer's factory.[340] Nothing is known of blackware produced by Joseph Mayer himself, if he did produce any at all.
Marks: (recorded on other wares) **JOSEPH MAYER & CO. HANLEY; MAYER & CO.; MAYER (?)**

Mayer and Newbold, Caroline Street, Market Place, Longton, Staffordshire, 1817-32
According to the directories the partnership of Thomas Mayer and Richard Newbold produced Egyptian blackware, but a trade card (Figure 305a) gives no indication of such manufacture and no blackwares have been identified. Painted marks on porcelain include the factory initials.
Mark: M & N (on porcelain, painted)

James Meakin, Newtown Pottery, Longton, Staffordshire, c.1846-52
Primarily a china manufacturer Jewitt suggests that James Meakin produced richly gilt 'jet ware'.[341] No 'jet' wares have been associated with this manufacturer.

William Mellor, Old Hall Road, Hanley, Staffordshire, c.1781-1801
According to Shaw, William Mellor was known for producing 'Black glazed or Shining Black' tea and coffee pots 'of the improved kinds of Pottery' in Hanley.[342] Jewitt suggested that Mellor made Egyptian black for the Dutch markets as did his successors Keeling, Toft & Co.[343] None of his blackwares has been identified.

Thomas Minshall, Stafford Street, Longton, Staffordshire, c.1852-54
Minshall was listed in *Kelly's Directory* of 1854 as producing 'Black and Rockingham' at Newbold Square, just off Stafford Street.[344] No wares have been identified.

Minton(s), Stoke-on-Trent, Staffordshire, c.1796-present
Minton appears to have produced basalt but no marked wares have been discovered to date. Minton was purchasing black teapots from Lockett & Co. from 1803-9[345] and black inkstands by the dozen from Chetham & Woolley in 1808[346] as well as

Figure 309. Teapot and cover, oval shape divided into panel by columns. The base has a diamond moulded relief pattern and the central sprig is Britannia. Mark: **MOSELEY**, c.1801-22, 7½in. high. Thomas collection.

Figure 308. Humidor and cover, cylindrical with a domed cover. The sprig relief is a hunting scene depicting hounds at the kill. Mark: **MOSELEY**, c.1801-22, 6¼in. high. City Museum and Art Gallery, Stoke-on-Trent.

'Blackware goods' and 'Egyptian blackware' from Brown & Cartlidge, Burslem in 1810.[347] but there is also evidence that Minton was actually manufacturing basalt a few years later. Minton purchased black clay in 1814 and there are listings for 'block moulds for 3 teapots, 1 sugar box and cream for Egyptian black…' in 1817.[348] The 1817 inventory lists of stock include quantities of teawares in Egyptian black in satin stripe and common fluted patterns. In 1836 the factory was one of the largest in the district with twenty ovens in operation.[349] Later nineteenth century blackwares were also produced. A pair of candlesticks with white enamel decoration was exhibited at the Imperial Institute in 1894.[350]

James Mist *see* **Abbott & Mist**

John Moseley (John and William Moseley) Cobridge and Burslem, Staffordshire; Cobridge 1801-18; Burslem 1809(?)-22
John Moseley was in partnership in a pottery business with William Dale in Cobridge until 9 November 1801.[351] Apparently John Moseley continued working the pottery in Cobridge on his own because on 14 November 1801 he took out an insurance policy on 'his part of a set of potworks at Cobridge brick and tiled £100. Stock and utensils £150'.[352] By 1808 Moseley had increased the insurance on the works to £240.[353] Some time after 1801 and prior to 1809 John Moseley took a partner, William Moseley,[354] in the manufacture of earthenware in Burslem. Their partnership was dissolved on 11 November 1809.[355] John and William Moseley continued to trade with London Staffordshire warehouseman Thomas Wyllie as partners from Cobridge until 1811 but they may simply have been utilizing outdated billheads. As records from the Wyllie papers indicate John Moseley and William Moseley carried on separately manufacturing pottery, both producing basalt from Cobridge and sending wares down to Wyllie until 1819.[356]

The blackwares sent by John Moseley down to London from 1812 to 1819 include a variety of shapes, some of the descriptions of which do not immediately conjure an

Figure 310 Teapot (minus cover), bamboo-shaped with five foot pads on base. Both the pads (Figure 310a) and the teapot shoulder show simulated bamboo cross sections. No strainer on spout. Mark: **MYATT**, probably Richard Myatt, Foley, Fenton, c.1770s, 5in. high. Blake collection.

Figure 310a. Base and mark on Myatt teapot in Figure 310.

Figure 311. Teapot and cover, cylindrical shape with fine-grained vertical satin stripes, small parapet, and cover with crudely modelled finial of a sibyl with head turned toward the handle. Mark: **MYATT**, probably Richard Myatt, Foley, Fenton, c.1790-95, 3⅜in. high. Victoria & Albert Museum, 2649-1901.

Figure 312. Teapot and cover, globular shape with undecorated body and parapet, the cover with a widow finial. Mark: **Neale & Wilson**, c.1783-91, 4¼in. high. Gunson collection.

image: satin stripe coffee pots (1813), oblong black teapots (1814), barrell [*sic*] teapots (1816), Dutch beaded teapots (1817), and Dutch casket teapots (1819). William and John Moseley were purveying oval black teapots in 1811 and William Moseley was selling round Dutch satin striped teapots in 1815.[357]

On 4 March 1820 the *Staffordshire Advertiser* published a notice:

Auction Lot 1, newly erected Church Yard Works, Burslem occupied by John Moseley, 3 hovels; Lot 2, wharf at Wheelock [near Sandbach, Cheshire], Lot 3, House at Wheelock. Apply Peter Joynson[358], Wheelock or Mr. Williams, Betley.

The pottery must not have sold in 1820. John Moseley was listed in the 1822-3 directory as a manufacturer of earthenware and Egyptian black at the Churchyard Works, (house, Longport). He died in 1824 at the age of forty-seven and was again described by the *Staffordshire Advertiser* as a 'manufacturer of Egyptian black and earthenware'.[357] In 1825 the manufactory was again advertised, this time to be let by the executors of the late John Moseley.[360]

It is impossible to determine if the basalt produced by the Moseleys was made by either John or William. The only mark recorded is the upper case **MOSELEY**. The texture of the wares produced is fine, smooth and not intensely black. Judging from the quantity and variety of the wares sent down to London and the few existing marked pieces the manufacture must have been a lively one. A rare and fine humidor (Figure 308) in the City Museum and Art Gallery, Stoke-on-Trent, hints at the range of wares produced at the Moseley factories. Perhaps the wares most commonly associated with the Moseley manufacture are the Trafalgar commemorative teawares (Figure 306). Nearly identical in moulded decoration to those produced by Elijah Mayer (Figures 296 and 297), the Moseley wares are distinguished by the band of Greek key decoration at the neck which marches to the right. On Mayer pieces the decoration goes in the opposite direction.
Mark: MOSELEY

Richard Myatt, Foley, Fenton, Staffordshire, c.1770s-1796; **Joseph Myatt**, Foley, Fenton, c.1796-early 19th century
Richard Myatt was the father of Joseph Myatt (b.1762) and their pottery was located in the Foley, Fenton. Richard Myatt was a well-known earthenware manufacturer at Lane End listed in both *Bailey's* 1781 and 1783 directories. He appears to be one of the major freehold owners in both Lane End and in Fenton in the 1780s and 1790s.[361] At his death in 1796 his son Joseph Myatt took over his father's works. Both apparently manufactured both red and black wares. Only a few teawares (Figures 310 and 311) impressed **MYATT** appear to have survived. Judging from the shapes they appear to have been the products of Richard Myatt's manufacture.
Mark: MYATT

Neale & Co., Church Works, Hanley, Staffordshire, 1778-1792; **Neale & Wilson**, c.1783-92
The figure most commonly associated with the Neale Pottery and Porcelain works in Hanley, James Neale, was in reality a London retailer of ceramics and glass in St. Paul's Churchyard from 1766 until his death in 1814. James Neale took over the beleaguered Church Works of Humphrey Palmer after his bankruptcy in 1778, having been a financial partner in the business for many years. It is said that Robert Wilson was the manager of the Palmer works, but this is impossible to prove. However, Wilson, who was manager of Neale's pottery and after 1792 the owner, has remained frustratingly obscure. He is largely unencumbered by biographical details so his role, undoubtedly a major one, is not fully recognized (*see* **Wilson**).

Although it is uncertain at what point James Neale contracted a formal partnership with Robert Wilson, an invoice exists dated 20 November 1783 with a printed letterhead for Neale & Wilson, Hanley.[362] *Bailey's* 1784 directory listed Neale and Wilson as 'Potters' in Hanley. The partnership was formally dissolved on 24 April 1792.[363]

Certainly the basalt and other earthenwares produced by the Church Works predominately bear the mark **NEALE & CO**. but it appears that the more rare

*Figure 313. Figure of Lucretia, polished basalt elegantly modelled. The figure is the heroine who committed suicide after being assaulted by Tarquin. The prototype is uncertain but may be taken from a bronze by Giambologna. Another Lucretia was produced by Lakin & Poole in pearlware c.1792-96. Mark: **NEALE & Co**., c.1780-90, 12 in. long. Zeitlin collection.*

*Figure 314. Figure of Cleopatra, polished basalt taken from a marble in the Vatican collection first recorded in 1512 when it passed from Angelo Maffei to Pope Julius II. The copies made of the original were numerous, produced in marble, plaster, bronze and wax. Mark: **NEALE & Co**., c.1790-1800, 11¾in. long. Zeitlin collection.*

Figure 315. Vase (minus cover), with simulated handles in the form of Cleopatra heads from which a floral swag falls. The pendant central cameo is Aesculapius. Mark: I. **NEALE HANLY** in wafer of base, c.1778-80, 7¾in. high. Private collection.

Figure 316. Left, vase (minus cover) on elevated polished basalt plinth with simulated handles in the form of Cleopatra, each head facing opposite directions. The pendant cameo depicts Inigo Jones. Mark: **NEALE & Co.** impressed in base, c.1780-85, 11⅛in. high. Right, vase (minus cover) modelled similarly but with a large minotaur cameo. Mark: **I. NEALE HANLY** in wafer of base, 11¾in. high. Rakow collection.

Figure 317. Vase (minus cover) with prominent bird's head handles suspending a floral swag. The undecorated body is relieved by a pendant cameo of the Minotaur. Mark: **I. NEALE HANLY** in wafer of base, c.1778-80, 11⅛in. high. City Museum and Art Gallery, Stoke-on-Trent.

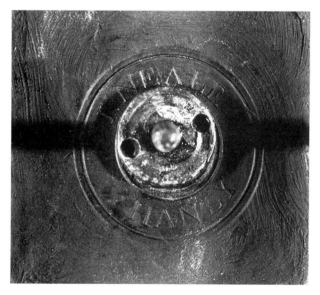

Figure 318. Ewer with applied floral and foliage bands and an elegant neck and scroll handle terminating in a female mask. Mark: **I. NEALE HANLY** in wafer of base, c.1778-80, 7½in. high. Kansas City (gift of Mr. and Mrs. F.P. Burnap), 41-23/138.

Figure 317a. Mark on vase in Figure 317.

Figure 319. Jug, pear-shaped with undecorated body and leaf-moulded spout and scroll handle. Mark: **NEALE & Co.**, c.1785-91, 6¾in. high. Private collection.

Figure 320. Portrait medallion of Shakespeare. Mark: **NEALE & Co.**, c.1780-91, 12⁵⁄₁₆in. x 9¹³⁄₁₆in. Private collection.

Figure 321. Pair of candlesticks with fluted columns and square stepped bases with floral relief on base and a swag around the candlestick. Mark: **NEALE & Co**. on both, c.1778-91, 4⅞in. high. Collection of the Newark Museum, New Jersey E57.198, gift of John B. Morris, 1957.

Figure 322. Kettle and cover with bail handle and spaniel finial. The relief sprigging is the bacchanalian boys utilized by many potters. Mark: **NEALE & Co.**, c.1778-91, 8¼in. high. Castle Museum, Norwich, Miller collection.

Figure 323. Teapot and cover, barrel-shaped body with engine-turned slats and bands. The cover has a rare finial of Elijah feeding the raven. Mark: **NEALE & Co.**, c.1780-91, 4⅛in. high. Middleditch collection, to Godden collection, now unknown.

Figure 324. Teapot and cover, oval body with fine bamboo reeding at base and applied swag relief decoration. The finial is a seated Fo lion. Mark: **NEALE & Co.**, c.1790, 6⅜in. high. Private collection.

Figure 325. Three covers from Town Road, Hanley (Church Works). Excavated in 1985, the waste tip was from the Church Works occupied by Humphrey Palmer until 1778, subsequently by Neale & Co. The covers include ones with the widow and recumbent lion finials, and one sliding cover (a rare find on a Neale teapot). City Museum and Art Gallery, Stoke-on-Trent.

*Figure 326. Teapots and covers of oval shape, undecorated except for a narrow band of husk relief decoration at the shoulder, widow finials. Mark: **NEALE & Co.**, c.1790, 3½in. high and 5in. high. Rakow collection.*

*Figure 327. Teapot and cover of oval bombé shape with wide engine-turned flutes at base and a narrow band of husk relief at the shoulder, widow finial. The relief sprigging includes scenes from Domestic Employment and various animals. Mark: **NEALE & Co.**, c.1790, 4⅞in. high. Rakow collection.*

*Figure 328. Teapot and cover, nearly square teapot with oval panels sprigged with chinoiserie scenes. A bold Medici-lion finial stands atop the cover. Mark: **NEALE & Co.**, c.1785-91, 5in. high. Castle Museum, Norwich, Miller collection.*

*Figure 329. Sugar box and cover en suite with teapot in Figure 328. Mark: **NEALE & Co.**, c.1785-91, 5¾in. high. City Museum and Art Gallery, Stoke-on-Trent, 405.*

*Figure 330. Two sugar bowls and covers and a cream jug, decorated with bacchanalian boys, widow finial and recumbent lion finial. Marks: sugar bowl (left) and cream jug, **NEALE & Co**; sugar bowl (right) **Neale & Co**., c.1780-91, sugars 4⅛in. high, cream jug 5¼in. high. Rakow collection.*

*Figure 331. Chocolate pot and cover with fine engine-turned fluted body broken by a horizontal band of swag relief half way up. A widow finial sits atop the fluted domed cover with a narrow band of acanthus-leaf trim. Mark: **NEALE & Co**., c.1785-91. Private collection.*

*Figure 332. Superbly potted tea cup and saucer in a waisted porcelain shape. Mark: **NEALE & Co**. on outside tea cup footrim, c.1780-91, cup 2¾in. high, saucer 5⅛in. diameter. Rakow collection.*

mark of **Neale & Wilson** (Figure 312) was used simultaneously, so specific dating by mark is not possible. The heritage of excellent quality basalt, as all other wares produced by the pottery, exemplified the high standards set by Humphrey Palmer and followed by Neale. The texture was fine and smooth, almost sensuous in nature. The potting or modelling, as in the case of the reclining Cleopatra and Lucretia (Figures 313 and 314), epitomized the fine tuning that was possible with the black fabric. Very few other manufacturers were able to maintain the consistent quality blackwares produced by the Palmer/Neale and Wilson ménage.

The range of wares was also extensive. Vases, following in the Palmer tradition (Figures 315-317) bear the mark **I. NEALE HANLY** in the wafer of the base, or very rarely **NEALE & Co**. One hallmark of Palmer/Neale vases, the central medallion, ubiquitously present on vases of Neale manufacture, continues with rare exceptions to be suspended from a loop which is secured by a simulated rivet, convincingly placed in the moulded frieze at the shoulder of the vase. In the case

*Figure 333. Coffee can and saucer of cylindrical shape with fine fluted base and saucer. The form is similar to the tea bowl base excavated in Williamsburg, Virginia (Figure 334). Mark: **NEALE & Co**., c.1790, can 3⅛in. high, saucer 5⅛in. diameter. Gunson collection.*

*Figure 334. Tea bowl base excavated in 1939 from the rear of the Golden Ball tavern, Williamsburg, Virginia. Mark; **NEALE & Co**., c.1790. Colonial Williamsburg Foundation.*

where there is no frieze the rivet looks like a staple driven directly into the vase. A variety of other wares in the form of ewers (Figure 318), portrait medallions (Figure 320), candlesticks (Figure 321) and figures, expanded the ornamental production. Tea and coffee wares display a wide range of shapes and decoration: neo-classical and chinoiserie teawares exist alongside those with practically no decoration. Finials include the distinctive widow, Elijah and the Raven, spaniel, sibyl, and recumbent and standing Fo Lions. Several covers with finials (Figure 325) and one sliding cover were excavated in 1985 from the Church Works site from levels which appear to postdate 1775. The sliding cover is a revelation. To date no marked wares have been discovered with sliding lids. Among the various teawares, cups and saucers, rarely seen in basalt, were produced in at least three different forms (Figures 332 and 333). One teabowl base was excavated in 1939 from the rear of the Golden Ball Tavern in Williamsburg, Virginia (Figure 334). The teabowl base is not the only indication of a blackware trade to America. An invoice from the retail partnership of Neale and Bailey operating from No. 8 St. Paul's Churchyard in London dated 28 November 1795 sold to 'Mr. Pierpoint's stores' (location not given) '2 black oval teapots 4/- and 2 ditto ditto 5/-'.[364] Naturally, one cannot assume these were Neale basalt teapots *per se*. Mintons (and probably other manufacturers) were also selling through Neale and Bailey in 1797-8, but not necessarily basalt. One can get an idea of the extensive size of the Neale and Bailey business which in 1788 was insured for a total of £8,400 and in 1789 £10,000.[365]

Neale apparently traded to the Continent but very little is known about that phase of the business. In some instances Wedgwood and Neale were amalgamating shipments abroad. A letter exists from merchants Menderop & Gevert in Rotterdam sent to Josiah Wedgwood II on 11 June 1802 in response to Wedgwood's arrangements to augment their shipment with wares supplied by James Neale.[366]
Marks: I.NEALE HANLY; NEALE & Co.; Neale & Wilson

Richard Newbold, Longton, Staffordshire, c.1833-37
Pigot's 1834 directory lists Richard Newbold as a manufacturer of 'Egyptian black'. In 1836 his factory paid taxes on four ovens.[367] From 1817 to 1832 Richard Newbold

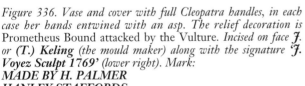

Figure 336. Vase and cover with full Cleopatra handles, in each case her hands entwined with an asp. The relief decoration is Prometheus Bound *attacked by the Vulture. Incised on face* **J.** *or* **(T.) Keling** *(the mould maker) along with the signature '***J. Voyez Sculpt 1769***' (lower right). Mark:*
MADE BY H. PALMER
HANLEY STAFFORDS.
on outside of plinth, 20¼in. high. Dwight and Lucille Beeson Wedgwood Collection, Birmingham Museum of Art, Alabama.

Figure 337. Vase and cover (left) with scroll handles. The body is modelled with a relief scene of Venus and Cupid at Vulcan's Smithy; *the reverse is a trophy of a wreath, quiver and vase. Incised signature:* **J. Voyez Sculpt** *with the plinth impressed on the outside:*
MADE BY H. PALMER
HANLEY STAFFORDS. E., *1769, 13in. high. British Museum, K11.*

was in a partnership with Thomas Mayer, also producing blackware (*see* Mayer and Newbold). Nothing is known about their wares.

Ouseburn Pottery *see* **Hyslop & Hall**

Humphrey Palmer, Church Works, Hanley, Staffordshire, c.1760 (or earlier)-1778
Humphrey Palmer has been discussed in Chapter II as the major rival of Josiah Wedgwood in the production of ornamental and useful blackwares in the last years

Figure 338a. Incised signature 'Voyez Sculpt' on Dionysus and Ariadne vase in Figure 338.

Figure 338. Vase and cover with scroll handles modelled with a sweep of Dionysus and Ariadne *circulating the body. Incised* **Voyez Sculpt**. *(lower right, Figure 338a). Mark:*
MADE BY H. PALMER
HANLEY STAFFORDS E., *impressed on outside of plinth, 1769, 17in. high. Mint Museum of Art, Delhom collection.*

of the 1760s and the early years of the next decade. Further material on Palmer is included under **James Neale** as well as in the book Neale *Pottery and Porcelain 1763-1820*.[368]

Palmer was among the most important of the early manufacturers of basalt. An excavation of the site labelled the Town Road, Hanley, took place in 1985 and yielded a wide variety of early earthenwares and stonewares which the archaeologists believe were associated with the Palmer manufactory.[369] A full analysis of this material will do much to expand the understanding of the Palmer occupancy of the Church Works, a period which has been largely delineated through the acrimonious letters written by Wedgwood about Palmer in the first years of the Industrial Revolution. One letter written from Bath by Wedgwood (who was looking for showrooms) to Bentley in London is illustrative of the business anxiety recurrent in their correspondence:

> Ld S. has certainly been at St. Paul's [at Neale's emporium] & they have told him, as they do everybody else, how much dearer our goods are than theirs, what hardships we have laid them under with our P—t [patent], ec, ec, as they pass for Manufacturers, this account for his Lordship's speech respecting other Manufacturers saying our things are dear...I suppose he has found their Vases more suitable to his idea in *Price*, but not in *quality* & wants to have *good things* from us as cheap as *ordinary ones* at other places.[370]

And the following year, 31 July 1773, Wedgwood wrote to Bentley:

> Our painted Etruscan T.pots painted as slight as possible, are ch d 12/- 10/6- & 9. Palmers I believe sell them at half the price painted with figures & borders both—-Have not you lowered these T. pots?[371]

*Figure 339. Pair of vases of unusual square form, the central panel modelled with a bacchanal on one side and a man being slain by a lion on the reverse. Mark: **H. PALMER HANLEY** (Figure 339a) around wafer of base, possibly modelled by John Voyez, c.1770, 6⅛in. high. Rakow collection.*

Figure 339a. Mark on vases in Figure 339.

As interesting as these letters are, and they are like a mercantile barometer, the voice and perspective is Wedgwood's, not Palmer's. More importantly the records do not provide us with an accounting of the actual wares produced by Palmer, a problem not encountered on the other side as documentation of Wedgwood and Bentley wares going from Etruria to London is extensive. When completed, an analysis of the Town Road sherds will help redress that balance.

Palmer employed a number of talented workmen: Thomas Greatbach was a turner at the Church Works, Enoch Wood was apprenticed under Palmer and it is said that Robert Wilson was his factory manager. Certainly his most famous employee was John Voyez, whose five signature creations would have immortalized Palmer even

Figure 341. Teapot and cover. The bamboo-moulded teapot has the unusual mark 'P' impressed in base. The shape is right for the period in which Humphrey Palmer was making teapots, but so far no teawares can be attributed to Palmer's occupancy of the Church Works in Hanley until Neale took over in 1778 and began marking wares. Possibly Humphrey Palmer, Hanley, c.1770-78, 5½in. high. Castle Museum, Norwich, Miller collection.

Figure 340. Vase with simulated handles in the form of Cleopatra portraits from which a husk swag falls. The central cameo is Athena, the reverse the cameo of Apollo and Marsyas. The vase can be found with either the Neale or the Palmer imprimatur. Mark: H. PALMER HANLEY, c.1770-78, 9in. high. Kansas City (gift of Mr. and Mrs. F.P. Burnap), 41-23/142

without his other important, finely executed vases. The five subjects definitely modelled by Voyez for Palmer were: The Prometheus Bound Vases (Figure 336), Venus and Cupid at Vulcan's Smithy (Figure 337), Dionysus and Ariadne (Figure 338) and Diana, goddess of the hunt. Other vases (Figure 339), not bearing the signature, may have been modelled by Voyez while he was working for Palmer (*see* **Voyez**).

The controversial John Voyez initially entered the pottery industry after Wedgwood hired him as a modeller in 1768. The friction surrounding his departure from Wedgwood and his subsequent hiring by rival Palmer was not nearly as contentious as the dispute engendered by the so-called encaustic patent taken out by Wedgwood on 16 November 1769.[372] Details of the infringement are available in other sources,[373] but the examples of Palmer encaustic wares are manifestly limited; the only known marked example is illustrated in Colour Plates 3 and 4.

While credited with numerous wares of an ornamental nature, there are no firmly documented useful basalt wares ascribed to Humphrey Palmer. That a useful wares manufacturing business existed is indicated by correspondence between Wedgwood and Bentley in the oft-cited, 'Nobody makes black T. pots but Palmers'.[374]

In a letter dated 25 February 1778, Wedgwood wrote:

Mr. Palmer sells his 3 sizes of black flat fluted Teapots with the Sibyl tops at 18/- the long dozns that is @ 9d. 12d. & 18d. Per pot which we sell at 50 or 60/-.[375]

Figure 341a. Plaque depicting Achilles in Scyros among the Daughters of Lycomedes, attributed to Pacetti and adapted from the sarcophagus of Alexander Severus and Julia Mammaea in the Capitoline Museum. Mark: PELLATT, c.1789, 4½in. x 9¾in. Private collection.

No surviving conventionally marked Palmer useful wares, if there ever were any so marked, exist. However, a bamboo shaped teapot, similar in form to those produced by Wedgwood & Bentley, William Clowes and John Turner, is in the Miller collection, Norwich Museum, marked on the base with a 'P' in relief (Figure 341). It is tempting to think that this might not only be an identifiable piece of Palmer basalt, but also an undocumented factory mark.

By 1773 Palmer was making and selling seals and undercutting Wedgwood's prices by half. An advertisement in the Birmingham newspaper indicated that there was to be an auction for intaglios to be sold for Palmer which 'I suppose' wrote Wedgwood's niece Miss A Brett, 'has caused some of our friends to desert us for the Present'.[376] Very few Palmer seals have been identified. One, mounted in gold, is in the Rakow collection.

Palmer basalt is dense, receives and is enhanced by a superficial polish, and meets harmoniously within the neo-classical métier its arch rival Wedgwood and Bentley. One of Palmer's primary exponents, Capt. M.S. Grant, sums it up:

> Of course, to manufacture classical vases at all was nothing but imitation: and Wedgwood himself was the arch-practitioner in the art. But Palmer and his successors [Neale and Wilson] contrived with such singular success to avoid repetition of the Etruria models, that,-and this can be said of no other potter in the Staffordshire school of that period-a glance is sufficient to attribute their vases to their true source of origin.[377]

Grant goes on to say: 'The shoulder masks are usually miniature works of art'.[378]
Marks: H. PALMER HANLEY; P (?) [in relief]

Apsley Pellatt & Co., 80 High Holborn, London, c.1789
Apsley Pellatt and Company were a large firm of chinamen operating from High Holborn. The London stock, including the retail establishment and two other warehouses, was insured for £1,400 in 1789.[378] Like Mist, Pellatt did not manufacture basalt but pieces are occasionally found with the retailer's impressed mark **PELLATT** (Figure 341a).

Benjamin Plant, Lane End, Longton, Staffordshire, late 18th century-early 19th century
Almost nothing is known about this potter. His wares are limited to a few known pieces in feldspathic stoneware and pearlware incised with the name 'B. Plant, Lane

End'. Benjamin Plant did leave a diary and in it was his recipe for black:

> 1 lb. of Magness [*sic*]
> 5 lb. of Oker [*sic*] to
> 15 lb. of Ball Clea [*sic*]
> Black is prepared by mixing a deep blue with Seven ounces of fine Varnish which is called oil of Stones.[379]

No basalt wares have been identified with the Benjamin Plant factory.
Marks: B. Plant, Lane End (incised in cursive), **Benjamin Plant, Lane End**

Pool(e) & Sutherland, Cornhill Passage and Heathcote Road, Longton, Staffordshire, 1859-1864; **Pool(e), Sutherland & Hallam**. 1865-post 1865
The directories list these partnerships as producing Egyptian black. No products have been identified with either one.[380]

Messrs. Pountney & Co., Temple Backs Pottery, Bristol, c.1813-72
This is the old Franks/Ring pottery operated in the eighteenth century successively by Richard Frank, Joseph Ring, and after Ring's death in 1788, by his widow Elizabeth. The partnerships which Pountney accrued were numerous in the nineteenth century and Jewitt said that they produced 'excellent imitations of Etruscan ware' during Mr. Pountney's lifetime[381] (Pountney died in 1852). The vases, imitations of Greek red-figured and black-figured originals, were decorated with red on a black body (coloured by a black slip on a redware body, so not technically qualifying as blackware), and black figures on a redware body. Examples of Pountney's Etruscan vases are in the Bristol Museum.[382]
Mark: P.A./B.P. incised

Felix Pratt, Lane Delph, Fenton, Staffordshire, c. late 18th century-present
The partnerships of Felix Pratt (& Co.) of Fenton are numerous and complicated. A number of them are listed in Geoffrey Godden's *Encyclopedia of British Porcelain Manufacturers*. The actual date of the onset of pottery manufacture by Pratt seems uncertain. John and Griselda Lewis suggest that the earliest documentary piece of marked **PRATT** pottery is a Lord Rodney mug dated 1785 made by Felix Pratt's father, William Pratt.[383] Felix Pratt (1780-1859) was in a partnership with William Coomer in the pottery manufacturing business in the early years of the nineteenth century. That dissolved on 11 November 1809 and Pratt continued on his own.[384] The only suggestion that Pratt ever made blackware was the publication of a notice in the *Staffordshire Advertiser* of 31 March 1838:

> Land for sale at Lane Delph next to Canning Inn, 600 square yards, buildings, hovel &c previously used for making Black Ware, beds of clay, marl &c., apply Felix Pratt, Fenton.

No blackwares have been identified from Pratt's manufacture.

Riddle & Lightfoot, Union Square, Longton, Staffordshire, 1841-51
James Riddle and Arthur Lightfoot listed 'Egyptian black' among the output of their

works in Pigot's 1841 directory. No blackware has been identified with the pottery.[385]

William Ridgway (& Son) or **(& Co.)**, Hanley, Staffordshire, c.1830-45
During the 1830s William Ridgway owned, or was working, six potteries in Hanley trading under various names. At least three of the potteries Ridgway was operating himself had previously been manufacturing basalt: Joseph Mayer's works, the former works of David Wilson, the Church Works, and another pottery, lately owned by Toft & May. Jewitt confirms that the firm produced all classes of fine useful wares, including 'jet', stone and jasper.[386] By 1836 William Ridgway & Co. were paying rates on twelve ovens in Hanley.[387] Considering their previous histories it is odd that no blackwares have been identified from any of the Ridgway potteries.

John and Richard Riley, Nile Street, Burslem, Staffordshire, c.1796-1828 (Hole House, Nile Street, c.1796-1811; Hill Works c.1811-28)
Roger Pomfret suggests that the Rileys began the operation of a pottery around 1796,[388] but the first concrete reference to any such Riley enterprise is an insurance policy taken out by the brothers on 11 February 1801 for 'stock and utensils in their manufactory, brick and tiled…£800'.[389] That the Rileys produced a considerable amount of black basalt seems to accord with both surviving pieces and the documentary evidence. A recipe for Black Egyptian or Black Lustre (a lead glazed blackware invented by John Riley in 1821) was put into the Riley recipe book on November 1823 with the following warning:

> It is easy to imitate, but difficult to discover.
>
> 600lbs blue clay
> 500lbs ochre
> 100lbs manganese costs £4/16/8d per ton.[390]
>
> This mixture now used November 1822; other mixtures rather too soft. It is of some importance that the articles be ground very fine, and well mixed together. Old clay works much better than clay newly made, therefore it is always necessary to have a stock of clay made before it is wanted.
>
> Black Luster. To give the Egyptian Black that fine polish, after it comes out of the biscuit, dip it very thin in the following mixture and fire it in a glost oven:-
>
> 130lbs white lead, 20 litharge, 10lbs red lead, 6lbs ground glass, and 1½ lbs tincal dissolved and put in—after this it becomes Black Lustre.[391]

An earlier recipe on page 88 of the Riley book gives a slight variation of the 1823 recipe:

> 1821 March   Black Egyptian or Black Lustre.
> 850lbs ochre
> 750lbs Blue Clay
> 160lbs Manganese   cost £4-9-7

Figure 342. Teapot and cover, glazed basalt with relief floral decoration in the London shape. Mark: **RILEY** impressed in footrim and an impressed '3' and 'H', 1821-28, 5¾in. high. Blake collection.

Figure 343. Cream jug en suite with the teapot in Figure 342. Mark: **RILEY 3**, 1821-28, 5½in. high. Gunson collection.

Figure 344. Teapot and cover, glazed basalt of rectangular shape with a pair of cornucopia baskets in central panel, floral swags and relief floral moulding overall. Mark: **RILEY** impressed in footrim, c.1821-28, 6⅛in. high. Castle Museum, Norwich, Miller collection.

Figure 345. Sugar box and cover en suite with teapot in Figure 344. Mark: '2' impressed in base, John and Richard Riley, c.1821-28, 5⅜in. high. Rakow collection.

Figure 346. Teapot and cover press-moulded in an unusual diamond-waffle design. This London-shaped teapot has a bifurcated handle. Mark: **RILEY** '6', c.1821-28, 6¼in. high. Castle Museum, Norwich, Miller collection.

Figure 347. Cream jug, glazed basalt, press-moulded with an overall floral relief. Mark: **RILEY** impressed in footrim, c.1821-28, 4¾in. high. Rakow collection.

The mixture made as follows:
587 teapots, 24 at 8½d.
103 do   30 at 6¾d
20 sugars at 8½d
120 creams called 3½ dozen

The cost in addition to the clay, for firing modelling, coals and workmanship, left a profit on the 830 teawares of a little over £9.[392]

On page 126 of Riley's Recipe Book:

Egyptian Black Ware was fired in the same oven, and though much the same colour as other ware that had been fired in the biscuit oven, having undergone about 50 hours constant firing; but in order to ascertain the solidity of the black which had undergone so sharp a fire, and to compare it with that of others that had been fired 50 hours, I took a piece of each and ground them on a grindle stone, and I found on inspection that those pieces which had undergone a quick fire were much more porous than the other that had had a long fire. Consequently it proves the necessity there is for all sorts of biscuit ware to have a long fire; otherwise the body will be more porous and open in its texture than it ought to be, and consequently more liable to craze…

The cost of making black lustre teapots (18's) turned out after all expenses were tallied to run at exactly 10/-per dozen; 24's ran 12/6d and 30's 11/6d per dozen.[393]

For some reason the Rileys do not appear in the Burslem land tax records until 1812 when they are shown to own and occupy one property. By 1819 they are either jointly or singly owners of three properties and occupying yet another which was owned by John Sherwin.

Figure 349. Teapot and cover, oval shape with wide satin engine-turned stripes on base and narrow elliptical chain at neck, widow finial. The relief sprigs include, Venus and Cupid, Apollo, and Poor Maria. The partial teaset, en suite with Figure 350, presents some problems in attribution because the signature on the sugar box is not totally legible. Unmarked, possibly Joseph Ring, Bristol, c.1786-88, 5½in. high. Blake collection.

Figure 350. Cream jug and sugar box and cover, en suite with the teapot in Figure 349, the underside of the sugar box cover impressed: JOSEPH P I / G ?, possibly Joseph Ring, Bristol, c.1786-88, 4¾in. high, 5⅛in. high. Blake collection.

*Figure 350a. Coffee pot, engine-turned basalt. Mark **Robinson** incised in cursive. John Robinson, Longton, c.1820, 9½in. high. Blake collection.*

Riley basalt was always moulded and apparently uniformly lead glazed, creating a hard, brilliant surface. If the recipe book is to be believed, the earliest wares must date to 1821, and no later than 1828, since the brothers both died in that year. A number of teawares are illustrated in Figures 342-8. The wares are frequently marked on the outside footrim.

Mark: RILEY (sometimes plus a number)

Joseph Ring, 9 Water Lane, Temple Street, Bristol, Somerset, 1784-88

In 1784 Joseph Ring, a rectifier and vinegar maker, married the daughter of a pottery manufacturer, Richard Frank, in Bristol. According to Jewitt, Ring purchased the business from his father-in-law and he and his wife Elizabeth continued the manufacture of pottery (apparently delftware). In addition, his address said that 'he continues the manufacture of Bristol Stone Ware...'[394]

In 1786, with the help of a Staffordshire creamware manufacturer Anthony Hassel (or Hassells) from whom he purchased stock and moulds, Ring began a fineware manufactory. Ring's business was cut short in 1788 when a building fell in on him and he was killed.[395]

There is no positive indication that Ring made basalt in any of the scanty documentation available. Grant suggested Ring made basalt in two pieces that he illustrated,[396] but neither have any mark which would link them with Joseph Ring. However, from 1784 to 1787 Ring was buying-in earthenware from many Staffordshire manufacturers, and specifically blackware from the Whiteheads, Hanley.[397]

There is a teaset, however, in Martin Blake's collection, which has a partially distinguishable mark which is tempting to attribute to Joseph Ring (Figures 349 and 350). The clearly impressed mark is **JOSEPH**. Partially impressed underneath is a short word which looks like **P I / G**. The shapes fit the 1786-88 period when Ring

would have been manufacturing fineware.
MARK: JOSEPH RING (?)

John Robinson, High Street, Longton, Staffordshire, 1819-20; **Robinson, Ash & Ball,** 1821; **Robinson, Ash, Ball & Goodwin,** 1821-25
Shaw referred to John Robinson as the 'highest character of tradesman and manufacturer'.[398] Robinson had previously been in partnership with the Locketts until 1818 and from 1822 onward he was a partner of Jonathan Lowe Chetham. Nothing is known about his other partners, Francis John Ash, Samuel Ball and John Goodwin. Few marked pieces are recorded (Figure 350a), but the directories corroborate the manufacture of Egyptian black.[399]

Rockingham Works *see* **Swinton**

Salopian Works *see* **Caughley Works**

Saracen Pottery, Possil Park, Glasgow, Scotland, 1875-c.1900
According to Jewitt, the Saracen Pottery established by Bayley, Murray and Brammer at Possil Park produced Egyptian black along with a wide range of other earthenwares and stonewares in the late nineteenth century. The wares were mostly useful wares and the mark included either the name of the pottery or the initials of the owners.[400] No blackware has been identified from the pottery.
Mark: B.M & Co., SARACEN POTTERY

Sayer & Bloor (Sayer & Co.), Tunstall, Staffordshire, c.1812
Indebtedness forced the sale of stock and utensils from the Sayer & Bloor works in Tunstall on 7 March 1812 according to the *Staffordshire Advertiser* of the same date. By May of 1812 Francis Sayer and Daniel Bloor were in gaol for debt.[401] A further sale took place on 13 June 1812 of their furniture and houses as well as stock and utensils[402] and the pottery itself was put up for lease the following month: 'Sayers and Bloor's potworks, Tunstall, to be let, small, suited to Egyptian Black, black printing, enamelling, lustre or gilding concern'.[403] Claims continued against the partners including a third one, William Sayer, until at least 1814.[404] No blackwares have been identified.

Senior and Morton Co., Sutcliffe's Yard, Hunslet, Yorkshire, c.1895-1949
James Wraith Senior was practically born into the pottery industry, beginning work at the age of eleven at the Leeds Pottery, Pottery Fields, under the management of the Brittons. After moving about within the industry he set up a tiny pottery in a stable at Sutcliffe's Yard off Balm Road, Hunslet, and began a pottery business that was to be almost in continuous operation until 1949.[405] It is not certain that James Wraith Senior was himself reproducing the creamwares associated with his name. It seems more likely that his son, George Wraith Senior and John Thomas Morton, who had joined the firm in 1907, were responsible for much of the creamware and basalt produced by the pottery. However, in an interview with George Senior made by Peter Walton, Senior indicated that his father had made some 'blackwares, the moulds being taken from genuine Wedgwood pieces...'[406] (Figures 351-354). These

*Figure 351. Cameo, of Francesco Albani taken from a Wedgwood & Bentley model produced at least by 1773. Mark: **LEEDS POTTERY**, Senior & Morton factory, late 19th-early 20th century, 2¼in. high. Royal Ontario Museum, 970.242.50. Brown collection.*

'blackwares', actually cameos and cameo-medallions, include more than sixteen subjects, but are less well articulated than the Wedgwood and Bentley originals. For some time they were thought to be the products of the earlier manufactory at Pottery Fields, but it is almost certain that the original Leeds pottery did not make cameos or portrait medallions.

The later partnership produced a catalogue of *Reproductions of the Leeds Pottery, Queen's Ware, Decorated and Silver Lustre, Basalt, &c, &c.* in 1913, marketing the wares through William Wood Slee from his antique shop at 30 Duncan Street in Leeds. The surviving catalogue contained twelve pages of photographs illustrating eighty-nine items numbered between 502 and 628. There must have been other catalogues which did not survive.[407] One basalt humidor, identical to some made in creamware (Figure 356), is a rare surviving product of the later factory, probably produced by George Senior and J.T. Morton in the early years of the twentieth century. The inferior quality and articulation, as well as the distinct character of the piece, separate it from the original Leeds Pottery wares. Basalt from the Senior and Morton partnership is usually marked in the upper case, sometimes twice in the formation of a cross (Figure 355a).

Mark: LEEDS.POTTERY

*Figure 352. Cameo of Pompey, another of the 'Leeds Revival' cameos of the Senior & Morton factory. Mark: **LEEDS. POTTERY**, late 19th-early 20th century, 2½in. high. Grigsby collection.*

*Figure 353. Cameo-medallion of 'Charity' (name dubbbed by Sarah Nichols, pending discovery of source), perhaps taken from a medal. Mark: **LEEDS.POTTERY**, late 19th-early 20th century, 3¼in. diameter. Temple Newsam House, 37.3/85.*

*Figure 354. Three cameos depicting Benjamin Franklin, Julia (daughter of Augustus by Scribbonia), and John Dryden. Marks: all **LEEDS POTTERY**, late 19th-early 20th century. 2⅞in. high. Temple Newsam House, 18/59, 18/25, 18/24.*

Figure 355a. Leeds pottery mark on figure 355.

*Figure 355. Plaque, diamond-shaped with two large cornucopias filled with fruit and flowers flanking a central panel depicting a Priestess over a sacrificial pyre; an upper panel surrounded by a wreath shows a ship under sail. This unusual plaque was intended to be hung with a pierced hole at the top. Mark: **LEEDS POTTERY** twice in the form of a cross (Figure 355a), probably Senior & Morton factory, late 19th-early 20th century, 6⅝ x 4¼in. Rakow collection.*

*Figure 357. Bowl with high flaring sides covered overall with a honeycomb roulette ground over which leaf decoration was applied. Mark: **SHORE** under an impressed crown, probably Shore & Co., Isleworth, Middlesex, c.1825, 4¼in. high. Rakow collection.*

*Figure 356. Tobacco box and cover (intended to have inner cover), of oval form decorated with moulded relief shields of the arms of Leeds, medallions containing figures of Bishop Blaise and ships with swags and wreaths. Mark: **LEEDS.POTTERY**, late 19th-early 20th century, Senior & Morton factory, 5⅛in. high. Rakow collection. Peter Walton points out that this form is based on a lead tobacco box produced in Leeds in the 1780s-1790s. Bishop Blaise was the Patron Saint of Woolcombers.*

John Hendley Sheridan, High Street, Lane End and Union Works, Market Place, Longton, Staffordshire, c.1807-21

John Hendley Sheridan was another of the anonymous manufacturers of basalt who left no intact, identifiable products of his work, but produced a variety of black wares including dipped, sprigged and turned black stonewares. Some of the basalt sherds excavated on the Gladstone Pottery site where he operated a manufactory may have been his wares.

Sheridan was in a partnership in Lane End with a John Hewitt which dissolved on 22 November 1808.[408] Nothing else is known of that partnership at present. Another partnership with William Hyatt, a coal proprietor,[409] ended in 1811, after which he carried on on his own.[410] In 1811 Sheridan opposed the proposed tax on earthenware with a subscription of £2.00. Sheridan was also buying in from Mintons who supplied him with a crate of earthenware in 1808.[411] From 1809 to 1811 Sheridan and Hyatt were sending wares to the London emporium of Thomas Wyllie. These included: 6 doz pressed teapots (24) 21/-, 10 doz Dutch teapots (24) 24/- [1809]; 1 doz satin teapots 12/- (no size given) [1810]; 9 doz round Dutch teapots (12,18,24) [1811] £6-6-0 (total).[412] Although not specified as basalt, Sheridan and Hyatt were also sending to London '5 doz bellied oval teapots 24/-, 1 doz diamond teapots £1.4s (1810), 4 doz prest oblong teapots, key border (no price), 3 doz Regency [teapots] (no price), 3 doz new silver shape [teapots] £3-12-0d. (1811)'.[413]

Sheridan was not one of the potteries' own. Of Dublin origin, his family were barristers, the father having been admitted to the Middle Temple in 1776 and called to the Bar in 1781. The youngest son, John Hendley Sheridan, was born at Middle Temple on 10 August 1780 and came to Longton by 1802, staying there until his death in 1859.[414]

Perhaps his legal heredity led him to assume the leadership and act as spokesman when sending a letter of protest to Josiah Wedgwood II in 1815 concerned with the proposed new taxes for manufacturers.[415] By 1820 Sheridan was looking for a buyer for his pottery. The *Staffordshire Advertiser* was advertising the auction of the works located between the Uttoxeter and Stone Roads as 'suitable for an Egyptian Black or China mfy…'.[416] By 1821 the manufactory was no longer in operation.

Shore & Co, Isleworth, Middlesex, c.1760-1825

A possible manufacturer of the bowl (Figure 357) is Shore & Co. Little is known

Figure 358. Milk jug and cover with fluted base and cover with widow finial. The sprig relief includes the Dipping of Achilles. This rare jug for hot milk stands as one of the few surviving pieces from this partnership so marked. Mark: **SHORTHOSE &** **HEATH**, c.1794-1810, 5½in. high. Private collection, ex Grant collection.

Figure 359. Sugar bowl and cover, oval base on a round spreading foot with a peaked cover, the body decorated with wide satin engine-turned stripes and narrow bands of roulette hatching at neck and on cover. A crude shapeless sibyl sits at the pinnacle of the cover. Mark: **SHORTHOSE & Co.**, c.1817-22, 6⅛in. high. Gunson collection.

about the factory or its wares and basalt has not been recorded.
Marks: SHORE & CO; SHORE over an impressed crown (?)

Shorthose and Co., Tontine Street, Shelton (Hanley), Stafforshire, c.1817-22; **Shorthose and Heath**, c.1794-1815 John Shorthose and Lewis Heath were in operation at least by 3 April 1794 when they took out an insurance policy on their business in Hanley:

> John Shorthose and Lewis Heath at Hanley near Newcastle in the County of Stafford, Earthenware Manufacturers. On their utensils and stock in their Warehouse only. Brick, tiled not exceeding £330. In their hovel only, brick and thatched, not exceeding £30. In their tiled warehouse only not exceeding £20.[417]

Shorthose and Heath occupied the Shelton property owned by the late Mr. Simpson (no. 3011 on the rate list) for which they paid rates in 1807 of £1.3.4 and another adjacent (no. 3012), a sliphouse owned by William Kenbright, assessed at

Figure 360. Cream jug, pear-shaped with spreading foot and engine-turned vertical and horizontal chequered decoration. Mark: **SHORTHOSE & Co.**, c.1817-22, 5½in. high. Private collection.

Figure 361. Teapot and cover of round shape with parapet and vertical and horizontal engine-turned chequered decoration. Mark: **SHORTHOSE & Co.**, c.1817-22, 4¾in. high. Royal Ontario Museum, 970.242.80. Brown collection.

Figure 362. Cream jug with bold basketweave body and feather and comb border. Mark: **SHORTHOSE & Co.**, c.1820-22, 5in. high. Thomas collection.

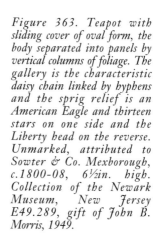

Figure 363. Teapot with sliding cover of oval form, the body separated into panels by vertical columns of foliage. The gallery is the characteristic daisy chain linked by hyphens and the sprig relief is an American Eagle and thirteen stars on one side and the Liberty head on the reverse. Unmarked, attributed to Sowter & Co. Mexborough, c.1800-08, 6½in. high. Collection of the Newark Museum, New Jersey E49.289, gift of John B. Morris, 1949.

£0.6.3. There appeared to be considerable business dealings between Shorthose and Heath and Wedgwood and Byerley.[418] Earthenwares decorated with Wedgwood borders are not infrequently found marked by one of the two Shorthose partnerships. As for the basalt wares, very few examples marked by the earlier partnership of Shorthose and Heath appear to have survived. One covered milk jug (Figure 358) attests to the quality of those wares they did produce. More blackwares exist from the Shorthose and Company partnership (Figures 359-362), but marked wares from either period are rare. In both cases the composition of the basalt is dense, a fine black, and nearly satin smooth. The later wares are nearly always engine turned whereas the one Shorthose and Heath jug (Figure 358) is decorated with both sprigged reliefs and engine turning. The last listing for John Shorthose and Co. as an earthenware manufacturer is in the 1822 directory, and by 1823 John Shorthose was bankrupt.[419] He died suddenly in 1828 in Brussels.[420]

Marks: SHORTHOSE & CO; SHORTHOSE & HEATH

J. & J. Snow, Pyenest Street Works, Hanley, Staffordshire, c.1877-1907
Jewitt claimed that the Snow's produced terracotta, 'jet' and other ordinary earthenware.[421] Nothing else is known of their 'jet' wares.

Sowter & Co., Mexborough Pottery, Mexborough, South Yorkshire, c.1800-08.
The pottery was discussed briefly in relation to the numerous Barker owned/operated potteries in Staffordshire and Yorkshire. However, initially the Mexborough Pottery was established by Robert Sowter in 1800 who operated it until 1808 when it was sold and Sowter became a merchant in Hull.[422] The Barkers operated the pottery from 1809 until its closing in 1848.

It has not been firmly established that the Sowter ownership produced basalt. However, stoneware teapots were reputedly made. The marked **S. & Co.** stoneware teapots have been tentatively attributed to the Sowter manufactory by both Heather Lawrence in her book *Yorkshire Pots and Potteries* (1974) and by me in 1982.[423] Independently we reached the conclusion that the dates and the Yorkshire nature of the wares marked S & Co. augured well for a Sowter attribution. No further substantiation or refutation has been advanced since those two books were published. However, the initials could easily be those of another manufacturer, such as Shore & Co, Isleworth or Sheridan & Co.

The relationship between the marked **S & Co** wares, some of which bear an additional number, especially 1, 6, or 8, and the large body of feldspathic and basalt wares simply impressed with numbers, is one which seems worth repeating. The impressed numerals on hitherto unattributed stonewares, both feldspathic and basalt wares, vary from 1-39. It is significant that many of the block moulds used on S & Co pots are identical to those used on pieces impressed only with numerals, and many of the details, such as galleries and finials, are also identical on **S & Co** pieces and those simply marked with numbers.

The relief wares with American symbols seem to fall into two categories: some utilize the exact block moulds as **S & Co** pieces, others vary greatly. The black teapot with the American eagle and thirteen stars (Figure 363) corresponds directly to moulds utilized on a marked **S & Co** sucrier in the Monmouth County Historical Society in New Jersey and should seriously be considered to be a product of that factory.[424] Whether the factory is Robert Sowter's is still in question.
Mark: S & Co (?) (accompanied by a numeral), numeral 1-39 alone (not necessarily from this factory); the full name has been noted on some earthenwares: **SOWTER'S & CO. MEXBRO**.

Josiah Spode, Stoke-on-Trent, Staffordshire, 1770-1833
Next to Wedgwood, Spode is the most thoroughly documented of the stoneware manufacturers. Major general monographs on the pottery history have been written by Arthur Hayden and Leonard Whiter.[425] Speciality books, dealing with one aspect of the manufacture, have been written by many others, and the Spode Society publishes regularly on all aspects of the factory history. Therefore, as has been the practice with other manufacturers about which monographs have been written, we shall dispense with the historical background.

By 1770, when Josiah Spode began manufacturing on his own, he had already had twenty-one years in the pottery business having been apprenticed to Thomas

Figure 364. Vase and cover similar to ones produced by Wedgwood & Bentley and Palmer and Neale, but rarely seen in Spode. The vase has prominent bird's head handles and sprig decoration of bacchanalian boys. Mark: **SPODE**, *c.1780-90, 7¼in. high. Polikoff collection.*

*Figure 365. Teapot and cover, cylinder-shaped with vertical engine-turned fluted body and seated spaniel finial. Mark: **SPODE**, c.1790-1800, 6⅝in. high. City Museum and Art Gallery, Stoke-on-Trent, 643P.1984.*

*Figure 366. Two teapots and covers, the left one oval and the right round with a parapet, both decorated with engine-turned flutes and sprig relief of swags and tassels. The teapot (left) with a spaniel finial, (right) a finial of a lion chewing a bone. Marks: (left) **SPODE** on outside footrim, c.1790-1800, 5¼in. high, on loan to the Spode Museum; (right) **Spode** on lower outside of handle, c.1790-1800, 5½in. high, Pulver collection, on loan to the Spode Museum, Stoke-on-Trent.*

Whieldon in 1749.

Black basalt must have constituted an important and early part of the Spode business. Although there is no large body of extant blackwares, the range is considerable and the forms seem to indicate that it was manufactured throughout the factory's existence. Certainly in 1823 basalt was still being supplied to both retailers and to private customers as indicated in an invoice discovered from Messrs. Spode and Copeland to Fiennes Wykeham of Leeds Castle, Kent: '2 Black teapots, 2 ditto stands,[426] 1 Black Coffee pot…2 Black Milk pots'.[427]

A black bank on the Spode site consisted of two bottle ovens for firing basalt and, according to Robert Copeland, 'some years ago when excavations were undertaken

Figure 367. Two bowls with spreading feet, engine-turned fluted bases and swag and tassel sprig relief. Marks: (left) SPODE, c.1790-1800, 3¾in. high; (right) NEALE & Co., c.1790, 3⅛in. high. Gunson collection.

Figure 368. Teapot (minus cover) and cream jug, both Yixing-inspired in form with chinoiserie reserve panels of figures in a landscape. The teapot is almost identical to ones produced by Neale & Co. (see Figures 328 and 329) and the cream jug ones by Turner (see Figure 390). Marks: both SPODE, c.1790, 5⅛in. high, 5in. high. Teapot Gunson collection, jug Thomas collection.

Figure 369. Teapot and cover, octagonal form with a dramatic finial of a boy riding a dolphin. This teapot is typical of the originally-conceived basalt wares produced by Spode, c.1790. Mark: SPODE, 6½in.high. Rakow collection.

Figure 370. Cream jug with elegant ear-shaped handle. This pear-shaped jug has a leaf-moulded spout and relief figures of Antonia and Andromache, and figures with a liberty cap. Mark: **SPODE**, c.1790, 2⅞in. high. Gunson collection.

Figure 371. Jug, silver-shaped with spreading foot and elegant handle, the body has fine fluting half way up. MARK: **SPODE**, c.1790, 9¼in. high. Robertshaw collection.

Figure 372. Coffee pot and cover of baluster shape with spreading foot and silver-shaped handle, the body and domed cover decorated with narrow horizontal and wide vertical engine-turned bands. The spout is elegantly moulded with vertical flutes and foliage. Unmarked, possibly Spode (compare handle with jug in Figure 371), c.1790-1800, 10⅜in. high. Thomas collection.

Figure 373. Teapot and cover of naturalistic shape in the Yixing manner with leaf and berry relief decoration and a crab stock handle and spout. The interior has a domed strainer indicating a nineteenth century date. Unmarked, probably Spode (see Figure 374), c.1805-10, 7⅟₁₆in. high. Castle Museum, Norwich, Miller collection.

Figure 374. Teapot and cover, buff-bodied stoneware with a Rockingham brown glaze. Mark: **SPODE**, c.1810, 3⅛in. high. Royal Ontario Museum, 921.54.1.

Figure 375. Cream jug, polished basalt with a silver-shaped body and spreading foot with a gadrooned edge and dramatic mermaid handle. Mark: **SPODE**, c.1790-1820, 4⅜in. high. Rakow collection.

Figure 376. Teapot and cover, polished basalt of dramatic form with arresting handle consisting of a winged female figure. The rectangular body is slipcast with a wide rising shoulder culminating in a scroll rim. The body and cover are shaped into panels divided by fluted or floral columns with a central moulded basket of flowers. Unmarked, possibly Spode, c.1820-30, 6¼in. high. Temple Newsam House, 11.47/41.

Figure 377. Coffee pot and cover, tall egg-shaped, with a spreading foot and engine-turned body with diagonal chequered decoration. Mark: **SPODE**, c.1810-20, 9½in. high. On loan to the Spode Museum, Stoke-on-Trent.

Figure 378. Teapot and cover of low round shape with engine-turned chequered body. The flat cover with button knop is barely visible above the roulette-decorated gallery. Mark: **SPODE**, c.1810-20, 3¼in. high. Royal Ontario Museum, 970.242.73, Brown collection.

238

*Figure 379. Sugar box and cover of low round form, engine-turned in diagonal stripes with ear handles and a button knop. Mark: **SPODE**, c.1810-20, 3½in. high. Spode Museum. Cream jug of low round form moulded with flowers. Mark: **SPODE**, c.1810, 2½in. high. Pulver collection, on loan to the Spode Museum, Stoke-on-Trent.*

*Figure 380. Incense/pastille burner of rare form and decoration in basalt with white stoneware Egyptian motif relief decoration. Mark: **SPODE**, c.1805-15, 4¼in. high. On loan to the Spode Museum. Cream jug lightly glazed, of low round form decorated in a similar style. Mark: **SPODE**, c.1810-20, 2⅝in. high. The Spode Museum, Stoke-on-Trent.*

to install underground arks (tanks for holding slip), huge quantities of black basalt sherds were discovered beneath the ground near one of the bottle ovens'.[428]

Spode was a retailer as well as a manufacturer. In 1779 a Sun Fire Insurance Policy described Josiah Spode as a 'Dealer in China, Glass and Earthenware: House £150, utensils £600, wearing apparel £50'.[429]

Although there is no accounting for the rarity of Spode basalt, the wares themselves are uniformly high in quality and exhibit (if I may beg to disagree with Grant who suggested that Spode was a major plagiarist in all ceramic areas)[430] an originality in many of the shapes.

Although the shapes were principally utilitarian, Spode produced a few ornamental wares. A rare vase (Figure 364) with bacchanalian boys and bird head handles is reminiscent of those produced by Neale, probably around the same time. Among the earliest wares one sees cylinder shaped vertically fluted teawares (Figure 365) with crisp solid handles and straight spouts. Neo-classical swag reliefs adorn a number of

*Figure 381. Teapot and cover of low round form decorated in a chinoiserie style with prunus and exotic floral reliefs. A similar one, made by Wedgwood in red stoneware, is in the same collection. Mark: **SPODE**, c.1820, 4in.high. Laver collection.*

*Figure 382. Jug, glazed basalt with bulbous body and flaring gilded spout, serpent handle with portions gilded. Mark: **SPODE** (very small 5mm impression), c.1825. Pulver collection, on loan to the Spode Museum, Stoke-on-Trent.*

pieces (Figures 366 and 367) in different shapes, some of which are again similar to those produced by Neale and Turner, as are the chinoiserie forms and decoration seen in Figures 368 and 369. Spode basalt is frequently solid in appearance (Figure 369); in other pieces silver shapes and elegant handles carry the day. If any single feature could be considered a hallmark of Spode basalt it should be the handles which are nearly always a focal point (Figures 371 and 375). Nevertheless, Spode produced its share of ordinary engine-turned wares which were the common denominator of most blackware manufacturers (Figures 377-379). Napoleon's Egyptian campaign provided fodder for exotica produced by Wedgwood and Spode in the form of blackwares with white stoneware relief (Figure 380) and chinoiserie continued to be popular into the nineteenth century (Colour Plate 18; Figure 381) sometimes with shapes which were popular thirty years earlier (Figure 374). Spode infrequently produced glazed basalt (Figure 382), but in general the wares were more effective when left unglazed.

Spode's debt to John Turner has often been cited because the wares are commonly confused. The Spode factory still possesses a large number of Turner sprig moulds, perhaps purchased after the Turner factory's bankruptcy in 1807 or more likely in 1829 when they were offered for public sale.[431] If indeed, they were purchased in 1829, the moulds would have impacted very little on the basalt production of the first Spode factory before it was taken over by Copeland and Garrett in 1833.
Mark: SPODE

Daniel Steel, St, James Street Works, Burslem, Staffordshire, c.1790-1818; Scotia Works, Burslem, c.1802; Nile Works, Burslem, c.1821-24
Although it seems probable that Daniel Steel was manufacturing basalt, no known marked examples exist. He billed himself in the 1822-3 directory a 'Jasper and Ornamental stoneware Manufacturer, Nile Street'. Examples of his jasper indicate that Steel was capable of competing successfully in that field and it seems likely that he was doing so in basalt as well. Daniel Steel does not make an appearance in the Burslem tax records until 1805 although he was reputedly operating from at least one works, the St. James Street works, before that. In 1805 he was listed as occupying a property owned by John Gilbert on which a tax of £0-3-9 continued to be paid until

1809. By 1812 that property was occupied by William and Thomas Bathwell. Steel's name disappeared from the tax records until 1820 when 'Daniel Steel & Co.' were occupying a property owned by Thomas Sherwin, which was previously occupied by J. & R. Riley. The tax was £0-5-0. Nothing else is known about this elusive pottery.
Marks: STEEL; STEEL BURSLEM

Benjamin Stubbs, High Street, Longton, Staffordshire, c.1849-51
Benjamin Stubbs was a decorator about whom very little is known. A recipe book of Benjamin Stubbs dated 1826 in the possession of Rodney Hampson, has a formula for Egyptian black (No. 97):

   90 lb ochre
   35 lb Manganese
   35 lb Iron Scales
  110 lb Blue Clay

William Stubbs, Eastwood Pottery, Hanley, Staffordshire, c.1857-97
Jewitt says that William Stubbs manufactured stoneware jugs and black teapots at the Eastwood pottery.[432] Little else is known about the factory. However, a list of other products manufactured by William Stubbs is in Malcolm Nixon's 'William Stubbs of Hanley', *Northern Ceramic Society Newsletter* No. 69.

Swansea *see* **Cambrian Pottery**

Swinton Pottery, Greens, Bingley & Co., Swinton, South Yorkshire, 1785-1806;
Brameld & Co., Swinton, 1806-26
Excavations made at the pottery site which date to the occupancy of Greens, Bingley & Co. uncovered some basalt sherds, but not large quantities.[433] In spite of the fact that fourteen teapot shapes from Swinton are indicated in the *Drawing Book for Black Ware* 1800 (Figure 383) produced by the Hartley, Greens and Co. pottery at Leeds, none of the excavated sherds and wasters corresponded to the Swinton shapes in the *Drawing Book*.
   Of the shapes in the *Drawing Book* of 1800 eleven of the fourteen have simple engine-turned decoration with either spaniel or widow finials.[434] Two other teapots have neo-classical swag , or scroll and urn relief decoration[435] and a third has classical figures incorporated along with the other acanthus leaf and scroll decoration.[436] According to the Coxes, wasters indicated firing problems.[437]
   A notebook with recipes from the pottery initialled 'J.G.' (probably that of John Green), gave a recipe for the Egyptian black body:

   70 Ochre calcined
   10 Manganese "
    8 Iron Scales "[438]

Only one piece of marked basalt has been recorded, a small plaque with an applied cupid in redware which was in the Sir. A.H. Church collection.[439] Curiously the plaque, whose present whereabouts are unknown, is impressed **ROCKINGHAM**. It

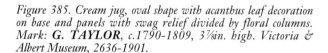

Figure 383. Swinton shapes in the Drawing Book for Black Ware, 1800 of Hartley, Greens and Company, Leeds.

Figure 384. Teapot and cover of oval form with the rose, thistle and shamrock and relief inscription TRIA JUNCTA IN UNO. Although unmarked, this teapot matches sherds excavated on the Swinton (Rockingham) site (see Eaglestone & Lockett, The Rockingham Pottery, 1964, Pl. X), c.1820, Brameld & Co., Swinton, 6½in. high. Gunson collection.

Figure 385. Cream jug, oval shape with acanthus leaf decoration on base and panels with swag relief divided by floral columns. Mark: **G. TAYLOR**, c.1790-1809, 3⅛in. high. Victoria & Albert Museum, 2636-1901.

may be a spurious mark but the Bramelds did produce some basalt ware.[440]

Thomas Brameld's notebook contained several recipes for Egyptian black gathered from other sources: Keeling's, Harvey's, Jas. Burnett's, Hollins's and J. Meyer's.[441] Brameld mentions production of the blackware in 1808 and 1809 and wares were sent to Wentworth House in 1816 and 1825, both described as 'Egyptian oval'. The Coxes report that excavated material included engine-turned wares, fragments from tall teapots with a band of moulded ivy leaves around the shoulder. Pieces were also found from a large oblong teapot with rose, thistle and shamrock devices and *Tria Juncta in Uno* motifs.[442] An extant example of the latter is in the Gunson collection (Figure 384). No marked basalt sherds were recovered from the site.

Tams & Lowe, St. Gregory's Works, High Street, Longton, Staffordshire, c.1865-74

John Tams and William Lowe were in a partnership from 1865 producing, according to *Keates'* 1865 directory, lustre and Egyptian black.[443] Although no blackwares have been identified from their manufactory, both Jewitt and Godden record marks

from the factory as being the first initials **T & L**, with the pattern name
Mark: T & L with pattern name

George Taylor, High Street, Hanley, Staffordshire, c.1784-1809; **George Taylor, jun.** c.1809-late 1820s
There were several Taylor families operating potteries in Staffordshire around the same time which is not surprising since the Taylors, like the Wedgwoods, Astburys and Tofts, were originally seventeenth century potters whose tradition in the industry had deep roots and generated several branches.

George Taylor is listed in *Bailey's Directory* of 1784 as being a potter in Hanley. In June of 1784 Taylor began incurring debts to Josiah Wedgwood in the form of bills which he found himself unable to pay. By 1785 these amounted to over £5.5.[444] After threatening to contact his solicitor, Mr. Sparrow, Wedgwood received payment from Taylor, but not until June 1788.[445]

George Taylor was one of the Subscribers to the Committee of Manufacturers of 1790.[446] He sold to Wedgwood (and had probably manufactured) black basalt by 12 February 1791:

2 Doz Black fluted Cream Ewers			30-
2 Doz	Do	Do	36-
1 Doz	Do	Sugars	18-
1 Doz	Do	Do	24-
1 Doz Stands to Teapots			12-
3 Doz	Do	Do	18-*
1 Doz	Do	Do	24-*
½ Doz	Do oval Do		12-*
1 Doz	Do	Do	18-*
½ Doz	Do	Do	24-*[445]

George Taylor was sending down wares to London Staffordshire warehouseman Thomas Wyllie in 1804-6 and in 1808.[448] The house he owned and occupied, along with the potwork, was No. 3984 in the rate list of 1807-8. He died in 1809 in Hanley and his son by the same name took over his father's business. By 1820 George Taylor, jun. was advertising for a young partner with capital to invest in his earthenware manufactory in Shelton.[449] Apparently he found his source because in August 1824 Edward Poulson, John Poulson, George Taylor, Thomas Glover and Joseph Lockyear, all of Stoke-on-Trent, took out an insurance policy on their China manufactory for £500.[450] The pottery on the High Street, operated by George Taylor, was absorbed by the Ridgways in 1830, about the same time as the two neighbouring ones previously operated by David Wilson and Elijah Mayer.

There are **G. TAYLOR** marked pearlware tewares which conform to stoneware shapes. Although George Taylor appears to have been manufacturing basalt as early as 1791, so far the only marked Taylor basalt to be identified is a creamer in the Victoria and Albert Museum (Figure 385).
Mark: G. TAYLOR

John Taylor, Hill Top Works and other locations, Burslem, Staffordshire, c.1798-1817 or later

Little is known of the John Taylor who for a time operated the Hill Top Pottery in Burslem (after Ralph Wood and before John and Richard Riley). Apparently he was a manufacturer of basalt. His first, or one of his first, partners was John Glass and they were sending wares of their own manufacture down to London by 1798.[451] In 1800 Glass & Taylor overcharged Thomas Wyllie on '46 Doz Round Black Tea Pots'.[452] John Glass and John Taylor dissolved their partnership on 4 January 1801.[453] In April 1804, John Taylor, Thomas Drewry, and Thomas Mellor, all of Burslem, dissolved another partnership.[454] Apparently Mellor continued on with Taylor because that liaison was not abandoned until 14 November 1808.[455] John Taylor contracted yet another partnership with James Wildblood, and they were listed in 1810 as manufacturers of earthenware in Cobridge in the dissolution of that partnership which occurred on 22 November of that year. John Taylor was said in the notice to have given up the whole interest in the partnership.[456] In 1817 Taylor was involved in the dissolution of two further partnerships: one with Joseph Stubbs (operating in Longport)[457] and another with Thomas Lindop.[458]

From 1809 to 1814 Lindop & Taylor were sending earthenware down to London Staffordshire warehouseman Thomas Wyllie.[459] A collection of John Taylor's ceramic recipes, twenty-seven of which are for black and shining black, appeared in 1847. Many of these recipes are listed in Appendix II. No basalt has been identified from any of John Taylor's partnerships.

George Townsend, High Street, Longton, Staffordshire, 1850-65
George Townsend was in an earlier partnership with George Everard but from 1850 until his bankruptcy in 1865 he was in business alone. Townsend occupied three works:

    1850-65 St. Gregory's Works, High Street
    1850-53 Gower Street
    1854-65 Chadwick Street

All the directories from 1850 to 1865 list Townsend as making 'black'. No blackwares have been identified with Townsend's manufactory.
Mark: G. TOWNSEND + the Royal Arms and Pattern Number (printed on earthenwares)[460]

Michael Tunnicliffe, Tunstall, Staffordshire, c.1828-43
John Ward in his 1843 book *The Borough of Stoke-on-Trent* listed Michael Tunnicliffe as being a manufacturer of 'China toys and black ware'. Nothing else is known of the business or its wares.

John Turner, Lane End, Longton, 1762-87; **William and John Turner**, 1787-1803; **Turner, Glover & Simpson**, 1803-06; *see also* **Abbott and Mist**
John Turner was a major basalt manufacturer. His stoneware output must have presented a serious threat to all the other manufacturers, both from the standpoint of the quality as well as the variety of the offerings. A good deal has been written about the Turner factory. The only monograph, *Master Potters of the Industrial*

Figure 386. Tripod oil lamp/pastille burner, consisting of three female figures holding up a globe-shaped container on their backs. A sibyl sits atop the domed fluted cover. Mark: TURNER on outside footrim, c.1790-1805, 11½in. high. Mint Museum of Art, Delhom collection, ex. Grant collection.

Figure 387. Teapot and cover in the Yixing-inspired bamboo shape. Mark: TURNER, probably John Turner, Sr., c.1770s, 3⅞in. high. Polikoff collection.

Revolution, The Turners of Lane End by Bevis Hillier (London: Cory, Adams & MacKay, Ltd. 1965), still stands as a major contribution in the field, although much has been added to the repository of material on Turner by more recent researchers, such as Rodney Hampson, Roger Pomfret, and Tony Thomas.

Turner, along with Neale and Wedgwood, was one of the early Staffordshire manufacturers to open up a London warehouse/showroom. He took out an insurance policy on 25 June 1770 on his London stock at the warehouse located at No. 10 Bennetts Hill, Doctor's Commons, for the substantial sum of £1,000.[461] By 1781 John Turner and his London partner Andrew Abbott were listed in *Bailey's Directory* as 'Potters to the Prince of Wales' (*see* **Abbott**). Turner prospered and after his death in 1787 his sons, John and William Turner, continued the business. By 1792 their two potworks, utensils and stock were insured for £4,700.[462] Turner wares were well enough known that they were specified through the retail trade by name. In 1798 merchant William Wills of Exeter ordered Turner wares through Wedgwood & Byerley, specifying Turner's 'Death of a Stag and Chase of the Hounds'.[463]

In 1803 the Turner brothers were joined in partnership by John Glover and Charles Simpson. Their partnership was officially organized on 10 February 1804 after a formal dissolution of partnership between William and John Turner on 12 December 1803 and the reorganization two months later under Turner, Glover and Simpson.[464] The partnership was further depleted in the autumn of 1804 with the retirement of John Turner;[465] by 1806 the Turner brothers were bankrupt.[466] The final dissolution of Turner, Glover & Simpson occurred on 27 March 1806 as published in the *London Gazette* on 1 April 1806.[467] By 1813 William Turner had fallen on hard times and his furniture was auctioned to pay debts. Shortly thereafter, John Turner II was again beleaguered and in 1815 his estate was assigned to creditors.[468]

It has been suggested that the Turners may have been producing his basalt from his own formula,[469] a not unusual practice for potters who, as has been shown, often utilized their own recipes. If so, no recipe seems to have survived.

The Turners produced a great many wares utilizing sprig-moulded relief decora-

Figure 388. Kettle of round form with wide satin stripes, bail handle, and cover with recumbent lion finial. Mark: **TURNER**, c.1785-95, 8in. high. Polikoff collection.

Figure 389. Teapot and cover (minus finial) of square form moulded with chinoiserie landscape in reserve panels. The cover has pierced naturalistic decoration and would have had a seated lion finial. A marked example with finial is illustrated in Neale Pottery and Porcelain (1987), Pl. 60. Unmarked, William and John Turner, Lane End, c.1790, 5⅛in. high, Robertshaw collection.

Figure 390. Cream jug of rectangular form with chinoiserie reserve panels, this jug is almost identical to ones produced by Spode (see Figure 368). Mark: **TURNER,** c.1790, 3¾in. high. Rakow collection.

Figure 391. Teapot (minus cover) octagon footed form consisting of concave panels with scenes of Domestic Employment. The form is unusual, seen in only one other manufacturer, Birch & Whitehead (see Figure 155). Mark: **TURNER**, c.1795, 4⅝in. high. Private collection.

Figure 392. Teapot and cover, round-bodied with vertical satin-striped base, relief sprig decoration of Venus on her shell. The flat, satin-striped cover has a sibyl finial. Mark: **TURNER**, c.1790-1800, 5in. high. The Board of Trustees of the National Museum & Galleries on Merseyside (Liverpool Museum), 1161M, Mayer collection.

Figure 393. Large teapot and cover. A substantial round-bodied teapot with vertical fluting and a band of Greek key rouletting at the shoulder. A lion sits atop the nearly flat fluted cover. Mark: **TURNER**, c.1800-05, 6¼in. high. Thomas collection.

Figure 394. Teapot, cover and stand of oval shape with wide horizontal and vertical engine-turned bands and a floral chain at shoulder. A sibyl finial sits on top of the domed fluted cover. Mark: **TURNER** in base of teapot; stand, unmarked, c.1800, 6¼in. high. Royal Ontario Museum, 970.242.66, Brown collection.

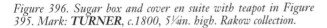

Figure 395. Teapot and sliding cover, press-moulded in an oval bombé shape with columns of flowers flanking the sprig relief of Maternal Affection and Domestic Employment. Mark: **TURNER**, c.1800, 5¼in. high. Gunson collection.

Figure 396. Sugar box and cover en suite with teapot in Figure 395. Mark: **TURNER**, c.1800, 5¼in. high. Rakow collection.

Figure 397. Jug of silver shape with vertical satin-striped base and horizontal wide floral band at mid-riff. The neck is engine-turned in fine horizontal bands and the strap handle has a simulated rivet at the neck and a leaf terminal. Mark: **TURNER**, c.1800, 6¾in. high. Gunson collection.

*Figure 398. Jug, similar in form to the one in Figure 397 but with a reduced spout and gilded rim. Mark: **TURNER**, c.1800, 7⅜in. high. City Museum and Art Gallery, Stoke-on-Trent, 2710.*

*Figure 399. Bust of Voltaire on a polished basalt pedestal (the bust of white feldspathic stoneware). Mark: **TURNER**, c.1790, 11⅜in. high. Laver collection.*

Figure 400. Figure of a classical woman reclining on an overturned urn. Mark: TURNER, c.1800, 8⅝in. x 12in. City Museum and Art Gallery, Stoke-on-Trent, 151P1965.

tion. More than 400 of these moulds marked **TURNER** found their way into the Spode works, perhaps at the sale in 1807 or at some later date.

The 1807 sale of William Turner sheds light on the variety of wares produced by the factory in the early years of the nineteenth century:

> A Large and elegant assortment of Earthenware, and China; comprising the different articles usually manufactured, both useful and ornamental; consisting of Cream Colour, China-glazed blue edge, china glaze printed and painted, Egyptian Black, Cane, Stone, Jasper, Pearl, and Patent China Goods; being the well known and highly reputed manufacture of Messrs TURNER and Co. of Lane-end aforesaid; ...[470]

Turner was no slavish imitator of Wedgwood and his basalt was refined and smooth textured. He produced a wide variety of useful and ornamental wares, including a few intaglio seals.[471] The tripod oil lamp in the Mint Museum (Figure 386), one of his most elaborate undertakings, successfully rivals similar ones produced by Wedgwood. Turner basalt also utilized red stoneware applied reliefs on some wares with equal effectiveness (Figure 406; Colour Plate 23). His basalt plinths, polished on a lapidary wheel, provide stunning bases for his stoneware busts and other figures (Figures 399 and 401). Turner wares excelled in lathe and engine-turned decoration and the necks and trim of his basalt were sometimes gilded (Figure 398). Turner produced satyr mugs similar to those by Neale (Figure 407), as well as hare (Figure 408) and hound's-head stirrup cups (Colour Plate 14). Many of Turner's stoneware mugs and jugs have silver or plate trim. Form is the only key to determining whether a piece was produced by John Turner I or by the two sons; even then it is difficult because styles seen in the 1780s lingered into the next decade. Apparently, William Turner continued to limp along after 1806, renting a manufactory from Joseph Myatt until 1813. No blackwares or other stonewares are attributable to William Turner during that period.[472]

Marks on basalt: TURNER; TURNER & CO.

*Figure 401. Candlestick figure, polished basalt on a separate drum pedestal. There is another pair of figures in caneware in the Royal Ontario Museum and another basalt example in the Victoria & Albert Museum. Mark: **TURNER** impressed in base, c.1790, 9in. high. Rakow collection.*

*Figure 402. Figure of Winter in polished basalt. The figure is taken from a model by Pierre Stephen (see Bevis Hillier, "The Child Seasons New light on the Bristol-Turner link, The Connoisseur, February, 1964). The base is hollow. Mark: **TURNER & Co.**, c.1790-1806, 10½in. high. Rakow collection.*

Figure 403. Pair of bulb pots and liners of rectangular form with sphinx heads at the four corners and ball and paw feet mounted on a square base. Marks: **TURNER**, c.1800, 7¼in. high. Rakow collection.

Figure 404. Two bulb pots and covers, almost identical to the pair in Figure 403 except for the pyramid-shaped covers. The reserve panels depict Charlotte at the tomb of Werther (left) and Domestic Employment (right). Marks: **TURNER**, c.1800, 8⅜in. high (left), 8in. high (right). Rakow collection.

Figure 407. Satyr mug similar to those produced by Neale. Turner mugs have a spreading foot with beading which the Neale ones lack. Mark: **TURNER**, c.1790, 4¾in. high. Thomas collection.

Figure 405. Vase on separate polished octagonal base. The bulbous lower body has vertical satin stripes over which leaves have been applied. The vase has a turned spreading foot and a flaring rim. The sprig relief includes a figure of Britannia. Mark: **TURNER & Co.**, c.1780-95, 8¼in. high. Rakow collection.

Figure 406. Jug of inverted cone shape with flared lip decorated with vertical satin stripes. The strap handle terminates in an acanthus leaf. Mark: **TURNER** impressed on outside footrim, c.1805, 4½in. high. Vase, ovoid-shape, undecorated basalt with red stoneware sprig relief of Poor Maria. Mark: **TURNER**, c.1800-05, 6⅝in. high. The Board of Trustees of the National Museums and Galleries on Merseyside (Liverpool Museum), 1162, 1164, Mayer collection.

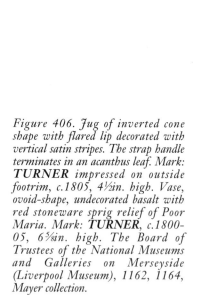

252

Figure 408. *Stirrup cup in the form of a hare. Mark:* **TURNER,** *c.1780-90, 7½in. long. Rakow collection.*

Figure 409. *Egg cup with spreading foot and turned stem, fluted and pierced bowl. Egg cups were produced in basalt at least from 1774. Mark:* **TURNER,** *c.1780-90, 2¾in. high. City Museum and Art Gallery, Stoke-on-Trent.*

Figure 410. *Inkwell with elegant bamboo body and narrow band of Greek key rouletting at base and top. Mark:* **TURNER,** *c.1790-1806, 2½in. high. Robertshaw collection.*

John Twemlow, Shelton (Hanley), Staffordshire, c.1794-99
The Twemlows were another family of the Potteries about whom little is known. They were certainly operating a pottery in 1769 as they were hiring well-known porcelain decorators from Liverpool and Worcester in that year.[473] A billhead in the Wedgwood archives indicates 'G. & T. Twemlow, Potters' were selling wares to Thomas Wedgwood around 1770.[474] Two undated books[475] in the Wedgwood archives list the Twemlows as subscribers for shares in the Trent and Mersey canal.

G. Twemlow, perhaps the father of John Twemlow, was listed as a potter at Shelton in *Bailey's Directory* of 1784.

In 1794 John Twemlow and John Weston dissolved their partnership in Shelton, which was possibly a pottery manufacturing business.[476] In 1795 John Twemlow took out an insurance policy on a set of potworks in Shelton, with stock and utensils totalling £890.[477] A 1797 invoice in Llewellynn Jewitt's possession (in 1883) includes the following basalt entries:

E. Black Teapots, capt., fest d and fig d; Oval E Black Teapots; ditto prest leaf, scollop top fest d and fig d and banded; ditto fluted; ditto coffee-pots;

Figure 411. Teapot and cover press-moulded in an hexagonal form with a central oval cartouche depicting scenes from Aesop's Fables. The mark JT at the base of the handle would ordinarily have been considered as modellers' initials had Grant not suggested in 1910 that this may be the product of John Twemlow's factory. Although nothing has intervened since to either substantiate or refute his suggestion, it seems likely that these are modellers' initials from some other factory. Mark: JT impressed at base of handle, c.1800, 6in. high. Blake collection.

octagon teapots with scollop top, and creams to match; oval plain teapots, (plus several other non-basalt entries).[478]

The *Staffordshire Advertiser* of 19 January 1799 advertised that the house and earthenware mnaufactory of Mr. Twemlow of Shelton was up for auction due to his retirement.

It was Grant who suggested the possibility that those teapots with the very rare initial '**JT**' (Figure 411) may have been the products of John Twemlow's factory.[479] No other pottery has successfully been forwarded to jettison that hypothesis. However, most of Twemlow's basalt must have been unmarked.
Mark: JT (?)

Twyford (John, Joshua and Charles), Shelton, Staffordshire, c.1740s-50s
The Twyford family were an old family of the Potteries who frequently intermarried with their business associates, the Astburys. John Twyford (1726-47) was a potter, his brother Joshua (b.1730) presumably one also, as well as a third son, Charles, who was a potter in Shelton in 1755.[480] It is, perhaps, worth while to lay to rest the attribution to the Twyfords of the two early basalt teapots in the City Museum and Art Gallery, Stoke-on-Trent (Figure 1), which for years were ascribed to them, but are now known to have been manufactured by John and Thomas Wedgwood before they built the Big House, Burslem. It is possible, however, that any one of the Twyfords or all three were making black stonewares, but impossible to attribute any of the early wares to them.

Henry Venables, Etruria Road Works, Hanley, Staffordshire, 1862-69
Jewitt described Henry Venables as manufacturing black basalt and jet glazed wares

Figure 412. Seal with monogram. Mark: **VOYEZ** *(see Figure 412a), c.1773-80, 1⅜in. long. City Museum and Art Gallery, Stoke-on-Trent, 75.1968.*

Figure 412a. Impressed mark on Voyez seal, Figure 412.

along with coloured jaspers.[481] No black wares have been identified from this pottery.

Joseph Vodril, Golden Hill, Tunstall, Staffordshire, c.1818-20
The *Commercial Directory* of 1818/19/20 lists Joseph Vodril of Golden Hill as a manufacturer of blackware. Nothing else is known of the pottery or its wares.

John Voyez, various locations, Staffordshire Potteries and London, 1768-80
John Voyez was a modeller with an itinerant career in the pottery industry, working for others as well as, from time to time, potting on his own. Knowledge of his history is gleaned largely from snatches in letters which Wedgwood wrote to Bentley about this gifted but ulcerative character. The first reference is 31 March 1768:

> I have hired a Modeller for three years, the best I am told in London, he serv'd his time with a silversmith, has work'd several years at a China Work, has been two or three years carving in wood & Marble for Mr. Adams [*sic*] the famous Architect, is a perfect Master of the Antique stile in ornaments, Vases, &ct, & works with equal facility in clay, wax, wood, metal or stone.[482]

By May 1768 Wedgwood had commissioned William Cox, his London showroom manager, to seek special commissions from Voyez until he was put on a weekly salary. Wedgwood suggested he begin by providing a model for a candlestick.[483] On Wedgwood's behalf Cox agreed the following month to pay Voyez 8/- a week plus 'as much more cash if he wants it as will buy him a featherbed'.[484]

Voyez moved to Burslem in July of 1768, into a house which, in anticipation of the modeller's arrival, Wedgwood had been paying rent for some weeks previously. By November relations were strained between Voyez and the Wedgwood family. Mrs. Wedgwood wrote to Bentley: 'I wish Voyez would either mind his business or go his own ways but I am affraid [*sic*] he will do neither'.[485]

By January 1769 Wedgwood had Voyez in the dock for stealing '11 Models of Clay val' 51s, 15 moulds of clay val' 50s and 15 Moulds of Plaister val 50s goods of

Josiah Wedgwood...'[484] Voyez was sentenced to seven years' transportation for theft but letters from prison indicate he served a jail term and was not transported. The sentence itself must have been modified because he was certainly working for rival Humphrey Palmer in 1769, producing the four vases which have served to immortalize their modeller: *Prometheus Bound, Venus and Cupid at Vulcan's Smithy, Dionysus and Ariadne* and *Diana* (*see* Figures 336-338). Apparently Voyez did not stay long with Palmer (*see* Palmer for speculation about other possible Voyez-designed vases produced by Humphrey Palmer). During 1770-1 he appears to have been in a partnership with one of the Hales, either John or Thomas, in Cobridge.[487]

Much to Wedgwood's dismay, in 1773 Voyez published a catalogue of seals he was manufacturing, irrefutably in competition with the Wedgwood market (Figures 412 and 412a).

> Voyez has published a little book Catalogue, or rather the Printer with whom he lodges his Seals, for him, which he calls an Historical Catalogue of all the Intaglios, being near 600. I have bo't this Mighty Volume & it contains about 200 names amongst those are Elius, Cesar, Mark Tully, Cicero, Caronda—Scipian, &tc.
>
> ...This Man's seals are wretched things, but by mere dint of application to the buyers I do not know whether he does not sell more than us [*sic*], but I suppose after Monday his carrier will be cut short at Birm'm & I think it would not be amiss if you had a store & advertis'd it amongst the jewellers & seal setters in the City—but that as you think proper: we can make from 10-20,000 £ worth Per Ann'm and I sho'd be glad to sell all we can, & all the world would have our seals in preference *to any other* if they could come as *easily* at them.[488]

A year later Wedgwood was seriously considering an advertisement to apprise the public that Voyez was defrauding them by placing the Wedgwood and Bentley name on his seals. Wedgwood wrote:

> I am now certain that Voyez puts our names in full length upon his seals, A Servant who worked for Voyez is now with Mr. Hales, & says he will, if we desire, take an oath to the fact...[489]

John Voyez' trade continued but he may not have been working in basalt. On 11 August 1778 Voyez placed an notice in the *Daily Advertiser*:

> COATS of Arms of any of the Families of the Commons of England, Scotland, and Ireland...elegantly engraved on Cornelain or other Stone, and beautifully set in a fine metal that nearly approaches to Gold, wearing like that Metal to the last; The Seal delivered compleat for 21s [or ? 27s]...J. VOYEZ M.R.S.A. at No. 379 Oxford-Street...[490]

By June 1780 Voyez had, at least temporarily, left the country and little else is known of his life. Wedgwood wrote to Bentley about the residue left by Voyez:

Figure 413. Teapot and cover, drum-shaped with vertical fluted engine-turned base and cover with widow finial. Mark: **W(***)**, c.1800, 5⅛in. high. Gunson collection.

Figure 414. Milk jug, pear-shaped with vertical engine-turned fluted body and acanthus leaf moulded spout. Mark: **W (***)**, c.1800, 4½in. high. Blake collection.

I have just now had a large lot of bas reliefs offer'd me which were left here by Voyez when he did our country the favor of turning his back upon it. He left the Models & Moulds in pawn for a debt, & has authoris'd the man to sell them for a trifle. They consist of Tablets & other things which he picked up in London but they are poor things in general, & I have refused them. Indeed, if they had been better…I should not have been under any violent temptation to purchase. The best thing among them was a group of sea horses, but with a Neptune which quite disgraced his cattle.[491]

Voyez exhibited in the Society of Artists in 1768 and 1791. He was described as John Voyer [*sic*], Wax Modeller. He also exhibited at the Free Society [of Artists] in 1767 and 1771.[492]

As a modeller Voyez was the most accomplished artist working in basalt of the period. His subjects, all the ones securely associated with him, are mythological, not unusual for the time. What is unusual is his treatment of the old themes. The fresh Voyez hand, never constrained by a medium which generally rendered its figures as stolid and inert, decorated the surfaces of his vases as a sweep in a landscape. The vases display a nervousness in composition which is more characteristic of the Romantic period than neo-classicism. In this sense, and many others, he anticipated his time.

The four known Voyez vases bear his signature **'I Voyez sculpt, 1769'** (Figure 336-338); but there is a pair of vases which were also produced by Humphrey Palmer (Figure 339) which are so unlike anything else Palmer produced as to be possible Voyez examples as well as another Palmer vase in the City Museum, Stoke-on-Trent (Colour Plate 6). The attribution of the latter vase to Voyez was first suggested by Robert Charleston in 1960[493] and this suggestion is considered to be the most compelling argument for attribution.[494]

Marks: 'I.Voyez, Sculpt. 1769'; VOYEZ

W(***) c.1798-1813

Speculation about the manufacturer of the class of wares which sometimes bear the mark **W(***)** has long remained a subject of conjecture. The range of manufactured wares included all the various earthenwares, a hybrid hard paste porcelain and basalt and the operation must have been of considerable size.

Figure 416. Kettle with replacement wicker bail handle, restrained engine-turning on lower third and on cover, otherwise undecorated, widow finial. Mark: W(***), c.1800, 8⅛in. high. Gunson collection.

Figure 415. Milk jug and cover with lower base and cover vertically fluted, widow finial. Mark: W(***), c.1800, 6⅝in. high. Johns Hopkins University, Homewood House Museum.

A number of possible manufacturers has been forwarded by Diana Darlington in the *Northern Ceramic Society Journal* 4 (1980-1) and by Geoffrey Godden in both his *Staffordshire Porcelain* (1983) and *The Encyclopaedia of British Porcelain Manufacturers* (1988) and by others. These arguments, well articulated as they are, are by no means conclusive and so I shall not reiterate them here. Suffice to say that the names of Wood, Wolfe, Warburton, and Whitehead are among the major contenders for the honour of claiming these fine quality earthenware, stone and porcelain wares.

The basalt identified previously is of fine, dense texture primarily with engine-turned decoration (Figures 413-415), but is occasionally left nearly undecorated (Figure 416) or with sprigged relief figures (Figure 417). A London shaped teapot (Figure 418) and a matching cream jug, discovered recently by Geoffrey Godden, has extended the period for the manufacture of these wares from what was previously considered to be confined to the first decade of the nineteenth century to about 1812 or 1813. Curiously this teapot has the beads on the tip of the spout seen only hitherto on some Mayer, Moseley and Davenport teapots. None of these manufacturer's names has been associated with the **W(***)** marked pots. Finials are not numerous and so far include only the widow and floral knops.
Mark: W(***)

Walker & Galley, Chemical Works, Tunstall, Staffordshire, c.1841
The *Staffordshire Advertiser* printed a notice on 13 November 1841 announcing the dissolution of partnership between George Walker and Samuel Galley as 'Egyptian and Shining Black Manufacturers' at the Chemical Works, Tunstall Bridge on 2 November 1841. Nothing else is known of the works or its wares.

Figure 417. Cream jug of oval form in panels divided by pilasters. The sprig decoration is a Dancing Nymph. Mark: W(***), c.1800-10, 5⅛in. high. Royal Ontario Museum, 970.242.37, Brown collection.

Figure 418. Teapot and cover of London shape with wide fluted base and a border of leaves and berries at the shoulder and on the cover. This teapot (en suite with a matching cream jug) was recently discovered by Geoffrey Godden, thereby extending the known dates of the W(***) manufactory. Mark: W(***), c.1812-13, 5¾in. high. Photograph courtesy Geoffrey Godden.

John Walton, Navigation Road, Burslem, Staffordshire, c.1822-34
John Walton, a well-known figure maker, is listed in both the 1822 directory and the 1834 *Pigot Directory* as a manufacturer of 'Egyptian Black'. No wares have been identified from his pottery.

The Warburtons
John Warburton, Hot Lane, Cobridge (Burslem), Staffordshire, c.1800-25
The Warburton family played a prominent role in Staffordshire in the eighteenth century, with family patriarch Jacob Warburton (1741-1826) setting the standard as a highly respected constituent of the community of potters. Jacob took over the works of his father-in-law Richard Daniel in 1769 and engaged all the men.[495] He was one of the original partners in the New Hall enterprise and subscribed to the

*Figure 419. Teapot with hinged cover, press-moulded oval teapot in panels with elliptical reserve panel of Sportive Love. The hinged cover has a swan finial. Mark: **WARBURTON**, probably John Warburton, Cobridge, c.1805-10; 6½in. high. Gunson collection.*

*Figure 420. Sugar box and cover of oval form divided by convex pilasters into panels with the central relief of Sportive Love. Mark: **WARBURTON**, probably John Warburton, Cobridge, c.1805-10, 4⅝in. high. Private collection, ex. Godden collection.*

Committee of Manufacturers in 1790,[496] but it is uncertain if he ever manufactured basalt. He lived until 1826 and appears from land tax records and other documentation to have been allied in various pottery ventures with his sons who did manufacture blackware. Indeed, in 1790 Jacob Warburton was enquiring about small jasper vases 'which are us'd in Germany at table...'[497] The production of jasper and basalt being very closely connected, Jacob Warburton must at least be considered a candidate for the list of manufacturers.

Jacob's mother, Ann Daniel Warburton, was herself a master potter and appears on the first land tax documentation in Burslem in 1781 as paying taxes on two properties. She continued in the listings until 1795 when her son (Jacob Warburton) began paying the taxes instead. She died in 1798, but Jacob Warburton is listed as occupying the sites himself. By 1799 there are three listings in the name of Jacob Warburton which continue until 1807 when Peter and John Warburton are installed in two of the properties and Jacob in the third.

Jacob Warburton had four sons, all of whom were at one time involved in pottery enterprises with each other: Peter, Francis, John and Benjamin.

The first mention of John occurs in 1799 after his return from Bristol where he was rebuffed by Josiah Wedgwood's sister Catherine. The apparent unhappiness caused by John's pursuit of Miss Wedgwood resulted in a letter to her brother promising no further communication with her.[498] Shortly thereafter, on 11 November 1800, Jacob Warburton and son John dissolved their partnership in the pottery at Cobridge with John continuing in business on his own in what had previously been his father's pottery.[499] In 1815 another partnership involving John Warburton was dissolved, this one including Benjamin Warburton and John Moseley. Their partnership traded as Warburtons & Moseley.[500] As previously mentioned, the name of John Warburton first appears on Burslem land tax records in 1807 and he continued paying a rate of £0-4-0 on the same property until 1820 when the rate dropped to £0-3-0. Since rates rarely changed he may have moved to a smaller pottery in 1820. His business, not a large one, was insured for a total of £800 in 1817.[501]

Although the directories in 1822-3 simply listed John Warburton as an earthenware manufacturer he apparently made the very good quality basalt impressed **WARBURTON** (Figures 419-420). The wares which have been identified are not numerous but make frequent use of a Venus and Cupid relief central panel or

*Figure 421. Sugar box and cover, engine-turned bamboo design on lower quarter and cover; sprigged decoration includes an adaptation of the Cage, Hebe and the Eagle, classical figures with urns, sibyl finial to cover. Mark: **P & FW**, Peter and Francis Warburton, c.1800, 5¼in. high. Robertshaw collection.*

cartouche. An elliptical shaped teapot in the Gunson collection (Figure 419) has a parapet collar with hinged lid and swan finial and the elliptical cartouche with relief decoration of Sportive Love. A sugar box (Figure 420) divided into panels popular in the first decade of the nineteenth century also has Sportive Love relief and a collar or neck composed of peaks alternating with floret roundels characteristically associated with Warburton basalt. Marked **WARBURTON** basalt is extremely rare. Probably a great deal was left un-marked.

MARK: WARBURTON

Peter and Francis Warburton, Bleak Hill, Cobridge, Staffordshire, c.1795-1802;
Peter Warburton, 1802-13
Very little is known about the partnership of Peter and Francis Warburton operating from Bleak Hill, Cobridge. An insurance policy taken out on 10 April 1801 covered their modest works:

> Messrs P. & T.[?F.] Warburton of Cobridge, Potters. Their Pottwork [at Cobridge] £200; Stock of Earthen-ware £150 Utensils £50. Total £400.[502]

Soon thereafter, in 1802, the dissolution of partnership between Peter and Francis Warburton occurred,[503] Francis Warburton establishing himself as a manufacturer of creamware at La Charité-sur-Loire in France and Peter continuing on in the pottery in Cobridge. Peter Warburton must have made some modest strides forward because by 1806 the pottery portion of his insurance policy was insured for a total of £600.[504] Peter Warburton died in 1813 and his wife leased the pottery, first to Robert Blackwell (in 1814) and after Blackwell died to Enoch Wood and Son in 1820.[505]

Few basalt wares have been identified as the products of Peter and Francis Warburton's Bleak Hill Works. An extremely rare covered sugar (Figure 421) marked **P. & F. W.** attests to the quality of the wares they did produce.

Marks: P.& F. W.; P. & F. WARBURTON; WARBURTON (?). The latter two have been noted on earthenwares.

Ralph Wedgwood & Co., Hill Pottery, Burslem, Staffordshire, 1789-97;
Knottingley Pottery, Ferrybridge, W. Yorkshire, 1798-1801
Ralph Wedgwood set up business in the manufacture of basalt as well as other earthenwares in Burslem probably in 1789, the year he first appeared as paying the taxes on three properties·[506] In 1790 he was included on the list of Subscribers to the Committee of Manufacturers.[507] The following year he placed a notice in the *Daily*

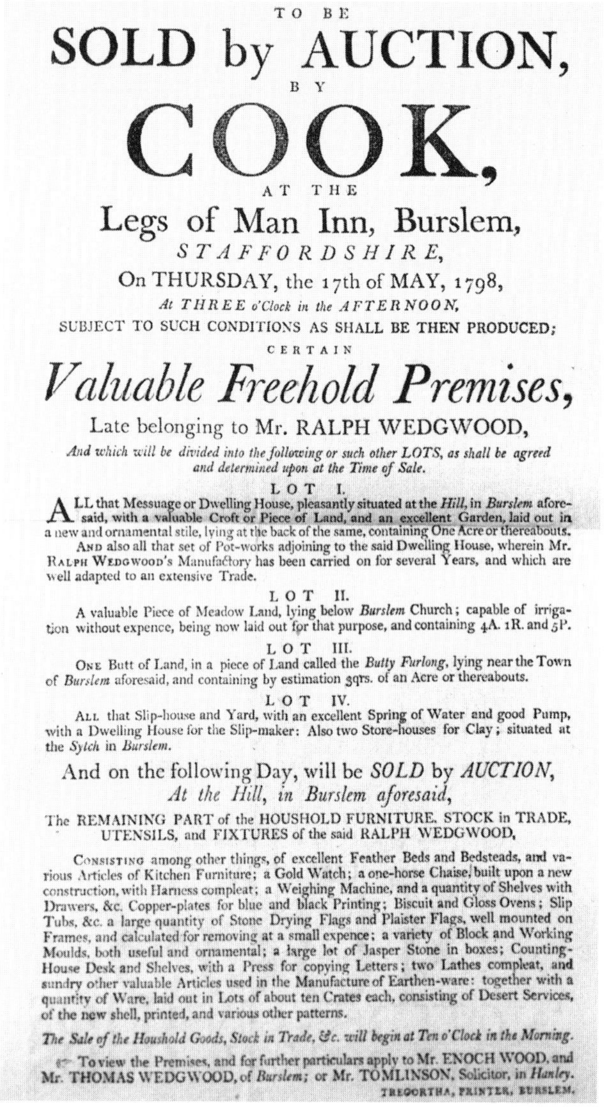

TO BE
SOLD by AUCTION,
BY
COOK,
AT THE
Legs of Man Inn, Burslem,
STAFFORDSHIRE,
On THURSDAY, the 17th of MAY, 1798,
At THREE o'Clock in the AFTERNOON,
SUBJECT TO SUCH CONDITIONS AS SHALL BE THEN PRODUCED;
CERTAIN

Valuable Freehold Premises,

Late belonging to Mr. RALPH WEDGWOOD,
*And which will be divided into the following or such other LOTS, as shall be agreed
and determined upon at the Time of Sale.*

LOT I.

ALL that Messuage or Dwelling House, pleasantly situated at the *Hill,* in *Burslem* aforesaid, with a valuable Croft or Piece of Land, and an excellent Garden, laid out in
a new and ornamental stile, lying at the back of the same, containing One Acre or thereabouts.
AND also all that set of Pot-works adjoining to the said Dwelling House, wherein Mr.
RALPH WEDGWOOD's Manufactory has been carried on for several Years, and which are
well adapted to an extensive Trade.

LOT II.

A valuable Piece of Meadow Land, lying below *Burslem* Church; capable of irriga-
tion without expence, being now laid out for that purpose, and containing 4A. 1R. and 5P.

LOT III.

ONE Butt of Land, in a piece of Land called the *Butty Furlong,* lying near the Town
of *Burslem* aforesaid, and containing by estimation 3qrs. of an Acre or thereabouts.

LOT IV.

ALL that Slip-house and Yard, with an excellent Spring of Water and good Pump,
with a Dwelling House for the Slip-maker: Also two Store-houses for Clay; situated at
the *Sytch* in *Burslem.*

And on the following Day, will be *SOLD by AUCTION,*
At the Hill, in Burslem aforesaid,

The REMAINING PART of the HOUSHOLD FURNITURE, STOCK in TRADE,
UTENSILS, and FIXTURES of the said RALPH WEDGWOOD,

CONSISTING among other things, of excellent Feather Beds and Bedsteads, and va-
rious Articles of Kitchen Furniture; a Gold Watch; a one-horse Chaise, built upon a new
construction, with Harness compleat; a Weighing Machine, and a quantity of Shelves with
Drawers, &c. Copper-plates for blue and black Printing; Biscuit and Gloss Ovens; Slip
Tubs, &c. a large quantity of Stone Drying Flags and Plaister Flags, well mounted on
Frames, and calculated for removing at a small expence; a variety of Block and Working
Moulds, both useful and ornamental; a large lot of Jasper Stone in boxes; Counting-
House Desk and Shelves, with a Press for copying Letters; two Lathes compleat, and
sundry other valuable Articles used in the Manufacture of Earthen-ware; together with a
quantity of Ware, laid out in Lots of about ten Crates each, consisting of Desert Services,
of the new shell, printed, and various other patterns.

The Sale of the Houshold Goods, Stock in Trade, &c. will begin at Ten o'Clock in the Morning.

☞ To view the Premises, and for further particulars apply to Mr. ENOCH WOOD, and
Mr. THOMAS WEDGWOOD, of *Burslem;* or Mr. TOMLINSON, Solicitor, in *Hanley.*
TREGORTHA, PRINTER, BURSLEM.

Figure 422. Notice of the auction of the Ralph Wedgwood pottery in Burslem 17 May 1798 (Wedgwood MS W/M 1820).

Advertiser advertising his London showrooms in St. Paul's Churchyard.

> Ralph Wedgwood and Co., respectfully informs the Publick, that they have opened a wholesale and retail Warehouse for all Kinds of Earthenware in St. Paul's Churchyard, No. 35, on ready Money terms, Coats of Arms, Cyphers, Crests and Services compleated on the shortest Notice, in Town, or at their Manufactory, Hill-Burslem, Staffordshire.[508]

The manufactory was a sizeable one with two sets of works, one on the Hill and another at Swan Bank, Burslem, another sliphouse and dwelling house for the slip maker at the Sytch, Burslem, and his London warehouse. The whole, including Wedgwood's own dwelling house next to the Hill Works, was insured for £4,150 in 1793.[509] By 1794 Ralph Wedgwood began cutting the amount of insurance on his properties, reducing the total valuation to £2,950.[510] The London venture was not a success and by 24 September 1794 was being advertised for auction.[511] It is worth noting that included in the list of the contents of the London showroom were 'black Figures' and 'Egyptian teapots', but one cannot be assured that they were products of the Hill Pottery. Ralph Wedgwood did make Egyptian black tewares but no black figures have yet been identified from his manufacture. By August 1795 the Swan Bank works had also been taken off the list of insured properties.[512] The business failed in 1797 and all the property owned by Wedgwood, including his personal effects, was sold by auction on 17 May 1798 by Cook auctioneers at the Legs of Man Inn, Burslem (Figure 422).[513] Not surprisingly, 1798 is the last year Ralph Wedgwood's name appears on the tax rolls for Burslem.

In June 1798 Ralph Wedgwood joined the partnership at the Knottingley Pottery, Ferrybridge, which consisted of William Tomlinson, John Foster and other silent or purely business partners trading under Tomlinson, Foster and Company. The partnership, which was intended to last ten years but in reality lasted less than three, was styled Tomlinson, Foster, Wedgwood & Co.[514] The pottery was an extensive one as described by several insurance policies taken out in 1795, 1801, 1806 and 1813.[515] The 1801 policy probably most accurately accounts for the size of the business when Ralph Wedgwood was there and indicates the pottery was insured for £8,000.[516] However, Ralph Wedgwood's experiments proved to be expensive; the partnership, which was not a success, was dissolved on 1 January 1801 and he was paid £1,025 to leave the concern and relinquish his partnership in the pottery.[517]

Very few basalt pieces have been found bearing the **WEDGWOOD & CO.**

Figure 423. Teapot and cover, press-moulded with basketweave base with vertical faceted panels above, reserve panel of St. George and the Dragon on one side and a horseman on the other. The gallery is moulded with a stylized floral relief and the cover has an unusual dolphin finial. Mark: **WEDGWOOD & Co**., c.1795, 6⅛in. high. Hacking collection.

Figure 424. Cream jug finely modelled with unadorned elegance. Mark: **WEDGWOOD & Co**., c.1795, 3½in. high. Holdaway collection.

Figure 425. Cream jug of high vertical shape nearly un-decorated except for a section of vertical fluting with horizontal beading at the base. Mark: **WEDGWOOD & Co**., c.1795, Fisk collection.

impressed mark. They are of generally excellent quality, fine and light in texture and some are interesting shapes. An oval sugar box with neo-classical swag relief decoration, formerly in the Grant collection, is illustrated by Grant, Plate XCII. A fine teapot in the Hacking collection (Figure 423) is an interesting form with a charming dolphin finial. The quality was so high that Ralph Wedgwood could leave his pots unadorned without fear of blemishes being discovered (Figure 424).

Figure 426. Teapot and cover of cylindrical form with engine-turned horizontal and diagonal stripes and horizontal rouletting on body, shoulder and gallery. The flat cover has a button knop. Mark: **FERRYBRIDGE**, *Ferrybridge (Knottingley) Pottery, Yorkshire, c.1800-10, 4½in. high. Wakefield Art Galleries and Museums.*

Figure 427. Coffee pot and cover (not mate), engine-turned in a chevron pattern with rouletting to body, shoulder and gallery. Mark: **FERRYBRIDGE**, *Ferrybridge (Knottingley) Pottery, Yorkshire, c.1795-1820, 4⅛in. high (without cover). Temple Newsam House, 4.67/46, Hollings collection.*

Two quite different tea and coffee pots exist marked **FERRYBRIDGE** (Figures 426 and 427). Instead of the moulded relief decoration seen on the **WEDGWOOD & Co** teawares discussed previously, they both have engine-turned decoration, tending to awkward, heavy forms. If they were made by the Knottingley Pottery during Ralph Wedgwood's tenure they are quite distinct from anything else we have hitherto associated with his work. Lacking the sophistication of **WEDGWOOD & Co** marked pots, it seems likely that they were made either after his association with the pottery or just before.

A curious cream jug in the Hacking collection (Figure 465) has an unusual mark with each letter of the **WEDGWOOD** name being stamped separately and askew, as if by a drunken workman. There is no reason to believe that this is the product of either of Ralph Wedgwood's factories, either from the shape, decoration or mark, all of which are dissimilar to other devices used by him.

A more detailed study about the wares of Ralph Wedgwood can be found in Dr. Minnie Holdaway's article, 'The Wares of Ralph Wedgwood', *English Ceramic Circle Transactions* Vol. 12, Part 3, 1986.

Mark(s): WEDGWOOD & CO.; FERRYBRIDGE (?)

Thomas and John Wedgwood, other sites and Big House, Burslem, Staffordshire, c.1730s-85

Distant cousins of Josiah Wedgwood, Thomas and John Wedgwood were in business as potters in Burslem before they built the Big House in Burslem around 1750. A handwritten notation in Enoch Wood's personal copy of William Pitt's *A Topographical History of Staffordshire* in the City Museum and Art Gallery, Stoke-on-Trent, indicates that the two blackware teapots in Enoch Wood's collection (Figure 1) were made by Thomas and John Wedgwood before they built the Big House. For further comments on the history of these two teapots see Chapter I, pages 26-27. No other blackwares have been specifically attributed to Thomas and John Wedgwood and by 1784 (John had died in 1776) Thomas was listed in *Bailey's Directory* as a

'Manufacturer of Cream coloured Ware and China glazed Ware, painted with Blue, &c. Big. House'. There was no mention of Egyptian black.

Thomas Whieldon, Fenton Low, Staffordshire, c.1740s and Fenton Vivian, c.1747-80
Thomas Whieldon's name is bantered about shamelessly as the manufacturer of all the early English stonewares and earthenwares. As a generic, Whieldon's hand has been associated with nearly every pottery type except black stoneware. In fact, a few sherds of wasters of black stoneware were excavated on the Fenton Vivian site (Figure 428). It is likely that he was experimenting with a black stoneware body and may have even produced some actual wares. Whieldon's recipe for Black survives (*see* Chapter I, page 33), but it appears to be a recipe for black-glazed redwares of the Jackfield type.

(Whitehaven) The Ladypit Pottery, Whitehaven, West Cumberland, c.1834
The Ladypit Pottery, Whitehaven, operated by Bell and Jackson, advertised on 25 July 1834 that they intended to make 'IRON-STONE-CANE WARE, BLACK GLAZED TEAPOTS, PORPHYRY & GROTTO WARE.'[518] Nothing else is known of the wares produced at the pottery.

James and Charles Whitehead, Old Hall Pottery, Shelton (Hanley), Staffordshire, c.1790-1810
The Whitehead family seem to have been involved in the pottery industry in Hanley earlier than 1790. Christopher Charles Whitehead was providing Messrs. Josiah and Thomas Wedgwood with '6 doz Tea kettles Plain red China', and 'Inlet plain black teapots' &c. in 1777.[519] Jewitt says the family were involved in white salt glaze manufacture prior to 1770.[520] In 1781 an account from the Whiteheads lists 'Teapots. leg'd with raised tops, Black Teapots, bowls, ewers, coffee pots Bowls sprigged other shapes'.[521] In 1787 an account of Chatterley & Whiteheads included 'Black inlet teapots, sprigged other shapes'.[522] In spite of all the above, Christopher Charles Whitehead was listed in the directories of 1784 and 1787 simply as a potter in Shelton.

As potters, his sons, James and Charles Whitehead, do not surface in documents much before 1792 when they took out an insurance policy with their uncle Ephraim Chatterley on a 'sett of Potworks in one connected range' and the stock of earthenware, utensils, blocks and moulds totalling £1,000.[523] In November 1793 Chatterley dropped out of the business in Hanley leaving the three Whiteheads, James,

Charles, and John to carry on alone.[524] James and Charles Whitehead were participants in the Potters Clay Company Copartnership of 1796 [525] and in 1798 they produced an outrunner or agent's catalogue of *Designs of Sundry Articles of Earthenware.* Subtitles included the following appendage: *At the Same Manufactory May Be Had A GREAT VARIETY OF OTHER ARTICLES, Both Useful and Ornamental, As Well Printed, Painted, & Enamelled, As Likewise DRY BODIES, Such as Egyptian, Black, Jasper, &c,&c.*[526] Ephraim Chatterley was linked importantly to European markets. Early in his career Elijah Mayer had been Chatterley's agent in Amsterdam. When Ephraim Chatterley died in 1811, the works, occupied by the Whiteheads, were still in his possession.[527] In 1810 James and Christopher Whitehead were bankrupt.[528] A meeting of their creditors was called to collect both local and foreign debts; the announcement of that meeting appeared in the *Staffordshire Advertiser* on 25 December 1813,[529] but apparently as early as 1810 James Whitehead was looking for other work. Mr. R. Pontiface of 46-47, Shoe Lane, London, requested a character reference for James Whitehead of Hanley of Messrs Wedgwood, saying in his letter that he was being considered for a position with them.[530]

Local tax records confirm that J. & C. Whitehead occupied Potworks 3759 owned by Ephm. Chatterley, plus a farm (3760), and brick ovens (3761), and paid a local rate on all of £4.9.8. In addition, there was a slip house, owned by Chatterley as well, on which a rate of £0.3.4 was paid.

Another letter suggests a sad end for Mr. C. Whitehead (Christopher), for someone who signed his name G. Smith wrote on 6 April 1818: 'I never knew or heard anything to the contrary of Mr. C. Whitehead being a very respectable character but I suppose he can have little capital to work with'.[531] Christopher Whitehead died of typhus at Shelton in 1818, aged forty-four.[532] James, who became a potter's merchant, was bankrupt again in 1821[533] and died at Shelton in 1825, aged sixty-three.[534]

The printed catalogue of Whiteheads of 1798 was not the first to be issued by the firm but is the only surviving copy. It is particularly important for the creamware shapes since the Whiteheads may not have marked their pottery.[535] The text is in English, German, Dutch and French, thereby identifying the firm's markets. Unfortunately, no dry bodied wares appear in the catalogue and since there were no wares marked, identification of Whitehead basalt is all but impossible.

Robert Wilson, Church Works, Hanley, Staffordshire, 1791-1801; **David Wilson (& Sons),** Church Works, Hanley, 1798-1817; West Pans Pottery, Scotland, c.1800-17

Robert Wilson is the unsung hero of James Neale's Church Works, having been manager probably from the time of Humphrey Palmer's tenure, that is before 1778. The Church Works passed from Neale to Wilson in 1791 when Robert Wilson, for the first time, assumed the taxes on the pottery. The official dissolution of partnership between James Neale and Robert Wilson did not take place until 24 April 1792.[536] Robert Wilson died on 3 February 1801 and the *London Gazette* printed a notice regarding the settlement of the estate:

> All persons who have any Demands upon the Estate of Mr. Robert Wilson late of Hanley...are requested to send an account thereof immediately either to James Neale. Esq. of St. Paul's Churchyard, London; the Reverend John

*Figure 429. Teapot, cover and stand, of cylindrical shape with wide vertical satin-striped base, a narrow band of deeply cut Greek key relief at shoulder, high, crimped gallery and widow finial. Aesop Fable sprig decoration is on both sides. Marked Wilson basalt is very rare, but an identical teapot is in the Blake collection. Mark: **WILSON** impressed in base of teapot, c.1795-1805, 5⅞in. high. Royal Ontario Museum, 970.242.81, Brown collection.*

Figure 430. Teapot and cover, boat-shaped with wide engine-turned satin striped body and a band of cross hatched rouletting at shoulder, crimped gallery and a slightly domed cover with a widow finial. The form is most unusual, but similar examples of the shape can be found in other Wilson-marked teapots (see Neale Pottery and Porcelain, Pl. 141). Unmarked, attributed to Wilson, c.1795-1805, 4⅞in. high. Royal Ontario Museum, 970.242.82, Brown collection.

Wilson of Market Drayton in the County of Salop, or to Mr. David Wilson of Hanley, aforesaid, the acting Executors…[537]

Wedgwood & Byerley were treated by some merchants placing orders as a sort of clearing house or emporium for other potters' wares. In 1798 William Wills of Exeter specified that he be sent wares of Wilson, Herculaneum and Turner manufacture as well as some items of unspecified manufacturer, presumably Wedgwood.[538] The practice of 'buying-in' between Wedgwood & Byerley continued probably because specific wares were being sought after as well as the common practice of filling out short orders. The Wedgwood & Byerley agent in these negotiations with Wilson and others, including John Davenport and Elijah Mayer, received a five per cent commission on the total order purchased from other manufacturers.[539]

By 1798 invoices and receipts appear headed with David Wilson's name. However, after Robert Wilson's death in 1801 his brother David Wilson officially succeeded him and, with his sons, traded as David Wilson & Sons. Land tax records for 1807-8 indicate that Wilson paid an aggregate of over £17 annually on three properties (Potwork 3972 £5.16.8; Land 3973 £11.7.0; Mill 3974 £0.3.4). A partnership of unspecified duration between William Breeze and David Wilson in the manufacture of earthenware in Hanley, trading as Breeze and Wilson, was dissolved by mutual consent in 1811 and reformed by David Wilson, the elder, as Wilson & Breeze in the same year.[540] The Wilsons became bankrupt and both the Hanley pottery and the West Pans Pottery, under the management of David Wilson, closed in 1817.

Unlike the previous regime, the quality of the wares varied under David Wilson's management, but could still be extremely high. Also unlike the previous regime very little basalt seems to have been manufactured, although the few marked **WILSON** examples are of superb quality (Figure 429). Some unmarked examples may also be from the Wilson era (Figures 430, 431).

With the exception of the widow finial, actual Wilson basalt bears no direct resemblance to previous Neale & Co basalt wares. Characteristic of the very few marked wares and some attributed ones is the bold fluted gallery and straight spout, very practically moulded for a metal fitting. Sprig relief decoration on the two

Figure 431a. Enoch Wood & Co. Trade Card. Courtesy The Winterthur Library; Joseph Downs Collection of Manuscripts and Printed Ephemera, 65x680.

Figure 431. Sugar box and cover of beaker shape with slightly wider top than base, ring handles and band of rouletting at shoulder. The flat cover is broken by a crimped gallery, widow finial. Unmarked, possibly Wilson, c.1795-1805, 6⅝in. high. Robertshaw collection.

marked **WILSON** teapots consists of Aesop fables not hitherto known on any Neale & Co. stonewares. For further information on the Wilson family and their pottery *see* **Neale Pottery and Porcelain.**
Mark: WILSON; 'W' (impressed)

Thomas Wolfe, Stoke-on-Trent, Staffordshire, c.1783-1818
Although there are no marked examples of Thomas Wolfe's basalt, he was listed in *Bailey's Directory* of 1784 as a 'Manufacturer of Queen's ware in general, Blue Printed, and Egyptian Black, Cane, &c.' His main attraction for ceramic historians has been his porcelain producing partnership in Liverpool with Miles Mason. However, since the manufacture of porcelain is outside the scope of this book it will not be rehashed. A thorough treatment of all the porcelain manufacturing partnerships of Thomas Wolfe is presented by Geoffrey Godden in *The Encyclopaedia of British Porcelain Manufacturers.*

Wolfe's pottery at the Big Works, Church Street, Stoke, must have been considerable because in 1807-8 he paid the large rate of £10.0.0 on Potworks No. 1802. By 1809 he was in a partnership with his son-in-law Robert Hamilton in a business described in their insurance policy as an 'earthenware and china' works.[541] Thomas Wolfe was further involved with Robert Hamilton and another son-in law, William Arrowsmith, in a retailing partnership in Dublin which was dissolved in 1810 when Arrowsmith left Robert Hamilton to continue alone in the business.[542] In 1811 Wolfe was listed by himself in a further insurance policy for the pottery still described as manufacturing both earthenware and china and insured for £3,000.[543] In 1810 the works were divided, with one son-in-law, Robert Hamilton working one part and Wolfe and another son-in-law, William Arrowsmith, the other.[544] Later Joseph Poulson, Stephen Folch and William Adams occupied various portions.

No marked Wolfe wares exist to help identify his products and at the sale of his stock, some five years after his death, in May 1823, no basalt wares were listed among the various earthenwares.[545]

*Figure 432. Bust of George Washington. Mark: **ENOCH WOOD SCULP./ BURSLEM**, c.1784-92. City Museum and Art Gallery, Stoke-on-Trent.*

*Figure 433. Bust of John Wesley. Mark: impressed on back of torso in a circular cartouche: **THE REV.D/ JOHN WESLEY M.A./ DIED MAR. 2. 1791./ AGED 88/ ENOCH WOOD SCULP. / BURSLEM**, c.1791, 9¾in. high. The National Museum of Wales, Cardiff, 659.*

Enoch Wood (& Sons), Fountain Place, Burslem, Staffordshire, c.1784-92 and 1818-46; **Wood & Caldwell**, 1792-1818

The firm of Enoch Wood and Sons is a major name in Staffordshire pottery history, primarily associated with the manufacture of earthenwares, particularly underglaze blue printed wares and pearlware figures. However, Enoch Wood did produce basalt in his various partnerships, from 1784 to post 1818.

Enoch Wood (1759-1840), son of Aaron Wood, is listed in *Bailey's Directory* of 1784 along with cousin Ralph [Wood] as, 'Manufacturers of all kinds of useful and ornamental Earthen Ware, Egyptian Black, Cane, and Various other Colours, also Black Figures, Seals and Cyphers, Burslem'. He was well-trained, having served an apprenticeship with Humphrey Palmer in Hanley before entering into business for himself with his cousin Ralph in Burslem in the early 1780s. The business grew rapidly, and by 1800 was occupying five properties in Burslem,[546] and insured for a total of £3,500.[547] In 1792 Enoch Wood took James Caldwell into partnership, trading until 1818 as Wood & Caldwell.

Wood & Caldwell marketed wares through London Staffordshire warehouseman Thomas Wyllie from 1794 to 1818.[548] They also traded privately, doing business with merchants such as Messrs Palmer Pearce in Tunbridge.[549] The Wood &

Figure 434. Bust of Wellington, Mark: **WOOD & CALDWELL**, c.1792-1818, 11¾in. high. Rakow collection.

Figure 435. Teapot and cover press-moulded oval shape with overall relief of stylized and meandering realistic flowers on a stipple ground. Mark: **WOOD** impressed in base, c.1790, 5¼in. high. Hacking collection. There is a teapot from the same mould in the Gunson collection in pearlware with a central band of coloured flowers also marked **WOOD**.

Figure 436. Teapot and cover of oval hexagonal shape with wide rising shoulder with a bold band of applied flowers. This sprig relief matches moulds from the Fountain Place factory illustrated in Falkner, Pl. XLI. The central relief is of bacchanalian boys with a floral swag on one side and with musical instruments on the reverse. Mark: 'W' at base of handle, possibly Wood & Caldwell, c.1800-10, 6¾in. high. Hacking collection.

Figure 437. Teapot and cover of octagonal shape with crimped gallery. The central sprig relief is of the Drunken Silenus after Duquesnoy. Mark: 'W' impressed, possibly Wood & Caldwell, c.1800-10, 6⅛in. high. Hacking collection.

Caldwell partnership dissolved on 17 July, 1818.[550] Final settlement of monies owed the partnership was still ongoing in 1821 when John B. Hostage, a solicitor representing Enoch Wood, wrote asking the intercession of Josiah Wedgwood II in settling the dispute over interest paid by a previous creditor in 1792.[551]

In 1818 Wood's sons, Enoch, Joseph, Edward and Thomas, were taken into the firm trading as Enoch Wood & Sons. A trade card, probably dating from that

Figure 438. Teapot and hinged cover of oval form with daisy chain gallery. The teapot is simply embellished with stiff floral spikes dividing the panels where a central shell is painted in opaque enamels similar to those used in Colour Plate 23. Mark: 'W' at base of handle, possibly Wood & Caldwell, c.1800-10, 4¾in. high. City Museum and Art Gallery, Stoke-on-Trent, 404.

Figure 439. Teapot and cover press-moulded with a stipple ground and raised panels divided by stylized floral columns with applied figures of sacrifice and mourning. A prominent lion finial sits atop a similarly decorated domed cover. The whole is picked out in blue and white enamels. Similar teapots were produced by both Spode and Neale, but a marked Wood example with the body from this same mould is in the Yorkshire Museum (see Miller, 1985, Pl. 1125). Unmarked, attributed to Enoch Wood, c.1790, 5¼in. high. Gunson collection.

period, illustrated in Falkner[552] offers 'Tables Services Enamelled with Arms, Crests or other Ornaments; Egyptian Black Tea-pots, Vases, Busts, Figures, Seal &c,&c.' In 1820 the business in Burslem was still occupying five properties, four of which were owned outright by Enoch Wood.[553] The firm had a large home and overseas market, primarily in printed earthenware, toby jugs, figures and busts, with a small basalt manufacture. At one time they even maintained a retail division, selling china, earthenware and glass from a shop in High Street, Belfast, but the partnership between Enoch Wood the Elder, Enoch Wood the Younger, Joseph Wood, Edward Wood, and Hamlet Wood was dissolved on 14 August 1827.[554] In 1836 they were the third largest manufactory in the Potteries paying rates on 21 ovens.[555]

Enoch Wood died in 1840 but the pottery continued in operation until 1846. The 1912 book by Frank Falkner, *The Wood Family of Burslem*, remains a standard and valuable source of information on all the Wood family branches.

Enoch Wood made a number of library size busts, now in public and private collections. A bust of George Washington (Figure 432) is excellently modelled. Grant, however, disparaged the 'inferior quality of the material employed', saying the basalt was 'rough and stoney, of an unpleasant blue-grey hue…'[556] Another bust of John Wesley (Figure 433) reputedly modelled in 1781,[557] could have actually been made at any time between that date and Wesley's death in 1791. A companion bust of the Reverend George Whitefield was produced by Enoch Wood in basalt.[558] A life-size bust of Enoch Wood modelled by himself is illustrated by Falkner,[559] and Wood produced a Statuette of Nelson as well as triton candlesticks.[560] Wood & Caldwell continued in the tradition and a masterful bust of Wellington (Figure 434) in the Roman style was one of their products. Compared with the Wesley and Wellington busts, the George Washington is, indeed, inferior in texture.

Some few useful wares are firmly attributed to Enoch Wood with impressed marks which, on basalt, mainly seem to be **WOOD**. A basalt teapot in the Hacking collection (Figure 435) is identical to one produced in pearlware in the Gunson collection. Both are impressed **WOOD**.

Other wares are less positively attributed. There are a number of teapots impressed with a '**W**' at the base of the handle which are often given to Enoch Wood

(Figures 436 and 437); however, the shape would suggest that they were later, and, if from the Fountain Place factory, from the Wood & Caldwell partnership. And two teapots in the City Museum and Art Galley (Colour Plate 23; Figure 438), finely executed with skilfully painted decoration, are suggested also to be his work.[561] One last teapot with relief decoration picked out in colours (Figure 439) was thought by the late Nancy Gunson to be possibly of Wood manufacture, even though both Spode and Neale made similar tewares in caneware. There have even been ideas bandied about rather fugitively that the **W(***)** wares were manufactured by Wood.
Marks: ENOCH WOOD SCULPT./ BURSLEM; WOOD; E. WOOD; E.W.; W(?); WOOD & CALDWELL (other marks exist on earthenwares)

John Wood, jun., Brownhills, Burslem, Staffordshire, c.1770-97
A cousin of Ralph Wood III, John Wood jun. was a manufacturer of white stone-ware, creamware, Egyptian black, and black-glazed wares as well as a variety of redwares and other earthenwares. A set of sales ledgers from Brownhills dating from 1770 to 1800 is in the City Museum and Art Gallery, Stoke-on-Trent.[562] No basalt has been identified from this manufactory.

Josiah Wood, Burslem, Staffordshire, c.1784-89 or later
Almost nothing is known about Josiah Wood and his business in Burslem. In 1789 he was operating the Swan Bank Pottery, Burslem, owned and insured by Ralph Wedgwood.[563] *Bailey's Directory* of 1784 lists Josiah Wood as a 'Manufacturer of fine Black, glazed, variegated and Cream-coloured Ware and Blue'. That he was still making variegated ware in 1788 is known from an invoice to Mr. Josiah and Thomas Wedgwood who were purchasing from him at the time.[564] No basalt was listed in the invoice. Josiah Wood was related to the Wedgwoods, probably by marriage, as his nephew was John Wedgwood, son of Thomas Wedgwood of Pepper House, Burslem, and mentioned in Wood's will of 1787.[565] No wares have been identified from his pottery.

Ralph Wood II, Hill Top Pottery, Burslem, Staffordshire, c.1789-1801
Ralph Wood, sen. (1715-72) was a modeller, rather than a potter and founded the Hill Top Pottery in 1754. Succeeded by his son, Ralph II, at the Hill Top, Ralph Wood was also for a short time in partnership with his cousin, Enoch Wood, in pottery manufacture in Burslem. Surprisingly little is known about Ralph Wood, in spite of the fact his name is commonly associated with the manufacture of pottery figures.

Ralph Wood's name is also elusive in Burslem land tax records. In 1800 he appears as an occupant for one year only of property owned by a Mr. Bierly [Byerley?].[566] The death of Ralph Wood occurred on 15 July 1801[567] and his works were to be let the following September.[568] The utensils from the pottery, which in 1811 became the J. & R. Riley works, were auctioned off in November 1802.[569] Ralph Wood II reputedly made basalt, but his wares are uncommon.
Marks: R. WOOD; Ra. WOOD BURSLEM; RALPH WOOD

Richard Woolley, Lane End, Longton, Staffordshire, 1809-11
After the death of James Chetham in 1807 Richard Woolley worked Turner's former pottery at Lane End, but was declared bankrupt in 1814. He died in 1825.[570]

*Figure 440. Teapot and cover, of oblong shape moulded with scrolls and stylized flowers. This ia a rare surviving piece from the John Yates factory, Hanley. Mark: **YATES**, c.1820, 6⅜in. high. Victoria & Albert Museum, C403-1918.*

It seems likely that Richard Woolley continued manufacturing basalt as he had done when in partnership with James Chetham. Although there are other stonewares associated with Richard Woolley's tenure at Lane End[571] after Chetham's death, no specific blackwares have been discovered.

Mark: WOOLLEY impressed or incised.

John Yates, the elder, Hanley, c.1770-96; **John (the younger) and William Yates**, Broad Street (High Street), Shelton (Hanley), Staffordshire, c.1794-1814

The 1818 Directory lists John Yates as an earthenware Manufacturer operating from Broad Street (or the High Street), Shelton. His father of the same name was listed in the directories of 1784 and 1787 as simply a 'potter'. The elder John Yates may have been much more important than the early listings indicated. He certainly was involved in early attempts to manufacture porcelain along with Baddeley, Littler and others. That a Yates did manufacture basalt is attested by a teapot in the Victoria and Albert Museum impressed **YATES** (Figure 440). Unfortunately, the teapot stands alone in documenting the manufacture of this family. However, there is a cream jug (Figure 441) which appears to be taken from the same mould, unmarked save for the potter's initials **'RD'** at the base of the handle.

Both John and William Yates worked together in the pottery industry for some

*Figure 441. Cream jug which appears to be en suite with the Yates teapot in Figure 440. Mark: **'RD'** (see Figure 441a) at base of handle, possibly John Yates, Hanley, c. 1820, 4in. high. Rakow collection.*

*Figure 441a. Mark **'RD'** at base of handle on cream jug in Figure 441.*

years. From 1791 to at least 1793 John and William Yates operated a warehouse in London at 31 St. Paul's Churchyard in partnership with Charles and Ephraim Chatterley.[572] An insurance policy was taken out on their 'Earthenware' manufactory in 1794.[573] Both were members of the Potter's Clay Company Copartnership of 1797.[574] Although their partnership was officially dissolved in 1808 with business to be exclusively carried on by John Yates,[575] it appears that John and William Yates continued to carry on some commercial activities together. Boston dealer Horace Collamore, anticipating the demand for English goods at the end of the Anglo-French War, placed large orders with John and William Yates in 1814, when he ordered more than one thousand dozen plates and sets of tea ware.[576]

Little else is known about the Yates as earthenware manufacturers. William Yates died in 1825 at the age of fifty-eight. He was a nephew of Ephraim Chatterley,[577] as was John Yates who died in 1828, aged sixty-eight.[578] The family continued to operate the pottery in Shelton until 1834 or later, and in 1843 it was trading as Yates & May.[579] Geoffrey Godden points out that a trade card exists in the British Museum for Yates & Co., located at 31 St. Paul's Churchyard. They are billed as 'manufacturers of Staffordshire earthenware in all its branches. Both useful and ornamental'.[580]

Mark: YATES, potter's initials **RD** (?)

CHAPTER V
Unmarked and
Unidentified Basalt

So long said Harold, and took some money out of a black Wedgwood teapot.
H. G. Wells, *Christina Alberta's Father* 1925[1]

Just as all black teapots are not Wedgwood, unmarked basalt, like the proverbial bull in a china shop, is a risky subject to encounter. Owing to the vast quantity of unmarked basalt, much of which appears featureless and undistinguished even to trained ceramic eyes, the subject has long been avoided, and for good reason. One principal reason is that a wealth of manufacturers of basalt never marked any wares, and therefore it will never be possible to make attributions to these manufacturers. Those unmarked wares about which it is possible to make an attribution are already included in the previous chapter listed by specific manufacturer. As a result this chapter includes a very few examples of pieces which are important either for reasons of form, decoration, or mark, even though they cannot be attributed.

One group of wares, impressed with the letter **'A'** (Figures 442-444) has been dis-

cussed in both the sections on **Adams** and on the **Cambrian Pottery**, Swansea. By no means the only two possibilities for their manufacture, these two factories stand as current possibilities for that group.

The thorny question of the maker of those tea-wares marked with numbers on the base, commonly 22, 36, 39, but ranging from 1-39, is one which has been discussed in the Sowter & Co. section and one which is also difficult to solve. That these wares have some relationship to those marked **S & Co** has been established since the numerals are occasionally seen in conjunction with the **S & Co** mark, particularly 1, 6 and 8. The largest single group of wares simply bear the numeral '22' (Figure 445). The attribution is often linked with the S & Co manufacturer (possibly Sowter & Co.), but it has not been conclusively proven.

Figure 442. Coffee pot and cover, pear-shaped on spreading foot with fine engine-turned vertical fluted body and domed cover with widow finial. Mark: 'A' impressed on base of handle, c.1800, 10in. high. Private collection. The 'A' marked wares (see also Figures 443 and 444) are not yet attributable and have been associated with at least two potteries, Adams and the Cambrian Pottery, Swansea. However, they could be the product of many other potteries, or from more than one pottery, if the initial is a potter's mark and not a manufacturer's mark.

Figure 443. Teapot and hinged cover, of high oval shape in vertical panels with stylized floral and swag moulding and a reserve panel of Pegasus. Mark: 'A' impressed in base, c.1800-10, 6¼in. high. Royal Ontario Museum, 970.242.64, Brown collection.

Figure 444. Inkwell, drum-shaped with engine-turned satin striped body. Mark: 'A' impressed in base, c.1780-1830, 2in. high. Royal Ontario Museum, 970.242.30, Brown collection.

Figure 445. Teapot and cover realistically moulded in the form of a swan, the neck acting as the handle and the tail the spout. Mark: '22', possibly Sowter & Co., Mexborough, c.1800-1805, 8in. x 11½in. Private collection.

*Figure 446. Teapot and cover, glazed basalt press-moulded in rectangular form with bold floral relief, the flat shoulder and upper spout rouletted in a fine waffle pattern. Mark: **WATERPROOF** impressed nine times in base, c.1820, 5¾in. high. Castle Museum, Norwich, Miller collection.*

Perhaps to prove that English manufacturers of blackware had a sense of humour, some manufacturer marked one 'shining black' teapot boldly on the base **WATER-PROOF** (Figure 446). No other mark appears on the pot which both in shape and in design is similar to Riley pieces (see Figures 342-348).

A handsome, heavily potted, vase presents a problem of attribution due to its bizarre form and unusual medallion of Atlas (Figure 447). The vase appears to be from the 1770s and the list of ornamental blackware manufacturers is limited to just a few names; it is tempting to suggest Voyez, but the suggestion is manifestly without any firm basis, emanating from the novel features on the vase.

Two beautiful large mugs, engine-turned, rouletted and sprig decorated with swags are also unmarked, probably dating to the 1770s (Figures 449 and 450). The mugs are the work of highly competent manufacturers. Wellington commemorative tea-

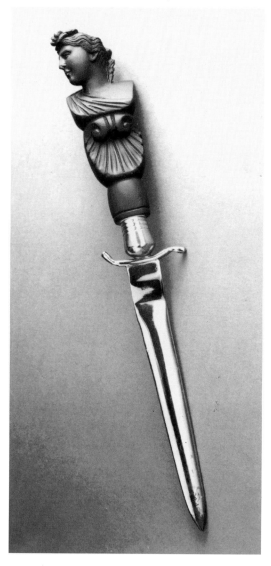

Figure 447. Vase of unusual form with striking applied naturalistic decoration. A central medallion depicts Atlas with the world on his shoulders. The vase is extremely heavily potted. Unmarked, c.1770s, 7½in. high. Photograph courtesy Geoffrey Godden.

Figure 448. Knife haft (mounted as a letter opener), basalt in the form of a female torso on a scroll shell socle, the head turned to the right. The quality of the basalt is coarse. The modelling of the head resembles some handles on a vase in the Zeitlin collection (see Neale Pottery and Porcelain, Pl. 28) made by the partnership of Voyez & Hales (Cobridge). Unmarked, c.1770, 9½in. long. (including opener). Royal Ontario Museum, 970.242.98, Brown collection.

278

Figure 449. Mug with skirt foot and a strap handle with acanthus leaf moulded relief (see Figure 449a). The body is engine-turned with satin stripes over which is applied a swag draped through rings. The top has a band on beading with a silver mounted rim. Unmarked, c.1770s, 6½in. high. Royal Ontario Museum, 970.242.99, Brown collection.

Figure 449a. Handle of mug in Figure 449.

wares are as plentiful as Nelson commemoratives. Often unmarked, Wellington commemorative teawares (Figures 451 and 452) must have been made by many manufacturers and since the subject sold the teawares, it was not necessary to sell by manufacturer's imprimatur.

Manufacturers were not constrained to standard forms, although there was a natural preponderance toward teawares, vases, and ornamental medallions and busts. Forms as diverse as pendulums (Figure 453), bed bolt covers (Figure 454), egg cups (Figures 14, 409), eye baths, wine tasters, salts and ladles (Figure 455), and candlesticks (Figure 456) were produced in basalt. Wares of enormous size must have been made as advertising gimmicks for display in shop vitrines, as one punch pot in the Liverpool Museum (Figure 457), fourteen inches high and over nineteen inches wide, would be too heavy to lift when full. Another fifteen and a half inch coffee pot in the same collection (Figure 458) would have overwhelmed the pourer had it been intended for use.

The tide of extremely popular beehive shaped tea and coffee wares (Figure 459) was not restricted to

Figure 450. Mug with slightly flared foot and rim and strap handle with floral terminal. The body is decorated with a band of rouletting at the foot and neck and two wide bands of vertical flutes, the centre is sprig-embellished with stiff swags and tassels and stylized rosettes. Unmarked, c.1770s, 5½in. high. Photograph courtesy Geoffrey Godden.

manufacturers who marked their wares although many, such as Wedgwood, Spode, Keeling, Toft & Co. and others did. Drawings of beehive shaped teawares occur in

Figure 451. Teapot and cover of oval hexagonal shape and cover with swan finial (head missing). The teapot commemorates Wellington's victory over Napoleon at Waterloo on 18 June 1815. Unmarked, c.1815-20, 7⅝in. high. Castle Museum, Norwich, Miller collection.

Figure 452. Teapot and cover of oblong shape with an elaborate ear-shaped handle and a bold relief of Wellington charging on Copenhagen. Unmarked, c.1825 perhaps Sewell, St. Anthony's Pottery, Newcastle-upon-Tyne, 5¾in. high. Castle Museum, Norwich, Miller collection.

Figure 454. Bed bolt cover (one of a pair) of un-polished basalt moulded as a flower. Unmarked, late 18th-early 19th century, 2¼in. high. Chellis collection.

Figure 453. Pendulum of unpolished basalt moulded with a central cartouche of a variation of a cupid representing Summer. Unmarked, late 18th-early 19th century, 6⅛in. diameter. Chellis collection.

Figure 455. Salt of oval fluted form with spreading fluted foot on a diamond-shaped base, along with a small ladle. Both unmarked, late 18th century, salt: 2⅛in. high, ladle: 4in. long. The Board of Trustees of the National Museums and Galleries on Merseyside (Liverpool Museum), 815M, 1158M, Mayer collection.

Figure 456. Pair of candlesticks fluted on square bases, one made in two parts with the upper candlestick secured to the base by a metal screw, the other made in one piece. Both are blistered on base and pitted on bottom indicating firing difficulties. Unmarked, c.1795, 9¾in. high. The Board of Trustees of the National Museums and Galleries on Merseyside (Liverpool Museum), 3027M, Mayer collection.

Figure 457. Large punch pot and cover with flared gallery and flat cover with wooden finial (which may be original). The round pot is decorated with vertical and horizontal engine-turning. Unmarked, c.1800, 14in. x 19¼in. Teapot with parapet and vertical fluting painted with a horizontal band of platinum around the midriff, widow finial, unmarked, c.1800, 4⅞in. high. The Board of Trustees of the National Museums and Galleries on Merseyside (Liverpool Museum), 3150M, Mayer collection, 29.9.87c.

Figure 458. Large coffee pot and cover with engine-turned diagonal satin stripes and high domed cover with sibyl finial. This coffee pot was probably used as an advertising gambit for a shop or manufacturer, as it would be too heavy when filled to lift comfortably. Unmarked, c.1790-1810, 15½in. high (smaller coffee pot without cover, unmarked, c.1790-1810, 6⅝in. high). The Board of Trustees of the National Museums and Galleries on Merseyside (Liverpool Museum), 3151M, Mayer collection 54.171.669.

Figure 459. Coffee pot and cover in the popular beehive shape. Produced from at least 1791, after 1796 beehive teapots came in 12s, 18s and 24s per potter's dozen. (Wedgwood MS 130-25920, 21 January 1808). Unmarked, c.1800-1810, 7in. high. Robertshaw collection.

Figure 460. Coffee pot and cover with swan spout and wings and serpent handle. Impressed '11' in base, c.1810-20, 9½in. high. Gunson collection.

Figure 461. Teapot and cover moulded in the shape of a wine cask (clearly a mixed metaphor, this may be a small punch pot instead of a teapot), on a rectangular footed base, the whole decorated with grape leaves and berries, berry knop to cover. Unmarked, c.1810-40, 5¾in. high. Gunson collection.

Figure 462. Teapot and cover of London shape moulded overall with dense foliage, the trees from which form the frame for the central cartouche of a milkmaid and a cow. Unmarked, c.1810, 5in. high. Collection of the Newark Museum, New Jersey, E49.290, gift of John B. Morris, 1949.

the *Don Pottery Pattern Book* of 1807 and reputedly Locketts & Co. also produced such wares.[2] Whimsical teapots, like the barrel shaped wine casket with grape vine relief decoration (Figure 461) provided a mixed metaphor, adding zest to a medium which, by the nineteenth century, had grown dull to many.

Pastoral relief decoration on basalt was most unusual. A teapot in the Newark Museum, New Jersey, has a central relief of a milkmaid and cow (Figure 462). The result is a teapot which looks like a piece of black Prattware.

A problem of attribution which may indeed be an English or European corruption are the series of intaglios, cameos and medals marked **WADGWOJD** (Figure 466). According to Leonard and Juliette Rakow,[3] a series of three inch basalt intaglios taken by direct impression from bronze medals of Bertrand Andrieu and marked **WADGWOJD** were made between 1815 and 1820. Other intaglios with high Tassie numbers impressed on the backs taken from the R.E. Raspé catalogues (1775 and 1786) were produced with the same mark.[4] It appears that these numbered intaglios were made about the same time, between 1810 and 1820. Further research will perhaps enlighten on the manufacturer of these intaglios and cameos.

A great deal of research remains to be accomplished comparing marked and unmarked blackwares, but it seems likely that there will always be unattributed pieces in abundance, owing to the vast number of manufacturers who left no identifiable products from their factories.

Figure 463. Teapot and cover of London shape with serpent spout, wide fluted base and strawberry moulded waist and shoulder. Unmarked, c.1810, 5⅞in. high. Blake collection.

Figure 464. Teacup and saucer of moulded body with wide shallow bowl and constricted foot, ear-shaped handle. The saucer and teacup all moulded with strawberries and leaves on a stipple ground. Unmarked, c.1820-30, cup: 2½in. high, saucer: 5½in. diameter. Royal Ontario Museum, 970.242.17, Brown collection.

Figure 465. Cream jug of oval form with panel divided by columns with a central panel of a male and female torso above a laurel wreath. This jug presents some problems in attribution due to an unusual mark: *W E D G W O O D* in an arc, each letter impressed individually, probably Yorkshire or Continental (see Chapter VII, Bodenbach and Vranov nad Dyji, for possible Continental manufacturers) c.1800-20, 4⅛in. high Hacking collection.

Figure 466. Cameo medallion of Richard I. Another problem of attribution which may indeed be an English or European corruption of Wedgwood is the series of *WADGWOƷD*-marked intaglios, cameos and medals. Mark: *WADGWOƷD*, English or Continental, c.1810-20, 2½in. high. Royal Ontario Museum, 970.242.48, Brown collection.

Figure 466a. Cream jug, basalt, old oval shape with fluted body. Mark: **WILKINSON,** c.1790-1810, 3½in. high. Blake collection

*Figure 467. Sugar box and cover of oval faceted shape with a large finial of a woman wrapped in a shawl. The basalt is crudely potted and coarse with a sprig relief sacrifice scene. Mark: **Beaumont,** Joseph Beaumont, Rheinsberg (Brandenburg) or Raciborz (Poland), c.1795-1800, 6½in. high. Rakow collection.*

CHAPTER VI
Continental and Foreign Blackware Manufacturers

Then he took her into the breakfast-parlour and showed her his present. It was a service of
Sèvres china,—very precious and beautiful. 'I got these things because Mr. Grey likes china.'
'So do I like china,' she said, with her face brighter than he had ever yet seen it.
A. Trollope, *Can You Forgive Her,* 1865[1]

English black basalt seems to have had considerable success on the Continent, such success that even a potter at Sèvres named Lambert produced blackware. Records of Wedgwood's European trade show quantities of basalt being imported into all the western European countries as well as some eastern European ones. This trade was discussed in Chapter II.

European manufacture of the popular blackware wafted naturally abroad when creamware potters, moving to the Continent to open up potteries, principally during the early years of the nineteenth century, brought with them the technology for manufacturing basalt. However, documentation for the manufacture of creamware abroad is scanty and for basalt it is almost non-existent. Certainly not all the creamware potteries produced blackware and the story as it is to be told is short, being narrated by published sources and by the existing marked wares.

Joseph Beaumont, Rheinsberg, Brandenburg, c.1793; Raciborz, Poland, c.1794-1803
According to Honey, Englishman Joseph Beaumont had reputedly been a potter at Leeds;[2] if so, his name has successfully eluded the biographers of the Leeds Pottery. In 1794 the Silesian industrial minister, Hoym, invited Beaumont, who was then working at Rheinsberg, to open a ceramics factory at Raciborz. Beaumont brought with him two assistants and they were allotted a group of buildings, an orangery and other derelict commercial buildings, for the pottery. In the absence of personal capital or subsidies Beaumont was forced to work alone, assisted only by his wife and brother. In 1803 he left the business without taking his wife and nothing else is known about him thereafter.[3]

That Beaumont produced basalt of a crude quality can be seen in a bombé-shaped sugar box and cover (Figure 467). The coarseness of the texture and potting wage war with an otherwise pleasant shape. The final is a woman wrapped in a shawl.
Mark: Beaumont

Bodenbach, Bohemia, c.1829-
W. Schiller and F. Gerbing produced a variety of wares in the Wedgwood style including a black varnished ware similar to basalt. In England the ware has from time to time erroneously been attributed to Shore and Goulding in Isleworth.[4]
Marks: S & G; FG; WS & S; WEDGWOOD impressed

*Figure 468. Teapot and cover, of low round form with a high parapet, basketweave engine-turned base and cover and moulded basketweave spout and handle. Mark: **CREIL**, c.1800-20, 4½in. high. Private collection.*

Burn & Co., Raneegungee, India, first quarter 19th century
Burn & Co. were listed among the English manufacturers because Thomas Burn was a Staffordshire warehouseman in a partnership with John Harrison in the Barbican, London, before going out to India and setting up his own pottery. Burn and Harrison dissolved their partnership in 1801 with the business to be carried on thereafter by Thomas Burn.[5]

Almost nothing is known about the business in India. An undecorated, ovoid shaped vase in Grant's collection and illustrated by him (Pl. XCVI), stands as a single monument to this pottery.
Mark: RANEEGUNGEE POTTERY WORKS; BURN & Co.

La Charité-sur-Loire, Nièvre, France, c.1802-12
This pottery was founded by Francis Warburton, who along with his brother, Peter had made black basalt in Cobridge (see Chapter IV, p. 261). According to several sources Francis Warburton moved on to France to begin a creamware manufactory at La Charité-sur-Loire, but black basalt was also produced at the factory in France.[6] Warburton was succeeded in the factory by another Englishman, Michael Willis.[7] Forms as diverse as eye baths were produced and finials manufactured at La Charité included sibyl and spaniel figures.[8]
Mark: La Charité (impressed)

Creil, Oise, France, c.1797-1875
In some respects the factories at Creil and at Montereau followed parallel paths. Both used raw materials from Montereau, Compiègne, and Chantilly and during certain periods were under the same management. Both factories produced similar wares, including blackware.

The Creil enterprise was started when Robert Bray O'Reilly erected a group of buildings on the River Oise for the manufacture of English creamware, basalt and

288

Figure 469. Sugar bowl (minus cover) of polished basalt with vertical satin stripes topped by a narrow band of rouletting, undulating gallery. Mark: **CREIL**, c.1800-20, 3⅜in. high. Rakow collection.

Figure. 470. Cream jug, round with high flaring spout and fine fluted base. Mark: **CREIL**, c.1800-20, 5⅝in. high. Rakow collection.

Figure 471. Teacup and saucer, decorated with fine engine-turned fluting. Mark: **CREIL**, c.1800-20, cup: 2½in. high; saucer: 5½in. diameter. Rakow collection.

Figure 472. Sugar box and cover of oval polished basalt moulded in panels with vertical floral columns, mock cherub handles and a sunflower with a female face in the centre. Mark: CREIL, c.1810, 5¾in. high. Rakow collection.

table glass. The management of the ceramics portion of the business was taken over by J.H. Stone. By 1799 Stone's brother-in-law A.M. Coquerrel had joined the firm and after 1800 Charles F. Saint-Cricq and Jacques Bagnall.[9]

The factory remained commercially strong throughout most of its life, producing mainly transfer-printed creamware but a not inconsiderable amount of basalt in the early years of the nineteenth century. The basalt was comprised primarily of useful wares decorated with engine turning, either in a basket weave pattern (Figure 468) or vertical fluted or satin stripes (Figures 469-471). Some very charming moulded relief decoration was executed on pieces which look more French than English (Figure 472). Ornamental wares were also produced: busts of the Emperor Napoleon, and of Voltaire, flower containers, and vases and cabinet cups decorated in colours and in gold. [10]

The quality of the basalt, which was executed between 1812 and 1827,[11] varied from a somewhat coarse texture to fine-grained and lustrous. The wares were sometimes burnished.

Mark (on basalt): **CREIL**

Douai (Nord), France, **Houzé de l'Aulnoit & Cie.**, c.1784-1820; **Martin Dammann**, c.1799-1804; **Brothers Boulé**, c.1800-06
The first of three Douai factories was started in 1784 by two brothers, Charles and Jacob Leigh, who had reputedly managed several factories in Staffordshire.[12] They traded under the name of Houzé de l'Aulnoit & Cie but were hard hit by the

Commercial Treaty of 1786. Nevertheless, they limped along until 1820 when they finally closed. Meanwhile, another factory was opened in Douai in 1799 by Martin Damman which lasted only five years. A third factory, owned by the Boulé brothers, but managed by a man named Halford, was operating in Douai from 1800 to 1806. The factories all produced creamware and basalt as well as red stoneware. The wares of Douai are usually unmarked.
Marks: (occasionally) **Leigh & Cie, Douai; Martin Dammann**[13]

Furstenberg, Brunswick, Germany, c.1747-present
Basalt was made at this porcelain manufactory during the neo-classical period under arcanist L.V. Gerverot who had previously worked at Sèvres, Wedgwood and other places before becoming manager of the works at Furstenberg in 1795. From 1807 to 1813 the Dukedom of Brunswick came under the rule of Jerome Bonaparte by marriage and his patronage was secured by Gerverot. However, after Bonaparte was deposed and the Dukedom restored in 1814, Gerverot also fell out of favour and the Wedgwood style wares were discontinued. Black basalt was made from 1796 to 1814 and many busts were made: Duke Frederick William of Brunswick and his wife were modelled by Schubert, Jerome Bonaparte and his consort by K.H. Schwarzkopf. Full classical ornaments, including fluting and acanthus leaf decoration, embellished the basalt produced at Furstenberg.[14]
Marks: on busts and reliefs 1796-1814, **an impressed figure of a horse at canter**

Gotha, Thuringia, Germany, c.1757-
According to their price list the factory at Gotha made vases in the style of l'étrusque.[15] These may have been inspired by the Furstenberg wares in the Wedgwood style or may have actually harked back to the Greek vases.

Hubertusburg, Saxony, Germany, c.1770-late 19th century
A pottery was founded here in 1770 by Johann Samuel Friedrich Tannich, apparently with the financial help of the Count of Lindenau, who in 1774 took over the direction of the manufactory. Around the turn of the century Count Marcolini took over the factory producing creamware and basalt in competition with the English wares which were flooding the Saxon market.[16] A coffee pot in basalt in the Westfälisches Landesmuseum für Kunst und Kulturgeschichte, Münster, is illustrated in Kybalová (Plate 96).
Marks: **K.S.ST.F. Hubertusburg; Wedgwood; 'R'** impressed; other marks were painted and probably not used on basalt

Konigsberg, East Germany, c.1775-85
Two factories existed in Konigsberg for the manufacture of ceramics, a faience factory (1772-1811) and another factory producing lead glazed earthenware and basalt (1775-85). The latter factory, which made wares in the so-called Wedgwood style, was operated by Paul Heinrich Collin and his brother who had lived in England. Black basalt was made in many forms including portrait medallions. A portrait medallion of Kant is among those produced by the factory.[17]
Marks: **frères Collin a Konigsberg**; Honey notes that other marks occur in both English and German on medallions but does not identify them.[18]

Lambert, Sèvres, France, 1797-1815

Very little is written about the potter operating from Sèvres in the last decade of the eighteenth century and early years of the nineteenth century who produced only the lovely quality basalt marked with his name. Lambert's manufactory, operated first by himself then by M. de Clavereau,[19] was independent from the Royal factory at Sèvres, and the quality of the wares pointed to the high level of competency achieved by the pottery (Figure 473). The chinoiserie gilding is like no other decoration seen on basalt, English or European. A bust of Napoleon Bonaparte was produced by Lambert which is currently in a private French collection.

There is a large, fine, Louis XIV-style vase in the Sèvres Museum attributed to Lambert.[20]

Mark: LAMBERT SEVRES (+ a number)

Montereau, Seine-et-Marne, France, c.1775-1836 (united with Creil thereafter)

A faience factory had been established on the Montereau site[21] before the creation, on 15 March 1775, of the factory by Clark, Shaw & Co. The Montereau site was famous for its natural deposits of white clays which would serve both the creamware and blackware interests. From 1775 on the factory was known as 'Manufacture de la Reine'. After the deaths of some of the principals in the business, John Hulme, known as Hall, became the sole owner in 1792. Following his death the factory was rented to Christopher Potter who owned another factory at Chantilly.

In the first quarter of the nineteenth century between 150 and 200 workers were employed at the pottery. After 1836 there was a gradual amalgamation between the factories at Montereau, Creil and Choisy-le-Roi.[22]

That basalt was produced seems likely but the wares were seldom marked or bore the marks of the Creil factory and so are difficult to identify.

Rendsburg, Germany, c.1764/5-1818

Originally a faience producing factory, in 1772 Rendsburg was established as a lead glazed earthenware manufactory by owners Christian Frederich Clar and Caspar Lorenzen. It is said that towards the end of the eighteenth century Clar introduced an imitation of English black basalt.[23]

Marks: REN.I; RF

Ulfsunda, Sweden, late 18th century-1843

In the late eighteenth century a small faience factory in Ulfsunda was converted to the production of black basalt and other stonewares in the Wedgwood style by sculptor Christian Arvid Linning.[24] The largest piece produced by the factory seems to be a clock with an ormolu pedestal bearing a representation in basalt of Kronos in his barque watching over the Hours, while Love with a golden oar propels the boat. Several clocks were produced; one in the Nordiska Museum is marked 'Ulfsunda, C. A. Linning fecit 1814'. Teawares were also produced in basalt, one of which is illustrated in Hannover, Vol. I Figure 616.[25]

Mark: CAL Ulfsunda

Vranov nad Dyji, Moravia, Czechoslovakia, c.1799-1860s

A large creamware manufactory which, during the 1830s, made black basalt in the

Figure 473. Part tea set decorated with gilded chinoiserie scenes and gilded sibyl finials. Mark: **LAMBERT SEVRES No. 2,** *c.1800-05, teapot: 6⅛in. high. Rakow collection.*

Wedgwood metier, existed at Vranov on the border between Austria and Czechoslovakia in the grounds of a neo-classical chateau. The factory was established by the Knight of Lilienhorn who owned the estate. Raw materials to manufacture the pottery were supplied by rich deposits of local clays. Lilienhorn sold part of his estate to his secretary Josef Weiss who took on several partners in the manufacture of the English-style wares. By 1818 the factory obtained a state permit to produce creamware and by 1820 the factory had eight warehouses and was sending examples of their wares to Vienna and Bruno for exhibitions. By the late 1830s the factory had warehouses in Prague and Vienna as well as in several other eastern European cities.

The 1830-1840 period was characterized by a concerted effort by the factory to imitate Wedgwood's output and simulate English prototypes. The imitation included plain or satin striped basalt, or wares with basket weave designs or applied relief decoration. A fine beehive shaped teapot was produced in basalt by the factory at Vranov as well as new oval shaped teawares with grape leaf borders, all of which were convincingly English in style and often impressed with a pseudo Wedgwood mark.[26]

Marks: WEDGWOOD

CHAPTER VII
Some Basalt Collectors

Among scientists are collectors, classifiers, and compulsive tidiers-up; many are detectives by temperament and many more explorers; some are artists, and others artisans.
Sir Peter Brian Medawar

Documentation on ceramic collectors is very limited. Lady Charlotte Schreiber's *Journals* recounting her European and English trips to acquire ceramics (and to a lesser extent fans and playing cards) stand as the solitary account of a collector's pursuit of pots which were, at that time, tantalizingly available and inexpensive. Although she did acquire a few examples, basalt was not a particular interest of Lady Charlotte's. However, Augustus Wollaston Franks, the famous nineteenth century collector of a multitude of antiquities including basalt, helped Lady Charlotte to catalogue her collection bequeathed to the Victoria and Albert Museum. About Franks more will be said presently as he is a shadow player in the lives of many nineteenth century collectors.

Enoch Wood, who died in 1840 at the age of eighty-one, was perhaps the first recorded collector of basalt and other Staffordshire ceramics. His collection was scattered into five parts, now gathered into three collections: the City Museum and Art Gallery, Stoke-on-Trent and the Victoria and Albert Museum in England and the Dresden Museums in Germany. While he was still living, in 1835,[1] Enoch Wood gave one part to the Royal Museum at Dresden and in 1838 he gave another part to the Pottery Mechanics' Institution at Hanley.[2] After his death, a part was sold to the Stoke-on-Trent Atheneum,[3] and is now re-united with the Hanley portion in the City Museum and Art Gallery, Stoke-on-Trent. Further portions were sold to the former Jermyn Street Museum in London, and to the South Kensington Museum, now gathered together at the Victoria and Albert Museum.[4]

Another collector, in the A.W. Franks fashion, was Joseph Mayer of Liverpool (1803-86) who had, by the 1840s, acquired a number of important pieces of Wedgwood with encaustic decoration, and by 1867, the year of his gift to the Liverpool Museum, amassed quantities of basalt and other dry bodied wares of Wedgwood, as well as other manufacturers. Mayer collected a wide range of other antiquities including business papers relating to the ceramics industry, a large portion of which is housed at Keele University under the management of the Wedgwood Museum. In 1887 antiquarian bookseller Rupert Simms wrote to Godfrey Wedgwood, Esq. about the sale of the Wedgwood business papers.

> They were discovered by Mr. Mayer in Birmingham 40 or 50 years ago in a Broker's shop. He had bought the whole of the Papers, Patterns, Letters, etc. of the Wedgwood firm up to the recent date—There were nearly a truck load of the [? word illegible] & acct. to be sold on 21st are all that was selected by Mr. Mayer and Miss Meteyard and of course are unique...It would be a pity to let them go out of the family.'[5]

A.W. Franks also encouraged Godfrey Wedgwood to buy the papers saying that he would bid on them himself if Wedgwood didn't want them.[6] Simms was commissioned to bid on the papers for Wedgwood and sent a telegram on 21 July 1887: 'Bought 244 Meet Cain Stoke to receive Cost 20+ paid. Send cheque to Newcastle…Simms'.[7]

In 1853, perhaps stimulated by his friendship with Franks, Joseph Mayer presented twenty-four pieces of Wedgwood to the British Museum.[8] As mentioned, the bulk of Mayer's collection of Wedgwood was given to the Liverpool Museum in 1867 and 1868, but he continued to add to the collection and in 1873 he presented them with twenty Wedgwood and Bentley period dies for basalt.[9] Mayer's original gift included 2,371 medallions. The remainder of his collection of cameos, necklaces, bell pulls, and seals was sold to a London dealer, a Mr. Wareham, who published a list of the remaining objects in 1879.[10] In 1879 the Liverpool Art Club Exhibition of the Works of Josiah Wedgwood included 1,491 exhibits comprising as many as 2,000 single items from the Mayer collection. The catalogue written by Charles Gatty, second curator of the collection, remains an important document in Wedgwood research.[11] Gatty was assisted in cataloguing the collection by Franks, Llewellynn Jewitt, Henry Willett and Eliza Meteyard.

Joseph Mayer was introduced to Eliza Meteyard by another collector, Charles Roach Smith, and Mayer immediately offered his ceramic knowledge to Miss Meteyard who, as an established author of novels and stories, was in the 1840s embarking on the study of Wedgwood.[12] In acknowledging his contribution to the field of ceramic history Eliza Meteyard said: 'Joseph Mayer of Liverpool has done more than any man living for the memory of Wedgwood…'[13]

Eliza Meteyard (1816-79) would herself soon eclipse Joseph Mayer in his own field by becoming the ultimate Wedgwood muse, an authority for collectors from all over the country to consult about their Wedgwood pieces. The Mayor of Sunderland, Robert Spence, sought her advice about a number of pieces in his collection: '50-60 seals in black Jasper [basalt], some Tea wares & Coffee wares and two Statuettes, Prior and Congreve…' saying, 'They are certainly by Wedgwood but have not the mark Wedgwood'.[14] In 1867 well-known Bath collector Sir William Holburne offered a photograph of his Prometheus Vase 'viewed by Mr. Chaffers who pronounced it unique' for one of Miss Meteyard's books (not specified).[15] The Prometheus vase (Figure 336) is the famous one modelled by John Voyez in 1769 and produced by Humphrey Palmer; one example is in the Holburne of Menstrie Museum, Bath, the other is in the Beeson collection, Birmingham Museum, Alabama. The photograph was despatched on 5 November 1887.[16]

There is no indication that Eliza Meteyard herself actually collected the wares about which she wrote, or basalt specifically. However, she had a particularly active correspondence with one important nineteenth century collector, Sir Isaac Falcke, whose collection of 450 pieces of Wedgwood and related wares was given to the British Museum in 1909. The surviving letters cover a period of at least three years (and perhaps longer as several are undated) from 1874 to 1877. Falcke queries Miss Meteyard on all Wedgwood subjects, displaying a critical eye for possible mistakes in her publications. On 21 February 1776 he wrote:

Dear Miss Meteyard,
In handbook folio 148 Nos. 241.2.3.4 are groups of Boys, panther's skins, arbours, festoons, etc by you stated as designs by Lady Diana Beauclerk which

I think is incorrect, as in Dr. Gibson's possession is a model in wax of part of the same Subject and which has the Artist's name I. Lignani 7. I think this is worthy [of] your attention for correction in future handbooks.[17]

Falcke's opinion was apparently respected by Miss Meteyard as she had sent him proof copies of her *Hand Book of Wedgwood Ware* (1875) in July 1874 to read for accuracy. Falcke suggested few changes, all apparently minor.[18]

In a letter in 1875, written perhaps to Falcke, but containing no salutation or address, Miss Meteyard tackles an oft discussed concern of hers, whether cameos and medallions were polished.

I do not think the finest cameos & bas reliefs were ever polished—There was a lapidary's wheel but I think it was only for polishing seals (chiefly black basalt) & bevelling & polishing the caps of cameos for setting—But I do not pretend to know.
I believe the fine, smooth waxy surface was a matter of material or fire or both.[19]

Falcke continued to edit Miss Meteyard's work, after it was published:

Dear Miss Meteyard,   20 May 1877
Looking over the Handbook the General History and remarks page 13. Speaking of Teapots you say (no Teapot Wedgwood ever made was worth that sum). May I suggest your qualifying the term by saying (no Teapot of Wedgwood's useful ware) was worth that sum [Meteyard was referring to a pearlware teapot].
Page 14 you say, In many instances particularly in the case of Busts in Basaltes (modern specimens compete most successfully with old ones) and you quote Voltaire and Mercury as examples. My criticism is as follows—
The modern black Busts & Plaques are crude & severe, whereas the old ones have a peculiar soft tint and feeling which gives them the appearance of the real Nero antico or black basalt marble and the distinction is easily made by the connoisseur. I don't know if you intend making any remark on the forgery by Wedgwood ['s] firm of the Wedgwood & Bentley mark![20]

On another occasion in 1877 Falcke calls to her attention an error on page 204 of the *Hand Book* where Miss Meteyard suggests the bust of Mercury is not Flaxman's but Grant & Hoskins.[21] As good as Falcke was he apparently did not recognize the difference between the mould making firm and the modeler.

The Falcke collection of basalt bequeathed to the British Museum is rich, including the famous Wine and Water ewers, a Pegasus Vase with pedestal, Triton candlesticks, and Vestal lamps together with four life size busts of Marcus Aurelius, Raleigh, Mercury, and Horace.[22] Several pieces from the Falcke collection are shown in Chapter II.

In concentrating on Wedgwood, Falcke did not fail to recognize the merits of many of the competitors. 'Turner and Adams both produced very fine examples [intaglios] in imitation. I have examples of both, the former I possess are equal to

Wedgwood's best period'.[23]

Augustus Wollaston Franks (1826-97) darts in and out of the lives of most of the major nineteenth century British collectors of antiquities and decorative arts. Consulted frequently by authorities and amateurs, Franks, like Joseph Mayer, is now little acknowledged for either his vast knowledge or the multiple collections he bequeathed to the British Museum, and other institutions. In 1851 he was appointed an assistant in the British Museum in charge of British and Medieval collections.

By 1866 he was Keeper of the Department of Medieval and Later Antiquities. The breadth of interests which kindled the imagination of Franks was staggering, from ethnographic items to manuscripts, Carolingian ivories, monumental brasses, portraits and prints and many other diverse objects.[24] Never a dilettante, as a collector Franks was a pure aesthete. His English ceramics collection, bequeathed to the British Museum in 1887, numbered 700 pieces and included every type of ware produced by the first Josiah Wedgwood, the single largest benefaction of its kind ever received by the museum.[25] A number of Franks basalt pieces are illustrated in Chapters II, III and IV. Like Falcke, Franks had the vision to see beyond the contributions of Wedgwood and collected the basalt of many manufacturers. Some rare examples such as the **S. GREENWOOD** vase (Figure 223) and the **ASTBURY** teapot (Figure 133) remain landmarks for those potters.

Knighted in 1894, Franks twice turned down offers of the directorship of the Victoria and Albert Museum and was offered the directorship of the British Museum which he also refused. As Director, and later President, of the Society of Antiquaries he was thrown into the society of both amateurs and professionals, and held in deep regard by both.[26]

Captain (later Colonel) Maurice Harold Grant (1872-1962) spanned the two centuries, and, unlike Mayer, Falcke and Franks, was a renowned collector of basalt, indeed the most celebrated collector, and author of the first authoritative work on the subject. *The Makers of Black Basaltes*, published in 1910, still stands as a bulwark on the subject.

In many circles, however, Grant has been more highly regarded for his work in English landscape painting, and his books on the subject remain currently in print.[27]

Grant relied heavily on the items in his own collection for compiling his impressive work on the manufacturers of black basalt. Over one quarter of the nearly 300 pieces illustrated were his own. The collection was eventually dispersed and sold to private collectors and many of the pieces have found new places in important contemporary collections.

As English ceramic research augmented the foundations laid by Meteyard, Jewitt, Church and other nineteenth century scholars, the gauntlet was taken up in the twentieth century by a number of enthusiasts who concentrated on collecting the basalt of manufacturers other than Wedgwood. The publication of Grant's monograph undoubtedly stimulated interest and appreciation for Wedgwood's contemporaries and successors.

Prominent North American collectors included Tillie S. Speyer, whose large bequest of basalt (mostly Wedgwood) was given by her children to the Museum of Art, Carnegie Institute in 1982. In a letter to Boston Wedgwoodian Jean Gorely, Mrs. Speyer spoke of herself as 'quite fanatical about black basalt'.[28] Canadian collector Hazel Egerton Brown gave her extensive collection of redware and basalt to the Royal Ontario Museum in Toronto in 1970. The basalt included examples from most of the manufacturers who marked their wares and many rare forms. Examples from Mrs. Edgerton Brown's collection are illustrated throughout Chapter IV.

The most extensive collection of marked wares by English (and some Continental) manufacturers is in the Rakow collection in New York. The late Dr. Leonard Rakow and Mrs. Rakow, in addition to a comprehensive Wedgwood collection, concentrated on purchasing documentary examples of dry bodies of all the English contemporaries. The result is a collection of some 700 marked examples by manufacturers other than Wedgwood in addition to the 2,000 or so Wedgwood items of all fabrics and periods. Their pieces are much in evidence throughout this book. There are numerous major North American Wedgwood collections containing quantities of fine basalt, of which some pieces are represented in Chapters II and III; others, such as the Kadison collection, are liberally represented in Robin Reilly's *Wedgwood* (1989).

In England in the nineteenth century, and early years of the twentieth century in some instances, one finds extensive basalt in the Sidebotham and Falkner collections at Peel Park, the collections of Edward Sheldon, Frederick Rathbone, George R. Burnett, C.B. Carruthers (from whose collection Falcke purchased Wegwood basalt, possibly at the Christie's sale of portions of the collection on May 16, 1870), Francis Sibson, Cornelius Cox as well as many others.[29] Among more contemporary collections was one formed by the late Nancy Gunson which contained a wealth of documentary pieces of both major and minor manufacturers. Philip Miller's collection, recently sold to the Norwich Museum, contains many important basalt wares as does Jack Hacking's collection. A less well-known, but extensive collection has lately been formed by Martin Blake in London.

Indebted to Eliza Meteyard as I am and to Maurice H. Grant, I should like to end on the same note which Grant ended his book in 1910, with a quote from Miss Meteyard:

> Their body [basalts] is so exquisite to the touch, their polish so fine, their decorations and forms so graceful and chaste,…Whether they adorn the library, the gallery, the hall, the drawing-room, or conservatory, their sober grace lends a charm and contrast to surrounding colours and objects.[30]

For myself, I chose the drawing-room and the library.

APPENDIX I

EGYPTIAN BLACK PRICES FROM STAFFORDSHIRE POTTERS PRICE FIXING AGREEMENTS

Notes by George L. Miller

August 1991

One of best sources of information on the prices and vessels available in basalt ware, or what potters more commonly called Egyptian black, are the Staffordshire potters' price fixing agreements. The earliest known price fixing list is a handwritten agreement dated 14 February 1770. At the bottom of that list is the following statement:

> To sell to the Manufacturers of Earthen wares at the above Prices & to allow no more than seven & a half p(cent) Besides Discount for Breakage & Prompt Payment'

Clearly, the 1770 list was just for white salt-glaze stoneware. Prices for pottery and other commodities were falling during the early 1770s. Josiah Wedgwood's correspondence to Thomas Bentley mentions the establishment of a potters' association in April of 1771 which appears to have led to the setting up of a price fixing agreement for earthenwares which may have included Egyptian black.[1] Unfortunately, copies of this price list do not seem to have survived.

Parts from printed price fixing agreements from 1783 and 1787 have survived which include a sheet of prices for shell edged and painted wares for both years and prices for cream coloured ware for the 1787 agreement. There is a good possibility that lists for Egyptian black wares existed for these years, but have just not survived. Evidence for this comes from the 1795 price fixing agreement for which we have extant lists for cream coloured, printed and Egyptian 'ware'. In any case, the Staffordshire potters had set the prices for Egyptian black (basalt) ware by at least 1795 if not as early as 1771.

Egyptian black wares are listed in the Staffordshire potters' price fixing agreements of 1795, 1796, 1814, 1825 and 1846. None of the price fixing agreements lists these wares as basalt. It is interesting to note that even in the Wedgwood price list of 1 August 1816 these wares are listed under a heading which reads 'EGYPTIAN BLACK, CANE RED'.[2] Under that heading are a listing of tea and coffee wares available plain, fluted, or bas-relief.

Potters' price fixing agreements after 1846 do not list Egyptian black or basalt. Lists examined included 1853, 1859, 1873 and 1881. Beginning with the 1881 pricing agreement, the potters changed from price fixing lists to pricing scales. Price fixing lists gave the prices for the various decorative types; however, the price scales only presented a series of prices for different types of vessel forms. Thus one was not able to price the different types of wares without knowing to which scale they were assigned. Therefore, it is possible that basalt wares could have been priced on the scales.

With the exception of some inkwells listed in the 1825 list, all of the Egyptian black wares are teawares dominated by teapots, sugars, creams, milk jugs, coffee pots, and some bowls. No cups and saucers were listed. The styles listed such as 'thread-fluted, imaged, satin stripe, and imaged' are long lasting, and the changes are few. Size ranges for teapots were in potters' dozen sizes which included 12s, 18s, 24s, and 30s. In 1796 the potters attempted to fix the potters' dozen sizes in terms of capacity. On that list teapot size capacities were listed as:

12s	=	1½	pints
18s	=	1	pints
24s	=	¾	pints

In that list, 30s were not listed, but they may have held a half-pint. One must keep in mind, however, that one of the ways that potters got around the price fixing agreements was to make larger sizes in the potter's dozen sizes. One occasionally sees hollow wares such as teapots, creams, and sugars with impressed numbers such as the above which are size marks.

The prices listed in the Staffordshire potters' price fixing agreements for basalt wares are presented at the end of this appendix along with the descriptions of the vessels as they appear in the price fixing lists. These prices, however, do not provide a good handle on the costs of the wares because we do not have the discount information for basalt wares. A price series with discount rates has been generated for Staffordshire earthenwares in 'A Revised Set of CC Index Values for Classification and Economic scaling of English Ceramics from 1787 to 1880.[3] In that article, index values were worked out for shell edged, painted, dipped, and printed wares in terms of their cost relative to CC (plain creamware) vessels. CC ware vessels were the cheapest type of refined earthenware available from the 1780s on through the 19th century.

The price of painted, printed, and basalt teapots in terms of their value relative to CC teapots have been generated from the potters' price lists which are presented in the following table:

THE COST OF PAINTED, PRINTED AND BASALT TEAPOTS RELATIVE TO THE COST OF THE CHEAPEST PLAIN CREAMWARE TEA POTS

	PAINTED		PRINTED		BASALT	
	low	high	low	high	low	high
1795			2.7 to 3.4		2.9 to 6.9	
1796	1.6 to 1.6		2.3 to 2.8		2.4 to 7.0	
1814	1.3 to 1.5		2.3 to 4.0		2.0 to 4.3	
1825	1.2 to 3.0		2.0 to 4.0		2.1 to 4.2	
1846	1.1 to 2.1		1.9 to 3.2		1.6 to 3.5	

The index values presented here indicate how much more expensive these teapots were than a plain CC (creamware) teapot from 1795 to 1846. In other words, in 1796, painted teapots were only 1.6 times more expensive than plain CC teapots whereas basalt ones ranged from 2.4 to 7 times the cost of a plain creamware teapot. One of the interesting things about this list is the relative fall in prices of painted, printed and basalt teapots in terms of how much more expensive they were than plain creamware teapots. By 1846, painted, printed, and basalt teapots began to be replaced by moulded white granite or ironstone wares which dominated the American market through the 1880s when transfer printed wares began to reappear. The relative declines in the basalt prices suggests the potters were trying to broaden their market for a ware whose time had passed. Probably by the 1840s its price had been lowered to the point where it was not worth continuing its production and the basalt which was popular and expensive in the late 18th century had become common and cheap with minimal demand by the mid-19th century

BASALT WARES AS LISTED IN THE STAFFORDSHIRE POTTERS' PRICE FIXING AGREEMENTS FROM 1795 TO 1846

TEA POTS

'Common round Tea Pots'	10/6		(1825)
'Low best Tea Pots round'	12/-		(1825)
'Drapery and Imaged, Tea-pots'	13/6		(1795)
	15/-		(1796)
'Round imaged, or figured Teapots'			
12s, 18s, 24s	16/-		(1814 & 1846)
30s	18/-		(1814 & 1846)
'Round Tea Pots figured'	14/-		(1825)
'Fluted Tea-pots, & c.'	10/-		(1795)
	11/-		(1796)
'Round Thread-fluted Teapots'			
12s, 18s, 24s	12/-		(1814 & 1846)
30'	14/-		(1814 & 1846)
'none to be counted more than 30 to a dozen'			(1814 & 1846)
'Round Satin stripe Teapots, lamp spouts'			
12s, 18s, 24s	14/-		(1814 & 1846)
30s	16/-		(1814 & 1846)
'Oval Pressed Tea-pots'	24/-		(1795)
large each	2/-		(1796)
second size each	1/6		(1796)
third size each	1/3		(1796)
'Oval Teapots, any shape,			
12s dozen	21/-		(1814 & 1846)
18s	24/-		(1814 & 1846)
24s	26/-		(1814 & 1846)
'none to be counted more than 24 to a dozen'			(1814 & 1846)
'Oval Tea Pots'	21/-		(1825)
'Oval Sliding-lid Tea-pots'	24/-		(1795)
large each	2/3		(1796)
second size each	1/9		(1796)
third size each	1/6		(1796)

COFFEE POTS

'Coffees' (Round imaged, or figured)	16/-		(1814 & 1846)
'Round Coffees figured'	20/-		(1825)
'Common round Coffee Pots'	10/-		(1825)
'Low best Coffee Pots round'	11/-		(1825)
'Coffees' (Round Thread-fluted)	12/-		(1814 & 1846)
'Coffees' (Round Satin stripe, lamp spouts)	14/-		(1814 & 1846)
'Oval Coffee pots	21/-		(1814 & 1846)
	20/-		(1825)

SUGARS

'Common round Sugar Boxes'	10/-		(1825)
'Low best Sugar Boxes round'	11/-		(1825)
Sugars 'Round imaged, or figured'	16/-		(1814 & 1846)

'Round Sugar Boxes figured'		13/-	(1825)
'Round Thread-fluted Sugars'		14/-	(1814 & 1846)
'Sugars (Round Satin stripe)'		14/-	(1814 & 1846)
'Oval-pressed Sugars'		24/-	(1795)
'Oval pressed Sugars'	each	1/6	(1796)
second size	each	1/3	(1796)
'Oval Sugars the same price as Teapots'			(1814 & 1846)
'Oval Sugar Boxes'		20/-	(1825)

MILKS AND CREAMS

'Common round Creams'		10/-	(1825)
'Low best Creams round'		10/-	(1825)
Creams 'Round imaged, or figured'		16/-	(1814 & 1846)
'Round Creams figured'		12/6	(1825)
'Round Thread-fluted Creams'		14/-	(1814 & 1846)
'Creams (Round Satin stripe)'		14/-	(1814 & 1846)
'Oval-pressed and Milks'		24/-	(1795)
'Oval Milks'	each	/10	(1796)
second size	each	/8	(1796)
'Oval Creams the same price as Teapots'			(1814 & 1846)
'Oval Creams'		18/-	(1825)

BOWLS

'Bowls thread-fluted, not figured'		15/-	(1814 & 1846)
'Bowls, figured'		18/-	(1814 & 1846)

MILK JUGS (PITCHERS)

'Round Milk Jugs and covers, not figured		15/-	(1814 & 1846)
figured		18/-	(1814 & 1846)
'Oval Milk Jugs and covers'		26/-	(1814 & 1846)

INKS

'Fluted round Inks'				
	No. 1	each	4d	(1825)
	No. 2	each	5d	(1825)
	No. 3	each	6d	(1825)
	No. 4	each	8d	(1825)
	No. 5	each	10d	(1825)
	No. 6	each	1/-	(1825)

Bibliography

Ann Finer and George, Savage, editors. *The Selected Letters of Josiah Wedgwood* London: Cory, Adams & Mackay Ltd. 1965.

George L. Miller. 'A Revised Set of CC Index Values for Classification and Economic Scaling of English Ceramics from 1787 to 1880.' *Historical Archaeology* 1991, Vol 24, no.1, 1-25.

Staffordshire Potters' price fixing agreements

1770 An untitled hand-written price fixing list for white salt-glazed stonewares which has been reprinted in Arnold R. Mountford's 'Documents relating to English ceramics in the 18th and 19th centuries.' *Journal of Ceramic History*, number 8, 1975, 4-8.

1783 'At a General Meeting of the Manufacturers of Queen's Earthen-ware, It was unanimously agreed, that no Manufacture thereof, should sell for less Prices than those respectively annexed in the List following.' Hanley 23rd September 1783. reprinted in Arnold R. Mountford's 'Documents relating to English ceramics in the 18th and 19th centuries.' *Journal of Ceramic History*, number 8, 1975, 9.

1787 'Hanley, 19th January, 1787 At a General Meeting of the Manufacturers of Queen's Earthen Ware, It was unanimously agreed, that no Manufacturer there of, should sell for less Prices than those respectively annexed in the List Following.'

'Prices of Queen's Ware, or Cream Coloured Earthen Ware established through the Potters, from February 2nd, 1787.'

Copies of the above two lists are in the Horace Banks Reference Library in Hanley, Staffordshire.

1795 'Staffordshire Potteries, 1795. Egyptian Ware.' 'Prices delivered in by the several Persons who have subscribed to the same, below which none of them are to sell any of the following GOODS after the 24th of June, 1795, in conformity to the Resolutions entered into at the General Meeting of Manufacturers held for that purpose.' reprinted in Arnold R. Mountford's 'Documents relating to English ceramics in the 18th and 19th centuries.' *Journal of Ceramic History*, number 8, 1975, 9.

1796 'At a Committee Meeting, held at the Legs of Man in Burslem, on Friday the 8th day of January, 1796, Mr. Caldwell in the Chair.'

'Staffordshire Potters. A LIST of PRICES. settled and finally agreed to, by the Manufacturers at large, as the LOWEST SELLING PRICES of the Articles of this Manufactory... April 21, 1796.'

Both of these lists are reprinted in Arnold R. Mountford's 'Documents relating to English ceramics in the 18th and 19th centuries.' *Journal of Ceramic History*, number 8, 1975, 11.

1814 'Price Current of Earthenware, as agreed to at a General Meeting of the Staffordshire Manufacturers, held at Hanley, on the 8th March 1814. reprinted in George L. Miller 'George M. Coates, Pottery Merchant of Philadelphia, 1817-1831.' *Winterthur Portfolio* Vol. 19, no.1, Spring 1984, 42-43.

1825 'Staffordshire Potteries, PRICE CURRENT OF EARTHENWARE. JULY 1, 1825.' Copy in the Ogden Day and successor companies, New-York Historical Society.

1846 'Staffordshire Potteries. PRICES CURRENT OF EARTHENWARE, 1814; Revised and Enlarged December 1st, 1843, and January 26th, 1846, in Public Meetings of Manufacturers.' reprinted in Arnold R. Mountford's 'Documents relating to English ceramics in the 18th and 19th centuries.' *Journal of Ceramic History*, number 8, 1975, 12-14.

1853 'PRICES CURRENT OF EARTHENWARE, 1853.' Wedgwood MS 47-29262.

1859 'PRICES CURRENT OF EARTHENWARE, 1859.' Wedgwood MS 42-29262.

1873 'EARTHENWARE GROSS LIST, FOR SOUTH AMERICAN AND SIMILAR TRADES, 1873.' George L. Miller collection.

1881 'EARTHENWARE PRICE LIST. Revised October, 1881. with Scales and Tables giving the number of pieces in various sets.' *The Pottery Gazette Diary*, 1882. 57-64.

Josiah Wedgwood and Sons

1816 'Josiah Wedgwood, of Etruria, and London. Price Current of Earthen-ware, August 1st, 1816.' Wedgwood Archives MS 47-29285.

APPENDIX II
ASSORTED RECIPES FOR EGYPTIAN BLACK

John Bourne, Burslem (n.d.)

blue clay	235
calcined ironstone	225
manganese	15
Cornish clay	15

'There is no body used in the ceramic art requiring more care in examination of the water than this, principally on account of the manganese, which ought not to come in contact with lime or any calcerous earth. It requires only one fire, after which it is scoured with fine sand, and afterwards rubbed with a little oil.'[1]

Cyples 1786

20 Ball Clay
5 calcined carr
1½ calcined manganese
These to be mixed by measure in the slip[2]

Cyples No. 400 *Egyptian Black*

1 Quart of White Slip, 3lbs. 3oz.
3 lbs. 8oz. of Manganese
3 lbs. 14oz. of Ochre[3]

Thomas Holland, Burslem 1815

Shining Black Glaze
60 lbs Litharge
18 lbs Flint
11 lbs Manganese
18 quarts White Slip, not too thin.[4]

L.H. Letillier, Burslem, 27 May 1845

'Black Shining Body'
15 Pecks of Soft Tom slip
15   do   of red marl
2   do   of Ball Clay slip
2   do   of Iron Stone

Shining Glaze to the Above
160 pound Lead
55 pound flint
26 pound good manganese free from iron
24 quarts Ball Clay slip[5]

Benjamin Plant, Lane End (n.d.)

1lb. of Magness [sic]
5lb. of Oker [sic]
15lb. of Ball Clea [sic]

Black is prepared by mixing a deep blue with Seven ounces of fine Varnish which is called oil of Stones.[6]

Richard Riley (*see* Chapter IV, pp. 222-225)

Benjamin Stubbs, Longton 1826

90 lb ochre
35 lb Manganese
35 lb iron Scales
110 lb Blue Clay[7]

(Swinton) John Green (?), Swinton, South Yorkshire (n.d.)

70 Ochre calcined
10 Manganese   "
 8 Iron Scales   "[8]

John Taylor, Shelton, c.1798-1817 or later

Egyptian Black No. 1
2 of Manganese
2 of Red Clay
2¾ of Iron Scales
2 of Blue Ball Clay
4 of Fine Marl
4 of Biscuit Pitchers

Egyptian Black, Rostrand No. 2
1 of Manganese
1 of Iron Scales
2½ of Fine Marl
1 of Red Clay
2½ of Blue Ball Clay

Egyptian Black, Rostrand No. 3
2 of Cobalt
2 of Oxide of Iron
4 of Good Marl
5 of Biscuit Pitchers, ground

Wash for Black Teapots
50 of Litharge
8 of Flint
20 of Manganese

Shining Black
25 of Lead
 9 of Stone
 5 of Flint

5 of White Shavings
5½ of Manganese

Glaze for the Above
25 Red Lead
9 of Stone
5 of Flint
5 of Red Shavings
1½ of Manganese

Black Body
10 of Red Clay
60 of Ochre
26 of Manganese
21 of Ball Clay

Encyclopedia Metropolitana (1817-45)[10]

Black Body, T.S.
24 of Ball Clay
20 of Calcined Ochre
7½ of Manganese
7½ of Iron Scales

Egyptian Black, H.M.
105 of Ball Clay
100 of Ochre
20 of Iron Scales
17 of Manganese

Egyptian Black, J.T.
22 Parts of Blue Clay
20 Parts of Ochre
8 Parts of Manganese
7 Parts of Iron Scales[9]

Dry Bodies.	Jasper.				Pearl.				Stone.				Chemical Utensils.				Cane.			Drab.			Black.			
	1	2	3	4	1	2	3	4	1	2	3	4	1	2	3	4										
Kaolin	18		32		30			40	50			30	40	30			18			25			10			8
Cornish stone		33		20		60	54			40	46				40	33		24	32		45	40		6		
China clay	7	17	30	14	32	22	36	12	25	10	12	16	30	30	20	20					6	10				4
Blue clay	40	17	28	18	14	14	4	44	25	30	24	54	30	40	25	25	18	16	24	46	27	16	37	36	40	36
Marl															5	11	64	60	44	26	20	40		14		16
Flint		6		12	10					5	12				10	11										
Flint glass				8	14	4	6	4		15	6															
																									Iron	
Barytes carbonate	35	27	10	28																					2	
Manganese																				3	2	4	5	4	8	6
Calcined ochre																							48	36	44	30

Art and History of the Potting Business (William Evans, 1836)

The Egyptian, best black, or vitrified basalt, is formed of these components:

(2) Fritt. — Felspar (greenish), sixty; borax, twenty-five; nitre, five; sal-ammoniac, ten. Body-Fritt, forty-five; china clay, forty; bone, fifteen; or, fritt. thirty-five; china clay, thirty; bone, thirty.[11]

Black Egyptian body
235 parts Blue Clay
225 of calcined ochre
45 of manganese
15 Cornish clay

The manganese sould be free from limesone and calcarious earths.[12]

The Manual of Practical Potting (1907)

Egyptian Black No. 14
50 lbs Blue Clay
40 "　Ochre
20 "　Ironstone
15 "　Manganese

Egyptian Black No. 15
240 lbs Blue Clay
120 "　Ochre
42 "　Iron scales
45 "　Manganese

Dry Black Body No. 16
120 lbs Ochre
120 "　Blue Clay
16 "　Manganese

Egyptian Black Body No. 17
65 lbs Ball Clay
60 " Ironstone
10 " Manganese

Egyptian Black No. 18
235 lbs Blue Ball Clay
 25 " Calcined Nickel
 45 " Manganese
 15 " China Stone

Egyptian Black No. 19
50 qts. Ball Slip at 24 ozs to pint
72 lbs Ironstone
22 " Manganese

Dry Smearing Black No. 57
16 lbs Ball Clay
 4 " Manganese
 4 " Ironstone
 8 " Red Clay

Egyptian Black No. 58
21 lbs BallClay
 3 " Red Clay
 4 " Manganese
 4 " Ironstone

Egyptian Black No. 59
30 lbs Blue Clay
40 " Ochre
50 " Manganese
10 " Iron Scales[13]

J.C.Fisher and His Diary of Industrial England 1814-51[14]

'I was greatly impressed by the skill with which both black and coloured crockery were embellished with charming embossed decorations and figures. The hollow moulds are derived from a metal casting. The pipe clay from which they are made is of very fine quality and has only been very lightly fired so that it absorbs a great amount of dampness. The clay, which is fairly soft, is pressed into these moulds and all the surplus clay is removed. If a very thin or fragile area requires trimming it is simply scraped smooth with a spatula. The ornaments made in this way are fixed to the main piece of chinaware by setting the spot to which they are to be attached. They are then pressed into position with the finger and the process is completed by means of a fine brush of camel hair.

I noticed that the clay, or the material from which the black crockery is made, has a dark rust colour before it is fired. This shows that the material used for securing a black colour is oxide of iron…I selected for my own use a dinner service and a black tea service.'

BIBLIOGRAPHY

The following bibliography is not intended to be a complete one on the various factories and subjects, merely a guide to works relating to the basalt production, or to the factory history. For example, works on Spode's blue printed wares would not appear in this list.

Andrew Abbott
Hampson, Eileen and Rodney. 'Pottery Manufacturers, 1800-1807.' *Northern Ceramic Society Newsletter* No. 68, December, 1987.

Robert Adam
Beard, Geoffrey. *The Work of Robert Adam*. New York: Arco Publishing Company, 1978.
Rykwert, Joseph and Anne. *Robert and James Adam*. New York: Rizzoli International Publications, Ltd., 1985.
Stillman, Damie. *The Decorative Work of Robert Adam*. London: Academy Edition, 1973, originally published 1966.

Adams
Deaton, Marjorie. 'Adams of Greengates.' *Apollo*, Vol. 57, 1953.
Turner, William. *William Adams An Old English Potter*. London: Chapman and Hall, 1904.

Alcock
Barnes, Dr. Geoffrey and Mrs. Alma. 'The Samuel Alcock porcelains c. 1822-1859.' *Staffordshire Porcelain*. London: Granada Publishers, 1983.
Halfpenny, Pat. 'Samuel Alcock & Co.' *Northern Ceramic Society Journal* Vol. 2, 1975-6.

Baddeley
Mallet, John. 'John Baddeley of Shelton.' *English Ceramic Circle Transactions* Vol. 6, Part 2, 1966.

B&W (Birch & Whitehead)
Gunson, Nancy. 'Another B&W Marked Piece.' *Ars Ceramica*, 1987.
Rakow, Juliette K. and Leonard S., M.D. 'B & W.' *Ars Ceramica*, 1986.

Bradley
Edmundson, R. S. 'Bradley & Co., Coalport Pottery.' *Northern Ceramic Society Journal* Vol. 4, 1980-81; 'Walter Bradley & Co. Coalport 1796-1800.' *Northern Ceramic Society Newsletter* No. 62, June. 1986.

Bullock
Clifford, Timothy. 'William Bullock—a fine fellow.' *Christie's International Magazine*, June 1991.

Cambrian Pottery (Swansea)
Armistead, Kathleen M. and Grant-Davidson, W.J. *Catalogue of the Kildare S. Meager Bequest of Swansea Pottery*. Swansea: Glynn Vivian Art Gallery, 1967?.
Grant-Davidson, W. J. 'The Early Pottery of Swansea.' *English Ceramic Circle Transactions* Vol. 7, Part 1, 1968.
Jenkins, Elis. *Dillwyn's Etruscan Ware*. Private Publication, 1971.
Jones, A.E. and Joseph, Sir. Leslie. *Swansea Porcelain Shapes and Decoration*. Cowbridge: B. D. Brown, 1988.
Nance, E. Morton. *The Pottery and Porcelain of Swansea & Nantgarw*. London: B.T. Batsford, Ltd., 1942.

Caughley
Godden, Geoffrey. *Caughley and Worcester Porcelains 1775-1800*. New York: Praeger Publishers, 1969.
Grant-Davidson, W.J. 'Excavations at Caughley.' *English Ceramic Circle Transactions*, Vol.6, Part 3, 1967.

Continental
Ariès, Maddy. *Donation Millet et Faïences Fines Du Musée*. Sceaux: Musée De L'Ile De France, Chateau De Sceaux, 1979; 'La Manufacture De Creil de 1737 à 1820.' *Cahiers De La Céramique Du Verre Et Des Arts Du Feu* No. 45. Sèvres, 1969.
Guineau, Bernard. *La Manufacture De Faïences Fines De La Charité-Sur-Loire*. Association des Amis de la Charité-sur-Loire, 1979.
Hannover, Emil. Pottery & Porcelain *A Handbook for Collectors. III European Porcelain*. New York: Charles Scribner's Sons, 1925.

Honey, W.B. *European Ceramic Art*. London: Faber & Faber, 1952.

Kybalová, Jana. *European Creamware*. London: Hamlyn, 1989.

Marien-Dugardin, A.M. *Faïences Fines*. Bruxelles: Musées Royaux D'Art et D'Histoire, 1975.

Nougarède, Claude. 'Faïences Fines De Sèvres.' *Cahiers De La Céramique Du Verre Et Des Arts Du Feu* No. 45. Sèvres, 1969.

Savage, George. 'The Influence of Wedgwood on Continental Pottery and Porcelain.' *The Third Wedgwood International Seminar*, 1958.

Castleford Pottery *see* **Dunderdale**

Chetham & Woolley

Halfpenny, Pat. 'The Chetham Family.' *Echoes and Reflections*. The Northern Ceramic Society, 1990.

Hollens, David. 'Some Researches into the Makers of Dry Bodies.' *English Ceramic Circle Transactions*, Vol. 11, Part 3, 1983.

Don Pottery

Don Pottery Pattern Book (1807) reprinted by the Doncaster Library Service, 1983.

Mandby T.G. 'Neglected Don Pottery'. *Antique Collector*, September, 1986.

Dunderdale

Edwards (Roussel), Diana. 'The Castleford Pottery and Other Stoneware Factories.' Proceedings of the 26th Wedgwood International Seminar, 1981.

The Castleford Pottery 1790-1821. Wakefield: Wakefield Historical Publications, 1982.

Lawrence, Heather. *Yorkshire Pots and Potteries*. Newton Abbot: David & Charles, Ltd., 1974.

Walton, Peter (preface) and Lawrence, Heather (historical note). *The Castleford Pottery Pattern Book* (1796). Reprinted by E. P. Publishing, 1973.

John Flaxman

Bindman, David (ed.). *John Flaxman*. London: Thames and Hudson, 1979.

Constable, W.G. *John Flaxman 1755-1826*. London: The University Press, Ltd., 1927.

Irwin, David. *John Flaxman 1755-1826*. London: Studio Vista/ Christies, 1979.

Foley Pottery

Barker, David. 'A Group of Staffordshire Red Stonewares of the Eighteenth Century.' *English Ceramic Circle Transactions*, Vol. 14. Part 2, 1991.

Greatbatch

Barker, David. *William Greatbatch, A Staffordshire Potter*. London: Jonathan Horne, 1991.

Hartley, Greens & Co., Leeds Pottery

Grabham, Oxley. *Yorkshire Potteries, Pots and Potters*. Wakefield: S. R. Publishers, 1971, originally published 1916.

Kidson, Joseph R. and Frank. *Historical Notices of the Leeds Old Pottery*. Wakefield: S.R. Publishers, 1970, first published by the authors 1892.

Lawrence, Heather. *Yorkshire Pots and Potteries*. Newton Abbot: David & Charles, Ltd., 1974.

Morley, Ron. 'Mr. Hartley of Hartley, Greens & Co.' *Journal of the Northern Ceramic Society* Vol. 8, 1991.

Towner, Donald C. *The Leeds Pottery*. London: Cory, Adams & Mackay, 1963; *English Cream-coloured Earthenware*. London: Faber & Faber, 1957; *Creamware*. London: Faber & Faber, 1978.

Walton, Peter. *Creamware and other English Pottery at Temple Newsam House Leeds*. Bradford: Lund Humphries, 1976.

Herculaneum

Smith, Alan. 'Herculaneum China and Earthenware.' *English Ceramic Circle Transactions* Vol. 7, Part 1, 1968; *The Illustrated Guide to Liverpool Herculaneum Pottery 1796-1840*. New York: Praeger Publishers, 1970.

Samuel Hollins

Robertshaw, Ivor. 'Samuel Hollins of Vale Pleasant.' *Northern Ceramic Society Newsletter* No. 54, June, 1984.

Knottingley Pottery (Ferrybridge Pottery) *see also* **Wedgwood & Co.**

Lawrence, Heather. *Yorkshire Pots and Potteries*. Newton Abbot: David & Charles, 1974.

Lakin

Blakey, Harold. 'Thomas Lakin: Staffordshire Potter 1769-1821.' *Northern Ceramic Society Journal* Vol. 5, 1984; 'Thomas Lakin in Staffordshire and Yorkshire'. *Ars Ceramica* No. 5, 1988.

Longton Potters

Hampson, R.S. *The Development of the Pottery Industry in Longton*. University of Keele Degree of Master of Arts. 1986. Published also as 'Longton potters 1700-1865'. *Journal of Ceramic History* Vol. 14, 1991.

Lowesby

Inder, Pamela, *Lowesby Pottery*. Leicester Museums Publcation, No. 12, 1977.

Mare

Mountford, Arnold. 'John Mare of Hanley.' *Echoes and Reflections*. Northern Ceramic Society, 1990.

Minton

Atterbury, Paul and Batkin, Maureen. *The Dictionary of Minton*. Woodbridge: Antique Collectors' Club, 1990.

Godden, Geoffrey. *Minton Pottery & Porcelain of the First Period 1793-1850*. London: Barrie & Jenkins, 1968.

Lockett, Terence A. 'Minton in 1810.' *Northern Ceramic Society Journal* Vol. 4, 1980-1.

Mist

Thomas, Tony. 'James Mist.' *Northern Ceramic Society Newsletter* No. 16. Reprinted in *Echoes and Reflections*, Northern Ceramic Society, 1990.

Neale and Palmer

Edwards, Diana. 'James Neale of St. Paul's Churchyard.' *Ars Ceramica*, 1986; *Neale Pottery and Porcelain, Its Successors and Predecessors, 1763-1820*. London: Barrie & Jenkins, 1987; 'Classical Competition'. *Collectors Guide*, November, 1987; 'Palmer and Neale-Imitators or Initiators?' *Proceedings from the 34th Wedgwood International Seminar*, 1989.

Godden, Geoffrey. 'James Neale's porcelains.' *Staffordshire Porcelain*. London: Granada, 1983.

Sutherland-Graeme, A.V. (Capt.). 'James Neale, potter.' *Connoisseur*, vol. cxx, 1947.

Benjamin Plant

Plant, Harold. 'Diary of Benjamin Plant, 18th Century Potter of Lane End.' *Pottery Gazette and Glass Trade Review*, July, 1855.

Pratt

Lewis, John and Griselda. *Pratt Ware*. Woodbridge: Antique Collectors' Club, 1984.

Ridgway

Halfpenny, Pat. 'John Ridgway's visit to America.' *Northern Ceramic Society Newsletter* No. 31, September, 1978.

Godden, Geoffrey. *Ridgway Porcelains*. Woodbridge: Antique Collectors' Club, 1985, originally published by Barrie & Jenkins, London, 1972.

Markin, Trevor. 'The Bankruptcy of William Ridgway in 1848.' *Journal of the Northern Ceramic Society* Vol. 6, 1987.

Riley

Pomfret, Roger. 'John and Richard Riley.' *Journal of Ceramic History* Vol. 13. Stoke-on-Trent: City Museum and Art Gallery, 1988.

Senior & Morton

Lawrence, Heather. *Yorkshire Pots and Potteries*. Newton Abbot: David & Charles, Ltd., 1974.

Morley, Ron. 'Leeds Pottery Plaques and Medallions.' *Northern Ceramic Society Newsletter* 79, September 1990; 'The Leeds Pottery Revival.' *Northern Ceramic Society Newsletter* 82, June, 1991.

Sowter & Co.

Edwards (Roussel), Diana. *The Castleford Pottery 1790-1821*. Wakefield: Wakefield Historical Publications, 1982.

Lawrence, Heather. *Yorkshire Pots and Potteries*. Newton Abbot: David & Charles, Ltd., 1974.

Spode/Copeland

Cleggett, Mavis. 'China for the new Castle.' *Northern Ceramic Society Newsletter* No. 82, June, 1991.

Copeland, Robert. *Spode-Copeland 1765-1965*. Exhibition catalogue Kunstindustrimusset Oslo (Norway), 27 April to 29 May 1966.

Copeland, Robert et al (Halfpenny, Pat, ed). *Spode Copeland 1733-1983*. Stoke-on-Trent: City Museum and Art Gallery, 1983.

Fisk, Geoffrey. 'Spode's Daisy Chain.' *Review*. The Spode Society, Vol. 1, 1989.

Hayden, Arthur. *Spode and His Successors*. London: Cassell & Company, Ltd., 1925.

Whiter, Leonard. *Spode*. London: Barrie & Jenkins, 1970.

William Stubbs

Nixon, Malcolm. 'William Stubbs of Hanley.' *Northern Ceramic Society Newsletter* No. 69, March, 1988.

Swansea *see* **Cambrian Pottery**

Swinton

Cox, Alwyn and Cox, Angela. 'Recent Excavations at Swinton Pottery.' *English Ceramic Circle Transactions* Vol. 11, Part 1, 1981; *Rockingham Pottery & Porcelain 1745-1842*. London: Faber & Faber, 1983.

Eaglestone, Arthur A. & Lockett, T.A. *The Rockingham Pottery*. Rutland, Vermont: Charles A. Tuttle Company, Inc., 1973, originally published 1964.

Lawrence, Heather. *Yorkshire Pots and Potteries*. Newton Abbot: David & Charles, 1974.

Rice, D.G. *The Illustrated Guide to Rockingham Pottery and Porcelain*. New York: Praeger Publishers, 1971.

John Taylor

'By the late John Taylor.' *The Complete Practical Potter or a Comprehensive Collection of Receipts for the Manufacture of China, Earthenware, Ironstone &c. &c...* Shelton, 1847.

Turner

Hillier, Bevis. *Master Potters of the Industrial Revolution, The Turners of Lane End.* London: Cory, Adams & MacKay Ltd., 1965.

Leese, Maureen E. 'John Turner II.' *Northern Ceramic Society Newsletter* No. 50, June, 1983; 'The Turner Moulds.' *Northern Ceramic Society Journal* Vol. 5, 1984.

Voyez

Charleston, Robert J. 'Jean Voyez.' *English Ceramic Circle Transactions* Vol. 5 Part 1, 1960.

Edwards, Diana. *Neale Pottery and Porcelain 1763-1820.* London: Barrie & Jenkins, 1987.

Grundy, A. H. 'John Voyez—some Masterpieces of Craftsmanship.' *Apollo*, October, 1958.

W(***)

Darlington, Diana. 'W(***)—a Mark of Reference.' *Northern Ceramic Society Journal* Vol. 4, 1980/1.

Godden, Geoffrey. *Staffordshire Porcelain* (Appendix VI). London: Granada, 1983.

Wedgwood

Adams, Elizabeth B. *The Dwight and Lucille Beeson Wedgwood Collection at The Birmingham Museum of Art.* Birmingham, Alabama: Birmingham Museum of Art, 1992.

Batkin, Maureen. *Wedgwood Ceramics 1846-1959.* London: Richard Dennis, 1982.

Bostock, E. 'Contributions of Josiah Wedgwood to the Technical Side of the Pottery Industry.' *Transactions of the Ceramic Society.* Stoke-on-Trent: The Ceramic Society, 1930.

Burman, Lionel. 'Joseph Mayer's Wedgwood Collection.' *Joseph Mayer of Liverpool.* London and Liverpool: The Society of Antiquaries in Association with the National Museums and Galleries on Merseyside, 1988.

Burton, William. *Josiah Wedgwood And His Pottery.* London: Cassell and Company, Ltd., 1922.

Buten, David. *18th-Century Wedgwood A Guide for Collectors & Connoisseurs.* New York: Methuen, Inc., 1980.

Chellis, Mrs. Robert D. 'Wedgwood & Bentley Source Books.' *The Seventh Wedgwood International Seminar*, 1962.

Clifford, Timothy. 'Some English Ceramic Vases and Their Sources, Part 1.' *English Ceramic Circle Transactions*, Vol. 10, Part 3, 1978.

Church, A. H. *Josiah Wedgwood.* London: Seeley and Co., Limited; New York: Macmillan, 1903.

Dawson, Aileen. *Masterpieces of Wedgwood in the British Museum. London.* Published by the Trustees of the British Museum, 1984.

Des Fontaines, John. 'Wedgwood's Pyrophorous Vases.' *English Ceramic Circle Transactions* Vol. 14, Part 2, 1991.

Farrar, Katherine Eufemia. *Letters of Josiah Wedgwood* Vols. I, II, III. Barlaston: The Wedgwood Museum, 1973 (originally published 1903).

Finer, Ann and Savage, George. *The Selected Letters of Josiah Wedgwood.* London: Cory, Adams & Mackay, 1965.

Hampson, Rodney. 'Josiah Wedgwood I Ceramic Historian.' *Ars Ceramica*, 1988.

Jewitt, Llewellynn. *The Wedgwoods.* London: Virtue Brothers and Co., 1865.

Johnson, Harwood A. 'Books belonging to Wedgwood & Bentley the 10th of Aug't 1770.' *Ars Ceramica*, 1990.

Kelly, Alison. *Decorative Wedgwood in Architecture and Furniture.* London: Country Life Limited, 1965; *Wedgwood Ware.* London: Ward Lock Limited, 1970; 'Josiah Wedgwood's London Banking Account.' *Proceedings of the Wedgwood Society* No. 9, 1975.

Macht, Carol. *Classical Wedgwood Designs.* New York: Gramercy Publishing Company, 1957.

Mankowitz, Wolf. *Wedgwood.* London: Hamlyn Publishing Group Limited, 1966 (originally published 1953).

Meteyard, Eliza. *Life of Josiah Wedgwood* Vol I, II. London: Hurst and Blackett, 1865, 1866; *A Group of Englishmen.* London: Longmans, Green and Co., 1871; *Wedgwood and His Works.* London: Bell and Daldy, 1873; *Memorials of Wedgwood.* London: George Bell and Sons, 1874; *Wedgwood Handbook.* London: George Bell and Sons, 1875; *Choice Examples of Wedgwood Art.* London: George Bell and Sons, 1879.

Miller, Lynn. 'The Oven Book: Oddities and Incidentals.' *Proceedings of the Wedgwood Society* Vol. 11, 1982.

Miller, Lynn and Des Fontaines, John. 'A Flash in the Pan Wedgwood's Pyrophorous Vase.' *Ceramics* III, May/June, 1986.

Morley-Fletcher, Hugo. 'Wedgwood Auctions in the Nineteenth Century at Christie, Mason and Woods.' *The Tenth Wedgwood International Seminar*, 1965.

Rackham, Bernard. 'Wedgwood Reconsidered.' *English Ceramic Circle Transactions* Vol. 3, Part 1, 1951.

Rakow, Dr. & Mrs. Leonard. 'Marks—Good, Bad and Indifferent.' *The Twenty-Sixth Wedgwood International Seminar*, 1981.

Roberts, Gaye Blake. 'Wedgwood in Russia.' *Ceramics Magazine*, July 1986.

Reilly, Robin and Savage, George. *Wedgwood Portrait Medallions.* London: Barrie & Jenkins,

1973; *Dictionary of Wedgwood*. Woodbridge: Antique Collectors' Club, 1980.

Reilly, Robin. *The Collector's Wedgwood*. New York: Portfolio Press, 1980; *Wedgwood I, II*. London: Macmillan Limited, 1989.

Smiles, Samuel. *Josiah Wedgwood*. New York: Harper & Brothers, 1895.

Smith, J. B. 'Baptismal Fonts in Black Basaltes.' *Proceedings of the Wedgwood Society*, 1957.

Tait, Hugh. 'The Wedgwood Collection in the British Museum.' *Proceedings of the Wedgwood Society* Vol. 5, 1963.

Tattersall, Bruce. *Stubbs & Wedgwood*. London: The Tate Gallery, 1974; 'Henry Webber, Art at the Service of Industry.' *Apollo*, July, 1985.

The Wedgwood & Bentley Catalogue (1779), reprinted by the Wedgwood Society of New York, 1965.

The Wedgwood Catalogue (1787), reprinted by the Wedgwood Society of New York, 1980.

Wedgwood & Co.

Blakey, Harold. 'Ralph Wedgwood: Decline and Bankruptcy in Staffordshire and arrival in Yorkshire.' *Northern Ceramic Society Newsletter* No. 53, March, 1984.

Des Fontaines, J. K. 'Ralph Wedgwood of Burslem and Ferrybridge.' *Northern Ceramic Society Newsletter* No. 49, March, 1983.

Holdaway, Dr. W.A.M. 'The Wares of Ralph Wedgwood.' *English Ceramic Circle Transactions* Vol. 12, Part 3, 1986.

West Cumberland Potteries

Sibson, Florence. *The History of the West Cumberland Potteries*. Published privately, 1991.

West Pans Pottery

Kelly, Henry. 'West Pans Pottery.' *Northern Ceramic Society Newsletter* No. 88, December, 1992.

McVeigh, Patrick. *Scottish East Coast Potteries 1750-1840*. Edinburgh: John Donald Publishers Ltd., 1979.

Quail, Gerard. *Northern Ceramic Society Newsletters* Nos. 44, 46, 63, 64, 66.

Whieldon

Mountford, Arnold. 'Thomas Whieldon's Manufactory at Fenton Vivian.' *English Ceramic Circle Transactions* Vol. 8, Part 2, 1972.

Whitehead

Haggar, Reginald (intro.). *Designs of Sundry Articles of Earthenware (James and Charles Whitehead, Hanley)*. Reprinted by David Drakard [n.d.], originally published 1798.

Wilson

Edwards, Diana. *Neale Pottery and Porcelain 1763-1820*. London: Barrie & Jenkins, 1987.

Wolfe

Markin, Trevor. 'Thomas Wolfe.' *Northern Ceramic Society Newsletter* No. 48, December, 1982; 'Thomas Wolfe: A Man of Property.' *Northern Ceramic Society Newsletter* No. 58, June, 1985.

Wood

Falkner, Frank. *The Wood Family of Burslem*. Wakefield: E.P. Publishing, Ltd., 1972, originally published 1912.

Halfpenny, Pat. 'The Wood Family.' *Ceramics Magazine*, May, 1986; *English Earthenware Figures 1740-1840*. Woodbridge: Antique Collectors' Club, 1991.

GENERAL REFERENCES

Adams, Elizabeth. 'Ceramic Insurances in the Sun Company.' *English Ceramic Circle Transactions* Vol. 10, Part 1, 1976.

Atterbury, Paul (ed.). *English Pottery and Porcelain An Historical Survey*. New York: Universe Books, 1978.

Barker, David and Halfpenny, Pat. *Unearthing Staffordshire*. Stoke-on-Trent: City Museum and Art Gallery, 1990.

Binns, Charles F. (ed.) *The Manual of Practical Potting*. London: Scott, Greenwood & Sons, 1907.

Blakey, Harold. 'Sun Fire Insurance Policies from the Country Department Registers.' *Northern Ceramic Society Journal* Vol. 3, 1978-9; 'Further Extracts from Sun Fire Insurance Policies.' *Northern Ceramic Society Newsletter* No. 42, June, 1981.

Brodeur, Paul. 'The Treasure of the DeBraack.' *New Yorker Magazine*, August 15, 1988.

Brown, Mrs. G. Edgerton. 'Black Basalt.' *The Fifth Wedgwood International Seminar*, 1960.

Charleston, R.J. and Towner, Donald. *English Ceramics 1580-1830*. London: Sotheby Parke Bernet Publications, 1977.

Collard, Elizabeth. *Nineteenth Century Pottery and Porcelain in Canada*. Kingston and Montreal: McGill-Queen's University Press, 2nd ed., 1984, originally published 1967.

Cushion, John. *Pottery & Porcelain Tablewares*. London: Studio Vista, 1976.

De La Beche, Sir Henry and Reeks, Trenham. *Catalogue of Specimens Illustrative of the*

Composition and Manufacture of British Pottery and Porcelain... London: Museum of Practical Geology, 1855.

Delhom, M. Mellanay. *The Delhom Gallery Guide English Pottery*. Charlotte: Mint Museum, 1982.

Detweiller, Susan Gray. *George Washington's ChinaWare*. New York: Harry Abrams, 1982.

Earle, Major Cyril. *The Earle Collection of Early Staffordshire Pottery*. London: A. Brown and Sons, Limited, 1915.

Eatwell, Ann and Werner, Alex. 'A London Staffordshire Warehouse 1794-1825.' *Journal of the Northern Ceramic Society* Vol. 8, 1991.

Edmundson, Roger. 'Staffordshire Potters Insured with the Salop Fire Office 1780-1825.' *Journal of the Northern Ceramic Society* Vol. 6, 1987.

Elliott, G.W. 'Staffordshire Red and Black Stonewares.' *English Ceramic Circle Transactions* Vol. 10, Part 2, 1972.

Emmerson, Robin. *British Teapots & Tea Drinking*, London: HMSO, 1992.

Godden, Geoffrey. *British Pottery and Porcelain 1780-1850*. Cranbury, New Jersey: A. S. Barnes and Company, Inc., 1964; *An Illustrated Encyclopedia of British Pottery and Porcelain*. New York: Bonanza Books, 1965; *Jewitt's Ceramic Art of Great Britain*. New York: Arco Publishing Company, Inc., 1972; *British Pottery An Illustrated Guide*. New York: Clarkson N. Potter, Inc., 1975; *Encyclopedia of British Porcelain Manufacturers*. London: Barrie & Jenkins, 1988.

Grant, M. H. *The Makers of Black Basaltes*. London: Holland Press, 1967, originally published 1910; *The Old English Landscape Painters*. Leigh-on-Sea: F. Lewis Publishers, Ltd., 1971, originally published 1926; *A Dictionary of British Landscape Painters*. Leigh-on-Sea: F. Lewis Publishers, Ltd., 1976, originally published 1952.

Graves, Algernon. *The Society of Free Artists of Great Britain 1760-1791. The Free Society of Artists 1761-1783*. Bath: Kingsmead Reprints, 1969, originally published 1907.

Greenslade, M.W. *Victoria History of the County of Stafford (VCH)*. Stafford: Staffordshire County Library, reprint, 1981.

Grigsby Leslie B. *The Henry H. Weldon Collection English Pottery 1650-1800*. London: Sotheby's Publications, 1990.

Guest, Montague (ed.). *Lady Charlotte Schreiber's Journals* Vol.I & II. London: John Lane, The Bodley Head, 1911.

Haggar, R.G., Mountford, A.R., and Thomas, J. *The Staffordshire Pottery Industry*. Stafford: reprinted by the Staffordshire County Library from The Victoria History of the County of Stafford, 1981, original reprint 1967.

Hampson, Rodney. 'Ovens Galore.' *Northern Ceramic Society Newsletter* No. 79, June, 1979.

Haslam, Malcolm. *Pottery*. London: Orbis Publishing, 1972.

Henderson, W.O. *J.C. Fischer and His Diary of Industrial England 1814-51*. London: Frank Cass, 1966.

Hillier, Bevis. *Pottery and Porcelain 1700-1914*. New York: Meredith Press, 1968.

Hobson, R.L. *Catalogue of the Collection of English Pottery and Porcelain*. London: The Trustees of the British Museum, 1903.

Holgate, David. *New Hall*. London: Faber & Faber, 1987.

Hollens, David. 'Some Researches into the Makers of Dry Bodies.' *English Ceramic Circle Transactions* Vol. 11, Part 3, 1983.

Hughes, G.B. *English and Scottish Earthenware 1660-1860*. London: Lutterworth, 1960.

Jewitt, Llewellynn. *The Ceramic Art of Great Britain*. Poole, Dorset: New Orchard Editions, 1985, originally published 1878.

Guide to The Lady Lever Art Gallery. Port Sunlight. Merseyside County Council [n.d.].

Lane, Arthur. 'The English Ceramic Collections in the Victoria and Albert Museum.' *English Ceramic Circle Transactions* Vol. 4, Part 4, 1959.

Lawrence, Heather. 'Yorkshire Newspapers.' *Echoes and Reflections*. Stoke-on-Trent: Northern Ceramic Society, 1990.

Lewis, Griselda. *The Collector's History of English Pottery*. Woodbridge: Antique Collectors' Club, 1977.

Lockett T. A. and Halfpenny, T.A. (eds.). *Stonewares & Stone chinas*. Catalogue of the Fourth Exhibition from the Northern Ceramic Society. Stoke-on-Trent: City Museum and Art Gallery, 1982.

Mankowitz, Wolf and Haggar, Reginald. *The Concise Encyclopedia of British Pottery and Porcelain*. New York: Frederick A. Praeger Publishers, 1968.

Miller Philip and Berthoud, Michael. *An Anthology of British Teapots*. Kent: Micawber Publications, 1985.

Nichols, Sarah C. *Black Basaltes Ware—The Speyer Collection*. Exhibition catalogue Carnegie Institute Museum of Art, 1983.

Nylander, Jane C. 'English Ceramics on Essex County Tables.' *Ceramics and Glass in the Essex Institute*. Salem, Massachusetts: The Essex Institute, 1985.

Pitt, William. *A Topographical History of Staffordshire*. Newcastle-under-Lyme: Printed by and for J. Smith, 1817.

Price, Robin. 'Three Dragons Redware, Blackware, and Cane-Coloured ware.' *English Ceramic Circle Transactions* Vol. 7, Part 3, 1970.

Pugh, Captain P. D. Gordon Pugh. *Naval Ceramics*. Newport, England: The Ceramic Book Company, 1971.

Rackham, Bernard. *Catalogue of English Porcelain Earthenware Enamels and Glass collected by Charles Schreiber Esq. M.P. and the Lady Charlotte Elizabeth Schreiber and presented to the Museum in 1884*. London: Published under the Authority of the Board of Education, 1928.

Shaw, Simeon. *History of the Staffordshire Potteries*. Hanley, 1829; *The Chemistry of the several Natural and Artificial Heterogeneous Compounds used in Manufacturing Porcelain, Glass, and Pottery*. London: Scott, Greenwood & Son, 1900, originally published 1837.

Sheldon, Harry. 'The Story of Black Basalt Ware.' *The Thirteenth Wedgwood International Seminar*. Charlotte, North Carolina: The Mint Museum of Art, 1968.

Smedley, The Rev. Edward, Rose, The Rev. Hugh James, Rose, The Rev. Henry John. *Encyclopedia Metropolitana* Vol. 6, 1845.

Solon, L.M. *The Art of the Old English Potter*. London: Bemrose & Sons, 1885.

Spanton, W.D., ed. *The Ancient Corporation of Hanley...1783-1900*. Hanley, 1901.

Sutton, Denys. 'Amateurs and Scholars.' *Apollo*. May, 1984.

Taggart, Ross E. *The Frank P. and Harriet C. Burnap Collection of English Pottery in the William Rockhill Nelson Gallery*. Kansas City: Nelson Gallery-Atkins Museum, 1967.

Valpy, Nancy. 'Extracts from 18th Century London Newspapers.' *English Ceramic Circle Transactions* Vol 12, Part 2, 1985; 'Extracts from the Daily Advertiser and additional manuscripts.' *English Ceramic Circle Transactions* Vol. 14, Part 1, 1990; 'Extracts from the Daily Advertiser 1792-1795.' *English Ceramic Circle Transactions* Vol. 14, Part 2, 1991.

Ward, John. *The Borough of Stoke-upon-Trent*. Hanley: Webberley, Ltd., 1984, originally published 1843.

Wilson, David M. *The Forgotten Collector*. London: Thames and Hudson, 1984.

CLASSICAL, ANCIENT AND MEDIEVAL SOURCES

Barton, K. J. *Pottery in England from 3500 BC- AD 1750*. Newton Abbot: David & Charles, 1975.

Boardman, John. 'Silver is White.' *Rev. Arch.*, February, 1987.

Caylus, Anne Claude Phillipe, comte de. *Recueil d'antiquités égyptiennes, étrusques, grecques, romaines et gauloises*, Vol. 1. Paris: Desaint & Saillant, 1756-1770, Vol. 2, Paris: Duchesne; Vols. 3-7, Paris: N. M. Tilliard; Vol. 8, *Recueil d'antiquités dans les Gaules...* Paris: Herissant le fils.

Del Chiaro, Mario A. *Etruscan Art from West Coast Collections*. Santa Barbara: University of California at Santa Barbara, 1967.

Forsdyke, E.J. *Catalogue of Greek and Etruscan Vases in the British Museum* Vol. 1, Part 1. London: The British Museum, 1925.

Mayo, Margaret Ellen. *The Art of South Italy Vases from Magna Graecia*. Richmond: Virginia Museum of Fine Arts, 1982.

Montfaucon, Bernard de. *L'antiquité expliquée et représentée en figures...* 2 ed. Paris: F. Delaulne, 1722.

Moon, Warren. *Greek Vase Painting in Midwestern Collections*. Chicago: The Art Institute, 1979.

Noble, Joseph Veach. *The Techniques of Painted Attic Pottery*. London and New York: Thames and Hudson, 1988.

Rackham, Bernard. *Medieval English Pottery*. London: Faber & Faber, 1972.

Rasmussen, T. B. *Bucchero Pottery from Southern Etruria*. Cambridge: Cambridge University Press, 1979.

Swan, Vivian G. *Pottery in Roman Britain*. Aylesbury: Shire Publications Ltd, 1988 (4th ed.).

Walters, H.B. *Catalogue of Greek and Etruscan Vases in the British Museum*, Vol. 1, Part II. London: The British Museum, 1912; *History of Ancient Pottery*, Vol. 1. Washington, D.C.: McGrath Publishing Company, 1973.

Williams, Dyfri. *Greek Vases*. London: The British Museum, 1985.

DIRECTORIES AND NEWSPAPERS

Bailey's Northern Directory 1781
Bailey's 1784 (Yorkshire)
Bailey's 1784 (Staffordshire)
Tunnicliff 1787 (Staffordshire)
The Universal British Directory 1795 (Yorkshire)

Leeds Directory 1798
Bailey's Commercial Directory (Staffordshire) 1818-20
Bailey's Commercial Directory 1814-15 (Yorkshire)
Bailey's Commercial Directory 1818-20 (Yorkshire)
Pigot's Directory 1822 (London)
London Gazette 1770-1835
Staffordshire Advertiser 1795-1863
Pottery Gazette 1884
Gazetteer and Daily Advertiser (London) 1769-1795
Dunlap & Claypoole's (Philadelphia) 1792-1796
New York Gazette 1762

UNPUBLISHED OTHER SOURCES

Catherall Papers, Flintshire (Clwyd) Record Office
Collamore Papers, Baker Library, Harvard University
Drawing Book for Black Ware 1800, Hartley, Greens & Co., Leeds Pottery, on deposit City Art Gallery Library, Leeds.
Land Tax Records (1781-1820), County Record Office Stafford.
Spode Papers, on deposit Keele University Library.
Sun Fire Insurance Policy Registers Hull (University Library) and London (Guildhall Library).
Wedgwood MSS, on deposit Keele University Library.
Wedgwood Shapes Books, Wedgwood Museum, Barlaston.

LITERARY REFERENCES

Byatt, A.S. *Possession*. New York: Random House Publishing, 1990.
Danziger, Katherine. *Dr. Johnson's Mrs. Thrale*. London: Century Publishing, 1984.
Medawar, Sir Peter Brian. *The Art Of the Soluble*. London: Methuen, 1967
Surtees, Virginia. *A Second Self the Letters of Harriett Granville 1810-1845*. Salisbury: Michael Russell, Ltd., 1990.
Trollope, Anthony. *Can You Forgive Her*. London: Oxford University Press, 1972, originally published 1865; *The Three Clerks*. New York: Dover Publications, 1981, originally published 1857.
Wells, H.G. Christina *Alberta's Father*. London: Hogarth Press, 1985, originally published by Jonathan Cape, 1925.

FOOTNOTES

CHAPTER I

1 *Possession* (New York: Random House, 1990), 312. The quote refers to the North Yorkshire coast.

2 Wedgwood MS E25-18521, 7 March 1774. All Wedgwood MS references are published with the kind permission of the Trustees of the Wedgwood Museum, Barlaston, England. The Wedgwood MSS are on deposit at Keele University Library.

3 *The Wedgwoods…* (London: Virtue Brothers and Co., 1865), 185.

4 Wedgwood MS E25-18208.

5 'Thanks for your discovery in favour of the black Teapots. I hope *white hands* will continue in fashion, and then we may continue to make *black Teapots* 'till you can find us better employment'. Wedgwood to Bentley, Wedgwood MS E25-18430, 26 December 1772.

6 Wedgwood MS 96-17667.

7 Josiah Wedgwood to William Cox, London, 31 August 1768, ibid.

8 Eliza Meteyard, *A Group of Englishmen 1795-1815* (London: Longmans, Green, and Co., 1871), x-xiii.

9 L.M. Solon, *The Art of the Old English Potter* (London: Bemrose & Sons, 1885), 129. Solon mentioned the teapots in the same text, without illustration, in his first edition, printed in London and Derby in 1883.

10 *Pliny* xxxvi (Holland, 1601), vii.

11 As quoted in the *OED*, 1933, 685.

12 E. Bostock, 'Contributions of Josiah Wedgwood to the Technical Side of the Pottery Industry', *Transactions of the Ceramic Society* (Stoke-on-Trent: The Ceramic Society, 1930), 48.

13 Wedgwood MS 39-28410 as quoted in R.S. Hampson, *The Development of the Pottery Industry in Longton*, University of Keele Degree of Master of Arts, 1986, 57.

14 Harry Sheldon, 'The Story of Black Basalt Ware', *The Thirteenth Wedgwood International Seminar* (Charlotte, North Carolina: Mint Museum of Art, 1968), 175.

15 Simeon Shaw, *History of the Staffordshire Potteries* (Hanley, 1829), 124.

16 Wedgwood MS E25-18208, 30 August 1768.

17 Ibid.

18 R.G. Haggar, A.R. Mountford, & J. Thomas, *The Staffordshire Pottery Industry* (Stafford: Reprinted by the Staffordshire County Library from *The Victoria History of the County of Stafford*, 1981 (original reprint

1967), 14-15.

19 Wedgwood MS E25-18622, 30 October 1775.

20 Letter from Robert Copeland 19th March 1990.

21 Kathleen M. Armistead and W.J. Grant-Davidson, *Catalogue of the Kildare S. Meager Bequest Swansea Pottery* (Swansea: Glynn Vivian Art Gallery, 1967?), 15.

22 Sheldon, 174-5.

23 H.B. Walters, *History of Ancient Pottery*, Vol.1 (Washington, D.C.: McGrath Publishing Company, 1973), 242.

24 Joseph Veach Noble, *The Techniques of Painted Attic Pottery* (London and New York: Thames and Hudson, 1988), 81.

25 H.B. Walters, *Catalogue of Greek and Etruscan Vases in the British Museum*, Vol.1, Part II (London: The British Museum, 1912), ix.

26 E.J. Forsdyke, *Catalogue of the Greek and Etruscan Vases in the British Museum*, Vol, 1, Part 1 (London: The British Museum, 1925), xii-xiv.

27 Mario A. Del Chiaro, *Etruscan Art from West Coast Collections* (Santa Barbara: University of California at Santa Barbara, 1967), 19.

28 Noble, 82.

29 T.B. Rasmussen, *Bucchero Pottery from Southern Etruria* (Cambridge: Cambridge University Press, 1979), 1-2.

30 Ibid, 20-1.

31 Walters, 1912, xxv.

32 John Boardman, 'Silver is White', *Rev. Arch.*, February, 1987, 288.

33 Warren G. Moon, *Greek Vase Painting in Midwestern Collections* (Chicago: The Art Institute, 1979), xvii.

34 Margaret Ellen Mayo, *The Art Of South Italy Vases From Magna Graecia* (Richmond: Virginia Museum of Fine Arts, 1982), 252.

35 Noble, 80.

36 Vivian G. Swan, *Pottery in Roman Britain*, 4th ed. (Princes Risborough: Shire Publications Ltd., 1988), 28-9.

37 K. J. Barton, *Pottery in England from 3500 BC-AD 1750* (Newton Abbot: David & Charles, 1975), 29.

38 Swan, 40.

39 Bernard Rackham illustrates several examples in *Medieval English Pottery* (London: Faber & Faber, 1972), pls. 92-95.

40 'Staffordshire Red and Black Stonewares', *English Ceramic Circle Transactions*, Vol 10, Part 2, 1977, 84-94.

41 Ibid, 91.

42 In the 1817 discussion of the Bradwell Wood site William Pitt also noted in *A Topographical History of Staffordshire* that only 'fragments of red broken china were found in the ground', 420.

43 Arnold Mountford, 'Thomas Whieldon's Manufactory at Fenton Vivian', *English Ceramic Circle Transactions* Vol 8 Part 2, 1972, 173.

44 W.R. Bourne, *A Collection of Ceramic Receipts for Many Years Used By The Late John Bourne, of Burslem, For Fifty Years A Successful Practical Potter* (Hanley: J. Hitchings, 1884), 17.

45 Wedgwood MS10-8987.

46 Undated draft letter from Josiah Wedgwood's lawyer defending Wedgwood's patent for encaustic painted vases, 1771, page 10, Wedgwood MS W/M 1829.

47 From a letter published by Josiah Wedgwood anonymously in 1788 or 1789. Rodney Hampson, 'Josiah Wedgwood I Ceramic Historian', *Ars Ceramica* No. 5, 1988, 24.

48 Wedgwood MS 1829, [n.d.], 2.

49 A creamware bowl marked 'EB' (Enoch Booth?) and dated 1743 is in the British Museum.

50 Elliott, 93.

51 Undated draft letter, page 6, 1771, Wedgwood MS W/M 1829.

52 Ibid. 5.

CHAPTER II

1 Josiah Wedgwood to Thomas Bentley Wedgwood MS E25-18269, 19 November 1769.

2 Ibid.

3 Wedgwood MS17-15862.

4 *New York Gazette* 24 May 1762. This advertisement is misquoted in G. B. Hughes, *English and Scottish Earthenware 1660-1860* to read 'Egyptian black…'(p. 81).

5 Wedgwood MS9-7001, 25 September 1764.

6 Wedgwood MS E25-18208, 30 August 1768.

7 Gori.

8 The notation indicates the copy is from Sir Watkin Williams Wynn, a gift from Wynn to Wedgwood and a duplicate in the library.

9 Wedgwood MS122-23591, 7 February 1774. Francis Grose' *The Antiquities of England and Wales, 1773-1777*, was published originally in Vols. 1-4 with four supplemental volumes following.

10 Wedgwood MS W/M 1441

11 Geoffrey Beard, *The Work of Robert Adam* (New York: Arco Publishing Company, Inc., 1978), 1.

12 Joseph and Anne Rykwert, *Robert and James Adam* (New York: Rizzoli International Publications, Ltd., 1985), 40.

13 Wedgwood MS96-17662, (n.d.) May, 1768.

14 *Gazetteer and Daily Advertiser*, 24 March 1769.

15 Ibid.

16 Wedgwood MS52-9527.

17 Quoted from the Hamilton-Nelson papers by Denys Sutton in 'Amateurs and Scholars', *Apollo* (May, 1984), 326.

18 *L'Antiquité Expliquée, et Représentée en Figures* (Paris: F. Delaulne, 1719).

19 Wedgwood MS L.H.P., 18 April 1770.

20 Wedgwood MS E25-18264.

21 Wedgwood MS E25-18266, 9 October 1769.

22 For a complete discussion of the editions and a brief description of the contents of the 1770 book list of Wedgwood and Bentley *see* Harwood A. Johnson, 'Books belonging to Wedgwood & Bentley the 10th of Aug't 1770', *Ars Ceramica*, 1990. The description of the Wedgwood and Bentley sources came from page 19.

23 Ibid, 21.

24 Carol Macht, *Classical Wedgwood Designs* (New York: Gramercy Publishing Company, 1957) is a valuable tool in working with the 1770 W & B book list.

25 Mrs. Robert D. Chellis, 'Wedgwood and Bentley Source Books', *The Seventh Wedgwood International Seminar* (Chicago: The Art Institute, 1962), 64.

26 Patent #939

27 Wedgwood MS W/M 1829

28 Wedgwood MS E25-18328.

29 Wedgwood MS E25-18266, 9 October 1769.

30 Wedgwood MS, W/M 1829, 8,9.

31 Wedgwood MS E25-18325, as quoted in D. Edwards, *Neale Pottery and Porcelain...* (London: Barrie & Jenkins, 1982), 36.

32 Notes written by Enoch Wood in his copy of William Pitt, *A Topographical History of Staffordshire*, printed for and by J. Smith, 1817, 416. I thank Pat Halfpenny for bringing this copy, in the City Museum, Stoke-on-Trent, to my attention.

33 Samuel Hollins' partnership with William Sutton in the earthenware business in St. Paul's Churchyard was dissolved in 29 June 1793 (*London Gazette* 13542, 29 June 1793).

34 Wedgwood MS 96-17659, 7 January 1768

35 Wedgwood MS L-17671, 30 March 1768.

36 Wedgwood MS 96-17660, 30 April 1768.

37 30th October 1771, The Sun Company #304306. Elizabeth Adams, 'Ceramic Insurances in the Sun Company, 1766-1774', *English Ceramic Circle Transactions*, Vol. 10, Part 1, 1976, 34.

38 13 August 1785, Sun Fire Insurance Policy #508865. Harold Blakey, Northern Ceramic Society *Newsletter* 42, June, 1981, 23.

39 Wedgwood MS W/M 1728.

40 A more thorough description of the Wedgwood London showrooms is provided by Robin Reilly and George Savage, *Dictionary of Wedgwood*, 1980, 314-6.

41 Wedgwood MS E25-18433, 2 January 1773.

42 Wedgwood MS W/M 1718.

43 Wedgwood MS W/M 1728.

44 Diana Edwards, *Neale Pottery and Porcelain* (London: Barrie & Jenkins, 1987), 36.

45 Wedgwood MS E25-18403, 13 September 1772.

46 In this statement I disagree with Robin Reilly who suggests that Wedgwood and Bentley were without serious rivals in the field of neo-classicism (*Wedgwood*, Vol. I, 1989), 98.

47 Wedgwood MS 96-17665, 18 July 1768.

48 Wedgwood MS 96-17667, 31 August 1768.

49 Wedgwood MS E25-18261, 27 September 1769.

50 Wedgwood MS E25-18264, 1 October 1769.

51 Wedgwood MS E25-18266, 9 October 1769.

52 Wedgwood MS E25-18263, 30 September 1769?.

53 Josiah Wedgwood to Thomas Bentley, Wedgwood MS E25-18485, 31 July 1773.

54 Wedgwood MS 31-306553.

55 Wedgwood MS 31-23287.

56 Wedgwood MS 96-17668, 14 September 1768.

57 Wedgwood MS W/M 1438, 10 August 1769.

58 Wedgwood MS W/M 1712.

59 Wedgwood MS 17-15689.

60 Wedgwood MS 12-10118, 6 March 1769.

61 Wedgwood MS E25-18269, 19 November 1769.

62 Josiah Wedgwood to William Cox Wedgwood MS 12-17672, 12 January 1769.

63 Sir Watkin Williams-Wynn lived at 20 St. James Square and this letter from Josiah Wedgwood to Mrs. Wedgwood was written on 7 March 1769, Wedgwood MS E25-18235.

64 Wedgwood MS 96-17681, 20 May 1769.

65 Wedgwood MS 96-17682, 28 June 1769.

66 Wedgwood MS 96-17677, 7 April 1769.

67 Wedgwood MS 96-17680, 2 May 1769.

68 Bernard Rackham, 'Wedgwood Reconsidered', *ECC Transactions* Vol. 3 Part 1, 1951, 27.

69 Wedgwood MS E25-18264, 1 October 1769.

70 Wedgwood MS 59-32508.

71 Wedgwood MS E25-18322, 29 August 1770.

72 Wedgwood MS E25-18324, 3 September 1770.

73 Nancy Valpy, 'Extracts From 18th Century London Newspapers', *English Ceramic Circle Transactions*, Vol. 12, Part 2, 1985, 172.

74 Ibid, 168. *Public Advertiser*, February, March, 1772.

75 Wedgwood MS W/M 1441.

76 Wedgwood MS E25-18403.

77 Wedgwood MS E25-18430, 26 December 1772.

78 Wedgwood MS E25-18404, 13 September 1772.

79 Wedgwood to Bentley, Wedgwood MS E25-18395, 31 August 1772.

80 Wedgwood MS E25-18407, 19 September 1772.

81 Wedgwood MS 96-17674, 22 March 1769.

82 Wedgwood MS E25-18365, 11 April 1772.

83 Wedgwood MS E25-18472, 14 June 1773.

84 Wedgwood MS W/M 1719, 10 August 1773.

85 Wedgwood MS E25-18404, 13 September 1772.

86 Alison Kelly, *Decorative Wedgwood in Architecture and Furniture* (London: Country Life Limited, 1965), 36-7.

87 Wedgwood MS E25-18548, 21 July 1774.

88 Ibid.

89 Wedgwood MS 2-30950.

90 Wedgwood MS 2-30951, 23 January 1771.

91 Wedgwood MS 1-112, January-December, 1773.

92 Wedgwood MS E25-18443, 6 February 1773.

93 Wedgwood MS W/M 1449. In footnotes from 1774-6 if there is only a date and no manuscript number the reference is to the above document file.

94 The shapes books are in the Wedgwood Museum, Barlaston.

95 Wedgwood MS W/M 1449, 19 and 26 November 1774.

96 3 December 1774.

97 26 November 1774.

98 3 and 17 December 1774.

99 Wedgwood MS W/M 1720, 1774.

100 Wedgwood MSS E25-4296; E25-4328.

101 Wedgwood MSS 78-13484; 78-13489.

102 Wedgwood MSS 100-18548; 100-18565.

103 Wedgwood MSS 100-18566; 100-18569.

104 Wedgwood MSS 100-18569; 100-18570.

105 Wedgwood MSS 100-18674; 100-18580.

106 Wedgwood MS W/M 1449, 15 March 1775.

107 Wedgwood to Mr. Cox, 2 March 1775, Winterthur MS 56.6.2. I am grateful to Arlene Schwind for bringing this order to my attention.

108 Wedgwood MS W/M 1449, 20 March

1775.

109 24 June 1775.

110 22 January 1776.

111 3 February 1776.

112 12 February 1776.

113 14 and 17 February 1776.

114 24 February 1776.

115 9 March 1776.

116 16 March 1776.

117 6 April 1776.

118 27 April 1776.

119 4 May 1776.

120 Wedgwood MS 96-17677, 7 April 1769.

121 Wedgwood MS W/M 1449, 11 May 1776.

122 26 May 1776.

123 1 June 1776.

124 8 June 1776.

125 15 June 1776.

126 28 June 1776.

127 Wedgwood MS W/M 1712.

128 Wedgwood MS W/M 1449, 27 June 1776.

129 6 July 1776.

130 Wedgwood MS E25-18847, (n.d.), probably 1776.

131 Wedgwood MS W/M 1449, 13 July 1776.

132 16 July 1776.

133 5 October 1776.

134 2 August 1776.

135 31 August 1776.

136 2 August 1776.

137 24 August, 1776.

138 28 December 1776.

139 Wedgwood MS E25-18433, 2 January 1773.

140 Wedgwood MS E25-18554, 22 August 1774.

141 Wedgwood MS E25-18591, 6 February 1775.

142 Wedgwood MS W/M 1449, 12 October 1776.

143 Cf. Fn. 93, 19 October 1776.

144 Wedgwood MS E25-18701, 30 September 1776.

145 Wedgwood MS 130-25950.

146 Wedgwood MS W/M 1449, 2 November 1776. Much previous research (Constable, Bindman, Reilly) has appeared to rely on the Wedgwood letter published in Farrar, vol. II, 419 (1973) which suggests that the first appearance of the 'Dancing Hours' relief decoration occurred in April, 1778. However, the original letter in the Wedgwood archives (E25-18847) is undated, intimating that Lady Farrar placed it in sequence contextually, not chronologically. Eliza Meteyard, *Wedgwood Handbook* (London: George Bell and Sons, 1875), 249, says that basalt vases decorated with the Dancing Hours were being sent down to London even earlier than the 2 November reference above, in September 1776.

147 Wedgwood MS W/M 1449, 2 November 1776.

148 David Bindman ed., *John Flaxman* (London: Thames and Hudson, 1979), 54.

149 Wedgwood MS E25-18847, n.d.

150 David Irwin, *John Flaxman 1755-1826* (London: Studio Vista/Christie's, 1979), 21-2.

151 W. G. Constable, *John Flaxman 1755-1826* (London: The University of London Press, Ltd., 1927), 17-18.

152 Wedgwood MS W/M 1449, 8 November 1776.

153 18 November 1776.

154 Wedgwood MS E25-18349, 31 July 1771.

155 Wedgwood MS W/M 1449, 30 November 1776.

156 14 December 1776.

157 17 December 1774.

158 14 December 1776.

159 21 and 28 December 1776 respectively.

160 Wedgwood MS E25-18742, 24 March 1777.

161 Wedgwood MS E25-18766, 21 June 1777.

162 Ibid.

163 Wedgwood MS 2-30951, 23 January 1771.

164 For further information on basalt baptismal fonts *see*, J. B. Smith, 'Baptismal Fonts in Black Basaltes', *Proceedings of the Wedgwood Society*, 1957, 64-66.

165 Wedgwood MS E25-18814, 25 February 1778.

166 The word Zingara is the feminine of Zingaro or Gypsy. The source for this model appears to be Maffei's *Raccolta di Statue antiche...* Pl. LXXIX (Rome, 1704) which was book twenty in the thirty-one books owned jointly by Wedgwood and Bentley in 1770. The identity of Chrispagnia is unknown.

167 Wedgwood MS 2-1352.

168 Wedgwood MS E.25-18792, 10 November 1771.

169 Wedgwood MS E25-18403, 13 September 1772.

170 The excavation has been published by David Barker in 'A Group of Staffordshire Red Stonewares of the 18th Century', *English Ceramic Circle Transactions*, Vol. 14 Part 2, 1991.

171 Wedgwood MS E25-18403, 13 September 1772.

172 *William Greatbatch, a Staffordshire Potter* (London: Jonathan Horne, 1991).

173 Wedgwood MS E25-18264, 1 October 1769.

174 Reilly, Vol. I, 349.

175 Wedgwood MS E25-18266, 9 October 1769.

176 Wedgwood MS E25-18264, 1 October 1769.

177 Reilly, Vol. I, 557.

178 Wedgwood MS E25-18263, 30 September 1769(?). Which sacrifice medallion is uncertain, but of the eight 'sacrifice' medallions in the 1779 catalogue, only one, #173, is labelled simply 'sacrifice'.

179 W. G. Constable, 8.

180 Eliza Meteyard, *Life of Josiah Wedgwood*, Vol. II (London: Hurst and Blackett, 1866), 322.

181 Reilly, Vol. I, 408.

182 Wedgwood MS W/M 1449, 2 November 1776.

183 Farrar, Vol. II, 419 (1973).

184 Wedgwood MS E25-18789, 29 October 1777.

185 Bindman, 56.

186 Wedgwood MS W/M 1449, 17 December 1774.

187 Wedgwood MS 2-1352.

188 Meteyard, Vol. II, 86.

189 Ibid., 80.

190 Wedgwood MS 96-17673, 20 March 1769.

191 Meteyard, Vol. II, 90.

192 Ibid.

193 Bindman (ed.), *John Flaxman*. Gaye Blake Roberts, 'A Selection of works by Flaxman's contemporaries working for Wedgwood', 67.

194 Wedgwood MS E25-18657, 24 February 1776.

195 Meteyard, Vol. II, 92.

196 Ibid.

197 Bruce Tattersall, 'Henry Webber, Art at the Service of Industry', *Apollo*, July, 1985, 36.

198 Ibid.

199 The treaty was signed on 26 September 1786 and ratified early in 1787.

200 Wedgwood MS 2-30193, 3 November 1786.

201 Wedgwood MS W/M 1526.

202 Meteyard, Vol. II, 590.

203 Wedgwood MS W/M 1526. These descriptions are foreshortened versions of the same wording used in the explanation of the bas-reliefs sent from Angelo Dalmazzoni in Rome to Wedgwood.

204 Ibid. Most of the designs provided by Webber, Pacetti, Angelini and Fratoddi were executed in jasper, but some were also produced in basalt or were the inspiration for sprig relief designs used by other manufacturers in basalt.

205 Hackwood seems to have been on four and five year contracts with Wedgwood and Bentley. In November 1777 Hackwood renewed his contract as a modeller for four years. The following November Hackwood's salary was one guinea and a half plus a house rent free (Wedgwood MS 2-1353A).

206 Bindman (ed.), *John Flaxman*. Gaye Blake Roberts, ' A Selection of Works by Flaxman's Contemporaries working for Wedgwood', 67.

207 Wedgwood MS E25-18608, 8 July 1775.

208 Bruce Tattersall, *Stubbs & Wedgwood* (London: The Tate Gallery, 1974), 78.

209 Wedgwood MS L.H.P., 12 November 1780.

210 Wedgwood MS 45-8007, 4 January 1790.

211 Timothy Clifford, 'Some English Ceramic Vases and Their Sources, Part 1', *English Ceramic Circle Transactions*, Vol. 10

Part 3, 1978, 162.

212 Lecture by Gaye Blake Roberts, 29th Wedgwood International Seminar, Washington, D.C., 1984.

213 Wedgwood MS E25-18203, 28 June, 1768.

214 Roberts, W.I.S., 1984.

215 Wedgwood MS E25-18237, 9 April 1769.

216 Wedgwood MS E25-18703, 6 October 1776.

217 Wedgwood MS E25-18433, 2 January 1773.

218 Wedgwood MS 17173-93, 7 January 1774.

219 Wedgwood MS E25-18264, 1 October 1769.

220 Meteyard, Vol. II, 217.

221 Wedgwood MS 30-32848, 28 January 1770.

222 Wedgwood MS 30-32849.

223 Wedgwood MS W/M 1444, 22 March 1771.

224 Wedgwood was actually made a present of a set of Cipriani/Bartolozzi prints in 1789, a gift from 'Sir W.[Hamilton] or Mr. Greville'. Letter from Josiah Wedgwood to Dr. Darwin, 17 November 1789, Wedgwood MS 26-18000.

225 Wedgwood MS 12-32853, 12 June 1786.

226 Wedgwood MS 97-17877, 27 April 1798.

227 Wedgwood MS 143-29453.

228 Wedgwood MS W/M 1851, n.d. 1774; also to be found in E25-4220, n.d.

229 Wedgwood MS 96-17719, 7 November 1790.

230 Alison Kelly, 'Josiah Wedgwood's London Banking Account', *Proceedings of the Wedgwood Society* No. 9, 1975, 66.

231 Wedgwood MS 21-3681, 24 December 1788.

232 Wedgwood MS 107-20044, 14 February 1789.

233 Wedgwood MS 8-6344, 19 September 1789 to Josiah Wedgwood from John Savaers, Bois le Duc.

234 Ibid.

235 Wedgwood MS 135-27032, 25 October 1804.

236 Wedgwood MS 96-17739, 11 July 1790.

237 Wedgwood MS W/M 1600.

238 Wedgwood MS 7-5564, 7 May 1777.

239 Wedgwood MS 7-5606.

240 Wedgwood MS 118-22653, 9 April 1788.

241 Wedgwood MS 102-18868, 12 October 1790.

242 Wedgwood MSS 74-12704, 25 April 1798; 74-12709, 26 October 1800.

243 Wedgwood MS 117-22496, 4 March 1802.

244 Wedgwood MS 135-27056, 29 July 1791.

245 Wedgwood MS 105-19552, 10 February 1802.

246 Wedgwood MS 7-5715, 3 August 1790.

247 Wedgwood MS 75-12875, 12 December 1783.

248 I am grateful to Arlene Palmer Schwind for sending me this entry, Baltimore County Probate Records, Liber 12, 277.

249 *Dunlap & Claypoole's*, 18 July 1795.

250 Joseph Downs Library, Winterthur Museum 54.37.88.

251 Susan Gray Detweiler, *George Washington's China Ware* (New York: Harry N. Abrams, 1982), 220.

252 Ibid. Although the text suggests that the coffee pot was of Turner manufacture, the author said it was unmarked.

253 Edwin M. Betts and James A. Bear, Jun., eds., *The Family Letters of Thomas Jefferson* (Columbia, Missouri, 1966), 277.

254 Personal communication Lucia C. Stanton, Director of Research, Monticello, 13 October 1993.

255 Baker MSS 830, Baker Library, Harvard University.

256 County Probate #7029, Rockingham County Court House, Exeter, New Hampshire.

257 Ibid. Probate #10999.

258 Alice H. Guerrant, ' Ceramics of the H.M.S. DeBraak', paper read at the Society for Historical Archaeology meeting Baltimore, Maryland, January 1989. In addition cf. 'The Treasure of the DeBraak', *New Yorker Magazine*, August 15, 1988, 33-60.

259 Wedgwood MS 117-22595, 14 December 1813.

260 The inventory is at Hampton, his home in Baltimore County, and was taken 29 August 1829.

261 Appendix III, Staffordshire Prices Current, Collamore Papers, MS 77, c. 697, Vol.12.

262 Flintshire (Clwyd) Record Office D/HC/C/47.

263 The proposals for the steam engine were for a date around 1782; however, it would seem that according to correspondence between Thomas Byerley and Josiah Wedgwood II as late as 17 January 1802 when Byerley refers to '...when our steam engine is up...' that the deed was yet to be accomplished. (Meteyard, *A Group of Englishmen*, 1871, 193.)

264 Wedgwood MS 15-14393, [n.d.] October, 1789.

265 Wedgwood MS 96-17704, 13 September 1786.

266 Wedgwood MS 2-1244, 20 July 1787.

267 Wedgwood MS 27-19328, [n.d.] 1789.

268 Wedgwood MS 11-6442, 18 June 1788; 11-10111, 6 May 1790; 132-26388-89, 25 September 1793.

269 Wedgwood MSS 5-794 and 11-10029 [n.d.].

270 Wedgwood MS 17722-96.

271 Wedgwood MS 39-28404, 16 July 1790. This was one of the last meetings of the Committee to be recorded, the last meeting being 27 July 1790. While the 1795 list for Egyptian Ware is from a General Meeting of Manufacturers, it is not mentioned in the minute book in the Wedgwood papers.

272 Wedgwood MS W/M 1566, 4 May 1797.

273 Joseph Downs Manuscript Collection No. 72x323.2, Winterthur Museum, 28 November, 1795.

274 Wedgwood MSS 38-6649, 29 November 1798; 38-6656, 30 March 1800; 38-6663, 26 December 1800.

CHAPTER III

1 Wedgwood MS 26-4374, 18 January 1800.

2 Wedgwood MS 102-19016, 10 October 1804.

3 Wedgwood MS 117-22496, 4 March 1802.

4 Wedgwood MS 130-25920, 21 January 1808.

5 *See* Spode Shape Book (1820), No. 304 as illustrated in Whiter, 1970.

6 Wedgwood MS W/M 1604, 1811 order book.

7 Ibid.

8 Wedgwood MS 146-30291, 3 August 1808.

9 Oxford dealer Mrs. Lydia Butler, Wedgwood MS 78-13527, 19 January 1812.

10 Bernard de Montfaucon, *L'Antiquité Expliquée et Représentée en Figures*, 10 Vols. (Paris, 1719).

11 *Recueil d'antiquités egyptiennes, etrusques, greques et romaines*, 1752-1761.

12 Wedgwood MS E25-18336, [n.d.] January 1771.

13 Wedgwood MS 96-17722, 22 December 1790.

14 Wedgwood MS 78-13529, 25 March 1812.

15 Wedgwood MS 78-13542, [n.d.] July, 1813.

16 Wedgwood MS 78-13544, 27 October 1813.

17 Wedgwood MS 78-13535, 16 February 1813.

18 Wedgwood MS 17-15861, 24 January 1795.

19 Aileen Dawson, *Masterpieces of Wedgwood in the British Museum* (London: British Museum Publications, 1984), 44.

20 Ibid.

21 Wedgwood MS 29-21187, 16 August 1813.

22 Ibid., 14 February 1829.

23 Virginia Surtees (Ed.), *A Second Self The Letters of Harriet Granville 1810-1845* (Salisbury: Michael Russell, Ltd.,1990), 269-70.

24 When queried about the date 2 Feb. 1805 Gaye Blake Roberts replied with the following: 'The particular significance of the date is not easy to explain. No documentary evidence for the application of this mark has been found, and the firing records (Oven Books) for this date which might have cast valuable light on the problem have not survived. One manuscript does, however, appear to be relevant to this problem. It

is a report about Alexander Chisholm, sent to Josiah II on 11th February 1805 with a covering letter from Josiah Byerley (MSS 95-17608 and 11-2058). Chisholm's report deals at some length with suggestions made by Josiah II for the improvement of Wedgwood's pyrometers...Josiah's letter dated 2 February 1805 has not been preserved. Attention to this correspondence was noted by Mrs. Jean Gorley in 1942 in the publication *Old Wedgwood* (pages 98-101). The bodies used for the four known shapes (Dolphin tripod Pastille Burner, Egyptian Tripod Pastille Burner, Tripod Vase/Candlestick and small vase on drum pedestal) are Jasper, Black basalt, Queen's ware and Pearl ware...The Diversity and extreme scarcity of these pieces are I think convincing grounds for assuming that they were trials and the shapes and decoration chosen suggests they were trials of firing methods...'

25 Lynn Miller and John DesFontaines, 'A Flash in the Pan Wedgwood's Pyrophorus Vase', *Ceramics* No. 3, 1986.

26 Reilly, Vol. II, 455.

27 Wedgwood MS 3-2617, [n.d.] September, 1813.

28 Order from Robert Davis & Co., Channel Islands, Wedgwood MS 26-4485, 3 May 1812.

29 I am grateful to Geoffrey Godden for making this list available to me.

30 Thanks to Gaye Blake Roberts for providing the reference to the article by Lynn Miller in *Proceedings of the Wedgwood Society* Vol. 11, 1982.

31 Wedgwood MS 11-1970, 20 January 1813.

32 Wedgwood MS W/M 1600.

33 The latter is illustrated in Plate 32 in Maureen Batkin's *Wedgwood Ceramics 1846-1959* (London: Richard Dennis, 1982), 28.

CHAPTER IV

1 Bevis Hillier, *The Turners of Lane End* (London: Cory, Adams & Mackay, Ltd., 1965), 55.

2 Ibid., 56.

3 31 January 1785 as quoted in Hillier, 59.

4 of Stafford, Chester and Lancaster.

5 In the Rakow collection, New York.

6 *London Gazette*, 6 April, 1792.

7 Dorset Record Office D/43, Colfox Papers; B/26, Business Accounts of Andrew Abbott as published by Eileen and Rodney Hampson, *Northern Ceramic Society Newsletter* No. 68, 29-30.

8 *London Gazette*, 3 June 1809.

9 Hillier, 66.

10 Tony Thomas, 'James Mist', *Northern Ceramic Society Newsletter* No. 16, as reprinted in *Echoes and Reflections*, Northern Ceramic Society, 1990, 39.

11 Hillier, 66.

12 For a complete breakdown of the four families it is necessary to consult William Turner, *William Adams An Old English Potter* (London: Chapman and Hall, 1904).

13 Sun Fire Insurance Policy 522140, 21 September 1786, as published by Harold Blakey, *Northern Ceramic Society Newsletter* No. 42, June 1981.

14 Burslem Land Tax Records, 1786-92.

15 William Adams of Cobridge was a major land owner in Burslem. By 1781 (the first year for which tax records exist) he owned three properties in Burslem. In 1788 he appears also on the tax records as occupying property formerly occupied by Thomas and Benjamin Godwin but owned by the Executors of the late Isaac Warburton. He continued occupying the same property owned by the Warburton family through 1809. By 1812 he had purchased that property and had been accumulating other properties all along, a total of eleven in 1812. He was not occupying all the properties himself. Several were let to other potters including John Rogers, Enoch Wood, Cartlidge & Co, and R. & J. Clews.

16 Turner, 8. An interesting article on Marjorie Deaton on the 'Adams of Greengates' appeared in *Apollo*, Vol. 57, 1953.

17 M.W. Greenslade, *Victoria History of the County of Stafford* (VCH) (Tunstall) (Stafford: Staffordshire County Library, reprint 1981), 100.

18 Turner, 8.

19 Wedgwood MS W/M 1566, 4 May 1797.

20 Wedgwood MS W/M 527, [n.d., c. 1877].

21 Several articles on Alcock have appeared: Pat Halfpenny, *Northern Ceramic Society Journal* No. 2, 1975-6; Dr. and Mrs. Geoffrey Barnes, 'The Samuel Alcock Porcelains c.1822-1859,' *Staffordshire Porcelain*, 1983, 307-25; Geoffrey Godden, *Encyclopaedia of British Porcelain Manufacturers*, 1988, 80-85.

22 Rodney Hampson, 'Ovens Galore', *Northern Ceramic Society Newsletter* No. 34, June, 1979, 18.

23 Harold Blakey, 'Sun Fire Insurance Records 1782-1793', *Journal of the Northern Ceramic Society*, No. 10, 1993, 190.

24 Both an Astbury and a Twyford are stated by Shaw, *History of the Staffordshire Potteries* (Hanley, 1829) 119, as having purloined the secrets of the Elers brothers at Bradwell Wood, Astbury by feigning idiocy and Twyford by acting indifferent.

25 Wedgwood MS 22-17949.

26 Anne Astbury Twyford had three sons who were potters: John Twyford (1726-47), Joshua Twyford (b.1730), and Charles Twyford, who was still living in 1755.

27 Greenslade, 164.

28 *London Gazette* 13034, 14 October 1788.

29 Rodney Hampson, 'Longton potters 1700-1865', *Journal of Ceramic History* Vol. 14, Appendix, 73.

30 Geoffrey Godden, *Jewitt's Ceramic Art of Great Britain* (New York: Arco Publishing Company, Inc., 1972),90.

31 *English Ceramic Circle Transactions*, Vol.6 Part 2, 1966, 124-66; Vol. 6 Part 3, 1967, 32 Ibid., 133.

33 Mallet, Vol.6 Part 3, 1967, 221.

34 *London Gazette* 16521, 10 September 1811 (partnership dissolved 29 August 1811).

35 No. 13135, 26 September 1789.

36 Wedgwood MS 113-21602.

37 M.H. Grant, *The Makers of Black Basaltes* (London: Holland Press, 1967, originally published 1910), 290 says 'invariably' stamped, but some wares are unmarked such as the coffee pot in the Gunson collection which is identical to Figure 138 marked **EASTWOOD**.

38 Ibid., 290, 293.

39 Jewitt, 1985, 549.

40 Wedgwood MS 96-17667.

41 Godden, *Jewitt's...*, 56.

42 Rodney Hampson considers this firm to be decorators and retailers supplying Thomas Wyllie with whatever he needed.

43 Ann Eatwell and Alex Werner, 'A London Staffordshire Warehouse 1794-1825'. *Northern Ceramic Society Journal* 8, 1991, 115.

44 Hampson, Appendix, 13.

45 Godden, *Jewitt's...*, 78.

46 Wedgwood MS 93-16986, March-July 1793.

47 Wedgwood MS 93-16987, July 1800.

48 *London Gazette* 17731, 31 July 1821.

49 Hampson, Appendix, 13.

50 Heather Lawrence, *Yorkshire Pots and Potteries* (Newton Abbot: David & Charles, 1974).

51 Ibid., 114.

52 Ibid., 115.

53 Hampson, Appendix, 16.

54 Ibid., 17.

55 Ibid.

56 *London Gazette* 15750, 30 October 1804.

57 Godden, *Jewitt's...*, 35.

58 Rakow, *Ars Ceramica* No. 3, 1986; Gunson, *Ars Ceramica* No. 4, 1987.

59 Ibid., Rakow, 27.

60 Ibid.

61 Reginald Haggar intro., *The Whitehead Catalogue 1798* (Milton Keynes: D.B. Drakard).

62 Wedgwood MS 30-22572, 11 September 1777.

63 The pottery of Messrs Chatterley and Whiteheads, Hanley was insured by the Salop Fire Office, policy #1638, on 1 December 1792.

64 *London Gazette* 13596, 12 November 1793.

65 Salop Fire Insurance Policy 1196, Roger Edmundson, *Northern Ceramic Society Journal* 6, 1987, 85.

66 *London Gazette* 15089, 15 December 1798.

67 Wedgwood MS 15-14516.

68 Wedgwood MS 15-14527, 8 May 1810.

69 Grant, 281.

70 Hampson, Appendix, 25.

71 Arranged by W.R. Bourne (Hanley: J. Hitchens Printers, 1884). I appreciate the kindness of Mollie Hosking in drawing this to my attention.

72 Greenslade, 100.
73 Wedgwood MS W/M 1506, 4 May 1797.
74 Terence A. Lockett, 'Minton in 1810'. *Northern Ceramic Society Journal* 4, 1980-1981, 33-34.
75 Wedgwood MS 6-4952, 12 May 1787.
76 Llewellynn Jewitt, *The Ceramic Art of Great Britain*, (Poole, Dorset: New Orchards Editions, Ltd., 1985), 487.
77 Grant, Pl. XCVI, Fig. 1.
78 Timothy Clifford, 'William Bullock — a fine fellow', *Christie's International Magazine*, June 1991, 14.
79 Ibid.
80 Mallet, op. cit., *English Ceramic Circle Transactions* Vol. 6, Part 2, 1966, 156.
81 Clifford, 14.
82 *London Gazette* 15415.
83 Grant, p. 365.
84 W.J. Grant-Davidson, 'The Early Pottery of Swansea', *English Ceramic Circle Transactions* Vol. 7 Part 1, 1968, 73.
85 Ibid.
86 A.E. Jones and Sir Leslie Joseph, *Swansea Porcelain Shapes and Decoration* (Cowbridge: B.D. Brown, 1988), 256-57.
87 Grant, 357.
88 *Staffordshire Advertiser*, 15 March 1828.
89 Ibid., 4 October 1828.
90 #17910
91 *London Gazette* 18079, 9 November 1824.
92 Catherall Papers, Clwyd Record Office, July 1815.
93 Ibid., 25 April 1815.
94 Grant, 350. This assertion is not supported by evidence produced by Edmundson in his excellent article on Bradley & Co, op. cit., *Northern Ceramic Society Journal* 4.
95 W.J. Grant-Davidson, 'Excavations at Caughley', *English Ceramic Circle Transactions* Vol. 6, Part 3, 1967, 271.
96 Personal communication Roger Edmundson, 20 May 1991.
97 Shaw, 208.
98 Grant, 369.
99 Mallet, '...Baddeley...', 161.
100 Hampson, Appendix, 46.
101 Ann Eatwell and Alex Werner, 'A London Staffordshire Warehouse-1794-1825', *Northern Ceramic Society Journal* Vol. 8, 1991, 100.
102 Ibid.
103 Hillier, 64.
104 Hampson, Appendix, 47.
105 Jewitt, 1985, 377.
106 Wedgwood MS 20-22821.
107 Lecture Keele University Summer Ceramics Seminar 1987 by George Miller; lecture American Ceramic Circle, Philadelphia by Nancy Dickinson 1988.
108 Salop Fire Insurance Policy 11,371 14 July 1817 is issued in the name of Mrs. Mary Warburton, Hanley, and indicates the earthenware manufactory is merely occupied by Ralph and James Clews. Edmundson, *Northern Ceramic Society Journal* 6, 1987.
109 Burslem Land Tax Records, Stafford. By 1812 William Adams of Cobridge owned eleven properties in the area.
110 Ogden appears to have been a major exporter. He represented a number of Staffordshire potters as well as Yorkshire potters such as David Dunderdale.
111 Personal communication Nancy Dickinson.
112 Nancy Valpy, 'Extracts from 18th Century London Newspapers', *English Ceramic Circle Transactions* Vol. 12 Part 2, 1985, 171.
113 Salop Fire Insurance Policy 501, 27 December 1781, Edmundson, 1987.
114 Land tax records for Staffordshire do not exist before 1781.
115 David Holgate gives a very good family background in his book *New Hall* (London: Faber & Faber, 1987), 22. The documents do not support Mr. Holgate's statement, however, that 'At no time was he [William Clowes] described as a potter'.
116 #15312.
117 Jewitt, 1985, 112.
118 Holgate, 13.
119 Jewitt, 1985, 468.
120 Illustrated in Diana Edwards (Roussel) *The Castleford Pottery* (Wakefield: Wakefield Historical Publications, 1982), Colour Plate V.
121 *London Gazette* 15457, 27 February 1802.
122 Sun Fire Insurance Policy 391/606061, Blakey, 1993, 196.
123 Jewitt, 1985, 377.
124 Godden, *Encyclopedia of British Porcelain Manufacturers* (London: Barrie & Jenkins, 1988), 260.
125 Godden, *Jewitt's...*, 110.
126 Rodney Hampson, 'Ovens Galore', *Northern Ceramic Society Newsletter* No. 34, June, 1979, 19.
127 Ibid., 18.
128 John Ward, *The Borough of Stoke-Upon-Trent* (Hanley: Webberley Ltd., 1984, originally published 1843), 266.
129 Hampson Appendix, 56-7.
130 Wedgwood MS 39-28410.
131 Hampson, Appendix, 57.
132 Jewitt, 1985, 451-6.
133 Published by Barrie & Jenkins, London, 1989.
134 Sun Fire Insurance Policy #587057, Blakey, 1993, 193.
135 Wedgwood MS W/M 1566, 4 May 1797.
136 Hampson, 1979, 19.
137 T.A. Lockett and G. Godden, *Davenport China, Earthenware and Glass 1794-1887* (London,: Barrie & Jenkins, 1989), 97.
138 Wedgwood MS 120-23152, 10 December 1807.
139 Hillier, 64.
140 Lawrence, 95-7.
141 Reprinted by the Doncaster Metropolitan Borough Council, 1983.
142 Ibid., historical background [p.1].
143 Grant, 334.
144 Geoffrey Godden, *Minton Pottery and Porcelain of the First Period 1793-1850* (London: Barrie & Jenkins, 1968) 4.
145 Grant, 305.
146 Diana Edwards (Roussel), *The Castleford Pottery 1790-1821* (Wakefield: Wakefield Historical Publications, 1982).
147 Sun Policy 1565810, 30 January 1790. Sun Office Policy Registers MS11, 936, Vol. 367.
148 Frank Faulkner, *The Wood Family of Burslem* (Wakefield: EP Publishing Limited, 1972, originally published 1912), 65-6.
149 The shapes book is reproduced in the Castleford Pottery monograph.
150 Montague Guest (ed.), *Lady Charlotte Schreiber's Journals*, Vol.1 (London: John Lane, The Bodley Head, 1911), 114.
151 Geoffrey Godden, 1988, 319-21.
152 I am grateful to Pat Halfpenny for providing the biographical material on Gordon Elliott.
153 David Barker's research is published as 'A Group of Staffordshire Red Stonewares of the Eighteenth Century', *English Ceramic Circle Transactions* Vol. 14, Part 2, 1991.
154 Robin Price, 'Some Groups of English Redware of the Mid-Eighteenth Century', *English Ceramic Circle Transactions* 4, Part 5, 1959.
155 Recalling that Wedgwood wrote to Bentley on 13 September 1772 'Nobody makes black T. Pots but Palmers.' (Wedgwood MS E.25-18403). Of course, it is likely that Wedgwood was not aware of all the manufacturers of black teapots at the time, especially if the pottery was a small one such as Thomas Barker's pottery at the Foley.
156 *London Gazette* 17880, 21 December 1822.
157 As described in the *Staffordshire Advertiser*, 23 March 1844.
158 *Staffordshire Advertiser*, 23 March 1844.
159 *London Gazette* 15099, 15 January 1799 (partnership dissolved 11 November 1798).
160 Jewitt, 1985, 542.
161 *London Gazette* 15534, 20 November 1802.
162 Lawrence, 178-9.
163 Ibid.
164 Godden, Jewitt's...., xxi.
165 *Pottery Gazette*, 1 November 1884, 1183 & 1234.
166 Blakey, Sun Fire Insurance Policy 666202, 4 April 1797.
167 Eatwell and Werner, 100.
168 Blakey, Sun Fire Insurance Policy 748567, 9 May 1803.
169 Wedgwood MS 39-28404, 16 July 1790.
170 Salop Fire Office 1576, 20 June 1792, Edmundson, *Northern Ceramic Society Journal* 6, 1987.
171 Ibid., policy #1833, 10 October 1795.
172 Ibid., 30 October 1797.
173 Eatwell and Werner, 100.
174 *London Gazette* 15529, 2 November 1802.
175 Eatwell and Werner, 94.
176 *London Gazette* 17669, 16 January 1821.

177 Wedgwood MS 13-2541, 20 May 1783.

178 Wedgwood MS 39-28404, 16 July 1790.

179 Policy 794220, 23 April 1806, as published by Harold Blakey in the *Northern Ceramic Society Journal* 3, 1978-9.

180 Ibid.

181 *London Gazette* 16538, 5 November 1811.

182 Ibid.

183 Wedgwood MS 13-2546, 26 May 1815.

184 Eatwell and Werner, 104.

185 *London Gazette* 19124, 31 January 1834.

186 Hampson, 1979, 18.

187 Godden, 1988, 364.

188 Published in London by Jonathan Horne, 1991.

189 Ibid., 271.

190 Grant, 301. Hollens also made this point in his paper in the *English Ceramic Circle Transactions*, 1983, 223.

191 *London Gazette* 18576, 15 May 1829 (partnership 'expired' 11 November 1827).

192 Ibid.

193 Godden, 1988, 385.

194 Hampson, 1979, 19.

195 Wedgwood MS 11-1970, 20 January 1813.

196 Grant, 321.

197 Acc.no. 4.64/46.

198 Collamore Papers MS77 C697, Vol. 12, Baker Library, Harvard University.

199 *London Gazette* 18773, 4 February 1831.

200 Godden, *Jewitt's...*, 141.

201 Ibid.

202 Geoffrey Godden, *British Pottery, An Illustrated Guide* (New York: Clarkson N. Potter, Inc., 1975), #215.

203 Lawrence, 17-24.

204 For a thorough treatment of William Hartley see Ron Morley's 'Mr. Hartley of Hartley, Greens & Co.', *Northern Ceramic Society Journal* 8, 1991, 1-13.

205 Ibid., 10.

206 Lawrence, 25.

207 Wedgwood MS 8-6979, 18 February 1789.

208 Wedgwood MS 20-17590, 27 September 1817.

209 Alan Smith, *The Illustrated Guide to Liverpool Herculaneum Pottery 1796-1840* (New York: Praeger Publishers, 1970), 9.

210 Harrington was named for the Dowager Countess of Sefton with sites available along the river frontage leased from the Earl of Sefton. (Smith, 14).

211 Sun Insurance Policy 663705, Blakey, *Northern Ceramic Society Journal* 3, 1978-9, 111. [Please note the misprint in the location is Harrington, not Hannington].

212 Smith, 123.

213 'Herculaneum China and Earthenware', *English Ceramic Circle Transactions* Vol. 7, Part 1, 1968, Plate 19.

214 Personal communication Ann Eatwell.

215 Greenslade, *Victoria History of the County of Stafford* (Hanley), 165.

216 The wares, received on 30 January 1774, consisted of 'Coffey pts' and 'Bowles'

of an unspecified body, but probably creamware. Wedgwood MS 31-23055, [n.d.] August, 1774.

217 Wedgwood MS 119-22921, 18 March 1809.

218 The Catherall Papers, Clwyd Record Office, 25 April 1815.

219 *London Gazette* 18866, 1 November 1831.

220 Ward, 1984 (originally published 1843), 266.

221 W.D. Spanton, ed., *The Ancient Corporation of Hanley...1783-1900* (Hanley, 1901), 9.

222 Shaw, 138.

223 Wedgwood MS E.25-18263, 30 September 1769.

224 Wedgwood MS 30-22429 [n.d.], 1777.

225 Wedgwood MS W/M 1506, 4 May 1797.

226 Wedgwood MS 115-22062, 24 September 1798.

227 Holgate, 17.

228 Eatwell and Werner, 100.

229 Policy #1438, Edmundson, *Northern Ceramic Society Journal* 6.

230 Ibid., Policy 5621, 15 July 1808.

231 Holgate, 17.

232 *London Gazette* 13542, 29 June 1793.

233 Ibid.

234 *English Ceramic Circle Transactions* Vol. 11, Part 3, 169.

235 Salop Fire Office 1575, 20 June 1792, Edmundson, *Northern Ceramic Society Journal* 6, 1987.

236 Ibid. Policy 5621, 15 July 1808.

237 Ibid., policy 5622, 15 July 1808.

238 Eatwell and Werner, 104.

239 Wedgwood MS 30-22436, [n.d.] December 1814.

240 On 17 July 1819, Richard Hollins signed a note for £72 owed to Job Meigh, John Ridgway, Charles Meigh, R. W. Newland, James Keeling, William Ridgway and Richard Hicks (Wedgwood MS 30-22440).

241 Wedgwood MS 30-22443, 26 July 1822.

242 Wedgwood MS 30-22446, [n.d.] October 1826.

243 *London Gazette* 17837, 23 July 1822.

244 Hampson, 1979, 19.

245 Jewitt, 1985, 566.

246 *London Gazette* 18934, 8 May 1832. The partnership was officially dissolved on 25 April 1832.

247 Godden believes the 'factory X' porcelains were manufactured by the Keelings (Godden, 1988, 449).

248 *Bailey's* 1784, *Tunnicliff* 1787.

249 Wolf Mankowitz and Reginald Haggar, *The Concise Encyclopedia of British Pottery and Porcelain* (New York: Frederick A. Praeger Publishers, 1968), 120.

250 Wedgwood MS 31-23001, 14 August 1764.

251 Godden, 1988, 442.

252 Wedgwood MS 31-30566, 18 March 1766.

253 Wedgwood MS W/M 1566, 4 May 1797.

254 Wedgwood MS 11-1852, 1 May 1798.

255 Wedgwood MSS 11-1861.

256 *London Gazette* 16297, 12 September 1809.

257 *Staffordshire Advertiser*, 4 July 1812.

258 *Staffordshire Advertiser*, 19 March 1814.

259 *Staffordshire Advertiser*, 21 January 1815.

260 Godden, 1988, 444-5.

261 Grant, 302.

262 Salop Fire Office Policy 2391, 16 July 1802. Edmundson, *Northern Ceramic Society Journal* 6, 1987.

263 *London Gazette* 15959.

264 Sun Fire Insurance Policy 722281, 14 September 1801, Blakey, *Northern Ceramic Society Journal* 3, 1978-9.

265 *London Gazette* 16803, 9 November 1813. According to *Parson's and Bradshaw's Directory*, by 1818 James Keeling was a packer and in partnership with Elijah Mayer as a dealer, but not a potter.

266 Godden, 1988, 454.

267 Eatwell and Werner, 102.

268 Personal communication Ann Eatwell.

269 Jewitt, 1985, 502.

270 Lawrence, 112-3.

271 Godden, *Jewitt's...*, 186.

272 Sun Fire Insurance Policy 636626, 10 January 1795, Blakey, 1978-9.

273 Salop Fire Office Policy 1637, Edmundson, *Northern Ceramic Society Journal* 6, 1987.

274 *London Gazette* 13862, 26 June 1796.

275 Sun Fire Insurance Policy 664594, 22 February 1797, Blakey, *Northern Ceramic Society Journal* 3, 1978,9.

276 Harold Blakey, 'Thomas Lakin: Staffordshire Potter 1769-1821', *Northern Ceramic Society Journal* 5, 1984, 85.

277 Ibid., 108.

278 *London Gazette* 16708, 2 March 1813.

279 *Staffordshire Advertiser*, 19 July 1814.

280 Jewitt, 1985, 467.

281 This information as well as all the other Burslem tax information was gathered at the County Record Office, Stafford.

282 Only owner, occupier and rate are listed in Land Tax Records. Since tax rates did not vary from year to year, often from decade to decade, the rate is often the major identifying feature of the tract of land occupied.

283 *London Gazette* 15314, 25 November 1800.

284 Hampson, Appendix, 106.

285 Ibid., 107.

286 Eatwell and Werner, 100.

287 Hampson, Appendix, 110.

288 Eatwell and Werner, 104.

289 Hampson, Appendix, 110.

290 Jewitt, 1985, 243.

291 Heather Lawrence, *Echoes and Reflections* (Stoke-on-Trent: Northern Ceramic Society, 1990), 37. *See also* Pamela Imber, *Lowesley Pottery*, Leicester Museums Publication, No. 12, 1977.

292 One John Mare filed a long, involved complaint in 1733 about the settlement of a

will made in 1721 (Wedgwood MS 22-17949-i).

293 Jewitt, 1985, 479.

294 *London Gazette* 12706, 6 December 1785.

295 Sun Fire Insurance Policy 515704, Blakey, *Northern Ceramic Society Newsletter* #42, June, 1981.

296 Wedgwood MS 39-28404, 16 July 1790.

297 Salop Fire Office Policy 1577, 20 June 1792, Edmundson, *Northern Ceramic Society Journal* 6, 1987.

298 Ibid. Policy 1576.

299 Ibid. Policy 1463, 24 January 1791.

300 Arnold Mountford, 'John Mare of Hanley', *Echoes and Reflections*, 1990, 30.

301 Ibid.

302 Ibid., 31.

303 Wedgwood MS W/M 1506, 4 May 1797.

304 Wedgwood MSS 11-1844, 1 September 1799; 11-1836, [n.d.] 1801.

305 Ibid.

306 Wedgwood MSS 11-1841, 2 July 1808; 11-1842, 23 April 1810; 11-1844, 1809-10.

307 Wedgwood MS 11-1844, 26 June 1812.

308 Hillier, 64.

309 Eatwell and Werner, 104.

310 #16887, 29 January 1814 appearing in print on 19 April 1814.

311 *London Gazette* 16864, 2 February 1814, published on 5 March 1814.

312 This must have been the son of John Mare as John Mare, Esq. died at Eastwood on 23 March 1819 according to the *Staffordshire Advertiser*, March 1819. He was described as an earthenware manufacturer from Hanley. No age was given.

313 Mountford, 31.

314 Ibid.

315 *Staffordshire Advertiser*, 25 February 1832: 'died Tuesday [21st], John Mare Market Street, Hanley, formerly earthenware mfr., aged 52.'

316 *Staffordshire Advertiser*, 8 March 1828.

317 *Staffordshire Advertiser*, 3 October 1829.

318 Hampson, 1979, 18.

319 Ward, 1984 (originally published 1843), 266.

320 Shaw, 209.

321 Salop Fire Insurance Policy 737, 25 March 1783, Edmundson, 1987.

322 Ibid.

323 Wedgwood MS 8-6785, 2 November 1790.

324 Wedgwood MS W/M 1566, 4 May 1797.

325 Wedgwood MSS 75-12825; 36-27829; 75-12830.

326 Wedgwood MS 36-27831, [n.d.] 1803.

327 Ibid.

328 Ibid.

329 *London Gazette* 16803, 9 November 1813.

330 Hawkins received five per cent commission on these transactions. Wedgwood MS 120-231152, 10 December 1807.

331 Godden, 1988, 520.

332 Greenslade, *Victoria History of the County of Stafford* (Hanley), 165.

333 Ibid.

334 Wedgwood MS 36-27832, 23 June 1814.

335 Wedgwood MS 75-12825, [n.d.] 1815.

336 Wedgwood MS 36-27842.B.

337 *Staffordshire Advertiser*, 1 December 1860.

338 *Staffordshire Advertiser*, 9 February 1861.

339 Personal communication Rodney Hampson.

340 Godden, *Jewitt's...*, 1971, 55.

341 Jewitt, 1985, 545.

342 Shaw, 208-9.

343 Jewitt, 1985, 503.

344 Hampson, Appendix, 126.

345 Ibid., 110.

346 Eatwell and Werner, 100.

347 Lockett, *Northern Ceramic Society Journal* 4, 1980, 33-4

348 Paul Atterbury and Maureen Batkin, *The Dictionary of Minton* (Woodbridge: Antique Collectors' Club, 1990), 36.

349 Hampson, 1979, 19.

350 Ibid.

351 *Staffordshire Advertiser*, 14 November 1801: 'Partnership dissolved, John Moseley and William Dale, Cobridge, potters 9 November 1801'.

352 Sun Fire Insurance Policy 724889, Blakey, 1978-9.

353 Ibid., Policy 822351.

354 William Moseley's name first appears on invoices of wares being sent down to London in 1809; John Moseley had been sending wares to Thomas Wyllie since 1806.

355 *London Gazette* 16408, 25 September 1810

356 Eatwell and Werner, 101-103.

357 Ibid., 104.

358 In discussing occupying potters of the Churchyard Works of Wedgwood, Jewitt mentions the property was conveyed out of the Wedgwood family when it was sold to Thomas Green in 1795. It remained in Green's hands until his bankruptcy in 1811 'when it appears to have been purchased by a manufacturer named Joynson, from whom it passed some years later on, to Mr. Moseley' (Jewitt, 1985, 439). The 'newly erected' works of 1820 must have meant additions on the site.

359 *Staffordshire Advertiser*, 4 September 1824.

360 *Staffordshire Advertiser*, 2 April 1825.

361 Barker, *English Ceramic Circle Transactions* Vol.14 Part 2, 1991.

362 Wedgwood MS 30-22808. See Diana Edwards, *Neale Pottery and Porcelain* (London: Barrie & Jenkins, 1987), 45.

363 *London Gazette* 13418, 19 May 1792.

364 Courtesy Henry Francis du Pont Winterthur Museum, Joseph Downs MS No. 72x323.2.

365 Geoffrey Godden, *Minton Pottery and Porcelain of the First Period 1793-1850* (London: Barrie & Jenkins, 1968), 4; Sun Fire Insurance Policy 353/543709, April 1788 and 361/557035, 2 May 1789, Blakey, 1993.

366 Wedgwood MS 117-22409.

367 Hampson, 1979, 19.

368 Diana Edwards, Barrie & Jenkins, London, 1987.

369 David Barker & Pat Halfpenny, *Unearthing Staffordshire* (Stoke-on-Trent: City Museum and Art Gallery, 1990), 17-8.

370 Wedgwood MS 25-18378, 14 June 1772.

371 Wedgwood MS 25-18485.

372 Patent number 939.

373 Meteyard, Vol. II, 1866, 78-80; Edwards, 1987, 36.

374 Wedgwood MS E25-18403, 13 September 1772. Clearly Wedgwood meant 'Nobody else' makes black teapots as he was producing them at least as early as August 1771 (Wedgwood MS W/M 1441).

375 Wedgwood MS E25-18814.

376 Wedgwood MS 6-4261, 13 July 1774.

377 Grant, 1967, 245-6.

378 Sun Fire Insurance Policy 264/562074, 16 October 1789, Blakey, 1993, 187.

379 Harold Plant, 'Diary of Benjamin Plant, 18th Century Potter of Lane End', *Pottery Gazette and Glass Trade Review*, July 1955, 1070-71. (I am grateful to Rodney Hampson for providing this material.)

380 Hampson, 203; Appendix, 133.

381 Jewitt, 1985, 232.

382 Illustrated in W.J. Pountney, *Old Bristol Potteries* (Bristol, 1920, reprinted 1972), Pls. XXII, XXIII.

383 *Pratt Ware* (Woodbridge: Antique Collectors' Club, 1984), 14-15.

384 *London Gazette* 16334, 16 January 1810.

385 Hampson, Appendix, 138.

386 Godden's, *Jewitt...*, 70.

387 Hampson, 1979, 19.

388 John and Richard Riley, (Stoke-on-Trent: City Museum and Art Gallery, 1988), 9.

389 Sun Fire Insurance Policy 716265, Blakey, 1978-9.

390 Pomfret, *Riley Recipe Book*, 87.

391 Ibid.

392 Ibid., 88

393 Ibid., 204-206

394 Jewitt, 1985, 210-11.

395 Ibid., 231.

396 Pl. XCI, Figs 2,3.

397 Reginald Haggar, 'Joesph Ring's Suppliers,' *Northern Ceramic Society Newsletter* No. 35, September 1979.

398 Shaw, 76.

399 Hampson, Appendix, 139.

400 Godden, *Jewitt's...*, 186.

401 *Staffordshire Advertiser*, 2 May 1812.

402 *Staffordshire Advertiser*, 13 June 1812.

403 *Staffordshire Advertiser*, 18 July 1812.

404 *Staffordshire Advertiser*, 11 June 1814.

405 Ron Morley, 'The Leeds Pottery "Revival"', *Northern Ceramic Society Newsletter* 82, June 1991, 12.

406 Ron Morley, 'Leeds Pottery Plaques

and Medallions,' *Northern Ceramic Society Newsletter* 79, September 1990, 18.

407 Lawrence, 38.

408 *London Gazette* 16204, 26 November 1808.

409 Hampson, Appendix, 147.

410 *London Gazette* 16494, 8 June 1811.

411 Hampson, Appendix, 147.

412 Eatwell and Werner, 115.

413 Ibid., 123.

414 Personal communication Rodney Hampson.

415 Wedgwood MS 49-29813, 2 March 1815.

416 *Staffordshire Advertiser*, 5 February 1820.

417 Sun Fire Insurance Policy 625880, Blakey, *Northern Ceramic Society Journal* 3, 1978.

418 Wedgwood MS 31-23292, 23 May 1814.

419 *Staffordshire Advertiser*, 16 August 1823 quotes 'Tuesday's Gazette': 'Bankrupt, John Shorthose & Co., Hanley, e/ware mfr.'

420 *Staffordshire Advertiser*, 14 June 1828.

421 Godden, *Jewitt's...*, 80.

422 Lawrence, 114.

423 Diana Edwards, *The Castleford Pottery 1790-1821*, 1982.

424 First published in 1982 in *The Castleford Pottery 1790-1821*, 43-4; the illustration of the **S & Co** sucrier is also in that book, Plate 90.

425 A. Hayden, *Spode and His Successors* (London: Cassell and Company. Ltd., 1925); L. Whiter, *Spode* (London: Barrie & Jenkins, 1970).

426 Delivered Christmas 1822 (invoice 24 Jan. 1823): Mavis Cleggett, 'China for the new Castle', *Northern Ceramic Society Newsletter* No. 82, June 1991, 35-6.

427 Ibid., 5 August and 25 August, 1823, respectively.

428 Personal communication 19 March 1990.

429 Policy #11936, Vol. 272, February 1779.

430 Grant, 265.

431 Whiter, 136-7.

432 Godden, *Jewitt's...*, 75.

433 Alwyn and Angela Cox, 'Recent Excavations at Swinton Pottery', *English Ceramic Circle Transactions* Vol. 11, Part 1, 1981, 66.

434 *Drawing Book* shape from Leeds number 4 is Swinton 5, Leeds 5=Swinton 9, Leeds 6=Swinton (obliterated in book); Leeds 7=Swinton 8; Leeds 8=Swinton 14; Leeds 9=(not distinguishable);Leeds 10=Swinton 13; Leeds 11=Swinton 10; Leeds 12= (not distinguishable);Leeds 13=Swinton 7; Leeds 14=Swinton 11.

435 Leeds 16=Swinton 1; Leeds 17=Swinton 3.

436 Leeds 15=Swinton 2

437 Cox and Cox, 1981, 66.

438 Alwyn Cox & Angela Cox, *Rockingham Pottery & Porcelain* (London: Faber & Faber, 1983), 247.

439 Illustrated in Grant Pl. LXXXIX, 4, 333.

440 Cox and Cox, 1983, 106.

441 Ibid.

442 Ibid. These sherds were also discussed and illustrated in Eaglestone & Lockett, *The Rockingham Pottery*, 1973 edn.

443 Hampson, Appendix, 154-5.

444 Wedgwood MS 11-2007, 2 June 1784-20 August 1785.

445 Wedgwood MS 11-2019, 14 June 1788.

446 Wedgwood MS 39-28404, 16 July 1790.

447 Wedgwood MS 10-9049, 12 February 179; * indicates fluted tewares.

448 Eatwell and Werner, 101.

449 Information supplied by Rodney Hampson.

450 Salop Fire Office Policy 12,554, 20 August 1824; Edmundson, 1987.

451 Eatwell and Werner, 100.

452 Ibid., 104.

453 *London Gazette* 15529, 2 November 1802.

454 *London Gazette* 15707, 2 June 1804.

455 *London Gazette* 16201, 15 November 1808.

456 *London Gazette* 16443, 12 January 1811.

457 *London Gazette* 17234, 25 March 1817 (partnership dissolved formally on 15 March).

458 *London Gazette* 17243, 22 April 1817.

459 Eatwell and Werner, 102.

460 Hampson, Appendix, 156.

461 Sun Fire Insurance Policy 286041, Elizabeth Adams, *English Ceramic Circle Transactions* Vol. 10, Part 1, 1976, 29.

462 Salop Fire Office Policy 1558; ibid., 17.

463 Wedgwood MS 38-6649, 29 November 1798. 'Death of the Stag and Chase of the Hounds' were probably only produced in feldspathic stoneware.

464 *London Gazette* 15675, 14 February 1804.

465 *London Gazette* 15755, 17 November 1804 (filed 10 November 1804).

466 Hampson, Appendix, 159.

467 *London Gazette* 15906.

468 Hampson, Appendix, 157-8.

469 Norman Stretton, 'The Turners of Lane End,' *Apollo*, October, 1958, 118.

470 Hillier, 74.

471 A pair of intaglios of Hippocampi impressed **'TURNER 4'** are in the Rakow collection. Sir Isaac Falcke also had a Turner intaglio in his collection which he claimed was 'equal to Wedgwood's best period'. (Wedgwood MS W/M 527.)

472 Hollens, *English Ceramic Circle Transactions* Vol. 11, Part 3, 1983, 226.

473 Bernard Rackham, 'Wedgwood Reconsidered', *English Ceramic Circle Transactions* Vol.3 Part 1, 1951, 27.

474 Wedgwood Ms 11-9635,[n.d.] c. 1770.

475 Wedgwood MSS 32-31013; 39-28417.

476 *London Gazette* 13725, 22 November 1794 (partnership dissolved 11 November 1794).

477 Sun Fire Insurance Policy 640135 1 April 1795, Blakey, 1978-9.

478 Jewitt, 1985, 488.

479 Grant, 369.

480 Wedgwood Ms 22-17949.

481 Jewitt, 1985, 507.

482 Wedgwood Ms 96-17671.

483 Wedgwood Ms 96-17661, 4 May 1768.

484 Wedgwood Ms 96-17664, 29 June 1768.

485 Wedgwood Ms LHP, 29 November 1768.

486 Several accounts deal with John Voyez. The most complete is R. J. Charleston's 'Jean Voyez,' *English Ceramic Circle Transactions* Vol. 5, Part 1, 1960. This was taken from the Crown Book of the Oxford Circuit and is published on page 12. Other accounts which deal extensively with Voyez are included in Diana Edwards, *Neale Pottery and Porcelain*, 25-35. 'John Voyez-some Masterpieces of Craftsmanship' by A.H. Grundy appeared in *Apollo*, October, 1958, 110-15.

487 Charleston, 31.

488 Wedgwood to Bentley 10 December 1773, Wedgwood Ms E25-18507.

489 Wedgwood Ms E25-18571, 4 December 1774.

490 Nancy Valpy, 'Extracts from 18th Century London Newspapers', *English Ceramic Circle Transactions* Vol. 12, Part 2, 1985, 185.

491 Wedgwood Ms LHP, 25 June 1780.

492 Algernon Graves, *The Society of Artists of Great Britain 1760-1791 The Free Society of Artists 1761-1783* (Bath: Kingsmead Reprints, 1969; first published 1907), 269.

493 Charleston, 22.

494 Edwards, 1987, Pl. 25.

495 Wedgwood Ms E25-18263, 30 September 1769. '...Mr. R. Danl's men were engaged all at once by Mr. Warburton who has taken the works'.

496 Wedgwood Ms 39-28404, 16 July 1790.

497 David Holgate, *New Hall* , (London: Faber & Faber, 1987), 19.

498 Wedgwood Ms 10-8080.

499 *London Gazette* 15311, 15 November 1800.

500 *London Gazette* 17119, 16 March 1816 (partnership dissolved 25 December 1815).

501 Salop Fire Insurance Policy 11,313, 26 February 1817, Edmundson, 1987.

502 Salop Fire Insurance Policy 2262, Edmundson, 1987.

503 *London Gazette* 15468, 3 April 1802 (dissolution on 29 March 1802).

504 Salop Fire Insurance Policy 5070, 25 March 1806, Edmundson, 1987.

505 Burslem Land Tax Records, County Record Office, Stafford.

506 Ibid. One property was let to a Mrs. Taylor and two, one referred to as 'Churchyard', were occupied by himself.

507 Wedgwood Ms 39-28404, 16 July 1790.

508 23 November 1791, Nancy Valpy, *English Ceramic Circle Transactions* Vol. 14, Part I, 1990.

509 Salop Fire Insurance Policy 1642, 1

January 1793, Edmundson, 1987.
510 Ibid. Policy 1745, 19 June 1794,
511 Nancy Valpy (with comments by Dr. W.A.M. Holdaway and Mr. J.K. des Fontaines), 'Extracts from the Daily Advertiser 1792-1795', *English Ceramic Circle Transactions* Vol. 14, Part 2, 1991, 230.
512 The Swan Bank Works and twelve adjoining houses must have been sold as they were off the list of insured properties by 8 August 1795 (Edmundson, 1987).
513 Wedgwood Ms W/M 1820.
514 Lawrence, 148-9.
515 Blakey, 1978-9.
516 Sun Fire Insurance Policy 716936, 1 April 1801.
517 Lawrence, 149.
518 Florence Sibson, *The History of the West Cumberland Potteries*, (published privately, 1991), 73.
519 Wedgwood Ms 30-22572, 11 September 1777.
520 Jewitt, 1985, 489.
521 Wedgwood MS 30-22600.
522 Ibid., MS 30-22596, 17 May 1787.
523 Salop Fire Insurance Policy 1638, 1 December 1792, Edmundson, 1987.
524 *London Gazette* 13596, 12 November 1793.
525 Wedgwood Ms W/M 1566, 4 May 1797.
526 Originally printed by Thomas Pearson, Birmingham, 1798; republished by D.B. Drakard [n.d.].
527 Introduction by Reginald Haggar, *James and Charles Whitehead Manufacturers Hanley Staffordshire* (Milton Keynes: D.B. Drakard, n.d.).
528 *Staffordshire Advertiser* 14 April 1810.
529 Ibid.
530 Wedgwood Ms 10-8209, 2 August 1810.
531 Wedgwood Ms 28-19940.
532 *Staffordshire Advertiser* 10 January 1818.
533 *Staffordshire Advertiser*, 24 November 1821.
534 *Staffordshire Advertiser*, 10 December 1825.
535 The Whitehead pottery is not marked unless one subscribes to the theory that the W(***) marked wares were made by the Whiteheads.
536 *London Gazette* 13418, 19 May 1792.
537 Ibid., 15335, 7 February 1801.
538 Wedgwood Ms 38-6649, 29 November 1798.
539 Wedgwood Ms 120-23152, 10 December 1807.
540 *London Gazette* 16484, 11 May 1811.
541 Sun Fire Insurance Policy 829176, 21 March 1809, Blakey, 1978/9.
542 *London Gazette* 16397, 14 August 1810.
543 Sun Fire Insurance Policy 857361, 10 April 1811, Blakey, 1978/9.
544 Trevor Markin, 'Thomas Wolfe: A Man of Property'. *Northern Ceramic Society Newsletter* No. 58, June, 1985, 11.
545 Godden, 1988, 783.

546 Burslem Land Tax Records, County Record Office, Stafford.
547 Sun Fire Insurance Policy 705680, Blakey, 1978/9.
548 Eatwell and Werner, 100-3.
549 Wedgwood MS 8-1461, 27 September 1807.
550 *London Gazette* 17384, 1 September 1818.
551 Wedgwood MS 28-20557, 21 December 1821.
552 Frank Falkner, *The Wood Family of Burslem* (Wakefield: EP Publishing Limited, 1972), Pl. XXXIX. Originally published 1912.
553 Burslem Land Tax Records, County Record Office, Stafford.
554 *London Gazette* 18309, 21 August 1827.
555 Hampson, 1979, 18.
556 Grant, 310.
557 No busts have actually been found dating from 1781; the earliest dated busts are from 1784, the year Enoch Wood began the pottery at Fountain Place, (Falkner, 46).
558 Illustrated in Falkner, No. 120.
559 Ibid., Nos. 109, 110.
560 Ibid., Nos. 123 and 150 respectively.
561 Attribution of David Hollens.
562 Pat Halfpenny, 'The Wood Family,' *Ceramics*, May/June, 1986, 122-126.
563 Sun Fire Insurance Policy 362/558222, 22 June 1789, Blakey, 1993, 186.
564 Wedgwood MS 12-2268, 19 July 1788.
565 Wedgwood MS 23-17959, 11 October 1787.
566 Burslem Land Tax Records, County Record Office, Stafford.
567 *Staffordshire Advertiser*, 18 July 1801.
568 *Staffordshire Advertiser*, 5 September 1801.
569 *Staffordshire Advertiser*, 6 November 1802.
570 Hampson, Appendix, 270.
571 There is a set of five flower vases in white feldspathic stoneware with blue enamel trim in the Fitzwilliam Museum, Cambridge (Glaisher Collection, 1266-1266d), impressed WOOLLEY (Richard Woolley, c.1809-10).
572 Blakey, 1993, 168.
573 Sun Fire Insurance Policy 629506, 11 July 1794, Blakey, 1978/9.
574 Wedgwood MS W/M1566, 4 May 1797.
575 *London Gazette* 16131, 26 March 1808 (dissolution on 25 March 1808).
576 Horace Collamore Letterbook/Order Book, 18 June 1814. MSS Collections, Old Sturbridge Village as quoted by Jane C. Nylander 'English Ceramics on Essex County Tables,' *Ceramics and Glass in the Essex Institute*, (Salem, Massachusetts, The Essex Institute, 1985), 26.
577 Haggar, Introduction to the Whitehead Catalogue (n.d.; n.p.).
578 Mankowitz & Haggar, 248.
579 Ibid.
580 Godden, *Encyclopedia...*, 1965, 704.

CHAPTER V

1 *Christina Alberta's Father* was published in London by Hogarth Press, 1985, 53; originally published by Jonathan Cape, 1925.
2 An earthenware example was illustrated in a photograph in Nancy Gunson's album of ceramic snapshots marked **Locketts & Co.**
3 'Marks — Good, Bad and Indifferent'. *Twenty-Sixth Wedgwood International Seminar*, 1981, 147-8.
4 Six of these intaglios are in the Beeson collection, Birmingham Museum of Art, Alabama.

CHAPTER VI

1 Plantagenet Palliser to Alice Vavasor on the occasion of her marriage to John Grey (London: Oxford University Press, Book II, 1972), 501.
62 W.B. Honey, *European Ceramic Art* (London: Faber & Faber, 1952), 62.
3 Jana Kybalová, *European Creamware* (London: Hamlyn, 1989), 193-4.
4 Honey, 79; George Savage, 'The Influence of Wedgwood on Continental Pottery and Porcelain'. *The Third Wedgwood International Seminar*, 1958, 100.
5 *London Gazette* 15415, 6 October 1801.
6 Bernard Guineau, *La Manufacture De Faiences Fines De La Charité-Sur-Loire*, Association des Amis de la Charité-sur-Loire, 1979, 27-29.
7 Emil Hannover, *Pottery and Porcelain A Handbook for Collectors* Vol. 1 (New York: Charles Scribner's Sons, 1925), 342.
8 Guineau, 28.
9 Kybalová, 63-4.
10 Personal communication Maddy Aries, the Musée de l'Ile de France, Sceaux.
11 Ibid.
12 Hannover, 338.
13 Ibid., 338-9.
14 Honey, 261-264.
15 Savage, 99.
16 Honey, 318.
17 Ibid., 348.
18 Ibid.
19 Claude Nougarède, 'Faïences Fines De Sèvres (1798-1815)', *Cahiers De La Céramique Du Verre Et Des Arts Du Feu* (Sèvres, 1969), 35-37.
20 William Chaffers, *Marks and Monograms on European and Oriental Pottery and Porcelain*, 14 Revised Edition (Los Angeles: Borden Publishing Company, 1946), 191.
21 Kybalová says that Englishmen had been involved in the factory site as early as 1749 when John Hill obtained permission to build a round English kiln [presumably a bottle kiln] to produce white ceramics [salt-glazed stoneware] on a contract for ten years, 59.
22 Ibid., 59-63.
23 Honey, 510.
24 Ibid., 630.
25 Hannover, 497.
26 Kybalová, 157-9; illustrations of basalt in figures 178-9.

CHAPTER VII

1 *Staffordshire Advertiser*, 11 August 1835; Falkner, 1912, 72.

2 Ibid., 1 August 1838; Falkner, Ibid.

3 *Staffordshire Advertiser*, 29 May 1847.

4 Arthur Lane, 'The English Ceramic Collections in the Victoria and Albert Museum', *English Ceramic Circle Transactions* Vol. 4, Part 4, 1959, 19-27.

5 Wedgwood MS W/M 600, 8 July 1887.

6 Ibid.

7 Ibid. Eliza Meteyard's account of Mayer's purchase of the Wedgwood papers in Birmingham varies somewhat from that of Simms, and since she was in a position to have heard the story directly from Mayer, her's is probably the more reliable version: E. Meteyard, *A Group of Englishmen 1795-1815* (London, 1871), x-xiii.

8 Lionel Burman, 'Joseph Mayer's Wedgwood Collection', *Joseph Mayer of Liverpool* (London and Liverpool: The Society of Antiquaries in Association with the National Museums and Galleries on Merseyside, 1988), 198.

9 Ibid., 198, 201.

10 Wareham's shop was at 14 & 15 Castle Street, Leicester Square, and the list was dated April, 1879. The brochure is among Henry Walters papers in the Walters Art Gallery, Baltimore, Maryland.

11 Burman, 201. The Liverpool Museum has first and second editions of the catalogue with annotations by Gatty.

12 Ibid., 200.

13 *The Life of Josiah Wedgwood* Vol. I, 1865, x-xi.

14 Wedgwood MS W/M 459, 20 June 1867.

15 Ibid., W/M 457, 23 October 1867.

16 Ibid.

17 Wedgwood MS W/M 527.

18 Ibid., 12 July 1874.

19 Wedgwood MS W/M 1243.

20 Wedgwood MS W/M 527, 20 May 1877.

21 Ibid, 20 January 1877.

22 Hugh Tait, 'The Wedgwood Collection in the British Museum'. *Proceedings of the Wedgwood Society* Vol. 5, 1963, 36.

23 Wedgwood MS W/M 527 [n.d.].

24 David M. Wilson, *The Forgotten Collector* (London: Thames and Hudson, 1984),16. Essentially a book on the collections of A.W. Franks in the British Museum, it is singular that Mr. Wilson never mentions the Franks bequest of 700 objects of English ceramics to that institution.

25 Tait, 32.

26 Wilson, 19.

27 Colonel M. H. Grant, *The Old English Landscape Painters*. (Leigh-on-Sea: F. Lewis, Publishers, Ltd., 8 vols. first published 1926, vol. 8 reprinted 1971). *A Dictionary of British Landscape Painters* (Leigh-on-Sea: F. Lewis, first printed 1952, second reprint 1976).

28 Sarah C. Nichols, *Black Basaltes Ware—The Speyer Collection*, exhibition catalogue, 1983.

29 *See* Hugo Morley-Fletcher's article 'Wedgwood Auctions in the Nineteenth Century at Christie, Mason and Woods', *The Tenth Wedgwood International Seminar*, 1965, 197-205.

30 Eliza Meteyard, *Hand Book of Wedgwood Ware*, 1875, 251.

APPENDIX I

1 Letters from Josiah Wedgwood to Thomas Bentley from April 21st and May 15th of 1771. *The Selected Letters of Josiah Wedgwood* edited by Ann Finer and George Savage, London: Cory, Adams & Mackay Ltd. 1965. 106 and 108.

2 'Josiah Wedgwood, of Etruria, and London. Price Current of Earthen-ware, August 1st, 1816.' Wedgwood Archives MS 47-29285, 4.

3 George L. Miller, 'A Revised Set of CC Index Values for Classification and Economic Scaling of English Ceramics from 1787 to 1880.' *Historical Archaeology*, 1991, Vol. 25, no.1, 1-25.

APPENDIX II

1 W.R. Bourne, *A Collection of Ceramic Receipts for Many Years Used By The Late John Bourne of Burslem, For Fifty Years A Successful Potter*. Hanley: J. Hitchings, 1884, 17.

2 Wedgwood MS 39-28410 as quoted in R.S. Hampson, *The Development of the Pottery Industry in Longton*, 1986, 57.

3 'By The Late John Taylor.' *The Complete Practical Potter or a Comprehensive Collection of Receipts for the Manufacture of China, Earthenware, Ironstone, &c.*...Shelton, 1847, 165.

4 From Mr. T. Simpson of Hanley passed to Henry Steel, The Catherall Papers, Clwyd Recod Office, 25 April 1815.

5 Wedgwood MS 10-8987.

6 Harold Plant. 'Diary of Benjamin Plant, 18th Century Potter of Lane End', *Pottery Gazette and Glass Trade Review*, July 1955, 1070-71.

7 Recipe Book of Benjamin Stubbs, owned by Rodney Hampton.

8 Cox & Cox, 1983, 247.

9 There are twenty-seven recipes for black in John Taylor's recipe book oly ten of which are included here. *The Complete Practical Potter, a Comprehensive Collection of Receipts...By the Late John Taylor* was published for the benefit of the Author's widow by William White, Hope Street, Shelton, 1847. The recipes for black are found on pp. 157-8, 161-2, 165-6, 169-70. Copies of the book can be found at the Manchester City Art Gallery and the Horace Barks Reference Library, Hanley (738.17.05).

10 The Rev. Edward Smedley, the Rev. Hugh James Rose, the Rev. Henry John Rose, eds., *Encyclopedia Metropolitana*, Vol. 6, 1845, 449. (The encyclopedia was issued in fifty-nine parts between 1817 and 1845; the precise date of this volume is unknown.)

11 As reproduced by Rodney Hampson in the *Journal of Ceramic History* No. 3, 1970, 28.

12 This is an earlier recipe (1826) published in the same source (ibid). Evans extracted his work from *The Popular Encyclopedia*. Glasgow: Blackie & Son, 1836, 42.

13 Charles F. Binns (ed.), *The Manual of Practical Potting*. London: Scott, Greenwood & Sons, 1907, 34-5, 42.

14 W.O. Henderson. London: Frank Cass, 1966, 139.

INDEX